American Business Leaders

Volume I

American Business Leaders

From Colonial Times to the Present

Volume I
A–L

Neil A. Hamilton

ABC-CLIO
Santa Barbara, California
Denver, Colorado
Oxford, England

Library of Congress Cataloging-in-Publication Data
Hamilton, Neil A., 1949–
    American business leaders : from colonial times to the present /
Neil A. Hamilton.
      p.   cm.
    Includes bibliographical references and index.
    ISBN 1-57607-002-6 (alk. paper)
    1. Businesspeople—United States Biography Dictionaries   I. Title.
HC102.5.A2H36   1999
338.092'272—dc21
[B]   99-27928
                                                                        CIP

05   04   03   02   01   00   99   10 9 8 7 6 5 4 3 2 1   (cloth)

ABC-CLIO, Inc.
130 Cremona Drive, P.O. Box 1911
Santa Barbara, California 93116-1911

This book is printed on acid-free paper∞.
Manufactured in the United States of America

Contents

List of American Business Leaders

Preface

American Business Leaders contains profiles of more than 400 prominent American men and women who built businesses important to the national economy. In many instances these people created new industries, developed resources on a massive scale, or took their original ideas and molded them into enterprises that changed the way people lived.

In addition to detailed biographical information, each profile places the leader within the context of his or her times. In this way the reader should gain a sense of how individual initiative combined with social forces to shape economic development. Names formatted in small capitals within entries indicate the person in question has his or her own entry within this book.

With the large number of business leaders in American history, deciding on which profiles to include has been no easy task. Any comprehensive listing would take many volumes. Here the decision was made to survey only the most prominent leaders—the movers and shakers, so to speak—in each category of development, such as finance, banking, heavy industry, food processing, broadcasting, communications, computers, and entertainment.

While the business world at its upper levels has long been a white male bastion, this encyclopedia includes several African Americans and women who contributed significantly to business development and made the American economy, and society, richer for the diversity they brought to it. Overall, particular attention has been paid to creating an en-

cyclopedia for general readers. Finally, while *American Business Leaders* covers entrepreneurs from colonial times to the present, it emphasizes developments beginning with the late-nineteenth-century industrial period.

The reader will find prominent figures in several categories. To name a few: early merchants John Jacob Astor, George Cabot, and John Hancock; industrialists Andrew Carnegie, Henry C. Frick, and John D. Rockefeller; retail store pioneers Rowland Macy, James Cash Penney, and Sam Walton; broadcasting executives Geraldine Laybourne, William Paley, and Ted Turner; fast-food entrepreneurs Debbi Fields, Ray Kroc, and Dave Thomas; food processors Frank Perdue, Gustavus Swift, and Rose Totino; entertainment moguls Richard "Dick" Clark, Louis Mayer, and Michael Ovitz; real estate developers Edward DeBartolo, Donald Trump, and William Zeckendorf; automakers Walter Percy Chrysler, Henry Ford, and Clement Studebaker; computer entrepreneurs Michael Dell, Bill Gates, and Steven Jobs; newspaper executives Frank Gannett, Al Neuharth, and Adolph Ochs; magazine founders Robert Guccione, Hugh Hefner, and Jann Wenner; and investors Peter Lynch, Michael Milken, and Ronald Perelman.

American Business Leaders includes such unusual stories as the food entrepreneur who took gelatin and, in the early twentieth century, made it into an everyday household item (Rose Knox); the world's richest man, who put a pay phone in his house for guests to use (J. Paul Getty); the immigrant who turned Polish face cream into a thriving cosmetics business (Helena Rubinstein); the indomitable African-American woman who said the idea for creating a product to straighten hair came to her in a dream (Sarah Walker); the ice cream makers who developed such strange-sounding flavors as Cherry Garcia and sacrificed profits to make a social difference (Ben Cohen and Jerry Greenfield); the private investigator who helped sneak a president, Abraham Lincoln, into Washington to avoid an assassination (Allan Pinkerton); the oil magnate with mysterious ties to Communist Russia (Armand Hammer), and the recluse who developed a candy empire (Forrest Mars).

They are all here, and many more, and they range from the upstanding to the scoundrels; from those who received public accolades to those who received prison time; from those with social consciences to those who knew only their ledger books. Readers who browse through *American Business Leaders* will get a better understanding of the events and people that led to the building of the world's most vibrant economy.

American Business Leaders

Volume I

Alexander, Mary Spratt Provoost

(April 17, 1693–April 18, 1760)
Merchant

Mary Spratt Provoost Alexander, a colonial businesswoman in the 1700s, was so successful that it was said virtually every boat that docked in New York City held goods for her to trade. Though she lived two centuries ago, Mary Alexander appears to have embodied the image of the modern woman; she was financially independent, maintained a flourishing business, bore 10 children, and supported her husband's role in politics.

Mary Spratt, born in New York City, New York, on April 17, 1693, came from a colorful immigrant family. Her mother, Maria DePeyster, was from a family of respected Dutch goldsmiths who became New York merchants. After a short marriage to Paulus Schrick, Maria married John Spratt, Mary's father. Spratt was a Scotsman who became a merchant and alderman in New York. When John Spratt died in 1697, Maria DePeyster Spratt married for the third time to David Provoost, a merchant whose primary activity was smuggling. Maria and "Ready-Money Provoost" (as the smuggler was known) had no children. In 1700, after Maria's death, Mary, her sister, and her brother went to live with their DePeyster grandmother.

Mary, nicknamed "Polly" by her indulgent grandmother, was a mischievous tomboy with dark curly hair and an early air of self-confidence. Acquaintances noted in letters and journals that this streak of pride in Mary would later come across as snobbish.

On October 15, 1711, Mary became the wife of Samuel Provoost, a merchant and younger brother of her mother's third husband. Mary participated in Samuel's business, investing her inheritance in his mercantile activities. The couple had three children—Maria, John, and David. John's son, also named Samuel Provoost after his grandfather, would later become the first Episcopal bishop of New York.

On January 5, 1721, two years after her husband Samuel's death, Mary married James Alexander, a lawyer and aspiring politician who had emigrated from Scotland in 1715. Mary, in an unusual action for a woman of her era, secured a prenuptial agreement to protect the inheritance of her Provoost children.

During the course of her 39-year marriage to Alexander, Mary bore another seven children, and participated extensively in the expansion of the Provoost trading business. In addition to sales of goods from her store, it is likely that she was involved during the French and Indian War in supplying horses, cannon, boats, and food for colonial troops. Of the seven children—Mary, James, William, Elizabeth, Catherine, Anne, and Susanna—only five lived to be adults. The surviving son, William, would later become known as "Lord Stirling," a general under George Washington during the American Revolution.

The Alexanders lived well. Their respective business ventures flourished, and their fortune was estimated at £100,000 in 1743. The Alexander residence was an ornate mansion on Broad Street in New York City. James Alexander was active during this time in opposing the colonial government, by using his position as a lawyer to support the newspaper of the contentious publisher John Peter Zenger in his battle for freedom of the press. While Mary's role in James' political career was not documented, it is clear that her wealth and social position provided James with useful connections to pursue his political agenda.

James Alexander died in 1756. Four years later on April 18, 1760, Mary died of pleurisy in New York City. As she had become an Anglican after her marriage to James, she was buried at Trinity Church in New York City.

BIBLIOGRAPHY

Miller, George G., "James Alexander and the Jews," *Publications*, American Jewish Historical Society, 1937; *Notable American Women, 1607–1950*, vol. 1, 1971; Provoost, Andrew J., *Biographical and Genealogical Notes of the Provost Family*, 1895; Van Rensselaer, Mrs. John King, *The Goede Vrouw of Mana-ha-ta*, 1898.

Annenberg, Moses

(February 11, 1875–July 20, 1942)
Publisher

A fierce and often unscrupulous business competitor, Moses Annenberg rose from an impoverished family to leadership within the communications industry as an executive with Hearst newspapers and owner of horse-racing publications, only to spend his last years in prison.

Moses was born on February 11, 1875, in Kalwischen, East Prussia (present-day Germany), to Tobias Annenberg and Sarah (Greenberg) Annenberg. After immigrating to the United States in 1882, Tobias Annenberg started a junk dealership, but he never made much money and always struggled to support his family. As a result, Moses left school at an early age to work in his father's business, then as a Western Union messenger and as a bartender. In 1899, he married Sadie Cecilia Friedman, daughter of a Chicago merchant; the couple subsequently had nine children.

The following year, Annenberg sold subscriptions for WILLIAM RANDOLPH HEARST'S Chicago newspaper, the *Evening American*. His success meant that when Hearst founded a morning newspaper, the *Examiner*, in 1904, he hired Annenberg as its circulation manager. Annenberg used gang warfare to obtain street-sale positions held by his competitors, a violent episode that marred his reputation.

Within a short time, he began an agency to distribute all of Chicago's newspapers, and over the next decade expanded his business into 20 cities. At the same time, Hearst hired Annenberg to publish the *Wisconsin News*. Shortly after 1920, Hearst made Annenberg circulation director for all his newspapers and magazines, and when the publisher founded the *New York Mirror* in 1924, he chose Annenberg to be its president.

Two years later, Annenberg quit the Hearst organization to concentrate on his own businesses. To the *Daily Racing Form*, which he had bought in 1922, he added other horse-racing newspapers, among them the *New York Morning Telegraph*. In 1927, he began providing bookies with race results via a wire service. He bought a half-interest in the General News Bureau and crushed his competition to form a monopoly in transmitting results from 29 racetracks. He then formed a rival company, called Nationwide News Service, to get rid of his partner in General News and another to get rid of his partners in the *Daily Racing Form*.

Annenberg prospered during the Great Depression and divided his holdings into different corporations. In 1936, he bought the prestigious *Philadelphia Inquirer*, an old newspaper, and changed its style to a sensationalist publication.

In 1939, a federal grand jury indicted Annenberg and his son WALTER ANNENBERG for income tax evasion. At the same time, American Telephone and Telegraph, Bell Telephone, and Illinois Bell telephone refused to continue carrying Annenberg's wire service.

Annenberg pleaded guilty in 1940 to one charge of tax evasion, while the charges against his son were dropped. He paid the government $10 million in back taxes and fines, and in July 1940 began serving a three-year prison sentence at a federal penitentiary in Lewisburg, Pennsylvania. Physically broken, his health deteriorated, and the government paroled him in June 1942. He died in Rochester, Minnesota, of a brain tumor on July 20 of that same year.

BIBLIOGRAPHY

Fonzi, Gaeton, *Annenberg: A Biography of Power*, 1970; Stern, J. David, *Memoirs of a Maverick Publisher*, 1962.

Annenberg, Walter

(March 13, 1908–)
Publisher

When Americans look to find out what is on television, they often turn to *TV Guide*, the largest of the publications begun by Walter Annenberg.

Walter was born on March 13, 1908, in Milwaukee, Wisconsin, to MOSES ANNENBERG and Cecilia (Friedman) Annenberg. In 1920, he moved with his family to Great Neck, New York, and after graduating from a prep school in New Jersey entered the Wharton School of Business at the University of Pennsylvania. He stayed only one year, however, before joining his father's business.

Annenberg Sr. owned publications and a wire service that provided bookies and bettors with horse-racing news and results. Walter Annenberg worked in his father's bookkeeping office before becoming vice president. In 1939, a federal grand jury indicted Annenberg Sr. for tax

Walter Annenberg (Archive Photos)

evasion and charged Walter Annenberg with "aiding and abetting" his father. Moses Annenberg pleaded guilty, paid $10 million in back taxes and penalties, and received a prison sentence. The government dropped the charge against Walter.

After his father died in 1942, Walter assumed the presidency of the family company, Triangle Publications. To the *Philadelphia Inquirer*, the *Daily Racing Form*, and other publications, Annenberg added, in 1944, *Seventeen*, a magazine aimed at teenage girls. The first issue sold about 400,000 copies.

In 1945, Annenberg bought WFIL-AM and FM, a leading radio station in Philadelphia. He then acquired radio and television stations in several locations. In 1953, he launched his most successful publication, *TV Guide*, which attracted the emerging mass of television viewers. By 1968, *TV Guide* had reached a circulation of about 14 million, and it withstood the rise of newspaper listings and the confusing array of cable television offerings to hold a position in the late 1980s among the three most popular magazines in America. Annenberg sold Triangle Publications, and with it *TV Guide*, to Australian businessman Rupert Murdoch in 1988 for $3 billion.

Over the years, critics have complained about Annenberg's autocratic behavior, evident in the large turnover of personnel at the *Philadelphia Inquirer*. They have disparaged his appointment by President Richard Nixon in 1969 as ambassador to Britain, saying his only qualification was the large sums of money he had donated to Nixon's campaign. Yet Annenberg displayed a philanthropic side when he founded Philadelphia Inquirer Charities, sponsored the Philadelphia Art Museum and the Philadelphia Orchestra, and began the Annenberg School of Communications at the University of Pennsylvania.

BIBLIOGRAPHY

Fonzi, Gaeton, *Annenberg: A Biography of Power*, 1970.

Arden, Elizabeth

(December 31, 1878–October 18, 1966)
Manufacturer

"I found I didn't really like looking at sick people," Elizabeth Arden said when she decided to quit nursing school. "I want to keep people well, and young, and beautiful." With that desire, she founded a cosmetics empire of salons and skin creams.

Elizabeth Arden was born Florence Nightingale Graham on December 31, 1878, in Woolbridge, a small town near Toronto, Canada. Her father, William Graham, worked as a tenant farmer. Her mother, Susan (Pierce) Graham, died when Florence was only five years old. Because of financial problems, Florence left high school before graduating, at which point she began her brief stay in nursing school. Although she disliked this work, during her studies she became interested in the use of creams, then newly developed to eliminate skin blemishes.

After working as a dental assistant for two years, beginning in 1907, Florence left Canada and followed her brother to New York City. Before long, she found work as a secretary in the office of Eleanor Adair's London-based cosmetic firm. Adair taught her to be a treatment girl, a job that required giving facial massages and applying creams to customers. Florence discovered she had a talent for this work, and she realized that the beauty business had enormous potential. Later in 1909, she met Elizabeth Hubbard, a maker of lotions, and the two agreed to enter a partnership. They opened a salon, but had numerous differences—some related to Florence's ambitious, even overbearing manner—and within a year, they decided to go their separate ways.

Florence Graham changed her name to Elizabeth Arden—she chose "Arden" from a Tennyson poem—and with capital provided by her brother, opened a beauty salon known for its attractive red door and fashionable clientele. She prospered immediately and, while providing facial massages, hired chemists to make compounds. Elizabeth Arden, Incorporated quickly emerged as the leader in skin care and cosmetics, and by 1915 Arden's salons held a secondary position to her lotions. Her advertisements in *Vogue* and other magazines attracted women through worry and hope:

> A slight change in contour, a faint wrinkling or marking of the skin, a noticeable fading of the complexion—these add *years* to one's *age*, that is, in the eyes of one's friends.

> Every woman can do what hundreds of Miss Arden's clients have done for years and keep the skin and complexion in the pink of condition . . . and youthful by devoting ten minutes each day to proper treatment with the Venetian products.

From 1915 to 1920, Elizabeth Arden introduced more preparations than any other cosmetics manufacturer, including a popular light and fluffy cleansing cream concocted by her chemist. She maintained an ongoing battle with her main competitor, HELENA RUBINSTEIN, and the two developed a lasting enmity.

In 1922, Elizabeth Arden opened her first foreign salon in Paris, and during that decade, she began promoting long-distance beauty analysis whereby women wrote to her about their skin problems and she proposed solutions. Her business grossed $2 million on domestic sales in 1925, and in 1930, she opened a lavish salon on New York City's Fifth Avenue—by then she had 150 salons in all, along with spas and worldwide sales of her products.

In the 1930s, she bought a farm in Maine and started raising horses and entering thoroughbreds in races. That same decade, the federal government cracked down on misleading advertising and forced Elizabeth Arden to end claims that her skin cream products were nutrients and that they lifted muscles and refined pores.

Despite this setback, her business continued to grow, fed by the ever fashionable, even compulsive, pursuit of youthful looks. After having for years denied mortality, Elizabeth Arden died on October 18, 1966, while still serving as chairman of the board of her company.

BIBLIOGRAPHY

Lewis, Alfred Allan, and Constance Woodworth, *Miss Elizabeth Arden*, 1972.

Armour, Philip Danforth

(May 16, 1832–January 6, 1901)
Meat Packer

Admirers and detractors alike said about Philip Danforth Armour that he built his giant meatpacking business by cutting up pigs and using "all but the squeal."

Born on May 16, 1832, in Stockbridge, New York, to Danforth Armour, a farmer, and Julia Ann (Brooks) Armour, Philip attended the Cazenovia Seminary and worked on the family farm before heading out to California in 1852 amid the gold rush to seek his fortune as a miner. He built sluices and sold supplies to miners and in 1856 returned home after having made a handsome profit. That same year, he went to Milwaukee and with Frederick B. Miles founded a wholesale grocery. In 1862, he married Malvina Belle Ogden.

Armour dissolved his partnership with Miles in 1863 and then joined John Plankinton to form Plankinton, Armour & Company, a grain dealer and meat packer. (Prior to 1857, meat packing was a seasonal operation, requiring the cold of winter for slaughtering in order to avoid spoilage. By 1863, the use of ice allowed year-round processing.) Armour made his first big deal when, as the Civil War neared its end, he decided to exploit an impending drop in pork prices. While pork hovered around $40 a barrel, he went to New York and signed contracts to deliver it at that price. Then when the war ended and pork dropped to $18 a barrel, he bought it at the new price and sold it at the contracted price—making a huge profit and, amid complaints he had acted immorally, netting about $1.5 million.

Upon his return to Milwaukee, Armour joined H. O. Armour & Company, a grain commission house founded by his brother. The firm added a pork-packing plant in 1868 and in 1870 changed its name to Armour & Company. By this time, Chicago had emerged as the nation's pork-packing center and railroad hub, and with Armour & Company having an increasing amount of its business there, Philip Armour moved to Chicago in 1875.

Armour pioneered in using waste from meatpacking to make products. He later described the situation:

> The packers were not aware of, or did not appreciate, the value of the offal, and the problem of how to get rid of it at the least expense was ever present. . . . In Chicago, the blood was allowed to run into the river, and men were paid five dollars a load to cart the heads, feet, tankage, and other waste material out upon the prairie and bury it in pits and trenches. . . .
> The large packing houses of today manipulate their own horns, hoofs, bones, sinews, hide-trimmings, etc., in their own glue works. The sweet fat of the cattle forms the basis of butterines made in their own butterine factories; the sheep pelts are scoured, and the wool removed in their own wool houses, cleansed and sold directly to Eastern cloth mills. The intestines are cleaned and salted and used for sausage casings in their own sausage factories. The blood and all animal residues are treated in their own fertilizer factories.

At a time when centralization marked the American economy and large industries devoured small businesses, Armour moved the nation from local slaughtering to central slaughtering and into transporting processed beef, mutton, and pork over long distances.

Refrigeration made this development possible. A dispute exists as to who first used refrigerated railroad cars—certainly GUSTAVUS SWIFT ranked among the leaders—but their widespread use by 1880 al-

Philip Danforth Armour (Library of Congress)

lowed Armour to expand his company's reach, and butchered meat now traveled from refrigerated cars to refrigerated plants. The processing of meat also changed, although slaughtering remained much the same. Carcasses hung along moving chains, making the meat cutting continuous, whereby each cutter removed certain parts as they came to him. "The killing is done by hand, " Armour said. He continued, "No mechanical means of wholesale slaughter having been evolved; but in the manipulation of the carcass many ingenious contrivances are utilized. . . . [A]s soon as life has left the animal he is hooked by the nose to an endless chain, passed through scalding vats and through an automatically adjustable scraper. . . . [H]e is then hoisted, head down, upon an inclined rail; and is disemboweled, beheaded, washed, trimmed, and whirled off to the chill-rooms at the rate of twenty hogs a minute."

Armour began canning meat and began sending refrigerated beef and pork to England, France, and Germany. He expanded his interests and in 1879 established the Armours' Bank in Kansas City, Missouri. Armour helped save several banks in Chicago during the Panic of 1893, when he bought $500,000 in gold from Europe and loaned it to the troubled institutions. By this time, his own wealth had reached $50 million, and Armour & Company had 230 branches and was shipping 7 million pounds of canned and refrigerated meat each week.

A scandal during the Spanish-American War, however, damaged Armour's reputation. Armour, and other companies, provided large amounts of meat to the army. As soldiers fell ill, the army accused the meat companies of having provided them with tainted meat. "The fresh whole quarters of meat issued to the army when not on marching rations was old meat," charged the military. "It had been treated (embalmed) with either one of the following two harmful meat preservatives: boric acid or salicylic acid. The canned 'roasted' beef issued as marching rations was nothing more than beef pulp. . . . The beef was unpalatable and nauseating. . . ."

An investigation eventually cleared Armour and the other companies, but nearly everyone at the time considered the report a political cover-up. The "embalmed beef scandal" reinforced a growing public view that unsanitary conditions prevailed in the meatpacking industry—a view reinforced a few years later by Upton Sinclair in his sensational novel, *The Jungle.*

Shortly after the scandal, Armour's health deteriorated. He tried to recover from the illness and from the mental anguish he felt from the scandal by traveling to Europe in 1899. He remained weak, however, and failed to resume his leadership at the company before dying two years later in Chicago on January 6, 1901.

Armour was generous with his money. He gave to charities, to the families of workingmen (while opposing unions and setting a paternalistic style), and to education—giving away millions of dollars. In his will, he provided substantial sums to his children and grandchildren, and a son, Jonathan Ogden Armour, succeeded him as head of the Armour firm.

BIBLIOGRAPHY

Leech, Harper, and John Charles Carroll, *Armour and His Times*, 1938.

Armstrong, Thomas Morton

(April 16, 1836–1906)
Manufacturer

Thomas Morton Armstrong's nest egg of $300 in 1860 launched a cork business that expanded rapidly, evolving to what is today Armstrong World Industries, a manufacturer of a wide range of interior furnishings with 13 plants in six foreign countries. Armstrong also pioneered the practice of selling merchandise that displayed the manufacturer's name. His motto, "let the buyer have faith," was a stark contrast to the standard operating procedures of the day, which advocated that the buyer should beware, as the seller acknowledged no responsibility for the quality of goods after purchase.

Thomas was born in New York City on April 16, 1836, to William and Nancy Armstrong, recent Irish immigrants of Scottish descent. He lived in Butler County, Pennsylvania, until the age of 5, when the family relocated to Pittsburgh. He received little formal education, though in later years he was a very studious man who was self-taught and well read. At age 12, Armstrong began working in a rope factory. After a short time, he became a shipping clerk at William McCully & Company, a glassmaker in Pittsburgh.

In 1860, Armstrong was presented with the possibility of joining with John D. Glass to purchase a small company that manufactured cork items, products devised from the outer bark of a type of oak tree that had proven valuable for centuries for many uses, including stopping up bottles. He furnished $300 of capital from his savings, and the two men agreed to go into business.

Under their original agreement made in 1860, Glass would run the firm, known as John D. Glass & Co., receiving both salary and half the profits. Armstrong, for his part, put up the capital and received the other half of the profits, but he continued for some time with his job at the glass factory. Armstrong's reluctance to leave the glass firm was based largely on his need for a steady income to support his wife, Martha Porter, whom he married on October 11, 1860. After a short time, with his wife's support, Armstrong threw himself full-time into the cork business.

The firm slowly gained its footing, making a little more headway in 1862 when it was able to abandon the practice of cutting cork by hand. The firm bought a machine for cutting stoppers that was a large investment but set the tone for an ongoing policy of discarding and upgrading outmoded equipment.

In 1864, Glass died of a heart attack. With the addition of Robert D. Armstrong, Thomas's brother, and William Standish, the company name was changed to Armstrong Bro. & Co. That same year, the Armstrongs adopted the practices of branding the company name on the corks and including with the product a written guarantee of quality. The early years of the business consisted of the sale of corks for soda-water bottles and fruit jars. The company grew rapidly and moved to a new location. During the 1870s, the company's insistence on quality enabled it to establish branch outlets for distributing the products. Prior to this time, customers of corks, such as breweries, would send representatives to the corkwood factories to choose the best-quality products. This limited the geographic range of customers to those who lived near the factories. By promoting the brand name of Armstrong and closely linking it to a guarantee of quality, Thomas was able to greatly increase his distribution network.

In 1878, Armstrong's factory was devastated by a fire. Fortunately, plans had already been under way for the purchase of land near the Allegheny River, and a new plant was quickly constructed. The business was also jarred by the death of Robert Armstrong the same year as the fire. Another brother, Andrew J. Armstrong, bought up Robert's interest in the company. Also during that year, Armstrong Bro. & Co. hired a representative in Spain for the direct purchase and preparation of raw cork, which until then had been purchased from American importers or European firms.

In 1891, the firm incorporated, though it changed its name again in 1895 to the Armstrong Cork Company. Thomas realized that the company needed to adapt in the face of increasing competition from the newly invented mason jar and spring stopper for soda bottles that threatened to make cork stoppers obsolete. The business began to research new products made from cork, and by 1902 had become a significant supplier of cork for insulating cold-storage rooms.

By this time, Thomas's son, Charles, was vice president of the company. In the last decade of his life, Thomas delegated much of the responsibility for running the firm to his son. Until the 1890s, Thomas was a hands-on manager who knew by name virtually every one of the 750 employees of the Pittsburgh plant. Just as Armstrong had helped encourage the notion of corporate responsibility for quality, he also believed in fair dealings with labor. Thomas Armstrong maintained an active interest in the company he founded until his death sometime in 1906.

BIBLIOGRAPHY

Muskowitz, Milton, et al., eds., *Everybody's Business*, 1980; *National Cyclopedia of American Biography*, vol. 25, 1921; Prentis, Henning Webb, *Thomas Morton Armstrong, 1836–1908: Pioneer in Cork*, 1950.

Ash, Mary Kay

(ca. 1915–)
Manufacturer, Merchant

With pink Cadillacs and heaps of praise, Mary Kay Ash turned housewives into salespeople and built a giant cosmetics company.

Ash was born Mary Kay Wagner in Hot Wells, Texas, around 1915. (She has refused to divulge her age.) When she was seven years old, her father contracted tuberculosis, and his incapacitation forced Mary Kay's mother to work long hours that required Mary Kay to take care of him. After graduating from Reagan High

Mary Kay Ash (UPI/Corbis-Bettmann)

School, she married Ben Rogers, a musician, and they had three children. Rogers, however, deserted her during World War II, and Mary Kay obtained a divorce.

She worked hard to support her family—first as a salesperson with Stanley Home Products and then, in 1953, with the World Gift Company, which sold home accessories. She earned $1,000 a month, and the firm rewarded her by making her its national training director. Over the next 10 years, she expanded the company's sales in several states, earned a comfortable income, and remarried. Something, however, angered her: the company bypassed her in order to promote men, and then it demoted her. Dispirited, she retired from the company and for the next few weeks worked as a housewife.

Always ambitious and energetic, however, Mary Kay decided to found a company in which everyone would be treated equally and in which salespeople would earn handsome profits. Shortly before her departure from World Gift, she had bought a skin care formula from the family of a cosmetologist. Now, with $5,000 in capital, she hired a manufacturer to make a skin care product and prepared to open a retail shop. Before her business could get under way, however, her husband died.

On the brink of financial ruin, she turned to her 20-year-old son, Richard Rogers, who agreed to help her with financial and administrative chores. With that, she founded Mary Kay Cosmetics in September 1963. She paid her salespeople (who were nearly all women) high commissions and rejected fixed territories in favor of allowing them to sell products wherever they wanted. She told her workers to live according to the motto: God first, family second, career third.

A dynamic speaker, Mary Kay energized her sales force at annual meetings at which she awarded prizes, most notably pink Cadillacs. She believed that for women to succeed they needed praise—and this she provided in abundance. Few of her salespeople earned large incomes, but many felt as if their lives had taken on new meaning, as if they no longer had to be confined to housewife chores.

Her company grew rapidly as it made its own products. Sales of $10 million in 1967 exceeded $50 million in 1977, and she expanded her Dallas manufacturing plant from 102,000 to 250,000 square feet.

Mary Kay's success rested on her motivational talent and on her decision to use a small product line, thus enabling her salespeople to carry and show each item to their customers.

After Mary Kay's third husband died of cancer in 1980, she devoted considerable time to fund-raising for groups dedicated to fighting the disease. She retired from Mary Kay Cosmetics in 1987, and in 1993 the Mary Kay Ash Center for Cancer Immunotherapy Research was founded in Dallas. Three years later, she established the Mary Kay Ash Charitable Foundation to provide funding for the research of cancers affecting women.

Today, Mary Kay Cosmetics has more than 500,000 salespeople in 26 countries and is the largest direct seller of skin care products in the United States.

BIBLIOGRAPHY

Ash, Mary Kay, *Mary Kay Ash*, 1981; Ash, Mary Kay, *You Can Have It All*, 1995; Sobel, Robert, and David B. Sicilia, *The Entrepreneurs*, 1986.

Astor, John Jacob

(July 17, 1763–March 29, 1848)
Merchant, Real Estate Developer

Icebound aboard a ship on Chesapeake Bay, John Jacob Astor struck up a conversation with a fellow passenger, a German immigrant, who told him about the fur trade in North America. With this information in hand, Astor decided to enter the business—and soon amassed the largest fortune in the United States.

Astor was born on July 17, 1763, in Waldorf, Germany. His father, Jacob Astor, worked as a butcher but, according to one popular account, spent more time drinking beer than tending to his trade. At age 17, John Jacob decided to seek his own fortune, and after working on a timber raft saved enough money to depart for England. There, he learned English and learned about a new nation, the United States.

In November 1783, Astor sailed to America, and at that time heard the German immigrant's story about the fur trade. Astor made his way to New York City the following year, and by 1786 owned a small shop where he sold musical instruments. He married Sarah Parton, worked hard, and developed big plans. Astor made frequent trips to the frontier and with great energy and considerable acumen developed his fur trade, mainly beaver skins. Typical for the time, he often obtained furs from Indians by plying them with alcohol, thus contributing to the destruction of Indian society. He also imported furs from Montreal and by 1800 had amassed a fortune of $250,000.

With a merchant friend, Astor sent a ship to the Orient—he was one of the founders of the American trade with China—and made $50,000. He invested his money in New York real estate, and over the years, he and his descendants acquired hundreds of acres on the Lower East Side, Upper West Side, and in Harlem.

After the Lewis and Clark expedition ended in 1806, Astor organized the American Fur Company and took his trade into the Far West. He developed an ambitious plan linked to his newly formed Pacific Fur Company, organized in 1810, and founded Astoria in Oregon country as a trading settlement, along with several posts from which he gathered furs. A fleet of ships then carried the furs to Canton, China, and on to Europe and New York. "The Astoria enterprise," claimed one historian, "represented an extraordinarily broad grasp of worldwide market conditions and a willingness to conduct business across the boundaries of several national states." The effort collapsed, however, when war erupted between the United States and Britain in 1812.

Astor made money during the war by joining with STEPHEN GIRARD in bond deals that financed the American effort. Afterward, he again pursued his fur trade, and by 1817 owned posts in the Mississippi Valley and the Southwest. Within ten years, he had developed a monopoly along the Upper Missouri and then penetrated the Rocky Mountains. Competition from the Rocky Mountain Fur Company, however, hurt Astor, and he grew tired of the enterprise. As a result, he sold all his fur interests in 1834 and concentrated on his real estate investments. When he died on March 29, 1848, he had by far more wealth than any other American.

BIBLIOGRAPHY

Haeger, John, *John Jacob Astor: Business and Finance in the Early Republic*, 1991; Porter, Kenneth Wiggins, *John Jacob Astor: Business Man*, 1931.

Ayer, Harriet Hubbard

(June 27, 1849–November 23, 1903)
Manufacturer, Journalist

Harriet Hubbard Ayer, a divorced mother with a flair for business, wrote one of the earliest American beauty advice columns. Her lifestyle served to encourage the independence of women, and her work earned her a part in the early days of the mass journalism movement.

Harriet, the third of four children, was born in Chicago, Illinois, on June 27, 1849, to a wealthy real estate dealer, Henry George Hubbard, and his wife, Juliet Elvira Smith. Although the Hubbards were Episcopalian, Harriet was educated at the Convent of the Sacred Heart, graduating at the early age of 15. She was, according to family accounts, a lonely child, considered plain even by her family.

In 1852, Harriet's father died, causing her mother to lapse into a long period of semi-invalidism. In June 1865, Harriet, then 16, married the son of a successful Chicago iron dealer, Herbert Copeland Ayer. The Ayers raised two daughters, Harriet and Margaret. A third daughter died in infancy in the Great Chicago Fire of 1871.

In the years after Margaret's birth, Ayer shed the "ugly duckling" label applied to her as a child. She became the epitome of the graceful society matron. Left to her own devices by a husband obsessed by work, she took part in amateur theatrical productions and became a patron of the arts. However, her pursuit of intellectual and theatrical society, a culture still tinged with an air of impropriety, caused the disintegration of her marriage. In 1882, Ayer moved to New York with her daughters.

The failure of Herbert Ayer's business in 1883 forced Ayer to assume responsibility for supporting her family. An energetic woman, she worked as a saleswoman and decorator just long enough to secure financial backing for her own venture. After she and her husband divorced in 1886, she began the manufacture and sale of a face cream product. Ayer, a shrewd merchandiser, began to come into her own. Capitalizing upon the snobbery of the upper class and her own social standing, she marketed the facial cream under both her own name and that of a famous beauty from the Napoleonic era, Madame Recamier.

The success of the product proved short-lived, however. James Seymour, a stockholder and the father-in-law of one of her daughters, charged that Ayer had mismanaged the company's funds. Seymour asserted that Ayer was mentally unbalanced and unfit to run the business. Ayer, not one to play the role of submissive female, brought a countersuit against Seymour, charging him with withholding stock and trying to drive her insane.

Though remaining records do not indicate the outcome or validity of the lawsuits, they do show that in 1893, Ayer was committed to a private insane asylum by her ex-husband and her daughter Harriet. After 14 months, Ayer was released and began to present a series of lectures to the public. Though these talks centered on her unjust imprisonment, they also called public attention to the horrible treatment of mental patients.

In 1896, Ayer embarked on a new venture, one that would secure her a role in the emerging mass media movement. Arthur Brisbane, the editor of the New York *World*, enlisted her to write a weekly women's page for the Sunday edition. Her articles were extremely popular, particularly to poor women who were happy to share in the mystique of the society woman's elegance. Although Ayer's advice was mostly common sense, her hints on hygiene, exercise, and nutrition encouraged a broader view of an active woman. Her columns—and her lifestyle—solidly rejected the image of the fragile, cloistered female.

In her later years, Ayer reconciled with her daughters and continued to write for the *World*. She died in New York on November 23, 1903, succumbing to pneumonia and chronic nephritis.

BIBLIOGRAPHY

Ayer, Harriet Hubbard, *Harriet Hubbard Ayer's Book: A Complete and Authentic Treatise on the Laws of Health and Beauty*, 1899; Ayer, Margaret Hubbard, and Isabella Taves, *The Three Lives of Harriet Hubbard Ayer*, 1957; Willard, Francis, *American Women: Fifteen Hundred Biographies with over 1,400 Portraits*, 1973; *Women of Achievement: Biographies and Portraits of Outstanding American Women*, 1940.

Ayer, James Cook

(May 18, 1818–July 3, 1878)
Manufacturer

James Cook Ayer, a medical doctor in the 1800s, used his successful home remedy called "Ayer's Cherry Pectoral" to build a business that dominated the patent medicine industry of the nineteenth century. He launched unprecedented advertising campaigns and was an early champion of including ingredient lists on product labels.

The son of Frederick Ayer Sr. and Persis Cook, James was born in Ledyard, Connecticut, on May 18, 1818. His brother, Frederick, would one day be a noted financier. The boys' father died when James was seven years old. James's early education came from schools in Preston and Norwich, and he received early mechanical training at his maternal grandfather's flannel mill. James attended high school in Lowell, Massachusetts, where he lived with his uncle, James Cook. After graduating, he was an apprentice in the apothecary shop of Jacob Robbins while studying medicine in his free time.

In 1841, shortly after receiving his medical degree from the University of Pennsylvania, Ayer borrowed money from his uncle to purchase Robbins's drugstore. During his early years of managing the store, Ayer developed a pulmonary remedy, known as "Ayer's Cherry Pectoral," that aided sufferers of lung problems.

The next few years were hectic, with Ayer's marriage to Josephine Miller Southwick in 1850 coinciding with his frantic advertising and product development push. Shortly after his marriage, he began to publish a journal designed to promote the virtues of Cherry Pectoral. His *American Almanac* was immediately popular and grew in circulation as additional products were included. He devised sugarcoated pills in 1854 and extract of sarsaparilla in 1855. That same year, he was joined by his brother Frederick in the business. In 1857, James developed an ague cure, and the brothers bought a large Lowell property to expand manufacturing capacity. In 1869, James introduced "Ayer's Hair Vigor," a hair growth tonic for men. All of these products were advertised extensively.

Ayer's patent medicine business continued to grow rapidly, becoming one of the largest in the industry by the end of the century. Circulation of the *Almanac* averaged 16 million copies per year at its peak, and it was published in 21 languages for global distribution. His creativity in advertising reached new heights as he enacted a policy of packaging special boxes of Cherry Pectoral to give foreign dignitaries as gifts. Notable recipients of his samples included the queen of Spain; the emperors of Siam, Japan, and China; and the czar of Russia.

In 1906, responding to political support for the passage of the Pure Food and Drug Act, Ayer voluntarily decided to start printing labels for his products with the full formula information stated clearly in plain English. Ayer also encouraged—though

James Cook Ayer (Archive Photos)

without success—his competitors to do the same.

With the continued growth of the patent medicine business, the Ayer brothers diversified their investments to include interests in textile companies. James was also a partner in the building of the Lowell and Andover Railroad in 1874, in addition to holding interests in the Lake Superior Ship Canal and Iron Company. Ayer remained active in all of his financial concerns until his death on July 3, 1878.

BIBLIOGRAPHY

Colbur, F. W., *History of Lowell and Its Peoples*, 1920; Cowley, Charles, *Reminiscences of James C. Ayer and the Town of Ayer*, 1879; Young, James Harvey, *The Toadstool Millionaires*, 1961.

B

Bache, Jules

(November 9, 1861–March 24, 1944)
Financier

From cashier to partnership in his uncle's brokerage house, Jules Bache amassed a fortune by financing large businesses and by appealing to middle-class investors in the stock market. He then used his money to build a world-renowned art collection.

Born on November 9, 1861, in New York City to Semon Bache and Elizabeth (Van Praag) Bache, Jules grew up in material comfort. His father, an immigrant from Bavaria, founded a business that made quality mirrors and other glass products. Jules obtained his education at the Charlier Institute in New York City and in Europe. In 1880, he joined his uncle's New York brokerage house, Leopold Cahn & Company, as a cashier and advanced quickly to treasurer in 1881 and then to partnership in 1886. In 1892, he became head of the firm, and its name was changed to Jules Bache & Company. That same year, he married Florence Rosalee Scheftel.

In 1893, the New York Stock Exchange accused Bache & Company of malpractice. Although a hearing cleared the firm, Bache sold his seat on the exchange. The controversy notwithstanding, Bache & Company prospered as it handled some of the era's most prominent financial deals, including the reorganizations of the American Spirits Manufacturing Company, the Distilling and Cattle Feeding Company (or "Whiskey Trust"), and the Cosmopolitan Fire Insurance Company.

Bache also expanded into branch brokerage and attracted middle-class investors. In the early 1900s, he opened offices in three towns in New York State and in Philadelphia, Pennsylvania; Newark, New Jersey; Montreal, Canada; and Liverpool, England. Prior to World War I, Bache's firm had the most extensive private wire system in the nation, and on several occasions the company transacted more than 200,000 shares in a single day.

Bache involved himself in other businesses as well. He served as vice president of the Chrysler Corporation from 1929 to 1943 and as president of Dome Mines from 1918 to 1943. Amid the Great Depression in the 1930s, he extended currency to customers in need of cash.

As his wealth grew, Bache collected art, mainly paintings. With the help of a great art dealer, Joseph Duveen, he acquired paintings by Botticelli, Raphael, Titian, Vermeer, Goya, and Gainsborough, among others. In the late 1930s, he opened a museum in his own home.

By the time of Bache's death on March 24, 1944, Bache & Company had 37 branches and more than 800 employees. Five years later, an arrangement with his estate resulted in his art collection being transferred to New York City's Metropolitan Museum of Art.

BIBLIOGRAPHY

Harrison, Mitchell C., comp., *N.Y. State's Prominent and Progressive Men*, vol. II, 1900.

Ball, Frank

(November 24, 1857–March 19, 1943)
Manufacturer

Even in an increasingly urban society, Americans canned food (preserves, pickles, and countless other items), and Frank Ball built a business on it. He made the Mason jars that housewives used for canning, an indispensable item for the family kitchen.

Born on November 24, 1857, in Greensburg, Ohio, to Lucius Ball and Maria Polly (Bingham) Ball, Frank grew up on a farm near Canandaigua, New York, where his family moved in 1868. A short time after he graduated from Canandaigua Academy, his father died, and an uncle helped him and his older brother begin a business. In 1880, they began making wood-encased tin cans for holding oils and varnishes. Later that year, they relocated the business to Buffalo, brought three other brothers into the firm, and named the company Ball Brothers.

Ball expanded his product line to include a metal tank fitted with a pump that grocery stores used to dispense kerosene—popular as a fuel for lighting—along with a metal kerosene can for family use and a glass oil jar. Then, in 1885, he acquired the expired patent for the "Mason Improved Fruit Jar" and began producing the distinctive glass containers and their caps, designed for canning.

Glassmaking required considerable fuel, however, and in 1887 Ball built a new factory in Muncie, Indiana, near the recently discovered midwestern natural gas and oil fields. Six years after moving to Muncie, Ball married a local woman, Elizabeth Wolfe Brady. The couple eventually had five children.

Meanwhile, the Ball brothers incorporated their business and appointed Frank Ball as its president. Sales grew rapidly, with Mason jars producing an annual company income of $10 million by the 1920s. Unlike many other companies, Ball Brothers saw its business expand during the Great Depression when, as the economy worsened, families resorted to preserving food.

In 1938, however, Frank Ball admitted to a congressional committee that his company had made secret agreements to stifle competition. Four years later, a federal court ruled that the Ball Brothers Company and seven other businesses had violated antitrust laws.

With their considerable wealth, Frank Ball and his brothers donated substantial money to the community. Among other gifts, they contributed $2 million to the Ball Memorial Hospital in Muncie and the same amount to Muncie Normal School, which years later became Ball State University.

Frank Ball remained president of the company until his death on March 19, 1943, in Muncie. Of the brothers, one observer said: "In their modesty and personal rectitude, combined with their rise from comparative poverty to great wealth, they fit perfectly the American success dream."

BIBLIOGRAPHY

Lynd, Robert S., and Helen Lynd, *Middletown in Transition*, 1937; White, Glenn, *The Ball State Story*, 1967.

Ballantine, Ian Keith

(February 15, 1916–March 9, 1995)
Publisher

Ian Keith Ballantine was a publisher whose quest to bring diverse reading material to the mainstream American public was the driving force behind innovations in the publishing industry. Ballantine's practice of simultaneously releasing an expensive hardbound book edition with an inexpensive paperback version changed the practice whereby quality literature was available only at a premium, while paperback titles were reserved exclusively for lower-quality works. Ballantine's endeavors, which include Penguin USA, Bantam Books, and Ballantine Books, have remained prominent segments of the publishing industry.

Ian, the son of Scottish actor Edward James Ballantine and an American theater publicist, Stella Commins Ballantine, was born on February 15, 1916, in New York City. Ian graduated from Stuyvesant High School in 1933. He then pursued a B.A. degree from Columbia University, followed by a year at the London School of Economics and Political Science.

Though Ballantine had never taken a particular interest in publishing, he wrote a thesis while in London on the possibility of creating an American market for low-cost British paperbacks. Until the advent of Pocket Books, Inc. in 1939, low-cost paperbound reprints of books were not common in the United States. Despite the emergence of this competitor, Penguin Books, Ltd. was impressed with Ballantine's ideas and established him in the United States as general manager of Penguin Books, Inc. One of the company's first releases was a paperback version of the H. G. Wells classic, *The Invisible Man.*

On June 22, 1939, the year Ballantine launched Penguin USA, he married Elizabeth Norah Jones, with whom he would have one son, Richard. In 1945, Ballantine left Penguin, and, along with his wife and investors from hardcover publishing houses, established Bantam Books, Inc.

During the initial years of Bantam, Ballantine conducted a number of innovative market research studies to determine reading patterns of the American public. Ballantine studied purchasing patterns to compile monthly best-seller lists, and Bantam aggressively marketed the best-selling titles. Ballantine also began to teach sociology part-time at Columbia University, where he focused on issues of mass communication and the influence of the media. Although Bantam's book list included modern classics such as *The Grapes of Wrath* by John Steinbeck and *The Great Gatsby* by F. Scott Fitzgerald, the dominant sellers at Bantam (and most of its competitors) were cheap, mass-produced paperbacks with lurid covers. One of Bantam's founders commented that, typical of the era, they even "had cleavage on [the cover of] *Little Women.*"

In 1952, a brainstorm of Ballantine's that would revolutionize the publishing industry inspired him to leave Bantam and form Ballantine Books. The new company focused on releasing both original fiction and nonfiction in hardback versions simultaneously with paperback versions that were lower priced for the newsstand market. Ballantine believed that his "simulprint" plan, combined with his ideas for changes in the way writers earned royalties, would enable high-quality original work to become accessible to the average person, who until then had to either pay more for an original hardbound edition or be content with a low-priced reprint of a classic or a low-quality piece of "pulp fiction."

In 1954, with Ballantine Books' release of *New Short Novels*, reviewers for *Time* magazine praised Ballantine's plan, stating that "paperback originals worth reading have been extremely rare . . . the news this week is that writing at a pretty high level has at last shown up between the covers of a thirty-five cent book." Ballantine Books focused on original work, publishing authors such as Ray Bradbury, Arthur C. Clarke, and J. R. R. Tolkien.

By 1963, the company was releasing 60 titles annually and continued to grow until 1974, when it was bought by Random House. The Ballantines returned to Bantam Books, where projects included books by Chuck Yeager and Shirley MacLaine.

Throughout his career, Ballantine maintained his early interests in international politics, becoming a member of the executive reserve of the State Department. He died on March 9, 1995.

BIBLIOGRAPHY

Current Biography, 1954; Muskowitz, Milton, et al., eds., *Everybody's Business*, 1980; *New York Times*, Book Review, May 18, 1952; *Time*, February 15, 1954.

Barber, Ohio Columbus

(April 20, 1841–February 4, 1920)
Manufacturer

In the late 1800s, there was one company in the United States that comprised almost 85 percent of the trade in the match industry. For most people, the coupling of the word "matches" with the company named Diamond is automatic. Ohio Columbus Barber was a key figure in the impressive national and international success of the Diamond Match Company.

Barber, the third of nine children, was born on April 20, 1841, in Middlebury, Ohio, a town that is now part of Akron. Barber's father, George, was a cooper from Connecticut, and his mother, Eliza Smith, was descended from Dutch immigrants. Barber left school at age 16 to assist his father, who had established a match manufactory, with the sale of his products.

Traveling by wagon, Barber distributed matches throughout Indiana, Michigan, and Pennsylvania. By 1862, Barber took over the company from his father. The business prospered, and in two years, the Barber Match Company was incorporated, offering public stock for the first time. In 1866, Barber married

Laura L. Brown, who would remain his wife until her death in 1894.

With his business thriving, Barber consolidated his company with many others into the Diamond Match Company in 1881, a merger that enabled the group to control around 85 percent of the match business. Barber served as vice president of the company until 1888, when he took over as president. Developing the scope of the company's business was the dominant activity of Barber's life and career. The work of "America's Match-King" paid off; the Diamond Match Company owned, in addition to its U.S. holdings, controlling interests in factories in England, Germany, Switzerland, Peru, and Chile.

In 1891, Barber developed the city of Barberton, Ohio, as the new location for his Akron manufacturing plant. He then began to diversify his product line, manufacturing packing boxes and straw board (the raw material of the packing boxes). He eventually established the American Strawboard Company. Another offshoot of the Diamond Match Company, the Diamond Rubber Company, would eventually be bought out by the tire-manufacturing giant, B. F. Goodrich Company.

Other business interests of Barber's included banking and the railroad industry. He founded the First National Bank of Akron and was president of both the original bank and its subsequent incarnation as the Second National Bank of Akron. He was also a key player in the construction of the Akron Barberton Belt Line Railroad.

In addition to business activities, Barber was an active philanthropist, supporting both local and national causes. He built a hospital for the city of Akron and designated $500,000 of his estate to

Ohio Columbus Barber (North Wind Picture Archives)

be used for industrial and agricultural education after his death.

Barber was described as a courageous and self-confident individual. He remained president of the Diamond Match Company until 1913, when he left the presidency to serve as chairman of the board of directors. In 1915, he married Mary F. Orr, with whom he lived until his death on February 4, 1920.

BIBLIOGRAPHY

Fleming, William Franklin, *America's Match King: Ohio Columbus Barber, 1841–1920*, 1981; Lane, S. A., *Fifty Years of Akron and Summit County*, 1892; Olin, O. E., *Akron and Environs*, 1917; Wright, G. Frederick, *Representative Citizens of Ohio*, 1913.

Barden, Don

(December 20, 1943–)
Entertainment Executive, Manufacturer

Don Barden parlayed $500 into a series of investments that in 1998 led to *Black Enterprise* magazine ranking his business among the 100 largest African-American-owned industrial or service companies.

Born on December 20, 1943, in Detroit, Michigan, to Milton Barden and Hortense (Hamilton) Barden, Don grew up in a blue-collar family. At various times, his father worked as a mechanic and a laborer in an automobile plant. At high school in Inkster, the town near Detroit where Don was raised, the youngster quarterbacked the football team and was the captain of the basketball team. After graduating from high school in 1963, he enrolled at Central State University, but he proved unable to afford college and was compelled to quit during his freshman year.

Barden then moved to Ohio, where he worked as a laborer in shipbuilding yards and also as a plumber. Ambitious, intelligent, and wanting more out of life, Barden took $500 he had managed to save and opened a record store in Lorain, Ohio. As his business grew, he began booking bands and promoting shows. He started his own record label and from there went into public relations.

Fortune came after he began investing in real estate. When in the mid-1960s the federal government was looking for a building to house its military recruiting station in Lorain, Barden found a suitable location and convinced the military to rent it. Government commitment in hand, he secured a bank loan and bought the building, later selling it and doubling his money.

Barden made several other real estate investments while founding the *Lorain County Times*, a weekly newspaper, and winning election to the city council, on which he served from 1972 until 1975. Two years later, he moved to Cleveland and hosted a talk show on WKYC-TV. While in that position, he learned about the advent of cable television and the potential it had to make money. Using his political connections, he convinced the city of Lorain to set aside a small portion of its cable television franchises for African-American investors. He subsequently invested in the cable system and then sold his interest for a considerable profit.

Over the next few years, Barden contracted with several predominantly African-American towns, including Inkster, to let him wire them for cable. He landed his biggest contract in 1983, when the city of Detroit granted him a franchise for its cable system. In partnership with a Canadian communications company, Maclean Hunter, Barden began wiring Detroit in 1986 and by 1994 had about 120,000 subscribers. That same year, he sold Barden Cablevision to the Comcast Corporation in a deal that netted him about $100 million.

In 1995, Barden, who had married Bella Marshall in 1988 and had a daughter, bid for and obtained a license from the Gary, Indiana, Gaming Commission to bring legal gambling to that city by opening a riverboat casino. Critics claimed that gambling would make already crime-ridden Gary worse, but Barden insisted, "I think it can only help because one of the by-products of poverty is crime. Now people will have a job and can earn a living." Barden's riverboat, the *Majestic Star*, became America's first African-American-owned casino.

Barden engaged in another controversial investment in 1998 when he and entertainer Michael Jackson opened a plant in the African country of Namibia to convert General Motors vehicles from left- to right-hand drive. His business, Barden Companies, also sold cars, drinks, canned food, and mattresses. The market, critics claimed, would prove too small, poor, and unstable. Where others saw limitations, however, Barden saw opportunities, and about Africa he proclaimed, "Once the free-market system permeates, this continent will be one of the world's most dynamic markets."

BIBLIOGRAPHY

McNeil, Donald G., Jr., "Black Pioneer Answers the Call," *New York Times*, July 7, 1998.

Barnum, P. T.

(July 5, 1810–April 7, 1891)
Entertainer

A 161-year-old slave, a midget, Siamese twins, and lastly a traveling circus—"The Greatest Show on Earth"—these characterized Phineas Taylor Barnum's career as a showman who used sensationalism and often proudly admitted to humbuggery.

Barnum was born on July 5, 1810, in Bethel, Connecticut, to Philo F. Barnum and Irena (Taylor) Barnum. At various times, his father worked as a tailor, farmer, and tavern-keeper, and ran a small express stage route from Norwalk to Bethel. As a boy, Phineas obtained little formal schooling and tried to avoid manual labor, which he always hated. Nevertheless, he did some odd jobs on the family farm, and when the elder Barnum opened a general store around 1823, he put his son to work in it.

After Barnum's father died in 1825, the young man, left with little money, obtained a job in another general store and gained a reputation as a shrewd trader. He soon moved to Brooklyn, New York, as a buyer for a grocery store and discovered an urban environment filled with attractions and opportunities. He returned to Connecticut in 1828 and opened a fruit and confectionery store in Bethel. The following year, he married Charity Hallett.

In 1831, he founded a newspaper in Danbury, Connecticut, the *Herald of Freedom*, dedicated to liberal ideas. Barnum's outspoken opinions resulted in libel suits being filed against him. In one case, a conservative court found him guilty and sentenced him to 60 days in jail. This conviction made him a martyr and public figure, but additional fines from other libel cases, along with mounting expenses, caused him to sell the newspaper.

Barnum found himself adrift in 1834 with nothing to do. Then, after opening a

P. T. Barnum (Library of Congress)

boardinghouse in New York City, a boarder told him about an unusual slave woman, Joice Heth. Barnum went to see her. Aged, toothless, and sightless, with eyes set far back in their sockets and a face overwhelmed by deep wrinkles, Heth could barely move. Barnum listened to her owners tell the story that she was indeed 161 years old—they showed him yellowed documents to prove it—and that she had nursed George Washington. Heth, despite her debilitation, still possessed a good mind and strong voice, and so confirmed the story, even revealing the details surrounding Washington's chopping down a peach tree as opposed to a cherry tree.

Although Barnum considered the story dubious, he saw a moneymaker and bought Heth for $1,000, thus beginning his career as a showman. In the year remaining before she died, Heth traveled around the nation with Barnum, who charged audiences to see and speak with her. His advertisements proclaimed: "Joice Heth is unquestionably the most astonishing and interesting curiosity in the world! . . . The most eminent physicians and intelligent men in Cincinnati, Philadelphia, New York, Boston and other places have examined this *living skeleton* and the documents accompanying her, and all, *invariably*, pronounce her to be, as represented, 161 *years of age!*"

After Heth died and the doctors who examined her estimated her age at 80, Barnum adeptly generated publicity by stating he had been misled. By this time, Barnum had tired of being on the road, and despite his success with Heth, his finances dwindled. As a result, he purchased Scudder's American Museum in New York City in 1841. The museum had opened in 1810 and featured many curios that Barnum continued to display. He took the museum in another direction, however, when he presented in its lecture room vaudeville-style acts—trained dogs, ventriloquists, and singers—and morality plays.

In a short while, his advertising—flamboyant and always intended to keep his name before the public—and his penchant to employ freaks as attractions drew larger and larger crowds. His museum featured a bearded lady and a mermaid, among others. He amused his audiences and made it clear that his entertainment included humbuggery. In fact, he and his customers delighted in it. In one famous incident, he advertised a horse appearing with its head where its tail should be. When customers viewed the horse, they indeed found it that way—Barnum had positioned the animal in its stall facing backward! In yet another incident, he placed a sign in the museum indicating the way to the "Egress." No animal awaited the curious, only a series of halls that led to the exit!

Barnum added the Siamese twins Chang and Eng as an attraction but scored his biggest success at the museum when in 1842 he displayed the midget Charles Stratton, whom he renamed Gen. Tom Thumb. Thumb (only five years old but promoted as older by Barnum) had stopped growing and at just over two feet tall, made for an extraordinary sight. Barnum taught Thumb to sing, dance, and tell stories, and the youngster displayed a keen talent for each. He took Thumb to Europe in 1844, obtained an audience in England with Queen Victoria—another event crafted for publicity—and had Thumb appear in Paris, riding in a miniature coach. (Thumb continued performing for Barnum on a regular basis until around 1852, although he married Lavinia Warren, another one of Barnum's dwarfs, in 1863 at a wedding noted for its extensive press coverage.) Barnum owed much to Thumb— the diminutive celebrity had made Barnum's reputation as a showman.

In 1850, Barnum staged a U.S. tour by Jenny Lind, a Swedish soprano who had tired of opera. The public flocked to her shows, making both her and Barnum wealthy.

Barnum entered politics and won election to the Connecticut state legislature in 1865. He considered retiring from show business, especially after his museum burned down that year but then decided to rebuild and kept the museum open until another fire struck in 1868. Barnum embarked on a new endeavor in 1871, when he founded a traveling circus, which held its first show in Brooklyn, New York. The Barnum circus included three rings under the big top. Barnum wasted no effort in finding odd people and strange beasts. He made headlines when, from Britain, he imported Jumbo, an enormous elephant that he billed as "The Only Mastodon on Earth." Barnum's circus grew—he called it "The Greatest Show on Earth"—and soon went from traveling in wagons to traveling on trains, and from torchlights to electric lights. This period was one of great change for Barnum, both personally and professionally. In 1873, his wife died, and the following year he married Nancy Fish. He briefly reentered politics as well and from 1875 to 1876 served as mayor of Bridgeport, Connecticut.

As competition in the circus business intensified, Barnum merged with his main competitor, James Anthony Bailey, in 1881. Barnum and Bailey's Circus had a gala opening that year with a pageant in New York City attended by thousands. The circus prospered, although marred by an accident in 1885 when a locomotive ran down and killed Jumbo. True to his bombast, Barnum claimed that Jumbo had run onto the tracks to save a baby elephant and had thus lost his life in a heroic act.

Barnum left no heir to carry on his business when he died on April 7, 1891. Always the showman, he had modernized entertainment in an era when developments in communication and a shift in population from farms to cities called for change. Barnum used newspapers to promote his bold advertising style and his moneymaking approach to publicity, and he attracted audiences in an urban society by playing to their desire for the unusual.

BIBLIOGRAPHY

Adams, Bluford, *E Pluribus Barnum: The Great Showman and the Making of U.S. Popular Culture*, 1997; Kunhardt, Philip B., *P. T. Barnum: America's Greatest Showman*, 1995; Root, Harvey W., *The Unkown Barnum*, 1927; Saxon, A. H., *P. T. Barnum: The Legend and the Man*, 1989.

Baruch, Bernard Mannes

(August 19, 1870–June 20, 1965)
Financier

As a Wall Street investor, Bernard Mannes Baruch had made $1 million by the time he was 30 and later became an influential voice in the national government.

Born on August 19, 1870, in Camden, South Carolina, to Simon Baruch and Belle (Wolfe) Baruch, Bernard grew up in a comfortable environment supported by his father's medical practice. At age 11, he and his family moved to New York City, where the elder Baruch continued as a general practitioner. After graduating from public school, Bernard entered the College of the City of New York in 1884. There he excelled at academics and sports, playing lacrosse and baseball. He received his B.A. degree in 1889 and, following several odd jobs, joined A. A. Housman & Company, a brokerage firm, in 1890.

Although Baruch began as a mere office boy, Wall Street excited him, and he devoured books about stocks and securities while learning all he could from the experts around him. Baruch soon bought bonds for himself and others successfully enough that in 1896 he obtained a one-eighth interest in the firm. He handled stock trades for clients, and in 1897, the year he obtained partnership, he made $40,000 on a $200 speculation in the sugar market. That same year, he married Annie Griffen; they eventually had three children.

Baruch continued to make money for all concerned, and his trade in tobacco, railroads, and copper earned him a legendary reputation. By 1900, he had made $1 million, and three years later, he retired from Housman to form his own brokerage firm, which specialized in industrial development.

Over the next several years, Baruch invested heavily in Texas Gulf Sulphur, Utah Copper, the Intercontinental Rubber Company, and the Alaska Juneau Gold Mining Company, all of which were leading businesses in the nation's rapid industrialization. Despite the money he made, he felt stung by those who attributed his success to luck or who derogatorily referred to him as a speculator. He craved respect from his peers, and after contemplating going into the field of law—and then rejecting it as impractical for a man his age—he decided to take an active role in government.

Partial to the Democratic Party, Baruch supported Woodrow Wilson in his 1912 presidential bid and despaired that the candidate might lose. "If Wilson is defeated," he said to a friend, "I don't know what I shall do." After Wilson's victory, however, Baruch visited him frequently at the White House as an unofficial adviser. In 1916, while World War I raged in Europe, Wilson appointed Baruch to serve on the advisory committee of the Council of National Defense, and the financier applied his expertise to determine which critical materials the United States would need in the event of being drawn into the conflict. (Baruch had previously liquidated his holdings to avoid any conflict of interest.)

In 1917, Baruch served on the Allied Purchasing Commission, which oversaw all purchases made in the United States for the Allied governments in Europe. After the United States entered the war later that year, he served as chairman of the War Industries Board, putting together a master plan for industrial development and making sure that bureaucracy did not hamper the war effort. Overall, he exerted an enormous influence on the nation's economic policies. In 1919, he traveled to Europe with President Wilson as a member of the U.S. delegation to the Paris Peace Conference, handling economics and reparations clauses.

In the early 1920s, Baruch addressed the problems facing American agriculture, which was then suffering from lagging productivity. Despite his Democratic politics, Republican President Warren Harding appointed him as a member of an agricultural conference. In 1925, Baruch pledged $1.5 million to help rehabilitate areas in South Carolina devastated by the boll weevil.

Baruch advised President Herbert Hoover on economic matters after the Great Depression began and, more importantly, became a confidential adviser to President Franklin D. Roosevelt.

Bernard Mannes Baruch (Courtesy: Harry S Truman Library)

Baruch played an important role in drafting the National Industrial Recovery Act of 1933, which was part of Roosevelt's early New Deal legislation. After World War II began, Baruch served as adviser to James Byrnes, Roosevelt's war mobilization director, and on several committees to which he was appointed by the president. From 1946 to 1947, he held the post of U.S. representative on the United Nations Atomic Energy Commission. Baruch died on June 20, 1965, and is remembered as one of the nation's leading financiers, an expert on industrial development, and a dedicated adviser to presidents.

BIBLIOGRAPHY

Baruch, Bernard, *American Industry in the War,* 1941; Baruch, Bernard, *Baruch: My Own Story,* 2 vols., 1957–1960; Baruch, Bernard, *A Philosophy for Our Time,* 1954; Coit, Margaret L., *Mr. Baruch,* 1957.

Bayard, William

(1760–September 18, 1826)
Merchant

Shortly after the American Revolution, William Bayard founded New York City's leading commercial house.

The son of William Bayard and Catherine (McEvers) Bayard, William was born in 1760 in Greenwich, New York. His father developed a prosperous colonial merchant business and owned extensive lands. When the American Revolution erupted, however, he sided with Britain and, as a result, his property was confiscated by the newly formed state of New York. The elder Bayard subsequently immigrated to England in 1783, but he left his son William behind, who had recently married Elizabeth Cornell.

Young Bayard entered into a partnership with Herman Le Roy in 1786, forming a merchant house. They traded first in liquor, importing it from overseas, and over the next few years developed one of early America's most important trading concerns. The two men added a third partner, thus creating Le Roy, Bayard & McEvers, but Bayard remained the firm's leader.

In the early 1800s, Bayard expanded his firm's trade even though incessant warfare between England and France made shipping precarious. Overall, the profits outweighed any losses from enemy attacks and confiscation. When Congress imposed an embargo on all overseas trade, Bayard's firm turned to land speculation, primarily in New York.

During the War of 1812, Bayard and his partners operated several privateers that made handsome profits. After the war, the merchant house traded extensively

William Bayard (North Wind Picture Archives)

with Europe and the East and West Indies. Amid the revolutions that swept South America during the 1820s, Bayard directed his firm in lucrative trade with the emerging nations.

Bayard's interests extended beyond his merchant house. A leader in economic modernization and diversification, he served as president of the Bank of America, the Chamber of Commerce of the State of New York, and the Morris Canal Company, among others. When merchants from the northern states met at Philadelphia in 1824 to protest a tariff increase, they made Bayard the group's chairman.

Bayard's two sons, William Jr. and Robert, eventually joined their father's merchant house but embarrassed him by engaging in a profiteering scheme that sullied the firm's reputation. Tension and depression from this errant action may have contributed to Bayard's death at Greenwich on September 18, 1826. His contemporaries remembered him for his business acumen, his commitment to honorable dealings, and for the fortune that made him one of the wealthiest men in the new republic.

BIBLIOGRAPHY

Nettels, Curtis, *The Emergence of a National Economy, 1775–1815*, 1962.

Bechtel, Stephen

(September 24, 1900–March 14, 1989)
Engineer

Known for his imagination and his ability to tackle projects others considered too difficult, Stephen Bechtel took his father's construction business and made it one of the largest construction and engineering firms in the world.

Stephen was born on September 24, 1900, in Aurora, Indiana, to Warren Bechtel and Clare Alice (West) Bechtel. Stephen served with the U.S. Army Engineers during World War I, after which he enrolled at the University of California, Berkeley. He left before graduating, however, in 1925, when his father formed the W. A. Bechtel Company, a construction business located in Oakland. Steve Bechtel worked as vice president and supervised railroad building and pipeline construction.

Bechtel became president of the company in 1936, and he and a friend, John McCone, formed the Bechtel-McCone Corporation. They specialized in construction projects for energy companies and, during World War II, built Liberty ships and tankers.

Bechtel dissolved Bechtel-McCone in 1946 and founded the Bechtel Corporation, for which he served as president and director. In 1947, Bechtel won a contract to build the Saudi Arabian portion of a pipeline stretching from the Persian Gulf to the Mediterranean. In 1952, he built a huge oil refinery in Aden for the Anglo-Iranian Oil Company. The following year, in a stunning feat that defied critics, Bechtel and the Trans Mountain Oil Pipeline Company completed a 718-mile-long pipeline across the Canadian Rockies from Vancouver, British Columbia, to Edmonton, Alberta.

Over the years, Bechtel guided the building of dams, the San Francisco-Oakland Bay Bridge, subway systems in Washington, D.C., and San Francisco, nuclear and hydroelectric power plants, and mining complexes. He retired from his company in 1960 and died in San Francisco on March 14, 1989. His son, by Laura Adaline (Pearl) Bernbach, whom he had married in 1923, continued to work for the company.

BIBLIOGRAPHY

McCartney, Laton, *Friends in High Places: The Bechtel Story, the Most Secret Corporation and How It Engineered the World*, 1988; "Stephen Bechtel, Sr. Obituary," *Time*, March 27, 1989.

Belmont, August

(December 8, 1816–November 24, 1890)
Banker

August Belmont, the son of a wealthy Austrian landowner, built a career as one of America's most influential bankers by securing the trust of the famous Rothschild family during the financial Panic of 1837. His flamboyant lifestyle made a tremendous impact on the staid New York society scene, and his business acumen and political intuition eventually earned him a reputation as a leader of the Democratic Party and as a person of tremendous character.

August, the son of Simon and Frederika Elsaas Belmont, was born on December 8, 1816, in Alzey, a village in the Rhenish Palatinate, a region known as the Paradise of Germany. August himself had early in life adopted the family's nickname for him in place of his given name, Aaron. In 1822, nine months after his mother's death, August moved to Frankfurt to live with his grandmother.

Though his family was wealthy, August chose to embark on a career at the young age of 14. Working without pay and initially entrusted only with sweeping the floors, he devoured everything he could learn at the Frankfurt branch of the banking House of Rothschild. August was extremely diligent, working late, conversing with the agents, and demonstrating his quick mind. After three years, he was rewarded for his efforts with an appointment to the Rothschilds' branch office in Naples, Italy.

His years in Naples were invigorating, with long days devoted to proving his growing expertise in finance and his leisure hours spent learning several languages, traveling, and becoming an aficionado of art and culture. At age 24, Belmont, en route to Cuba for an assignment, stopped over in New York City on May 14, 1837. Arriving just as the financial Panic of 1837 began, Belmont was astonished at the eerie stillness of the city. Over the next few days, he witnessed the chaotic economic crisis unfold and hastened to the offices of the Rothschilds' American agents, only to find that it had already gone bankrupt.

Realizing that communication to Europe would take weeks, Belmont took the risky decision of canceling his Cuban trip. Sensing the opportunity in front of him, he rented a small room on Wall Street for an office and established August Belmont & Company. In the financial ruin that was New York at this time, he was able to secure everything he needed on the strength of the Rothschild name. Using his acquired acumen in international banking and finance techniques, he threw himself into the impoverished market, buying and reselling commodities, using only the Rothschild name to secure credit. In doing so, he not only steadied the debt left by the previous Rothschilds' agent, but eventually secured their approval and won a handsome salary to continue as their American representative.

During his first year in this role, Belmont speculated in the cotton industry, Bank of Arkansas notes, and Missouri securities, succeeding so well in these ventures that the Rothschilds made a considerable profit. Within three years of his arrival in America, Belmont himself was one of the richest men in New York City. He was considered one of the three most significant private bankers in the United States, renowned for his skill at arbitrage. For this talent, he earned the nickname, "King of the Money Changers."

His wealth and career well in hand, Belmont became a social butterfly, eager to spend his money to live in the sumptuous style that he had come to associate with the European aristocracy. He hosted lavish dinners, developed a reputation as a playboy, and embraced entertainment of all forms with abandon. He cut a dashing, yet somewhat frightening, image in the staid society of New York, a subculture dominated by the long-standing, elitist Knickerbocker family. He was consequently excluded from a number of society functions. His entanglements caused some friction with the Rothschilds when word reached them of a duel Belmont fought—and won—to protect his good name from criticism by his opponent, William Hayward.

Despite the controversy, Belmont exerted a great deal of influence over the social norms of the day. In time, Bel-

August Belmont (Library of Congress)

mont's reputation softened, and he came to be regarded as a gentleman. It was noted in his obituary that Belmont "taught New Yorkers how to eat, how to drink, [and] how to dress."

In 1844, Belmont became a naturalized American citizen. That same year, he was appointed as the Austrian consul general in the United States, a post he held until 1850. His business continued to grow, with investments in new corporations, state bonds, and railroads. He cultivated a strong relationship with clients by taking as much care with small loans as he did with large investments. He preferred not to do business with slave owners; though he disliked slavery on a moral basis, he primarily believed that it was not a sound economic institution.

On November 7, 1849, Belmont married Caroline Slidell Perry, with whom he had three children. As Belmont's personal and business lives continued to run smoothly, he became increasingly more interested in politics. In 1851, Belmont led the Democratic campaign in New York to elect James Buchanan to the presidency. When Buchanan lost the primary to Franklin Pierce, Belmont threw the weight of his influence to Pierce. After Pierce was elected to the presidency in 1852, Belmont was rewarded for his efforts with an appointment as American minister to the Netherlands.

By 1857, Belmont was widely considered one of the most influential younger leaders of the Democratic Party. During the Civil War, he threw himself into the Union cause, proving particularly useful in keeping his European contacts aware of what transpired during the war. Belmont withdrew from political activity in 1872, though he continued to follow politics from a distance. In the latter period of his life, before his death from pneumonia on November 24, 1890, Belmont became an avid art collector and was an enthusiast of horse racing.

BIBLIOGRAPHY

Black, David, *The King of Fifth Avenue: The Fortunes of August Belmont*, 1981; Katz, Irving, *August Belmont: A Political Biography*, 1968; Sears, Louis M., "August Belmont: Banker in Politics," *The Historical Outlook*, April 1924.

Bennett, James Gordon, Jr.

(May 10, 1841–May 14, 1918)
Editor

James Gordon Bennett Jr. was the heir to the *New York Herald*, a paper that his father JAMES GORDON BENNETT SR. had started in the 1830s. Bennett Jr. took over the paper shortly after the Civil War, and although under his tutelage the *Herald* remained one of New York's leading papers, Bennett failed to recognize the growth of fierce competitors in New York's journalist market. Bennett himself, however, became one of the best-known newspaper publishers of the nineteenth century.

James Jr. was born in New York City on May 10, 1841, and was educated primarily in Europe, at first by his mother, Henrietta Agnes (Crean) Bennett, and then at the École Polytechnique in Paris. He served in the U.S. Navy during the Civil War, after which he worked in several departments at his father's newspaper, the *New York Herald*.

The elder Bennett made his son managing editor in 1867. When Bennett Sr. retired, young James inherited a newspaper whose circulation had reached 90,000 daily and whose profits had reached $400,000 annually. That same year, he founded the *Evening Telegram*, a sensationalist paper.

As the *Herald*'s chief executive officer, Bennett directed several notable journalistic assignments, most notably when he sent Henry M. Stanley to Africa in 1871 to search for David Livingstone, a story that held the *Herald*'s readers spellbound. After his father died in 1872 and following a scandal involving the family of his fiancée (a woman he never married), Bennett moved to Paris and managed the *Herald* and the *Telegram* via cable. In 1883, he joined financier John W. Mackay and founded the Commercial Cable Company, which laid a cable line across the Atlantic and ended the then-existing cable monopoly.

Bennett's long-distance management worked poorly. Overbearing and temperamental, he hired, demoted, and promoted people with little thought, and his absence kept him from understanding the competition raised by the *New York World* under JOSEPH PULITZER and the *New York Times* under ADOLPH OCHS. Even as Bennett moved the *Herald*'s headquarters from Broadway and Ann Street to Broadway and Sixth Avenue—Herald Square—in 1893, circulation declined.

Bennett married Baroness de Reuter in 1914. She was the former Maud Potter of Philadelphia and the widow of Baron George de Reuter. He died in France on May 14, 1918.

James Gordon Bennett Jr. (Library of Congress)

BIBLIOGRAPHY

Crouthamel, James L., *Bennett's New York Herald and the Rise of the Popular Press*, 1989; O'Connor, Richard, *The Scandalous Mr. Bennett*, 1962.

Bennett, James Gordon, Sr.

(1795–June 1, 1872)
Editor

From a one-penny paper printed in a cellar, James Gordon Bennett and his son, JAMES GORDON BENNETT JR., developed the *New York Herald* into a prestigious publication that reflected the advent of a consumer society.

The elder James Gordon Bennett was born in Keith, Scotland. Records do not indicate his exact date of birth, although it is thought to have been in 1795. He was educated to join the Roman Catholic priesthood, but he never had much

James Gordon Bennett Sr. (Library of Congress)

enthusiasm for joining the clergy, and in 1819 he immigrated to Halifax, Nova Scotia, in Canada. Within a short while, he moved to Boston and later, in 1822, to New York City, where he obtained a job as a newspaper reporter. The following year, a newspaper in Charleston, South Carolina, hired him to translate foreign articles.

Bennett returned to New York City in 1825 and wrote for the *Courier* before the *Enquirer* hired him the following year as an associate editor. Bennett won a national audience with his articles about Washington politicians. At that time, newspapers and their editors had a close attachment to political candidates and often openly declared themselves to be the voice of one political party or an-

other. Bennett committed himself in 1828 to Andrew Jackson, the presidential candidate of the newly formed Democratic Party, and praised the Jacksonian appeal to the common man. (Bennett's support had its limits, however—a few years later, he joined the Jacksonians in criticizing the national bank, but abruptly changed his position when a principal figure in the bank invested in his newspaper.)

Bennett brought his enthusiasm for the common man to his work in stories that exposed the foibles of the elite. After the *Enquirer* merged with the *Courier* in 1829, Bennett directed the newspaper to greater growth. He left, however, in 1835 when the paper shifted its political allegiance. Two years earlier, the *New York Sun* had emerged as the first penny press newspaper, and Bennett entered the field by founding the *New York Herald*. He produced it from a cellar on Wall Street, while sitting behind an office desk that consisted of a plank propped atop two barrels. Bennett wasted no time in achieving success—his intensive, blunt coverage of local news found a large audience. The *Herald* stood above all other papers in its extensive use of telegraphy in reporting, in its assigning of foreign correspondents, and in its coverage of financial news from Wall Street.

Bennett pioneered in another area, too, one that complemented his indebtedness to a teeming, commercially driven society: advertising. Traditionally, newspapers had devoted little attention to creativity in advertising, but Bennett stunned his competitors in 1848 by requiring that all advertisements be renewed daily—meaning their content had to be changed. As Bennett's managing editor said: "The advertisements of the *Herald* are a feature. They are fresh every day."

During the Civil War, Bennett employed 63 correspondents to cover the conflict. He supported the Union, but frequently expressed views sympathetic to the Confederacy. Bennett supervised the *Herald* until he retired in 1867, at which time he turned the paper over to his son. The elder Bennett died on June 1, 1872.

BIBLIOGRAPHY

Crouthamel, James L., *Bennett's New York Herald and the Rise of the Popular Press*, 1989; O'Connor, Richard, *The Scandalous Mr. Bennett*, 1962.

Bernbach, William

(August 13, 1911–October 1, 1982)
Advertising Executive

In 1983, *Harper's Magazine* claimed that William Bernbach "had a greater impact on American culture than any of the distinguished writers and artists who have appeared in [our] pages . . . during the past 133 years." To earn this accolade, Bernbach led an advertising agency that created some of the most innovative advertisements in modern history.

Born in New York City, New York, on August 13, 1911, to Jacob Bernbach, a designer of women's clothes, and Rebecca (Reiter) Bernbach, William obtained a bachelor's degree in English from New York University in 1932.

He had his first experience in developing advertising when, while working for Schenley Distillers as an office boy during the Great Depression, he wrote an advertisement for the company's American cream whiskey. He acquired more experience as a writer when he worked for the New York World's Fair in 1938, a job that led to his being hired by the William H. Weintraub Agency. While working for the agency, he learned about art and graphics.

During World War II, Bernbach worked as a copywriter for Grey Advertising, where he met Ned Doyle, an account executive. They developed a plan to start their own agency with Doyle's friend Maxwell Dane, and in 1949 they founded Doyle Dane Bernbach.

Bernbach blazed new ground when he insisted that market researchers be cast aside for innovation. He believed that reliance on market surveys resulted in bland advertisements, and he wanted his staff to use its own creative instincts. Bernbach replaced the prevailing style of strident advertisements with low-key, ironic ones, and by all accounts his work produced an advertising revolution. He applied his technique in 1963 with a campaign in New York for Levy's rye bread. On billboards and in magazines, he posed African Americans, Native Americans, and Asians next to the slogan, "You don't have to be Jewish to love Levy's." The subtle humor made Levy's the biggest selling rye bread in New York.

On a national level, Bernbach gained his greatest recognition developing advertisements for Volkswagen and Avis Rent A Car. For Volkswagen, he developed a minimalist style—a photo of the car, a VW Beetle, dwarfed by a white backdrop and accompanied by a brief comment and the slogan "Think Small." The advertisements made what many considered an ugly car into a cultural icon.

For Avis, Bernbach took the company's status as second to that of the leading car rental agency, Hertz, and turned it into an advantage when he developed the slogan "We try harder. We're only number 2." Again, in the advertisements he used an uncluttered, modern look, one that soon permeated the advertisements presented by other companies and that has since remained a distinguishing feature of American advertising.

An ardent promoter of world peace, Bernbach developed advertisements for the Committee for a Sane Nuclear Policy. They featured the prominent author and baby doctor Benjamin Spock pictured with a child on his knee and the simple caption: "Dr. Spock is worried."

Bernbach retired as CEO of Doyle Dane Bernbach in 1976 after having attracted accounts worth millions of dollars. After his departure, the firm lost its creativity and several of its large clients. Bernbach died on October 1, 1982, in New York City from leukemia.

BIBLIOGRAPHY

Fox, Stephen, *The Mirror Makers*, 1984; Kinsley, Michael, "William Bernbach," *Harper's Magazine*, January 1983; Mayer, Martin, *Madison Avenue*, 1958.

Bethune, Gordon

(1941–)
Airline Executive

In the 1990s, Gordon Bethune won acclaim as an outstanding executive for taking Continental from among the worst to among the best airlines.

Born in 1941, Bethune spent his adult life around airplanes. After graduating from high school, he joined the U.S. Navy, where he fixed aircraft engines. He later obtained a B.S. degree from Abilene Christian University in Abilene, Texas, and held positions as vice president of engineering and maintenance at Braniff and Western airlines; senior vice president for operations at Piedmont Airlines; and, from 1988 to 1994, a vice president at Boeing Aircraft.

He left Boeing to become chairman and CEO at Continental, an airline that had gone through two bankruptcies, with questionable management under FRANK LORENZO, and had a reputation for flying shoddy planes, losing luggage, and seldom keeping to schedules. Bethune said: "Continental . . . had become a lousy, unreliable airline, and people had stopped using [it] and for good reason. An airline has no real value unless it's predictable and reliable, but for a decade management had been cutting costs. . . . Our service was lousy, and nobody knew when planes might land."

Many doubted that Bethune could do anything with the company. Within two years, however, Continental, which had previously finished last in the Department of Transportation's ranking for on-time flights and customer satisfaction, finished in the top third. Company profits rose as more business travelers began to use Continental.

Bethune accomplished the transformation by ordering immediate upgrades in the company's planes, by demanding they fly on time, and by hiring talented assistants, among then Gregory D. Brenneman, who became president in 1996. Brenneman and Bethune formulated what they called their "Go Forward Plan," meaning "Fly to Win, Fund the Future, Make Reliability Reality, and Work Together." Said Bethune: "We all knew what needed to be done. But the difference between those guys [his predecessors] and me is that I get enough people to help me get it done."

Bethune earned considerable money for his labor. In 1995, he received $1.1 million in salary and bonuses, and over $1 million to keep him from accepting an offer from United Airlines. Whether his success at Continental stemmed more from his talents or from the nation's strong economy in the late 1990s remains to be seen, although many consider his managerial style an example of how a corporation should be run.

BIBLIOGRAPHY

Bethune, Gordon, *From Worst to First*, 1998; Bryant, Adam, "The Candid Mr. Fix-it of the Skies," *New York Times*, November 12, 1996.

Birdseye, Clarence

(December 9, 1886–October 7, 1956)
Manufacturer

Clarence Birdseye invented the method to produce frozen food after an unusual encounter with a fish.

Clarence was born on December 9, 1886, in Brooklyn, New York, to Clarence Frank Birdseye, a lawyer and legal scholar, and Ada (Underwood) Birdseye. As a youngster, taxidermy interested him, as did food preparation: in high school at Montclair, New Jersey, he enrolled in a cooking class.

Around 1905, Birdseye entered Amherst College in Massachusetts, where he earned money by trapping black rats at $1 each, to be used by a professor at Columbia University for breeding experiments. Birdseye left Amherst before graduating, and in 1910 began working as a field naturalist for the Biological Survey of the U.S. Department of Agriculture. In 1912, he wrote a scientific book, *Some Common Mammals of Western Montana in Relation to Agriculture and*

Spotted Fever. That same year, he moved to Labrador, where he trapped silver foxes and sold them in the United States as breeding stock and entered the fur trade. On a visit to the United States in 1915, he married Eleanor Gannett; the couple soon had a son.

Birdseye had his encounter with the fish in 1916, after he returned to Labrador. While ice fishing, he dropped his catch next to him. The fish froze immediately, but, to Birdseye's amazement, when he took it home and put it in a pail of water, it began to swim. The fish had revived because its cells had frozen so quickly that there had been no time for deadly large ice crystals to form.

From this incident, Birdseye went on to discover that in slow-frozen fish and in game large ice crystals caused a coarse texture and produced fluids that ruined the flavor. He found that if fish could be frozen rapidly—what he called "quick-freeze"—the bad taste would be avoided. Birdseye believed this applied to other foods, too. He discovered a problem, however, in trying to develop quick-freezing: different foods froze at different rates, and it was difficult to control the desired temperature for each one.

World War I interrupted Birdseye's experiments, and from 1917 to 1919 he worked as a purchasing agent for the U.S. Housing Corporation. In 1923, after a brief stint as president of the U.S. Fisheries Association, he opened a small shop in New Jersey and invented a machine for quick-freezing. His method involved pressing thin amounts of food under metal plates cooled to –25° F. With this machine, exposure to temperatures could be precisely controlled. At first, Birdseye quick-froze haddock in small blocks and packed it in cardboard boxes.

The following year, he opened a development lab in Gloucester, Massachusetts—a fishing port—that he called the General Foods Company and improved his quick-freezing technique. He applied it to fish, poultry, and meat. In 1929, the Postum Company (a food distributor) and the Goldman Sachs Trading Corporation bought Birdseye's patents and assets for about $20 million. Presently, Postum bought Goldman Sachs' interest and adopted the name General Foods, but applied "Birds Eye" in bold print to many of its frozen foods.

By the 1940s, vegetables and precooked foods joined the list of quick-frozen items. The use of frozen foods improved diets by making vegetables available all year long. Freezing within a few hours of harvest made them tastier and more nutritious than fresh vegetables transported from farm to distant market, and, with the new industry, farmers began growing crops specifically for it. With their popularity, Birdseye's foods resulted in nearly every home having a freezer.

After his deal with Postum, Birdseye continued working and developed an infrared heating lamp and a new type of harpoon gun. In 1951, he and his wife authored *Growing Woodland Plants*, and two years later, he went to Peru to research making paper from sugarcane stalks. While there, he suffered a heart attack. When he died in New York City on October 7, 1956, he owned about 300 patents.

Shortly before his death he said about his accomplishments: "I am intensely curious about the things which I see around me, and this curiosity, combined with a willingness to assume risks, has been responsible for such success and satisfaction as I have achieved. Only through curiosity can we discover opportunities, and only by gambling can we take advantage of them."

BIBLIOGRAPHY

Clark, William H., and James H. S. Moynahan, *Famous Leaders of Industry*, 1955.

Bloch, Henry Wollman

(July 30, 1922–)
Tax Preparation Entrepreneur

As tax laws became more complex in the 1960s, millions of middle-class Americans turned to a tax preparation service, H&R Block, founded by Henry Wollman Bloch and his brother Richard A. Bloch.

Henry Bloch was born on July 30, 1922, into one of the leading families in Kansas City, Missouri. He earned his bachelor's degree from the University of Michigan and served in the U.S. Army Air Corps during World War II as a combat navigator. He went on to attend the Graduate School of Business at Harvard and then worked as a stockbroker.

In 1946, Henry and his brother Leon started the United Business Company (UBC) with $5,000 borrowed from a great-aunt. UBC provided advertising, bookkeeping, and accounting services for small businesses, but struggled so much in its first year that Leon left it to attend law school. UBC then expanded slowly before Henry invited his brother, Richard, to join the firm—an excellent choice, for Richard, who had obtained a degree in economics from the Wharton School of Finance at the University of Pennsylvania, possessed the go-getter qualities that balanced Henry's preference for management. Together, the brothers formed H&R Block, changing the spelling of their last name out of concern that people would otherwise pronounce it "Blotch."

Henry and Richard stumbled inadvertently into preparing tax returns for others. At first, they did so only as a favor to a few clients and found the service such an impediment to their other interests that they considered dropping it. A client at the *Kansas City Star*, however, convinced them in 1955 to run an advertisement to see if tax preparation might have a larger appeal. After the advertisement appeared, hundreds of customers jammed the H&R Block office, seeking help with their tax forms. As it turned out, the Blochs had run their advertisement at an opportune time, for that same year, the Internal Revenue Service decided to end its practice of completing tax forms for free.

From that beginning, H&R Block grew quickly into the nation's largest tax preparation business. This expansion met formidable opposition, however, from accountants and lawyers who considered the company an intruder.

As the federal government made tax laws more complex in the 1960s, H&R Block gained more customers, largely from a confused and harried middle class. During the 1970s, the company began its first large-scale advertising campaign, and its promotional budget soon reached $20 million. In 1978, Richard, stricken with cancer, left the firm.

By 1985, H&R Block had 9,000 offices operating during the tax season, hundreds of them as franchises. Henry Bloch had already realized, however, that the seasonal nature of his company's business necessitated diversification to increase profits. In 1978, he acquired the Florida-based Personnel Pool of America, an industrial, medical, and clerical employment agency. Two years later, he acquired CompuServe, a computer information services company, for $23 million. CompuServe's revenues in 1985 reached $68 million, making the company a tremendous asset to H&R Block.

Also in the 1980s, Bloch bought 80 percent of Hyatt Legal Services, a company that provided legal advice much the same way that Bloch provided tax services—in small offices readily available to middle-class Americans. The following year, however, Bloch sold back the business to its original owner.

In the mid-1980s, H&R Block prospered to the point of accumulating a $120 million cash reserve. By that time, Tom Bloch, Henry's son, assisted Henry in guiding the firm. In 1993, H&R Block founded the Block Financial Corporation as a subsidiary to provide credit card and on-line financial services and to publish such software programs as Kiplinger TaxCut. H&R Block sold CompuServe in 1997 in a deal valued at $1.2 billion.

BIBLIOGRAPHY

Goldwasser, Thomas, *Family Pride: Profiles of Five of America's Best-Run Family Businesses*, 1986.

Boeing, William Edward

(October 1, 1881–September 28, 1956)
Manufacturer

A new era stirred William Edward Boeing, an aircraft design and manufacturing pioneer, its spirit captured by *Aircraft* magazine: "You cannot tether time nor sky. / The time approaches, Sam must fly."

William was born on October 1, 1881, in Detroit, Michigan, to Wilhelm and Marie (Ortman) Boeing. His family had lucrative connections to the mining and lumber industry, and he obtained his education at private schools in the United States and Europe. Boeing entered Yale University in 1899 but left three years later without graduating. He then pursued his family's lumber business, and his interests in the Pacific Northwest resulted in his moving to Seattle in 1908.

Boeing took his first airplane ride in 1914 and the following year learned how to fly at a school operated by GLENN MARTIN. Regarding an early aircraft, he remarked to his friend Conrad Westervelt: "There isn't much to that machine. . . . I think we could build a better one." He soon did. While maintaining his involvement in the lumber industry, in July 1916 Boeing joined Westervelt, an engineering officer in the Navy, and another friend, Herb Munter, to form the Pacific Aero Products Company, later renamed the Boeing Airplane Company, to manufacturer aircraft.

At first, business boomed—when the United States entered World War I in 1917, Boeing obtained government contracts to build Curtiss flying boats. The war ended, however, before the aircraft could be completed, and hard times set in. To remain in business, Boeing had to resort to building furniture. At about the same time he married Bertha Potter Paschall in 1921, his company negotiated a contract with the government to rebuild 50 wartime de Havillands.

In 1923, Boeing began making his own experimental pursuit aircraft, the PW-9, and sought to enter the commercial field, a plan soon aided by the government's decision to transport airmail via private carriers, and by public interest in aviation, intensified in the wake of Charles Lindbergh's dramatic transatlantic flight in 1927. That July, Boeing Air Transport began flying mail and passengers from San Francisco to Chicago on planes designed and built by Boeing, a fleet of 25 M-40s that could carry up to four passengers and 500 pounds of mail. The venture immediately made money.

In February 1928, Boeing joined with Fred B. Rentschler (the head of Pratt and Whitney aircraft engines) and Gordon Rentschler (the head of National City Bank) to form United Aircraft and Transport, a combination that also included Hamilton Standard Propeller and several airframe firms. Boeing's planes soon made United the leader in commercial air transportation. In 1928, United introduced the Model 80, a passenger plane complete with upholstered seats, reading lamps, and other amenities, and with in-flight stewardesses to serve the riders. Two years later, the Monomail revolutionized aircraft construction with its streamline, all-metal design. The company replaced the Model 80 in 1933 with the twin-engine 247, the world's first modern passenger transport. For the military, Boeing manufactured the B-9 bomber, which increased airspeed from 100 to 186 miles per hour.

In 1934, however, a scandal involving government airmail contracts resulted in Congress passing legislation that required corporations involved in aviation manufacturing and transportation to separate their interests. Consequently, United divided into three companies: Boeing Aircraft, United Aircraft, and United Airlines. Embittered by this development, Boeing retired from business. He moved to a large estate in Fall City, Washington, where he continued to live until, suffering from declining health, he died on September 28, 1956, while sailing on his yacht.

Over the ensuing years, Boeing Aircraft remained a leader in manufacturing commercial and military planes. The company built the P-26 Peashooter in the 1930s and from the 1960s through 1990s developed the first stage of the Saturn V rocket, lunar orbiters, the lunar rover, and part of the space shuttle system. In 1996, Boeing merged with Rockwell International, a space and defense contractor.

BIBLIOGRAPHY

Mansfield, Harold, *Vision: The Story of Boeing, A Saga of the Sky and New Horizons of Space*, 1966.

Boesky, Ivan

(March 6, 1937–)
Financier

In the 1980s, 20-hour workdays and an enormous amount of time on the telephone—a console telephone with 300 buttons—reflected Ivan Boesky's wheeling and dealing in stocks and securities. His no-holds-barred tactics—"Ivan the Terrible" some called him—enabled Boesky to amass a fortune, but also earned him time in prison.

Born in Detroit, Michigan, on March 6, 1937, to a Russian Jewish émigré whom Boesky later described as poor (a point on which stories differ), Boesky began earning money at age 13 when he began selling ice cream from a truck he drove illegally, because he was underage. After graduating from high school and briefly attending college, he obtained a degree in 1963 from the Detroit School of Law. While at the school, he married Seema

Ivan Boesky (Reuters/Peter Morgan/Archive Photos)

Silberstein (they would eventually have four children), whose father owned the Beverly Hills Hotel.

Boesky moved to New York City in 1966 to pursue a career in arbitrage. In the early 1970s, he headed the arbitrage department for Edwards & Hanly and, in an incident that foreshadowed his later troubles, was fined $10,000 for selling securities short in excess of the firm's ability to deliver.

With $350,000 from his wife's mother and stepfather and a like amount from his wife and himself, Boesky launched his own investment firm in 1975 and made substantial profits, until two large deals turned sour in 1980. Despite the setback, Boesky had increased the firm's capital from its initial $700,000 to $94 million.

In 1981, Boesky withdrew from his company to form Ivan Boesky Incorporated. The first year, he made more than $12 million. The following year, he lost more than $11 million in a bad deal with oil company Cities Service. In 1983, however, he rebounded after earning a huge profit in a merger between Getty Oil and Texaco, bringing him more than $76 million.

In disparagement, his enemies portrayed Boesky as gluttonous and gave him the nickname "Piggy." The shrewd arrangements he had with the investors in his corporation meant he always got a large chunk of profits while suffering little from any losses. For example, in 1982, the year Boesky endured reverses, the outside investors lost $9.3 million while he lost only $1.8 million. "Greed," said Boesky in the 1980s to a group of college students, "is healthy. You can be greedy and still feel good about yourself." Observers marveled at Boesky's tenacity and his long workdays, claiming that "He's like a machine. He never gives up. He digs and digs until he gets the answer."

To obtain more capital for arbitrage, in 1982 Boesky bought control of several companies that provided him with $130 million, among them Cambrain & General Securities. He also obtained money from a subsidiary that owned the Beverly Hills Hotel. When some investors and reporters wondered if Boesky had acted illegally to amass his fortune, he retorted: "We buy and sell securities every day, always properly."

But, in fact, Boesky colluded with MICHAEL MILKEN and engaged in insider trading, an illegal activity whereby he received secret tips from officials in investment houses concerning corporate mergers and buyouts. (Although Milken pleaded guilty to criminal charges, he always denied having engaged in insider trading.) An investigation by the federal government resulted in Boesky cooperating with law enforcement in exchange for a plea bargain. On December 18, 1987, before a crowd of 200 spectators who came, said one newspaper, "to watch the disgraced tycoon be sent to jail," a judge sentenced Boesky to three years in prison. In addition, Boesky paid a $100 million civil penalty to the Securities and Exchange Commission and was barred from Wall Street for life. Boesky served his time at a minimum-security prison in California until December 1989, and at a halfway house in New York City until his release the following April. In the end, the Boesky investigation exposed "rampant criminal conduct" on Wall Street.

Despite the penalties levied against Boesky, loopholes still allowed him to buy and sell stocks for himself and to operate a small firm; in addition, rumors abounded that he had millions in a secret bank account in Switzerland. Two years out of prison, he divorced his wife and then rebounded financially, managing around $1 billion for clients on Wall Street. To a reporter, Boesky said, "I am comfortable and quite content."

BIBLIOGRAPHY

Byron, Christopher, "Happily Ever After," *Esquire*, April 1995; Kinkead, Gwen, "Ivan Boesky, Money Machine," *Fortune*, August 6, 1984; Marcial, Gene, *Secrets of the Street*, 1995; Stewart, James, *Den of Thieves*, 1991; "Stock Trader Shoots for the Moon," *U.S. News & World Report*, April 15, 1985.

Boit, Elizabeth Eaton

(July 9, 1849–November 14, 1932)
Manufacturer

It was not uncommon in Wakefield, Massachusetts, at the turn of the century to hear the sentiment voiced that "the smartest man in Wakefield is a woman." Elizabeth Eaton Boit, a textile manufacturer, is remembered for her business expertise and her philanthropy.

Elizabeth Boit was born on July 9, 1849, in Newton, Massachusetts, where her father, James Henry Boit, was the janitor of a school. Boit's mother, Amanda Church, was from Bridgton, Maine. Boit and her five sisters attended the public schools of Newton.

Though never particularly gifted in mathematics, Boit's career in business began at the early age of 18, when she was hired as timekeeper at the Dudley Hosiery Knitting Mill. Although textile factories during that time hired an increasing number of women, it was rare for one to become as successful in the industry as Boit. Within five years, she had become the forewoman of the sewing department, and by 1883 she was the superintendent of Allston Mills.

In 1888, Boit and a colleague, Charles N. Winship, following the advice of her brother-in-law George W. Morse, formed a partnership in a textile manufactory. Winship, the more inventive of the two, managed production, while Boit oversaw financial and administrative affairs.

Winship, Boit and Company established the Harvard Knitting Mill in Cambridge, Massachusetts. Specializing in the manufacture of women's underwear, the company began with 25 employees. By the next year, Boit and Winship moved the mill to the suburb of Wakefield.

By 1897, the mill did $250,000 worth of business annually, employed 360 people, and owned its own plant. The company continued to grow rapidly, expanding its line of garments to include men's and children's underwear. The garments were marketed under the names Merode and Forest Mills, and were sold by William Iselin & Company of New York, Lord & Taylor of New York, and Brown, Durrell of Boston.

Boit, by this time the leading businesswoman of Wakefield, lived in a style befitting her wealth. She built a large stucco house on an extensive property, which she shared with a companion, Emma May Bartlett. She was also a generous benefactor, contributing to such local charities as the Wakefield Home for Aged Women and to all of the town's churches. An important figure in Wakefield's business community, Boit also served as a director of the Wakefield Cooperative Bank.

The mill and its employees were the center of Boit's life. At the height of its success, the firm occupied eight and one-half acres, employed 850 people, and finished 2,000 garments daily. In 1920, with business booming, the company instituted a profit-sharing plan. Boit's personal interest in the welfare of her employees, however, is better illustrated through small actions; for example, it was her habit on rainy days to send a streetcar for the girls who worked in the mill to take them to their homes after work.

Although many considered Boit old-fashioned, her family knew her to be generous and devoted to family and work. Due to illness, Boit turned her interest in the mill over to Charles Winship in the late 1920s. She continued to visit the mill as often as her health allowed. On November 14, 1932, four years of illness came to an end when she died of a combination of circulatory ailments and diabetes. She was buried in Lakeside Cemetery in Wakefield.

BIBLIOGRAPHY

Conklin, Edwin P., *Middlesex County and Its People*, 1927; Howe, Julia Ward, *Representative Women of New England*, 1904; *Notable American Women, 1607–1950*, vol. 1, 1971.

Borden, Gail

(November 9, 1801–January 11, 1874)
Manufacturer

Gail Borden, who developed the process for making condensed milk and consequently altered dairy farming, advertised his product as every bit as good as that obtained straight from the cow: "For use in Tea and Coffee, and for Ice Creams, Custards, Puddings, and all other articles of cookery requiring both milk and sugar, it will be found excellent. It cannot, when diluted, be distinguished from the best country milk. . . ."

Gail was born on November 9, 1801, on his family's farm near Norwich, New York, to Gail Borden and Philadelphia (Wheeler) Borden. As a child, Borden did his farm chores and grew up in a period when Americans were carving out new settlements in the West. His parents joined that migration in 1815, and for a brief period, Borden lived in Covington, Kentucky. While there, he helped his father farm and learned how to survey. When his family moved to Indiana in 1816, he received his only schooling, lasting under two years.

In 1822, Borden, beset by poor health, moved on his own to Amite County in southwestern Mississippi. There, he taught at two frontier schools, one in Bates, the other in Zion Hill. He married Penelope Mercer in 1828 and the following year, moved to Texas, then still part of Mexico, where he farmed and raised cattle. To Borden, Texas appeared the land of opportunity, and it soon fulfilled his expectations. Stephen Austin, who headed the American colony in Texas, appointed Borden to superintend the official land surveys and, with his father-in-law, Borden obtained a land grant that exceeded 4,000 acres.

He gained a reputation from his surveying work and over the next few years contributed greatly to the Texas independence movement. In 1833, he helped write the state constitution that propelled Texas toward independence from Mexico, and two years later, he was one of six men who signed a proclamation saying the crisis necessitated war. After the battle with Mexico began, Borden published the only newspaper in Texas, the *Telegraph and Texas Register*.

With Texas independence gained in 1836, Borden made a survey for Galveston and laid out the city. In 1837, he became Galveston's collector of customs, the most important customs post in the Texas Republic and a busy position that soon made it among the most important of all government positions. Although Borden lost the collector's job for a short while, he later regained it and held it until 1849. During these years, his first wife, who had borne his children, died, and in 1845 he married Augusta Stearns.

At the same time, between 1839 and 1851, Borden worked as an agent for the Galveston City Company that sold land on which Galveston was built. As settlers came into Texas and moved beyond, across the towering Rocky Mountains into Oregon and California, he learned more and more about their hardships, particularly about how they often lacked food in the sparsely inhabited territory. Seeing a way to help them—especially after the California gold rush began in 1849—and a way to make money, Borden began experimenting with producing a meat biscuit that could be transported easily or even carried in saddlebags, if needed. In 1850, he obtained a patent for his biscuit. He made his product by boiling meat to separate it from its broth, creating a dense syrup. He then mixed the whole concoction with flour and baked it.

In 1851, Borden traveled to London, where he displayed his meat biscuit at the Great Exhibition and won the top award, a gold medal, for his contribution to foodstuffs. *Scientific American* magazine called his meat biscuit "one of the most valuable inventions that has ever been brought forward."

As a moneymaker, however, the meat biscuit failed, largely for two reasons. First, the U.S. Army issued a report condemning it; second, many people simply disliked the way it tasted. "We all tried it once," said one trail-weary consumer, "then turned unanimously to . . . watery potatoes. Once afterwards . . . we tried again [and] then left all we had purchased to the birds."

From meat biscuits, Borden plunged quickly and forcefully into condensed milk. An apocryphal story tells why: while aboard a ship sailing back to America from Europe, Borden supposedly witnessed babies unable to obtain milk and dedicated himself to correcting the problem.

Borden produced condensed milk through a process that used a vacuum pan. When he applied for a patent for the process in 1853, however, he was turned down. The government claimed he had invented nothing new, and, indeed, work elsewhere, especially in France and England in the 1820s and 1830s, had led to concentrated milk that was similar to Borden's. He proved, however, that he was innovative when he showed that his process required that air be excluded from milk from the time the evaporation began until the milk was sealed in cans. The government eventually agreed, and in 1856 he received his patent.

Condensed milk provided the nutrients found in fresh milk without having to keep the product in a cooler. Canned condensed milk could be stored for months on a shelf. Borden believed this characteristic made his product salable. His biggest problem became locating the financing he required to produce canned condensed milk in substantial quantities.

Help came in 1857 when on a train in the Northeast, he accidentally met Jeremiah Millbank, a wholesale grocer. Borden told Millbank about the condensed milk, and Millbank agreed to provide the capital to produce it.

Borden began a small condensary for making the milk and founded the New York Condensed Milk Company for distributing it. In 1861, he established a larger condensary up the Hudson River in Wassaic, New York. Farmers brought their milk to the two-story wooden building where the female workers wore all white, the men wore white aprons and white gloves, and the whitewashed walls and floors sparkled.

The turning point for Borden came during the Civil War, when the federal government ordered condensed milk for its troops as a regular field ration. In the summer of 1862, Borden sold 50,000 quarts of condensed milk. Within one year, his dairy had expanded to such an extent that it could produce the same quantity in three days. Sales boomed as many Americans came to accept canned condensed milk after the U.S. Army accepted it. In 1863, Borden complained that he could not meet the demand, and he opened branch factories.

Borden dropped his own name from his condensed milk in 1866, after it had been infringed on by competitors, and began calling his product Eagle Brand, the name it still carries. He also obtained patents for producing concentrated fruit juices, tea, coffee, and cocoa.

In the late 1860s, he returned frequently to Texas and built a schoolhouse for freedmen (although he had once owned slaves) and another for white children. He died at his home in Texas on January 11, 1874. After his second wife had died in 1860, he had married Emeline Eunice, and she survived him, as did children from his first marriage.

Borden's development of condensed milk did more than improve diets; it changed dairy farming. He required that farmers who supplied milk to him meet requirements concerning the cleanliness of their cows, and as Borden needed more milk, farmers moved away from selling it informally to selling it within an efficient, industry-driven operation—the essence of America's modern economy.

BIBLIOGRAPHY

Comfort, Harold W., *Gail Borden and His Heritage since 1857*, 1953; Frantz, Joe B., *Gail Borden: Dairyman to a Nation*, 1951.

Bradley, Milton

(November 8, 1836–May 30, 1911)
Manufacturer

From "The Checkered Game of Life," Milton Bradley developed a toy and game company that still contributes to American recreation.

Milton was born on November 8, 1836, in Vienna, Maine, to Lewis Bradley and Fannie (Lyford) Bradley. His father operated a starch mill until the family moved to Lowell, Massachusetts, in 1847. After high school, young Milton worked as a draftsman, saved his money, and entered Lawrence Scientific School at Cambridge. In 1856, he moved with his family to Hartford, Connecticut, before he could graduate, and then relocated to Springfield, Massachusetts, where Bemis & Company, a locomotive works, hired him. There he labored for two years, until the firm closed.

Bradley then opened his own business as a mechanical draftsman and securer of patents, but after learning lithography he decided to set up a lithograph shop. Good fortune came his way when Samuel Bowles, publisher of the *Springfield Republican*, urged him to print a portrait of Abraham Lincoln. Bradley took the artwork, converted it into a lithograph, and printed it just in time for Lincoln's rise to prominence as a candidate for president in the election of 1860.

The lithograph sold well, but Bradley's business declined so much during the Civil War that he resorted to printing games. After he distributed an English parlor game called "The Checkered Game of Life," its popularity led to his forming Milton Bradley & Company with two partners in 1864. Bradley's games often promoted a moral message: good deeds bring rewards, bad deeds bring trouble. He made money, however, from games geared strictly to entertainment and joined the croquet craze by making sets and printing manuals for players.

In 1867, while his line expanded to playing cards, checkers, backgammon, and dominoes, Bradley patented and made "Zoetrope—or Wheel of Life," an optical toy that consisted of a small drum into which a user placed strips of paper that had pictures printed on them. The user then whirled the drum and looked through a slit that revealed a moving picture, repeated over and over again. Bradley followed this device in 1868 with "Historoscope," a flat box with a handle that, when cranked, revealed panoramic color drawings depicting scenes from American history.

In 1869, Bradley embraced the kindergarten movement and its belief that children could learn through play at an early age. As a result, he began making kindergarten materials—alphabet blocks, paints, and weaving sets—and publishing children's books. He published a children's magazine, too, titled *Work and Play*, and over the years wrote several books devoted to using color as a teaching tool, including *Color in the School Room* and *Color in the Kindergarten*.

When Bradley's partners retired in 1878, he changed the firm's name to Milton Bradley Company and continued to expand his market with toys made from wood, paper, and cardboard. His model houses and railroads sold well, as did his 1880 jigsaw puzzle, the "Flag Ship," that, he claimed, was "drawn from an instantaneous photograph of the U.S. cruiser *Chicago.*" He also reinforced gender roles by manufacturing a toy that taught girls how to design dresses. Bradley wanted to make buying toys and games a year-round activity, and so to his customers he wrote, "We wish to present to your notice the fact that the idea is no longer entertained that the sale of Games and Home Amusements is confined to the Holiday Trade. There never was any reason why Games, if of any value in themselves, should not have as steady and continual a sale as books."

Bradley, who had married Villona Eaton in 1860 and, after her death, Ellen Thayer in 1864, died on May 30, 1911. His company continued, though, and later manufactured "Scrabble," a game invented in the 1930s by Alfred M. Butts and, after rejection by every major game company, was originally produced by James Brunot. Today, Milton Bradley is a part of Hasbro, a large corporate toy and game company.

BIBLIOGRAPHY

McClintock, Inez, and Marshall McClintock, *Toys in America*, 1961; Milton Bradley Company, *Milton Bradley: A Successful Man*, 1910.

Braniff, Thomas Elmer

(December 6, 1883–January 10, 1954)
Airline Executive

A pioneer of the passenger airline industry, Thomas Elmer Braniff originated many of the first foreign commercial routes, initiated the first major air routes within South America, and configured airplanes to allow for tourist and first-class service aboard the same flight. In addition to his reputation as an imaginative businessman, Braniff was devoutly religious, and an active participant in social welfare and civic causes.

The pioneering instinct was innate to Braniff, as his parents, John and Catherine Baker Braniff, had left the fertile land of Pennsylvania to settle on the prairie of Salina, Kansas. Thomas Braniff was born in Salina on December 6, 1883. In 1900, when John Braniff migrated to Oklahoma to start an insurance company, Thomas remained in Kansas, supporting himself through his sophomore year of high school by working as a copyboy for the *Kansas City Star.*

After completing his sophomore year, Braniff parlayed a short stint helping his father into the establishment of his own insurance agency. The eager 17-year-old tornado insurance salesman learned his first business lessons the hard way. Tornadoes were a common occurrence in Oklahoma, and one night an exceptionally intense storm resulted in high claims that wiped out his company. Undaunted, young Braniff continued to try new ventures, eventually establishing the Braniff Investment Company and Prudential Fire Insurance.

On October 26, 1912, after a four-year engagement, he married Bess Thurman. She remained Braniff's lifelong companion and confidante in both private and business matters. The deep religious faith shared by both would be called upon frequently; both of their children—Thurman and Jeanne—died young.

In 1927, with the country captivated by Charles Lindbergh and his transatlantic flight, Braniff entered into a partnership with four other men to purchase an airplane. Shortly thereafter, Braniff bought out his partners' interest and, with his brother Paul, a former World War I pilot, started ferrying passengers between Oklahoma City and Tulsa. The two cities were part of the hub of the developing oil-producing industry, and there was a great deal of business travel between the two. In a short time, the frequency of flights on this route was greater than that between New York City and Chicago.

In 1930, Braniff Airways was incorporated. Though passenger routes expanded quickly, revenue from passengers was less significant than steady income from competitive contracts from the U.S. Post Office to deliver air mail in these early years of aviation. The company struggled to remain solvent, with paydays frequently overdue. Despite hardships, Braniff built a solid base of employee loyalty. It is a measure of Braniff's personality and conviction that three of the employees from those early days remained with the company to eventually sit on the board of directors. After four lean years, Braniff Airways got its first of many airmail contracts.

In 1935, Braniff acquired a Texas airline, Long and Harmon, Inc., which had mail routes throughout Texas. This purchase allowed Braniff to institute the first direct service from Chicago to the Gulf of Mexico. Braniff's inventiveness, combined with the growth of the Southwest, enabled the company to flourish.

During World War II, Braniff Airways operated a military transport service and conducted training schools for pilots and mechanics. By the postwar period, there was greater national appreciation for the role of a strong air transportation system, and new routes appeared rapidly. Braniff pushed relentlessly for acquisition of new service areas and in 1946 was authorized to fly internationally. Braniff's routes in Central and South America expanded quickly. In 1949, he established a nonstop route from Lima, Peru, over the Andes to Rio de Janeiro, Brazil. It was billed as the first service of its kind and the longest regular commercial nonstop service in the world.

Envisioning a reduced rate for travel was another Braniff innovation. His tourist fares on Latin American routes preceded the development of a domestic coach fare. It was also Braniff Airlines that began the practice of having both first-class and coach travelers on the same plane. In addition, Braniff popularized the use of commercial airborne radar systems. In 1952, with the acquisition of Mid-Continent Airways, Braniff Airways became the sixth largest airline in the United States, with assets exceeding $35 million.

In addition to his involvement with airlines, Braniff devoted a great deal of time to civic interests. A devout Roman Catholic, he was deeply committed to religious tolerance and served as the Catholic co-chairperson of the National Conference of Christians and Jews. He also worked with its European branch, the World Brotherhood. Georgetown University honored Braniff for his involvement with these organizations and for his other contributions in international affairs. He was also an active member of the U.S. Inter-American Council on Commerce and Production.

Despite being a high-school dropout, Braniff placed great value on education and culture, and he served as director of the Dallas Symphony Orchestra and the Grand Opera Association. He was also a trustee for several universities and a member of the National Advisory Council of the Institute of Fiscal and Political Education. Braniff was interested in promoting health and social welfare issues as well. He served as a director and chairperson of the board of directors of the Texas division of the American Cancer Society, was a member of the advisory committee of the Pilot Institute for the Deaf, and sat on the executive board of the Boy Scouts.

In 1944, Braniff established the Braniff Foundation, an institute devoted to supporting religious, educational, and scientific endeavors. Both Thomas and Bess Braniff willed the bulk of their estates to the foundation. Braniff's interest in others, and his engaging personality, earned him a warm reputation among people of all walks of life.

Aviation, which dominated Braniff's business career and captivated his imagination, also caused his death. On January 10, 1954, Braniff was killed while returning from a hunting trip when his plane struck a power line and crashed near Shreveport, Louisiana.

BIBLIOGRAPHY

Beard, Charles E., *Thos. E. Braniff (1883–1954): Southwest Pioneer in Air Transportation*, 1955; Davies, R. E. G., *A History of the World's Airlines*, 1964; Kelly, Charles J., Jr., *The Sky's the Limit*, 1963; *New York Times*, Obituary, January 11, 1954; Smith, Henry L., *Airways*, 1942.

Bronfman, Edgar

(1955–)
Manufacturer, Entertainment Executive

Edgar Bronfman sometimes tells the story of how when he was a child he flew alone on his family's company jet to a boarding school in New England. "Are you here with your father?" one headmaster asked. "No," Edgar replied, "I'm here with my pilot." So Bronfman lived, a child of wealth who, after struggling to find himself, inherited Seagram liquor, diversified it, and brought it to Hollywood as the parent company of a major studio.

Edgar was born in 1955 in Purchase, New York, an upscale town in Westchester County, to Edgar M. Bronfman and Ann (Loeb) Bronfman. Bronfman Sr. headed Seagram, a liquor company founded in the 1920s in Montreal, Canada, by Samuel Bronfman. Surrounded by wealth, Bronfman Jr. had every material

Edgar Bronfman (Reuters/Peter Morgan/Archive Photos)

advantage and attended the prestigious Collegiate School in New York City, near his home on Park Avenue. He did well at school, although he had no interest in it and vowed never to attend college. Bronfman's vow may have reflected a desire to be creative rather than herded onto a business track.

In fact, at age 15, at a time when his father owned a large share of MGM movie studios, Bronfman read a screenplay and convinced the elder Bronfman to finance its production. The resulting film, *Melody*, featured David Putnam as director and young Bronfman as production assistant.

After graduating from high school, Bronfman moved to Hollywood and worked as a producer, with modest success in the 1970s. In 1979, he married an African-American actress, Sherry Brewer, a union that caused tension with Bronfman Sr., who disliked racial mixing.

Bronfman produced his most successful movie, *The Border*, in 1982, after which the elder Bronfman asked his son to join Seagram with the view to eventually heading it. Young Bronfman hesitated—he feared a corporate structure that would stifle him, but he ultimately decided that he could use his talents at Seagram and so joined the firm.

After working at Seagram in New York City, Bronfman went to Europe, where he arranged the purchase of Oddbins, a retail liquor store chain, and played a role in acquiring Matheus Muller, a sparkling-wine manufacturer. Bronfman returned to the United States in 1984 as president of the House of Seagram, a division that oversaw the distilled-spirits operation of a Seagram subsidiary. He launched an appealing advertising campaign featuring actor Bruce Willis that boosted the company's wine cooler sales. A few years later, however, the wine cooler market collapsed, costing the company substantially, and overall alcohol consumption in the United States declined. As a result, Bronfman cut jobs and sold off Seagram's low-end labels while promoting its more expensive products, such as Chivas Regal.

Bronfman's ascension to president and chief operating officer of the Seagram Company in 1989—shortly after acquiring Tropicana Products—gave him day-to-day control of the firm, although the elder Bronfman watched all as CEO. Bronfman Jr. purchased Martell cognac for $732 million and, in 1993, obtained the right to distribute Absolut Vodka in the United States.

As Seagram's profits grew, Bronfman decided to diversify into a business that promised great expansion: the entertainment and communications industry, where he had first exhibited his creative interest. He tried and failed to gain control of Time Warner. Then, after succeeding his father as Seagram's CEO in 1994, he set his sights on MCA, a faltering Hollywood conglomerate most noted for its recording and video companies, and for Universal Studios. Bronfman sold Seagram's interest in DuPont Chemical—a move widely denounced by investors—and with the money bought 80 percent of MCA from a Japanese firm, the Matsushita Electric Industrial Company, for $5.7 billion.

Bronfman, who had divorced Brewer and, in 1994, married Clarissa Alcock, the daughter of a Venezuelan oil company executive, found many critics in Hollywood who portrayed him as a spoiled rich man interested in MCA only as an expensive hobby. Under Bronfman's leadership, however, Universal produced the box-office hit *Dante's Peak*, and he made such impressive deals as buying half of Interscope Records for $200 million and half of the sitcom production company Brillstein-Grey for $100 million.

Soon, former critics were saying about Bronfman: "How refreshing it is to have so much new blood at Universal." It remained to be seen, however, whether MCA would prove to be as profitable as the investment in DuPont had been for Seagram's, and whether Bronfman, who had his fourth son in September 1996, would be able to pass along to his children a Seagram company equal to if not better than that which he had inherited.

BIBLIOGRAPHY

Rose, Frank, "The Love Song of E. Bronfman, Jr.," *Esquire*, June 1977.

Brown, Alexander

(November 17, 1764–April 3, 1834)
Banker

Alexander Brown and his sons built one of America's leading financial institutions in the nineteenth century and amassed fortunes that ranked them among the nation's earliest millionaires.

Born on November 17, 1764, at Ballymena in County Antrim, Ireland, Alexander Brown immigrated to Baltimore, Maryland, in 1800 with his wife Grace (Davison) Brown and his eldest son, William. The couple's other three sons (George, John, and James) remained temporarily in Ireland. Brown had operated a successful linen business in Belfast, and in Baltimore, he set himself up as a linen importer. Within a short time, he expanded his line of products, and in addition to selling goods on his own account, he sold them for others on a commission basis, an activity that soon dominated his business. The firm became known as Alexander Brown & Sons.

Within a few years, Brown's other sons arrived in America from Ireland and joined him in the family business. In

1809, William moved to Liverpool and founded Brown, Shipley & Company, thus providing an important contact that enabled the Browns to expand their transatlantic trade. By 1810, Brown & Sons had increased its capital to $121,000, a sum that a decade later exceeded $1 million.

Under Brown's auspices, each son eventually established a branch of the company in a new location, with George assisting his father in Baltimore, while John opened a branch in Philadelphia in 1818 and James opened a branch in New York City in 1825. The latter firm expanded so rapidly—boosted by the city's economic expansion as the Erie Canal opened—that in time the Browns made it a separate company. Another branch of the firm opened in Boston shortly thereafter.

Alexander Brown combined boldness with his conservative maxim that a firm should never outpace its capital. By the 1820s, he had begun exporting substantial amounts of cotton to Britain and had bought several ships. As a ship owner, he displayed great talent in sailing his cargoes across waters made turbulent by weather, war, and pirates. At the same time, he and George were instrumental in founding the Baltimore & Ohio Railroad as a means to revive Baltimore's economy, damaged by steamboat transportation and traffic along the Erie Canal.

Outside the business realm, Alexander Brown supported numerous improvements in Baltimore, including the founding of the city water works and the formation of the Maryland Institute of Art. At his death on April 3, 1834, his fortune reached $2 million—a considerable sum in that era.

Alexander Brown & Sons continues today in Baltimore as an investment banking firm. The other branches of the Brown enterprise merged with the Harriman investment banking house in 1931 to form Brown Brothers Harriman & Company, which remains an important financial institution.

BIBLIOGRAPHY

Kouwenhoven, John A., *Partners in Banking: An Historical Portrait of a Great Private Bank, Brown Brothers and Harriman & Co., 1818–1968*, 1968; Perkins, Edwin J., *Financing Anglo-American Trade: The House of Brown, 1800–1880*, 1975.

Buffett, Warren

(August 30, 1930–)
Financier

Brought up in a wealthy family, Warren Buffett dabbled in stocks as a child and as an adult transformed Berkshire-Hathaway from a struggling textile company into a prosperous investment firm.

Buffett was born on August 30, 1930, in Omaha, Nebraska, to Howard Homan Buffett and Leila (Stahl) Buffett. His father earned a fortune as a grocery store owner and, after that, as a stockbroker, and won election to Congress as a Republican.

Warren bought his first stock at age eight, and his interest in finance—he often dreamed about becoming the world's richest person—followed him into college. After earning a bachelor of arts degree from the University of Nebraska in 1950, he continued his studies at Columbia University's School of Business in New York City. During those years, he read *Security Analysis*, a book written in 1934 by Benjamin Graham and David Dodd. At the same time, he was studying under Graham at Columbia. Buffett was so taken by Graham's financial plan that he even offered to work at the professor's investment company for no pay. After Graham rejected the offer, Buffett returned to Nebraska and married in 1952. Two years later, Graham hired Buffett, and the young man moved to New York City.

In most of his dealings, Buffett enthusiastically applied the Graham formula for success on the stock market, which meant buying stocks at no more than two-thirds of net capital—stocks that were trading at low prices relative to book value and that other investors were ignoring—and then waiting for them to gain a following and rise in price.

Buffett moved back to Omaha in 1956 and with $5,000 of his own money and $100,000 from others, founded Buffett Partnership, an investment firm. His success on Wall Street attracted additional investors and led him to purchase American Express stock in 1963, a time when scandal and financial reverses had damaged the company. American Express soon corrected its problems, and Buffett and his partners reaped an enormous profit.

In 1965, Buffett acquired Berkshire-Hathaway, a textile company in New

Warren Buffett (Reuters/Str/Archive Photos)

Bedford, Massachusetts. Although the company never turned a good profit on its textile manufacturing, Buffett used it as a device to make more stock investments, especially after he dissolved Buffett Partnership in 1969. Over the next two decades, he purchased an interest in See's Candies, the Nebraska Furniture Mart, and Omaha-based insurance companies, all, again, in agreement with the strategy in *Security Analysis*. He said: "Those who read their Graham and Dodd will continue to prosper." By 1984, his pretax operating earnings from these businesses reached $88 million.

That same year, Buffett bought 740,000 shares in the American Broadcasting Company (ABC) and expanded his holdings in

Time, Incorporated to 1.6 million shares. Shortly thereafter, he also invested heavily in the Exxon Corporation and the Washington Public Power Supply System. Then, in 1985, he participated in the spectacular Capital Cities takeover of ABC and obtained an 18 percent interest in the new company, Capital Cities/ABC. This move went against the Graham formula, for the stock was already a glamour stock, not an undervalued one. Buffett, however, considered the potential for future profits tremendous—an estimate that proved accurate.

The following year, Buffett invested $700 million in Salomon Brothers, the largest investment banking house on Wall Street, and stuck with it through the crash of 1987—a typical move for him since he believed in holding onto stock rather than quickly reselling it. Known for the advice he gave to others in essays he wrote for Berkshire-Hathaway, Buffett made these observations:

> Candor benefits us as managers. The CEO who misreads others in public may eventually mislead himself in private.

> Predicting rain doesn't count; building arks does.

> Casino-type markets and hair-trigger investment act as an invisible foot that trips up and slows down a forward-moving economy.

Buffett's most prominent deal took place in 1995 when, with Berkshire-Hathaway as the largest stockholder in Capital Cities/ABC, he helped engineer the acquisition of the latter firm by Disney. This transaction produced the world's largest media company, a status reflective of the consolidations that swept the media industry from the mid-1980s to the mid-1990s.

Under Buffett, Berkshire-Hathaway's value jumped from $450 per share in the 1980s to $36,000 in 1997, while his personal wealth exceeded $2 billion. Beginning in July 1997 and continuing into 1998, Buffett bought more than $900 million worth of silver in a move that puzzled financial experts. Was he trying to manipulate the precious metals market or just betting that the future portended a great demand for silver? Whatever the answer, Buffett's action showed his clout as he pushed silver prices higher and investors marveled at the "Wizard of Omaha."

BIBLIOGRAPHY
Hagstrom, Robert G., and Peter Lynch, *The Warren Buffett Way: Investment Strategies of the World's Greatest Investor,* 1995; Smith, Adam, *Supermoney,* 1972; Train, John, *The Money Masters,* 1980.

Bulova, Arde

(October 24, 1889–March 19, 1958)
Manufacturer

Arde Bulova began his career as a salesman for the jewelry business started by his father and eventually assumed control of the company. Under his leadership, it produced fine watches and acquired other jewelry and watch companies. Bulova, an avid fan of radio, manufactured radio receiving sets in the 1930s and was instrumental during World War II and the Korean War in making precision components for the military.

On October 24, 1889, Arde Bulova was born to Joseph and Bertha Eisner Bulova in New York City. Joseph Bulova had emigrated from Bohemia at the age of 18 and settled in New York City, where he opened a small jewelry manufacturing operation in 1875. Arde attended New York public schools and began his first job in 1905 as a salesman for his father's business, the J. Bulova Company. The company prospered and was incorporated in 1911 with the elder Bulova holding the presidency, while Arde served as vice president and treasurer.

Initially, the jewelry manufacturing was carried out at a small plant in New York City, but by 1911 Arde had established a second plant in Providence, Rhode Island. In 1913, Arde made the important decision to expand the product line to include fine watches made with imported parts from Switzerland.

In 1919, product demand was great enough to warrant the establishment of a Bulova plant in Bienne, Switzerland, to produce the watch mechanisms. Another factory was then opened in Woodside, New York, to manufacture and assemble the remaining pieces of the watches. In 1923, the company was reincorporated as the Bulova Watch Company, and in 1930 Arde Bulova was elected chairman of the board, a position he would hold until his death.

In the 1930s, Bulova continued to expand operations by acquiring several subsidiaries, including Sag Harbor Guild and the Westfield Watch Company. Additional plants were opened in Valley Stream, New York, in 1941 and in Jackson Heights, Michigan, in 1952. A new modern factory was also built in 1952 in Flushing, New York. All operations from the old Woodside plant as well as the executive offices were transferred to this new site.

During this period of expansion, Bulova continued to emphasize quality and service. He invented several improvements such as special tools, gauges, and machines to produce standardized parts and mechanisms that required little maintenance and repair. Bulova products were sold only to licensed jewelers to maintain a high standard of service. During the Great Depression, the company extended many months of credit to its customers to allow for better inventory flow.

Bulova developed a love for the radio industry at its inception and began manufacturing radio receivers during the 1930s. He also became a pioneer of radio advertising by producing the first radio spot advertisements in 1926. Bulova acquired financial interests in a number of radio stations including WOV, WNEW, and WWRL in New York City.

At the outbreak of World War II, the Bulova Watch Company aided the war effort by manufacturing military timepieces and other precision devices for aviation and explosives. The company served a similar function during the Korean War, leading Bulova to establish a permanent research lab to develop mechanisms for guided missiles, cameras, gyroscopes, and munitions. He assisted disabled veterans after World War II by creating the Joseph Bulova School of Watchmaking in 1945. The school allowed handicapped veterans to retrain for jobs in Bulova's factories, with all costs covered by the Bulova Watch Foundation. Bulova had always encouraged the employment of handicapped workers at the company, and in 1955 he was appointed the chairman of the President's Commission on Employment of the Physically Handicapped.

In 1952, Bulova married Ilcana Marie Kevcia Pociovolosteanu from Romania. By the time of his death on March 19, 1958, the Bulova Watch Company had sales of over $76 million and assets totaling $46 million.

BIBLIOGRAPHY

Ingham, John N., ed., *Biographical Dictionary of American Business Leaders*, 1983; Loomes, Brian, *Watchmakers and Clockmakers of the World*, 1989; *National Cyclopedia of American Biography*, 1921.

Burpee, Washington Atlee

(April 5, 1858–November 16, 1915)
Merchant

As a teenager, Washington Atlee Burpee stood amid cooing pigeons, clucking chickens, and honking geese and decided he would start a mail-order business. The way it turned out, it led to forming the world's largest seed company.

Atlee was born on April 5, 1858, in Sheffield, New Brunswick, Canada, to David Burpee and Anna Catherine (Atlee) Burpee. After his father, a doctor, moved the family to Philadelphia, Atlee attended Friends' Central School. This was when he began breeding pigeons, chickens, geese, and turkeys as a hobby, and gained enough experience to write articles for poultry trade journals. At age 17, he started selling purebred fowl through the mail. His father, however, wanted him to follow in his footsteps and practice medicine, and in 1875 Atlee enrolled as a premedical student at the University of Pennsylvania.

Burpee stayed only a year. He disliked college, and when a businessman agreed to provide $5,000 for him to start a new poultry mail-order firm, the young man agreed. Burpee and his partner soon argued over policy, and sluggish sales worsened the relationship. With financial backing from his father, Burpee went off on his own, and in 1878 founded the W. Atlee Burpee Company that, like his earlier business, sold purebred fowl by mail order, along with some seeds.

Much to Burpee's surprise, his customers wanted seeds more than they did fowl, and in 1880 he revised his catalog to offer tomato, cucumber, turnip, and other seeds. He recruited people across the country to sell for him when he offered a free sewing machine to those who sold 300 seed packets, at 25 cents per packet. The orders soon quickened to some 400 daily.

Over the next few years, Burpee traveled through Europe searching for new seeds that would produce plumper tomatoes, sweeter berries, and more beautiful flowers. He introduced iceberg lettuce, Golden Bantam corn, and Bush lima beans, along with new varieties of tomatoes, onions, and celery. Burpee bought a farm at Doylestown, Pennsylvania, to test his seeds and, later, additional farms in New Jersey and California. For several years, he served as president of the American Seed Trade Association.

Burpee eventually won a large audience for his catalog. In its 200 pages, he did more than sell seeds—he told stories about his travels and interjected humor, as when he said that Spanish peanuts could be used "for fattening hogs and children." Many a farmer and small-town person sat on their porches reading Burpee's catalog, eyeing the pictures of fruits and vegetables and chuckling at the remarks.

By the time Burpee died on November 16, 1915, he had 300 employees and sold nearly 3,000 orders daily. Burpee had married Blanche Simons in 1892, and one

Washington Atlee Burpee (Library of Congress)

of his two sons, David Burpee, continued the seed business. Under David, the business expanded further, with sales increasing from $900,000 annually to more than $6 million, making Burpee the largest seed mail-order house in the world.

BIBLIOGRAPHY

Kraft, Ken, *Garden to Order*, 1963.

Burr, Donald Calvin

(May 8, 1941–)
Airline Executive

As a youngster, Donald Calvin Burr loved to stop at the local airfield and watch planes take off and land. He hoped someday to be involved in flying. As it turned out, he founded People Express Airlines and ranked among the most successful businessmen of the 1980s—until his competition outdid him.

Burr was born on May 8, 1941, in South Windsor, Connecticut, where his father worked as an engineer and his mother as a social worker. He considered entering the ministry but changed his mind after he decided he could make more of an impact by doing something else. After graduating from Stanford University in 1963—where he had served as president of the Flying Club—with a bachelor's degree in economics, Burr, who had recently married, obtained his M.B.A. in 1965 from the Graduate School of Business at Harvard.

Burr first worked as a securities analyst on Wall Street at the National Aviation Corporation, which specialized in aerospace investments. He advanced rapidly and in 1972 became president. The following year, an acquaintance, FRANK LORENZO, asked Burr to help save an airline he headed, Texas International. Burr agreed and joined the firm as its executive vice president. In 1977, he provided Lorenzo with an idea that contributed to the airline's turnaround: "peanuts fare," or super-low fares. The tactic caused Texas International's net income to increase from $2.5 million the previous year to $41.4 million in 1979.

Burr was named company president in June 1979, but he chafed under Lorenzo's dictatorial style and believed that the federal government's deregulation of the airline industry provided new opportunities. In late 1979, he resigned and within weeks embarked on a bold experiment: he would create an airline based on the lowest fares to date combined with a progressive personnel policy that gave every employee an important financial stake in the company.

For capital, Burr and several associates used their savings accounts, and investor William R. Hembrecht helped him raise $25 million through a stock sale. Burr then went to work establishing the important elements that made his new airline, which he named People Express, successful. First, he based his operations at Newark Airport, where he obtained space at the terminal for a low rate. Second, he purchased 17 used Boeing 737s at $4.5 million each, less than a third of the price for new models. Third, as he hired staff, he forbade any corporate bureaucracy. No one had a secretary, and everyone had to rotate in and out of jobs—pilots even worked at such ground duties as booking passengers. Fourth, all employees had to buy company stock, at a discount, thus giving them a vested interest in the business. Finally, People Express provided no-frills service that enabled it to offer superlow fares. Thus, passengers did without hot meals, computerized reservations, and free baggage handling.

Burr's company had an inauspicious start—a strike by air traffic controllers in 1981 caused it to lose $6 million over a two-month period. Burr revamped his route system, however, and in 1982 the airline carried more than 2.8 million passengers and made a small profit. Over the next several years, People Express experienced dramatic growth, and college business schools hailed Burr as an exemplar of a humane and innovative capitalism. The airline's growth, however, had a drawback as service deteriorated and passenger complaints skyrocketed.

At the same time, controversy enveloped Burr when he fought an attempt by the pilots to unionize. He suspended profit-sharing checks and froze salaries and all hiring. Complaints emerged that despite Burr's avowed enlightened policy that said all employees should have an influence in the company, he made all the decisions and fostered a personality cult.

Nevertheless, revenues at People Express continued to grow, and in 1985 Burr out-maneuvered Frank Lorenzo to buy Frontier Airlines. That purchase, however, along with the purchase of small commuter lines, burdened People Express with debts. At the same time, Lorenzo's Continental Airlines cut into Burr's profits, and in 1986 Burr decided to attract more passengers by moving away from his no-frills approach. The move failed. In August, Burr filed for protection under Chapter 11 of the federal bankruptcy code, and a few weeks later swallowed his pride by selling both People Express and Frontier to Lorenzo's Texas Air.

BIBLIOGRAPHY

Ramsey, Douglas K., *The Corporate Warriors*, 1987.

Burroughs, William

(January 28, 1855–September 15, 1898)
Manufacturer

In discussing late-nineteenth-century America, a prominent historian has called William Burroughs a "spectacular industrial success story." Burroughs invented and manufactured the modern adding machine, and in doing so, made possible extensive and accurate quantification.

William was born on January 28, 1855, in Auburn, New York, to Edmund Burroughs and Ellen (Julia) Burroughs. His father made patterns for castings and models for inventions—neither of which earned much money. Raised in poverty, young Burroughs obtained a limited education and at an early age worked in banks and general stores.

At one Auburn bank, Burroughs kept records of transactions and found the task so laborious and fraught with errors, and so time-consuming with its need for checks and cross-checks, that he decided to develop a machine that could do the job. In this, he was encouraged by the inventors he saw at his father's shop, creative men who wanted to make a difference.

While working at the bank, Burroughs contracted tuberculosis, and at age 26, in search of a different location that might improve his health, he moved to St. Louis, Missouri, where he worked briefly for his father and then in a machine shop.

After joining several investors to form the American Arithometer Company, Burroughs worked diligently on his invention and in 1887 built 50 recorder-adder machines. These lacked durability and he scrapped them, but the following year, he obtained a patent for a machine that recorded the final result of a calculation. In 1893, he obtained a patent on an improved version that recorded both the separate items and the final result.

In 1895, he sold 284 machines—he called them "Registering Accounts"—mainly to banks. The following year, he sold the English patent rights for $200,000. Unfortunately, his tuberculosis grew worse, and on September 15, 1898, he died in Citronelle, Alabama. He was survived by his wife, Ida Selover, whom he had married in 1879, and by four children.

Burroughs, however, had started a revolution in business that led to the widespread use of adding machines and allowed more efficient record keeping. His invention helped provide businessmen "with their own private, accurate, up-to-the-minute statistics about their enterprises." After Burroughs died, Joseph Boyer headed American Arithometer, and in 1900 the company sold 1,500 adding machines. That number increased to 4,500 in 1903, and in 1905 the business changed its name to the Burroughs Adding Machine Company and moved its headquarters to Detroit. Shortly before World War I, the firm had annual sales exceeding $8 million, more than its competitors combined, and Burroughs's machines could be found in many countries.

BIBLIOGRAPHY

Boorstin, Daniel, *The Americans: The Democratic Experience*, 1973.

Busch, Adolphous

(July 10, 1839–October 10, 1913)
Brewer

Adolphous Busch cut a wide swath with his full figure, prominent mustache, trim goatee, and deep voice. He looked like a German brewer, and with his engaging personality and ambitious drive, he earned many sales for the company he built into the leader among American beer manufacturers.

Busch, born on July 10, 1839, in Mainz, Germany, a town on the Rhine, hailed from a wealthy family. His father, Ulrich Busch, supported the 21 children he had by two wives by operating a lucrative brewers' supply company. Adolphous attended the finest schools in Europe. In 1857, he immigrated to the United States

Adolphous Busch (Library of Congress)

and lived in St. Louis, a city that had attracted many German settlers.

At first, Busch clerked on a steamboat, but when his father died in 1859, he took the money he inherited and, with his brother Ulrich, opened his own brewers' supply store. Since St. Louis teemed with breweries, he had a solid market. Among Busch's customers was Eberhard Anheuser, and in a double wedding on March 7, 1861, Adolphous and Ulrich married Anheuser's daughters, Lilly and Anna.

Anheuser had recently acquired a bankrupt brewery, E. Anheuser & Company, and Adolphous Busch now joined it as a partner. He served briefly in the Union Army during the Civil War, and obtained his U.S. citizenship in 1867. In working to expand the brewery, he traveled as a salesman to many cities and handed out a distinctive "calling card"— a jackknife bearing the firm's logo. Busch increased sales from about 8,000 barrels a year in the late 1860s to 25,000 barrels a year by 1873. After the business incorporated in 1875 as Anheuser-Busch, Busch served as secretary.

Yet, other than aggressive promotion, nothing distinguished Busch's beer until in 1875, Carl Conrad, a St. Louis restaurateur, brought home from the German village of Budweis a distinct brewing recipe. Conrad gave the recipe to Busch, a close friend, and he, in turn, began making the beer for Conrad. Unlike most beers sold in America at the time, this beer, which Conrad named Budweiser, had a light texture with a hop flavor and a carbonation that caused it to retain its smoothness and taste longer than other brews.

Shortly after Budweiser appeared, Anheuser died, and Busch became the company's president. When Conrad's finances proved inadequate to market Budweiser, Busch arranged to take over the beer while developing a pasteurization process that allowed him to ship it long distances without refrigeration.

In an era that knew few limits in mass advertising, Busch plastered the nation with corkscrews, matchboxes, and Budweiser girl posters. His plant in St. Louis expanded to 70 acres with 6,000 workers, and he shipped 1.6 million barrels of beer per year. He founded a glass-bottle factory to supply his beer company, and when refrigerated railroad cars became important, he acquired an interest in the St. Louis Refrigerator Car Company.

In 1896, Busch began marketing a premium beer, Michelob, which he sold only in draft. He further diversified his business interests in the late 1890s when, after seeing a diesel engine at work in Europe, he obtained the exclusive right to manufacture it in the United States and founded the Busch-Sulzer Diesel Engine Company.

Busch built the Hotel Adolphous in Dallas, Texas, where he also constructed a 16-story office building. He owned several mansions and developed the famous Busch sunken gardens at his winter resort in Pasadena, California.

A multimillionaire, Busch donated large sums to charities and colleges. When he died on October 10, 1913, from cirrhosis of the liver, he left several children who continued the company. The firm struggled through Prohibition in the 1920s—barely hanging on by selling yeast and soft drinks—and the strain in maintaining the business caused its president, Busch's son August, to commit suicide in 1934. Under Adolphous Busch's grandson, August Busch Jr., the Busch label made its first appearance in 1955. Adolphous Busch had made Anheuser-Busch the nation's leading brewery, a status his successors maintained.

BIBLIOGRAPHY

Robertson, James D., *The Great American Beer Book*, 1978.

Butterfield, John

(November 18, 1801–November 14, 1869)
Financier

John Butterfield was a financier in the nineteenth century who founded the original American Express Company. Butterfield and the American Express Company established the Overland Mail Company, the first mail service to run on the longest stagecoach line in America. Under Butterfield's direction, the Overland Mail was a success. After his death, the company was absorbed by another notable business in American history, the Wells Fargo Company.

John, the son of Daniel Butterfield, was born in Berne, New York, near Albany, on November 18, 1801. He was descended from Benjamin Butterfield, who immigrated to Massachusetts in 1658, and other relatives who had fought in the American Revolution. He received very little formal schooling and at an early age began working as the driver of a stagecoach.

An ambitious young man and a hard worker, Butterfield advanced rapidly, soon owning a share in the stagecoach company. He had a keen interest in transportation services and followed the activities of the packet boats and steamboats on New York's many canals. Butterfield was instrumental in developing the street-trolley railway in Utica, New York, and was a strong proponent of the expansion of the nation's railroad system.

In February 1822, Butterfield married Malinda Harriet Baker. The couple had nine children together. Their son Daniel would later become a general for the Union army during the Civil War.

Butterfield stayed involved with the era's constantly evolving technology. With a few associates, Butterfield started the New York, Albany & Buffalo Telegraph Company. In addition, though he was not the first to develop an express business for mail delivery, he was one of the first to take advantage of the potential of such a service, with his formation in 1849 of the Butterfield, Wasson & Company express business.

The American Express Company, which eventually grew to be the financial giant it is today, emerged originally as a consolidation of Butterfield's express company and two smaller firms. An act of Congress in 1857 paved the way for the establishment of the first transcontinental stagecoach line, which was planned to extend from St. Louis to San Francisco by way of El Paso, Tucson, and Los Angeles. This decision was critical to the American Express Company, as Butterfield and his partners received the contract for implementing the mail service for the line. The

$600,000-per-year contract was an enormous sum for that time.

Butterfield followed this success with the establishment of the Overland Mail Company. Its success, which was later commended by President James A. Garfield as "a glorious triumph for civilization and the Union," was largely due to Butterfield's aptitude for planning.

Outside of business interests, Butterfield was active in the community of Utica, New York. He pursued real estate and land development, served as director of the Utica City National Bank, built the Butterfield House, and was mayor of the city in 1865.

Two years after becoming afflicted with paralysis, Butterfield died in Utica on November 14, 1869.

BIBLIOGRAPHY

Butterfield, Julia Lorillard, *A Biog. Memorial of Gen. Daniel Butterfield*, 1904; Conkling, Roscoe Platt, *The Butterfield Overland Mail, 1857–1869; Its Organization and Operation over the Southern Route to 1861; Subsequently over the Central Route to 1866; And Under Wells, Fargo and Company in 1869*, 1947; Hicks, Sam, *Butterfield Overland Mail: Longest Stage Line in the World*, 1979; Reed, Ralph Thomas, *American Express: Its Origin and Growth*, 1952.

C

Cabot, George

(January 16, 1752–April 18, 1823)
Merchant

George Cabot led a diverse and colorful life. After leaving Harvard College to become a cabin boy, he advanced to become a highly successful seafaring privateer, established himself as a bank director and wealthy merchant, represented Massachusetts as a U.S. senator, and served as one of the driving intellectuals of the Federalist Party.

George, the seventh of the 11 children of Joseph and Elizabeth Higginson Cabot, was born in Salem, Massachusetts, on January 16, 1752. Born into a wealthy merchant family, George was given an excellent education. In 1766, he entered Harvard College, ranking upon admission seventeenth out of an incoming class of 42 students. Even in his early days at Harvard, George demonstrated a spirited, independent streak, taking the lead in protests over the rank butter served at meals and being admonished by faculty for neglecting study in favor of "idle behavior." On March 19, 1768, he withdrew from the college, choosing to sign on as a cabin boy aboard a ship owned by his elder brothers, John and Andrew.

The brothers, who used their ships to carry out their father's rum, fish, and iron trade, attempted to reign in the restless Cabot by assigning him to work under a demanding captain. This strategy was effective, and within two years George had become skipper of *Sally*, a schooner belonging to his brothers that transported salt codfish. Over the next few years, he commanded a number of different schooners.

In 1774, Cabot was married to his first cousin, Elizabeth Higginson. Her ener-

George Cabot (North Wind Picture Archives)

getic and commanding disposition is credited with completing Cabot's transition from rowdy youth to responsible adult, a shift her family rewarded by entrusting Cabot with the command of some of their finest ships.

By 1777, weary of seafaring, Cabot joined his brothers in the administration of the business, which had grown to include 40 privateers and letters-of-marque ships. During the American Revolution, those merchant ships outfitted with armaments continued their trade with Spain. The Cabot brothers' Spanish trade was headquartered in Bilbao, where, unlike most other privateers, the Cabots deposited into a bank the proceeds of all sales.

Cabot began to diversify his own business interests, and in 1784 became the director of the Massachusetts Bank, the first bank in the state. The following year, he entered into partnership with his brother-in-law Joseph Lee to pursue additional shipping and mercantile activities. In 1788, he also supported two significant industrial ventures in Massachusetts—the building of the Essex County bridge and the cotton manufacturing factory in Beverly.

During these successful business years, Cabot had also begun to make a reputation for himself in politics. His initial political activity involved a group of Essex County merchants and lawyers who ultimately became the core members of the Federalist Party. Over the next decade, he participated in a number of state and constitutional conventions, as well as serving for a short time in 1783 as the state senator for Essex County. His interests increasingly drew him into the arena of federal politics, and in June 1791 Cabot was elected to the U.S. Senate to represent Massachusetts.

Cabot's dignified and gracious style, combined with his understanding of business issues, assisted him greatly in his public role. He was a close adviser to Alexander Hamilton, sharing with him an abhorrence of the French Revolution and a preference for maintaining peace with Britain.

In May 1796, Cabot gave into his growing weariness with public life. Having retired the year before from his mercantile and shipping enterprises, Cabot, who had amassed a fair fortune, moved to a farm in Brookline, outside of Boston. Unable to remain still for long, however, Cabot spent his remaining days serving as the president of the Boston branch of the United States Bank and director of the Suffolk Insurance Company. Around 1809, he became the president of the Boston Marine Insurance Company. Though he was hesitant to become politically active again, Cabot was the trusted sage of the Federalists, becoming "one of those rare men who, without ambition, without effort, almost without the consciousness of admitted superiority, control, and become, the oracles of communities." Cabot and the other early Essex Federalists were significant voices on the Massachusetts political stage.

After the election of Thomas Jefferson to the presidency in 1800, Cabot, motivated largely by a belief that Jefferson was an anarchist, reluctantly accepted several public offices before his death from a gall-bladder disease on April 18, 1823.

BIBLIOGRAPHY

Briggs, L. V., *History and Genealogy of the Cabot Family*, 1927; Davis, James S., *Essays in the Earlier History of American Corporations*, 1917; Hamilton, John C., *History of the Republic*, 1859; Howe, O. T., "Beverly Privateers in the Am. Revolution," *Publications of the Massachusetts Colonial Society*, vol. 24, 1932; Lodge, Henry Cabot, *Life and Letters of George Cabot*, 1877.

Candler, Asa

(December 30, 1851–March 12, 1929)
Manufacturer

Asa Candler (The Coca-Cola Company)

Asa Candler did not invent Coca-Cola, but he recognized the product's potential as a refreshing drink and established the company's modern foundation.

Born on December 30, 1851, to Samuel Candler and Martha (Beall) Candler near Villa Rica, Georgia, Asa grew up on his family's farm and obtained an education that was good enough to qualify him for the state university. Rather than attend college, however, Candler briefly studied medicine and then, in 1873, went to Atlanta and worked for a druggist. He showed keen ability and developed a thriving drugstore business. Candler married Lucy Elizabeth Howard in 1878. (After Lucy's death, he married Mary L. Reagin in 1923.)

In 1886, an Atlanta pharmacist, John Stith Pemberton, invented Coca-Cola. No one knows exactly how he developed the concoction, but he sold it as a cure-all for headaches, sluggishness, and indigestion. Within the year, however, Pemberton fell ill and sold his business.

Candler knew about Coca-Cola from having drunk it to alleviate his headaches, and in 1887 he bought the formula for the drink for $2,300. At first, he, like Pemberton, promoted Coca-Cola for its supposed medicinal value, but he soon realized that it had greater potential as a fountain drink. Consequently, he began selling his syrup to drugstores equipped with soda fountains and invested heavily in advertising. Across the South, painted Coca-Cola signs appeared on barns, along with fans, bookmarks, and glasses all displaying the Coca-Cola name. Candler produced his syrup in Atlanta, and at plants in Chicago, Dallas, and Los Angeles.

Interestingly, Coca-Cola never manufactured the drink itself, but rather sold the syrup that others made into the drink—a secret formula whose precise ingredients remain unknown. What has been deciphered is that the product contains 99.8 percent sugar and water, probably mixed with coca leaves, cola nuts, some spices, citrus oils, and glycerin.

When some people urged Candler to take Coca-Cola beyond the soda fountain and bottle it, he demurred, never thinking it would sell in such form. In 1899, he signed a contract that for $1 gave two Chattanooga lawyers the right to bottle Coca-Cola in nearly the entire nation. The lawyers bought the syrup from Candler and then resold it to bottlers elsewhere, thus beginning the franchise bottling system that remains a part of the Coca-Cola operation.

In 1909, the federal government sued Coca-Cola, claiming that the drink's caffeine level posed a health risk. Candler agreed to reduce the ingredient. Meanwhile, he bought real estate in Atlanta, and used his increasing fortune to help the community. When a real estate panic threatened the city in 1907, he bought houses and resold them to families of modest income for only 10 percent down and low-interest payments. He resigned his presidency at Coca-Cola in 1916 to serve as mayor, and over the following year helped reorganize the city administration and provided money for many civic improvements. He contributed land to Emory University to build its campus and gave an initial $1 million endowment, followed by several million more. In addition, he built a hospital to train doctors that adjoined Emory's medical school.

Candler sold Coca-Cola in 1919 for $25 million to a group of businessmen led by Ernest Woodruff. Four years later, Woodruff's son, ROBERT WOODRUFF, took over as president and expanded Coca-Cola through advertising that portrayed it as a national institution. Candler died on March 12, 1929. Coca-Cola's next great period of growth occurred in the 1980s and 1990s under ROBERTO GOIZUETA. Today, Coca-Cola is heavily indebted to Pemberton's formula and Candler's business acumen for its current position as the most widely sold product in the world.

BIBLIOGRAPHY

Kahn, E. J., Jr., *The Big Drink*, 1959; Oliver, Thomas, *The Real Coke, the Real Story*, 1986.

Carnegie, Andrew

(November 25, 1835–August 11, 1919)
Manufacturer

Rising above his impoverished childhood, Andrew Carnegie built the largest steel company in the United States and gave millions of dollars to educational and cultural institutions.

Andrew was born on November 25, 1835, in Dunfermline, Scotland, to William Carnegie, a weaver, and Margaret (Morrison) Carnegie. From an uncle, Andrew learned pacifist beliefs, which stayed with him as an adult. When industrialization began to overtake Scotland, William Carnegie, wedded to his traditional craft, found it difficult to find work. Consequently, the family immigrated to the United States in 1848 and settled in Allegheny, Pennsylvania, near Pittsburgh. There, Andrew found a job as a bobbin boy at Blackstock's cotton mill for $1.20 a week.

Ambitious and hardworking, Carnegie quickly advanced. In 1849, O-Reilly's (a telegraph office in Pittsburgh) hired him as an office boy. He soon learned to work the telegraph and took messages by ear;

that is, he read the sound without writing the code, an unusual feat. Over the wire rattled messages dealing with business consolidations and financial agreements—developments and techniques he absorbed.

In 1852, THOMAS ALEXANDER SCOTT hired Carnegie as his secretary and personal telegrapher. Scott, who directed the western division of the Pennsylvania Railroad, became Carnegie's mentor, and the 17-year-old gained expertise in management and finance. Writing in *Andrew Carnegie and the Rise of Big Business*, historian Harold C. Livesay asserts that Carnegie's later success rested on his ability to take the managerial methods he had learned from railroads and apply them to manufacturing. For example, Scott used cost control and cost data to discipline his superintendents and pit one against the other in a drive for bonuses and promotions. Carnegie later applied this strategy to his own business.

So much did Scott trust Carnegie that, while away in 1855, he put him in charge for 10 days. When Scott advanced to company vice president in 1859, he made Carnegie superintendent of the Pittsburgh division. Carnegie held this position for six years, during which time the Pennsylvania Railroad quadrupled its traffic and increased its efficiency, in part due to him.

Carnegie used the money he earned from the Pennsylvania Railroad to make shrewd investments, some under Scott's guidance. In 1861, he bought a farm in Pennsylvania for $40,000 and started drilling for oil. His well came in and he formed the Columbia Oil Company, capitalized at $200,000, which was soon the most profitable oil firm in the state. Carnegie, however, thought the oil business too chaotic and so left it. He bought and

Andrew Carnegie (Library of Congress)

sold stocks and bonds and within a short time owned securities worth nearly $500,000. He quit the railroad in 1865 to join with John Piper in expanding the Keystone Bridge Company, a firm he and several other partners, including Scott, had founded three years earlier. Carnegie believed that, for railroad traffic, iron and steel made better bridges than wooden ones, hence Keystone entered this endeavor. The company built a bridge across the Mississippi River at St. Louis—the largest steel arch bridge in the world, and as railroad construction boomed after the Civil War, so too did Keystone.

That same year, Carnegie began the Union Iron Company to provide beams and plates for Keystone Bridge, a step in vertical integration. Carnegie displayed his talent for innovation by bringing the entire iron and steelmaking process together under one roof. Until this time, companies typically made iron in scattered locations, with each location dedicated to one stage of production. As usual with him, Carnegie applied a strict cost accounting system and based his investing, marketing, and personnel decisions on it.

In 1867, Carnegie united with GEORGE PULLMAN to form the Pullman Pacific Car Company that built railroad sleeping cars. At the same time, he invested heavily in the Western Pacific and Union Pacific railroads. Carnegie wholeheartedly adopted Spencerianism, a philosophy advanced by the Englishman Herbert Spencer and widely popular in the United States. Spencer applied Charles Darwin's scientific theory of evolution to society and declared life to be a test of "survival of the fittest." Reformers called this individualistic creed nothing more than justification by the wealthy to exploit others, but Carnegie thought competitive struggle moved society forward, and he said: "'All is well since all grows better' became my motto, my true source of comfort."

Carnegie moved into the steel industry with characteristic fortitude, convinced that steel, stronger and more durable, would supplant iron as the nation's primary metal. Despite a deep economic depression that struck the nation in the 1870s, Carnegie completed his Edgar Thomson Steel Works in 1875 at a cost of $1.25 million, a plant that used the Bessemer process, by which air blasted across molten iron produced steel. Carnegie built the mill primarily to make steel rails for the railroads, but it made other steel, too. For example, in 1878, Carnegie got a contract to provide steel used in building the Brooklyn Bridge.

In 1881, Carnegie began a partnership with HENRY C. FRICK, who owned the Frick Coke Company. Frick (who was known to be headstrong) and Carnegie (who was given to outrageous demands) saw in each other something they needed—Frick wanted an infusion of capital and Carnegie wanted coke. As it turned out, Frick supplied Carnegie with most of the coke needed in the steel mills. Carnegie controlled Frick's company and, four years later, acquired a competitor, the Homestead Works, which made steel structural beams and angles in the most modern rail mill and Bessemer steel plant in the country.

Carnegie merged Keystone Bridge, Union Iron, and the Edgar Thomson Works in 1886, under the Carnegie Brothers Company, named after himself and his brother Tom, who over the years helped guide the numerous business ventures (and for which Andrew repaid him with invective). Andrew Carnegie kept Homestead and Frick Coke as separate businesses. He made Frick chairman of Carnegie Brothers in 1889 and placed him in charge of operations. He insisted, however, that all cost sheets be sent to him. He said: "I have known . . . that our hope for profit lay for some time to come in the fact that our cost was less than others."

Carnegie continued to watch for innovations that would allow him to best his competition. Thus, he obtained the rights for his company and others, as part of a trade group called the Bessemer Association, to employ the Thomas process, an improvement over the Bessemer process since it used ore high in phosphorous. When it was shown that the Thomas process worked better in an open hearth furnace than in the Bessemer converter, he ordered Homestead, and later the Edgar Thomson plant, to change technology.

By this time, Americans read insatiably about Carnegie and other industrialists, and in 1886 he wrote an essay, published in *Forum*, in which he stated that labor strife could be avoided by accepting unions. He warned, too, about using strike breakers. "The employer of labor," he said, "will find it much more to his interest, wherever possible, to allow his works to remain idle and await the result of a dispute than to employ a class of men that can be induced to take the place of other men who have stopped work." There followed in 1889 his essay "The Gospel of Wealth," widely read when it appeared in the *North American Review*. In it, Carnegie proclaimed a responsibility to spend his money to help society. The man who died rich, he said, died disgraced.

Yet, in 1892, Carnegie's compassion seemed more fiction than fact. That year, he consolidated his holdings, including the Homestead Works, into the Carnegie Steel Company. He then went to Scotland, leaving Frick in charge. Carnegie and Frick wanted to change the wage scale at Homestead and destroy the union. The two men purposefully precipitated a crisis to obtain these goals. Frick decided he would not bargain with the union in good faith, and bloodshed drenched the strike that followed when Frick hired guards to attack workers who, in reaction to the crisis, had occupied the plant. Although Frick busted the union, the episode badly damaged Carnegie's reputation. Newspapers throughout the United States and Britain, both conservative and liberal, assailed him for the bloodshed. The *St. Louis Post-Dispatch* intoned: "Three months ago Andrew Carnegie was a man to be envied. Today he is an object of mingled pity and contempt."

A policy dispute caused Frick to leave Carnegie in 1894. The following year, Carnegie reached a deal with JOHN D. ROCKEFELLER, who controlled iron ore deposits in Minnesota. Carnegie Steel leased the ore lands for 50 years and agreed to send specified amounts over Rockefeller's railroads and boats, with an upper limit set on the shipping rates. One observer called this Carnegie's greatest achievement since it assured his company primacy in steel production.

Carnegie Steel earned a profit of $4 million in 1895, compared to its nearest competitor who earned $360,000. Within five years, Carnegie's profits reached $40 million, and the tycoon set his sights on continued expansion when he decided to start making finished products, such as wire and nails.

By this time, financier J. P. MORGAN SR. had started forming steel trusts—large, integrated corporations. In 1901, Carnegie sold Carnegie Steel to Morgan for $480 million. Carnegie Steel formed the centerpiece for the largest corporation to that time, United States Steel.

Carnegie retired from business and supervised giving his money to various institutions. In his lifetime, he donated more than $350 million to educational, cultural, and peace groups. He endowed nearly 1,700 libraries in the United States and Britain and contributed funds to help build the Peace Palace at the Hague in the Netherlands. In this way, Carnegie fulfilled his "Gospel of Wealth."

Carnegie, who at age 50 had married Louise Whitfield, the daughter of a New York merchant, died from pneumonia on August 11, 1919.

BIBLIOGRAPHY

Livesay, Harold C., *Andrew Carnegie and the Rise of Big Business*, 1975; Swetnam, George, *Andrew Carnegie*, 1980; Wall, Joseph Frazier, *Andrew Carnegie*, 1970.

Carr, Julian Shakespeare

(October 12, 1845–April 29, 1924)
Tobacco Executive

One of the most prominent citizens of North Carolina in his time, Julian Shakespeare Carr made his fortune in the tobacco industry as owner of the Blackwell Durham Tobacco Company, which sold the popular Bull Durham brand. After selling the company for $4 million in 1898, Carr became an executive for a host of other companies ranging from cotton textile manufacturers to banks and railroads.

Julian Shakespeare Carr (North Wind Picture Archives)

The son of John Wesley and Eliza P. Bulloch Carr, Julian was born on October 12, 1845, in Chapel Hill, North Carolina. His father was a merchant, planter, and county court judge. Julian attended the local schools and went on to the University of North Carolina for two years before interrupting his education to enlist

with the Confederate cavalry at the beginning of the Civil War. After the war, he returned to the university, graduating in 1866. He worked in his father's business for three years and then briefly moved to Little Rock, Arkansas, to work for an uncle.

Upon returning to Chapel Hill, Carr purchased a one-third share in the Blackwell Durham Tobacco Company with $4,000 given to him by his father. Carr married Nannie Graham Parrish in 1873, and the couple eventually had six children, two of whom succeeded their father in his later textile ventures.

Carr headed an aggressive marketing campaign to gain worldwide recognition for the Bull Durham brand name. He placed the Bull Durham logo in numerous newspapers and on ubiquitous signs, and Bull Durham was soon the most popular brand of smoking tobacco in the world. With this success, the Blackwell Company rose to be the largest manufacturer of smoking tobacco. Carr later bought out Blackwell to became sole owner and president until he sold the firm in 1898 to the American Tobacco Company for $4 million.

After leaving the tobacco industry, Carr became actively involved in many other endeavors, ranging from textiles to banking. He was owner and president of the Durham Hosiery Mills, which included mills in Durham, High Point, Chapel Hill, and Goldsboro, North Carolina. At the time of his death, there were 4,000 employees at 14 mills, making the company the largest producer of hosiery in the world. Carr founded the Golden Belt

Manufacturing Company, which was the main supplier of tobacco pouches to American tobacco companies. He also owned Occoneechee Farm, a large stock and grain farm, and was president of the Ormond Mining Company, the North Carolina Bessemer Company, two railroad companies, the Durham Electric Light Company, and the Commonwealth Cotton Manufacturing Company. Carr also organized and was president of the First National Bank of Durham and served as vice president of the Durham Cotton Manufacturing Company and the Greensboro Blast Furnace Company.

As a prominent Methodist, Carr was successful in having Trinity College (which would later become Duke University) moved to Durham. He financially supported African-American colleges and churches and established an endowment for the Greensboro Female College. As a staunch Democrat, Carr served as a delegate at 14 Democratic national conventions and was a member of Herbert Hoover's food administration staff during World War I. He died on April 29, 1924.

BIBLIOGRAPHY

"Business Leader—The Business Leader Hall of Fame," http://www.businessleader.com/blnov96.cover.html; "Durham: The Town Tobacco Built," *The News & Observer*, August 11, 1996; Ingham, John N., ed., *Biographical Dictionary of American Business Leaders*, 1983.

Carrier, Willis Haviland

(November 26, 1876–October 7, 1950)
Manufacturer

As an engineer, Willis Haviland Carrier, the "father of air conditioning," defined cooling systems technologically and explained them in these words: "Air conditioning," he said, "is the control of the humidity of air by either increasing or decreasing its moisture content. Added to the control of humidity is the control of temperature by either heating or cooling the air, the purification of the air by washing or filtering the air, and the control of air motion and ventilation."

Willis was born on November 26, 1876, to Duane Williams Carrier and Elizabeth (Haviland) Carrier in Angola, a town in western New York, where he grew up on his family's farm. As an only child, he took to tinkering with mechanical devices, a pastime enjoyed by his mother. In fact, he later said that what talent he had in mechanics, he inherited from her.

In 1894, Carrier graduated from Angola High School. He wanted to attend college, but a severe economic depression gripped the nation at that time and so pinched his family's finances that he taught school in order to earn money. Three years later, though, he won a scholarship to Cornell, from where he graduated in 1901 with a degree in electrical engineering.

Carrier then worked as a research engineer for the Buffalo Forge Company.

He designed a system for drying lumber and another for testing and rating heaters. When the Sackett-Wilhelms Publishing Company sought a way to reduce humidity in its plant, Carrier designed an innovative system that not only lowered the humidity—a procedure already achieved by others—but also held it at a constant level—a feat never before accomplished. He did this by balancing the temperature of the coils, through which cold air passed, with the rate of airflow to reach the desired dew-point level. Sackett-Wilhelms installed his system, complete with fans and ducts, in its Brooklyn, New York, plant in 1902, an event Carrier's biographer, Margaret Ingels, says "marked the birth of the air conditioning industry because of the addition of humidity control."

In 1907, Buffalo Forge accepted Carrier's idea to create a subsidiary, the Carrier Air Conditioning Company, to develop and market air-conditioning systems. Carrier served as vice president and applied his engineering talent to improve cooling devices and bring down their cost. He emphasized marketing the systems to industries and sold several to tobacco factories that needed to clean and cool the air within their buildings.

Carrier won national attention in 1911 when, at a conference, he presented his paper, "Rational Psychometric Formulae." In it, he offered calculations that became the basis for the air-conditioning industry—his charts even appeared in college textbooks. With this recognition, Carrier sold more air-conditioning systems—63 in 1912, 93 in 1913, and 130 in 1914.

When Buffalo Forge decided to discontinue engineering, Carrier joined with several partners in 1915 and, with $32,600 in capital, formed the Carrier Engineering Corporation. Within its first few months, the firm sold air-conditioning systems to textile mills, tobacco factories, bakeries, munitions plants, and all types of businesses—big and small. "We took every type of contract we could handle," Carrier said. "We needed to bring cash in for our company."

Carrier made another advance in 1920 when he designed a revolutionary compressor that used a centrifugal chiller, a direct drive, and dilene (a nontoxic refrigerant different from the old ammonia compressors). The compressor lowered costs and allowed Carrier to take air-conditioning beyond factories and to the masses. After first installing the compressor at the Whitman Candy Company in 1923, he installed another at Detroit's Hudson Department Store in 1924 and later that year at movie theaters in Dallas and Houston, Texas. One theater owner claimed, "The cooling plant is revolutionizing picture show attendance . . . !" Carrier's first important theater installation occurred, however, in 1925 at New York City's famed Rivoli. Success at that location—block-long lines formed to experience the coolness—led to widespread publicity, and by 1930 resulted in more than 300 theaters using his system. Carrier's bypass downdraft design that prevented patrons from feeling moving air won praise.

In 1925, Carrier obtained a contract to freeze the ice-skating rink at New York City's Madison Square Garden. The successful application of his compressor there showed that it could be used for heavier cooling jobs.

Carrier merged his firm with York Heating and Ventilating and with the Brunswick and Knoeshell Company in

1930 to form the Carrier Corporation, whose board he chaired. In the early 1930s, he brought air-conditioning to railroad cars and thus further popularized it. In 1937, the Carrier Corporation consolidated its several plants into one, located at Syracuse, New York. Two years later, Carrier introduced the "Conduit Weathermaster System" as a way to cool high-rise buildings. The system pushed air through steel conduits at high speed and through vents into individual rooms.

Although Carrier had developed unit air conditioners in the late 1920s, they did not obtain popularity until after the Great Depression when, buoyed by post–World War II prosperity, consumers bought them for use in their homes. At the same time, builders began installing central air-conditioning in houses.

After a heart attack in 1948, Carrier retired from business. He died two years later, on October 7, 1950, in New York City while formulating grandiose plans to air-condition streets and even entire towns. His wife, Edith Marsh White, whom he had married in 1941, survived him (two previous marriages had ended when his wives died), as did his two adopted sons.

The Carrier Corporation continued to innovate, providing air-conditioning systems for nuclear-powered submarines, airplanes, and the Houston Astrodome. In 1980, Carrier merged with the United Technologies Corporation.

BIBLIOGRAPHY

Ingels, Margaret, *Willis Haviland Carrier: Father of Air Conditioning*, 1952, reprt. 1972.

Carter, Edward

(1912–)
Merchant

When America erupted into suburban expansion after World War II, Edward Carter made his Broadway stores a part of that growth and developed one of the largest department store chains in the nation.

Little information exists regarding Carter's early life, but he was born around 1912 in Maryland. In 1932, he graduated from the University of California, Los Angeles. He obtained his M.B.A. from the Harvard Graduate School of Business in 1937 and then joined May Department stores in California. By the start of World War II, he was the firm's merchandise manager.

Carter left May stores in 1946 when Blyth & Company hired him to revive its stagnant Los Angeles–based Broadway stores. By that time, suburban development had overtaken southern California, and Carter decided Broadway should expand with the middle class. He jettisoned the traditional idea that a department store chain must have a main downtown store and auxiliary stores elsewhere.

Instead, he remade Broadway so that its downtown store and its stores in suburban shopping centers offered the same merchandise—with the suburban stores sometimes exceeding the downtown store in size. By 1957, he expanded Broadway from three to eight stores, including a huge 1.15-million-square-foot building in a shopping center.

Carter merged Broadway with the Hale Brothers chain in the 1950s and thus acquired stores in northern California. The Hale stores fared poorly, however, and he had to close them in the 1960s. Despite this, he continued his presence in the region through the Weinstock stores he had also bought.

Carter kept aiming his stores at the middle class, on the one hand avoiding budget items and on the other avoiding luxury items. In addition, he kept expanding through buyouts. In 1967, Broadway-Hale, as his company was then known, bought Emporium Capwell, the largest department store chain in San Francisco. This was followed by the purchase of Neiman-Marcus in Dallas, Texas, a store designed for the wealthy and thus a new dimension for Carter. In 1968, he acquired Waldenbooks, a bookstore chain. Sales at Broadway-Hale consequently exploded, from $220 million in 1964 to $640 million in 1969.

Carter expanded Neiman-Marcus into Bal Harbor, Florida, and Atlanta, Georgia, and in 1972 he expanded his luxury store empire by buying Bergdorf-Goodman, a New York store that catered to the wealthy. Two years later, he acquired Holt-Renfrew & Company, the leading department store in Canada.

Carter had digressed from his original plan to serve middle-class suburbanites, and he accentuated the change when, in the mid-1970s, he built a new Broadway store in downtown Los Angeles, complete with a 500-room Hyatt House Hotel, an office building, and a 2,000-car garage. Broadway-Hale changed its name, too, and became Carter Hawley Hale stores (CHH), reflecting Carter's influence and his position as CEO, and the appointment of Philip Hawley as president.

Soon after, though, in 1977, Carter stepped down. Through the 1980s, CHH faced enormous financial difficulties from overexpansion. As a result, the corporation sold Neiman-Marcus, Bergdorf-Goodman, Holt-Renfrew, and Waldenbooks. Carter, meanwhile, focused on civic affairs as a regent for the University of California and chairman of the Los Angeles County Museum of Art.

BIBLIOGRAPHY
Moskowitz, Milton, et al., eds., *Everybody's Business*, 1980.

Casey, James E.

(March 29, 1888–June 6, 1983)
Shipping Executive

With $100 borrowed from a friend, James E. Casey founded the American Messenger Company. Today, the firm leads all other parcel delivery companies—as the United Parcel Service (UPS).

Casey was born on March 29, 1888, in Candelaria, Nevada, where his father prospected for gold. He grew up, however, in Seattle, Washington, and lived there his entire life. Casey quit school at age 11 after his father took ill and his family needed more income. He began work as a delivery boy for a department store and as a messenger for a telegraph company. For a short while, he followed in his father's footsteps and prospected for gold, but then he returned to Seattle.

In 1907, he and two partners formed the American Messenger Service with $100 borrowed from a friend. At that time, few Americans had telephones, and the U.S. Post Office had not yet started its parcel post system. As a result, people had to rely on private messenger and delivery services. Thus, Casey's business met a need, although other entrepreneurs had the same idea and he had to face stiff competition.

Casey at first had six messengers and two bicycles, before switching to motorcycles and a Model T Ford refitted for carrying packages. In 1913, he merged with a competitor, Evert McCabe, to form Merchants Parcel Delivery, which concentrated on delivering packages via truck for retail stores. Within five years, Casey counted Seattle's largest department stores among his customers. He pioneered "consolidated delivery"—combining packages addressed to a certain neighborhood onto one delivery vehicle, thus promoting efficiency.

Casey expanded operations into Oakland, California, in 1919 and changed the company's name to UPS. Rapid expansion followed, and by 1930 UPS dominated urban parcel delivery along the West Coast. In the latter year, Casey took UPS to New York City, and in 1931 gained an enormous advantage when he convinced the prestigious Lord & Taylor department store to ship with him. UPS adopted innovations, including the first mechanical system for package sorting, conveyor belts for moving parcels, and delivery by airplane—although financial problems forced the latter to be discontinued after only eight months.

By the early 1950s, Casey decided to broaden UPS's market by picking up and delivering packages for anyone, both businesses and private residences. Using planes owned by various airlines, the company resumed its air service in 1953, offering two-day delivery to major cities on the East and West Coasts.

An impeccable dresser, Casey ordered a strict dress code for his workers—they all had to wear brown uniforms, neatly pressed, with shoes shined. Striving for cleanliness, he ordered that all the trucks be painted brown—he considered it a distinguished color—and washed everyday.

"Ideals of our company cannot be carried out from the top alone," Casey said. Thus, he arranged that whenever a UPS driver earned promotion to supervisor, the driver received stock. In this way,

UPS was owned exclusively by the company managers.

Casey, a lifelong bachelor, seemed consumed by package delivery. He talked about it incessantly and worked at it unfailingly. By the time he died on June 6, 1983, UPS was delivering 6 million packages a day. Despite competition from Federal Express and other carriers, UPS continued its growth into the 1980s and 1990s, and remained the largest parcel delivery company. In 1988, UPS began operating its own aircraft, called UPS Airline, and it entered the international shipping market—today, it operates in some 185 countries. A tumultuous labor dispute and strike in 1997 left the company shaken but still dominant.

BIBLIOGRAPHY

Moskowitz, Milton, et al., eds., *Everybody's Business*, 1980.

Chandler, Harry

(May 17, 1864–September 23, 1944)
Publisher

Harry Chandler, the conservative and antiunion president of the *Los Angeles Times*, greatly contributed to the newspaper's success during the first 40 years of the twentieth century. He was influential in attracting both jobs and people to the growing city of Los Angeles, and through his dual role as newspaper president and real estate developer, he spearheaded efforts to create the suburban region of the San Fernando Valley.

Harry was born to Moses Knight and Emma Jane Little Chandler in Landaff, New Hampshire, on May 17, 1864, and was educated in the nearby town of Lisbon. After an illness changed his plans to attend Dartmouth College, Chandler moved to southern California in 1882 to regain his health. He was quite poor and lived in a tent in the San Fernando Valley, earning his food by training horses and helping a farmer in return for a share of the fruit crop.

In 1885, Chandler became a clerk in the circulation department of the *Los Angeles Times*, a newspaper owned by HARRISON GRAY OTIS. An ambitious youth, Chandler—without his boss's knowledge—established his own delivery routes and collection methods. Meanwhile, he regularly used his earnings to buy stock in the *Times*.

In 1888, Chandler married Magdalena Schladar, to whom he remained married until her death in 1892. Otis was impressed with Chandler's vitality and efficiency. In 1894, Chandler was promoted to business manager. Later that year, he also became the owner's son-in-law by marrying Otis's daughter Marian.

During the last decade of the nineteenth century, Chandler also began what would become a lifetime involvement in real estate ventures. Initially gaining a number of contacts through his position at the newspaper, in 1899 Chandler purchased a swath of land in the

Colorado desert, encompassing an area just north and south of the Mexican border. By 1902, he had established two corporations, the California-Mexico Land and Cattle Company and the Colorado River Land Company. Over time, the latter company would acquire more than 800,000 acres of land south of the border in the Mexicali Valley.

Otis delegated an increasing amount of responsibility to Chandler. Shortly after taking the reins as assistant general manager in the early 1900s, Chandler, who was adamantly opposed to unions, aggressively campaigned against labor interests. He helped establish the radical antiunion Merchants and Manufacturers Association, a group that largely determined the economic policies of Los Angeles businesses over the next three years. The *Times* itself had remained nonunion based on employee-friendly policies such as high wages and rewards for loyalty and seniority. It was the first newspaper to have a human resources department and was an early proponent of the 40-hour workweek.

As the antiunion commentaries of the *Times* had made the paper the focus of vicious labor-related boycotts before the turn of the century, Chandler's public, adversarial stance was both antagonist and dangerous. The year 1910 was one of widespread national violence against nonunion workers and vandalism of companies using nonunion labor. On June 1, Los Angeles ironworkers went out on strike, unleashing months of violence in the city and a flood of antiunion commentary from the *Times*. On October 1, an explosion tore through the *Times* building, killing 20 people. Officials of the Bridge and Structural Workers Union were indicted for the bombing,

and Chandler adeptly used the incident to create sympathy and increase the popularity of the newspaper.

Within two years, the newspaper had moved into a newly built, state-of-the-art facility, and Chandler ushered in a new era of community interest for the *Times*. As the city of Los Angeles experienced rapid growth and development, Chandler was an active proponent of bond issues to divert water from the Owens Valley to secure a water supply for the city. Chandler's efforts were not solely based on civic interests; for several years he had been quietly purchasing large tracts of land in the San Fernando Valley that were inexpensive because of the lack of water. Otis, Moses Sherman, and Chandler formed the Suburban Homes Company and subdivided their 60 million acres into both residential and industrial properties serviced by the new water supply. To facilitate the annexing of the new city of San Fernando by Los Angeles (which occurred in 1915), the group built a new highway. For all of his extensive real estate and development ventures, Chandler earned the title, "California's landlord."

After Otis' death in 1917, Chandler assumed full control of the *Times*. Over the next few decades, he greatly expanded the scope of the paper's operations. In the early 1940s, the paper's daily circulation was over 320,000, with Sunday edition circulation soaring above 600,000. He was adept at attracting advertisers and added the *Times' Sunday Magazine* and motion picture page to the newspaper's contents.

Chandler used the newspaper as a promotional tool for increasing the influx of people to southern California, advertising to the nation the beneficial climate and the availability of land, jobs, and homes. His efforts, which earned him the Realty Board's "Most Useful Citizen" title, most likely lured hundreds of thousands of people from the Midwest to southern California. His contribution to the growth of jobs included his aggressive lobbying of businesses such as the motion picture industry and the aviation industry. With Chandler at the helm, the *Times* led an effort that resulted in the construction of the San Pedro harbor, which quickly became one of the West Coast's biggest ports. Chandler was also a conservative Republican and did not hesitate to use the paper as a mouthpiece for his partisan politics.

Although Chandler was a savvy marketer, he did not closely track the eco-nomics of the paper. In 1941, when Norman, one of Chandler's eight children, took control of the daily operations, he found the paper to be financially shaky. Over the next decade, Norman turned the *Times* into one of the nation's most profitable newspapers. Harry Chandler died on September 23, 1944.

BIBLIOGRAPHY

Ainsworth, Edward, *History of the Los Angeles Times*, 1940; Ainsworth, Edward, *Memories in the City of Dreams: A Tribute to Harry Chandler, Gran Benefactor de la Ciudad*, 1959; Bonelli, William G., *Billion Dollar Blackjack*, 1954; Gottlieb, Robert, and Irene Wolt, *Thinking Big*, 1977; Halberstam, David, *The Powers That Be*, 1979.

Chrysler, Walter Percy

(April 2, 1875–August 18, 1940)
Manufacturer

Walter Percy Chrysler took over the troubled Maxwell Motor Company and turned it into the highly profitable Chrysler Corporation.

Born on April 2, 1875, in Wamego, Kansas, to Henry Chrysler and Anna Maria (Breyman) Chrysler, Walter first worked as a manual laborer. After graduating from high school in Ellis, Kansas, he first took a job in a grocery store and later worked as an apprentice machinist for the Union Pacific Railroad, the company for which his father worked as a locomotive engineer.

After completing his apprenticeship, Chrysler moved about the West, riding freight trains, going from one railroad shop to another, and earning a reputation as an outstanding mechanic. In 1901, he was made roundhouse foreman of the Denver, Rio Grande & Western Railroad in Salt Lake City, Utah. That same year, Chrysler married Della Viola Forker.

Chrysler advanced rapidly in the railroad business, and in 1908 the Chicago Great Western Railroad appointed him superintendent of motive power. He left the firm in 1910 and joined the American

Walter Percy Chrysler (Library of Congress)

Locomotive Company in Pittsburgh, Pennsylvania, as assistant manager. Two years later, he advanced to manager, but by that time he had become fascinated by the new automotive industry, and he accepted a position as works manager at the Buick Motor Company division of General Motors (GM), even though it meant a reduction in pay. He introduced efficiency at the Buick plant, implementing the economies of assembly-line production found at the Ford Motor Company. In 1916, William Durant, who that year regained control of GM, made Chrysler president of Buick with a salary of $500,000 a year.

A dispute with Durant, however, caused Chrysler to resign in 1920, and the following year, he accepted the presidency of the financially troubled Maxwell Motor Company. While producing Maxwells, he and three designers worked on a new car that would incorporate many innovations, such as four-wheel hydraulic brakes. Chrysler exhibited the car in New York City in 1924, and it was an immediate hit. Company profits topped $4 million in 1925, and the firm changed its name to the Chrysler Corporation.

Chrysler acquired the Dodge Brothers Company in 1928 and months later introduced the DeSoto and Plymouth lines, which boosted the Chrysler Company into serious competition with Ford and GM. In another project, one Chrysler undertook independent of his company, he built the Chrysler Building, completed in 1930 as the tallest skyscraper in New York City.

Chrysler retired from the presidency of his company in 1935 but continued as chairman of the board. He died on August 18, 1940, at his estate in Great Neck, New York, and was survived by his four children. The Chrysler Corporation nearly collapsed in the late 1970s and 1980s but was saved by a government bailout orchestrated by LEE IACOCCA.

BIBLIOGRAPHY

Breer, Carl, *The Birth of Chrysler Corporation and Its Engineering Legacy*, 1995; Chrysler, Walter, *Life of an American Workman*, 1950; Stout, Richard H., *Make 'Em Shout Hooray!*, 1988.

Claiborne, Elizabeth

(March 31, 1929–)
Manufacturer

While other fashion designers created dresses, Liz Claiborne broke new ground with mix-and-match separates and in doing so developed one of the most successful businesses ever headed by a woman.

Elizabeth was born on March 31, 1929, in Brussels, Belgium, to Omer Villere Claiborne and Louise Carol (Fenner) Claiborne, both American citizens. Her father, a banker, took her to museums and educated her in art, while her mother taught her to sew. The family moved to New Orleans in 1939 when the Nazis threatened to invade Belgium. As a result of her travels, and because her father wanted to educate Liz himself, she never finished high school.

In 1947, Claiborne returned to Europe and studied art in France at the insistence of her father, who expected her to pursue an art career. Although Claiborne learned to draw and later applied this to her business, she rejected art for fashion design. In 1950, she began working in New York City's Seventh Avenue garment district and the following year was hired as a sketch artist and model. At this time, she married Ben Schultz, a designer for Time-Life Books, and they had a child shortly thereafter.

In the early 1950s, Claiborne worked at Omar Kiam's fashion business as his assistant before moving on to the Junior Rite Company and the Rhea Manufacturing Company. At the latter firm, she met design executive Arthur Ortenberg, and they began a relationship that resulted in their divorcing their respective spouses and, in 1957, getting married.

By this time, Claiborne had gained a reputation as a talented dress designer, and in 1960 the Jonathan Logan Company hired her as chief designer for its junior dress division. Over the next 15 years, she worked at Logan and tried to convince the firm to make moderately priced outfits for the increasing number of women who were working in offices.

Logan, however, refused to heed her advice, and in 1976 after leaving the company, she and her husband, along with a third partner, founded Liz Claiborne, Incorporated. Sales took off immediately as she produced pants, knickers, sweaters, and other clothes, all meant to be mixed and matched. Working women liked the colorful relaxed outfits—clothes meant for average figures rather than for fashion models—and the reasonable prices. By the summer of 1977, Liz Claiborne, Incorporated grossed $7 million, and one year later, revenues reached $23 million.

Growth continued rapidly with few setbacks. In 1981, Claiborne took her firm public and raised over $6 million in the sale of stock. She kept her clothes current by planning new lines several years in advance, by marketing the new lines six times a year rather than the traditional four, and by using a computer system that gave her weekly reports on the sales of styles, colors, and sizes at different department stores. She diversified her lines, too, and in 1981 introduced her petite sportswear, followed in 1982 by dresses. In 1985, she bought Kaiser-Roth Corporation, the company that markets handbags and other accessories under the Liz Claiborne label. Her entry into men's clothes, however, fared poorly, the victim of shabby quality and unappealing designs, and a children's line, begun in 1983, struggled and had to be discontinued four years later.

Liz Claiborne, Incorporated made history in 1986 when it cracked the *Fortune* 500 list of large companies, the first time for a business founded and led by a woman. In 1987, the company's stockholders added two offices to go along with Claiborne's presidency, those of chairman of the board and CEO.

After a recession damaged sales in the late 1980s, Claiborne expanded a chain of boutiques and opened a First Issue store that sold lower-priced casual sportswear. In 1989, she and her husband owned company stock worth nearly $100 million. That year, they announced their retirement from the business and their desire to devote more time to environmental issues. The Claibornes created a bird sanctuary on Fire Island, and today they operate a foundation that supports environmental groups and causes.

BIBLIOGRAPHY

Silver, A. David, *Entrepreneurial Megabucks: The 100 Greatest Entrepreneurs of the Last Twenty-Five Years*, 1985.

Clark, Catherine Taft

(December 31, 1906–May 1986)
Manufacturer

Catherine Taft Clark, a personnel office clerk and housewife, parlayed a favorite recipe for bread bought from a local bakery into a highly profitable baked goods business that sold for $12 million when she retired as president of Brownberry Ovens in 1972.

Catherine, who was born in Whitewater, Wisconsin, on December 31, 1906, was the daughter of Warren Joseph Taft, who died while she was still young, and Clara Louise West Taft. After receiving an education in Whitewater's public schools, Catherine took a job in Milwaukee to help pay for her brother to attend college.

For the next few years, Catherine worked in the personnel department of a department store. During this time, she met Russell J. Clark, a University of Wisconsin graduate who left Milwaukee to earn an M.B.A. from Harvard University. On September 5, 1931, several years after he finished his degree, Russell and Catherine were married. The Clarks moved to the suburb of Oconomowoc, Wisconsin, where they eventually had three children—Sue, Cassidy, and Penelope Anne.

Clark continued to work as a personnel clerk until the birth of her first child. While raising her children, she frequented a local bakery whose bread she found delicious. Eventually, she made an offer to Marsh, the owner of Delafield Bakery, to purchase his recipe for whole wheat bread. He also sold her some bread-baking equipment. Clark rented a store, bought an old truck, and began a small-scale bread delivery service that would eventually become Brownberry Ovens.

In 1943, the Clarks mortgaged their home and solicited additional investment capital from friends. Clark officially designated her fledgling company Brownberry Ovens in 1946. Her initial customers were grocery stores in Milwaukee. Demand for the product soon grew, however, and by the end of the first year, Clark was able to invest in new equipment to increase production capacity.

Brownberry Ovens continued to expand, with both Catherine and Russell traveling on weekends to investigate new retail outlets. Though the company grew every year, its products were only marketed in the Midwest, due to Clark's insistence on offering baked goods free of the preservatives and artificial ingredients that would be required to sell the product in more distant markets. After several years, Clark began to advertise extensively, beginning the Brownberry campaign with advertisements in the *Milwaukee Journal*. The company eventually marketed a bread-making cookbook, *Bread Baking: The How and Why*.

Sales escalated annually and the Brownberry workforce multiplied from a staff of 2 in 1946 to 72 employees in 1954. The product line expanded to include 12 types of bread, 6 kinds of rolls, stuffing, and croutons. Emphasis was placed on producing high-quality baked goods at a higher price. According to Clark, a higher price was suitable for a distinctive product, stating that the goal was to "be original and different—and then convince the public this difference was something they needed."

In 1972, Clark sold Brownberry Ovens to the Peavy Corporation for $12 million, although she remained an active member of Brownberry's board of directors. Shortly after the sale, Clark retired to San Francisco, California, where she died in May 1986.

BIBLIOGRAPHY

Ingham, John N., ed., *Biographical Dictionary of American Business Leaders*, 1983; MacDonald, James R., "Catherine T. Clark," in *The New Millionaires and How They Made Their Fortunes*, 1960; McCoy, Louise Riel, *Millionairesses: Self-Made Women of America*, 1978.

Clark, Richard "Dick"

(November 30, 1929–)
Entertainment Executive

When most Americans think of Richard "Dick" Clark, they recall his memorable teenage rock 'n' roll television show *American Bandstand*. Clark went well beyond spinning records, however, and founded a diverse television production company.

Born on November 30, 1929, in Bronxville, New York, the son of Richard and Julia Clark, Dick grew up in Mount Vernon, New York, where he attended A. B. Davis High School. As a teenager, he avidly listened to the radio, and after his father moved the family to Utica, New York, in order to accept a job at radio station WRUN, Dick worked at the station in the summer, helping out in the mail room.

His first on-air experience occurred when he filled in for a vacationing announcer. In 1945, Clark enrolled at Syracuse University and majored in advertising while pursuing a minor in radio broadcasting. After Clark graduated in 1951, his father, then manager at WRUN, hired him as a summer replacement announcer.

Clark wanted to go on his own, however, and soon accepted a job as announcer

Dick Clark (Archive Photos)

singers. He also bought and established music publishing companies. His business activity got him into trouble when the federal government investigated him and other deejays in 1960 for accepting payments from record companies in return for playing their artists. The investigation never found Clark guilty of any crime, but ABC required him to sell his business interests in order to avoid any appearance of impropriety.

After the invasion of British rock groups in 1964, *American Bandstand* remained on the air, but faded in popularity. Clark responded by diversifying and in the 1970s produced numerous TV shows, including *Dick Clark Presents the Rock and Roll Years* (a weekly show that ran during the 1973–1974 season) and specials such as *Hollywood's Private Home Movies*. He began hosting and producing *Dick Clark's New Year's Rockin' Eve*, that ushered in each new year with a broadcast from Times Square in New York City.

By the 1980s, he had founded Dick Clark Productions, located in Burbank, California. In 1984, the company produced more than 170 hours of TV programming. At the same time, he produced and hosted radio shows, especially *Dick Clark's Rock, Roll and Remember.*

Critics accused Clark of producing mindless entertainment; one labeled his shows "the McDonald's of television." Clark knew what many in middle America wanted, however, and by the mid-1980s, his wealth topped $100 million, while Dick Clark Productions amassed annual profits exceeding $12 million. Clark took his company public in 1986 and listed it on the New York Stock Exchange.

In the 1990s, Dick Clark Productions continued to develop programs for TV

at WKTV, Utica's only television station. In 1952, he moved to Philadelphia, Pennsylvania, and worked at radio station WFIL. His television career resumed three years later when a local station fired the host for its *Bandstand* show and hired Clark. Young and handsome, Clark seemed the perfect choice to attract teenagers to a show that consisted of playing rock 'n' roll records and focusing its cameras on dancing youths. Clark's all-American image counteracted the criticism from adults about rock 'n' roll's threat to morals.

In 1957, the ABC television network decided to air Clark's show nationwide and renamed it *American Bandstand.* At about the same time, Clark began investing in the record industry, buying record labels and forming a company to manage and cable networks and through Dick Clark Restaurants operated Dick Clark's American Bandstand Grill, a chain of family eateries. Clark, married in 1977 to Kari Wigton, his third wife after two divorces, and the father of three children, remained at the helm of his business and was prominent on television shows and in commercials.

BIBLIOGRAPHY

Clark, Dick, *Rock, Roll & Remember*, 1976; Jackson, John A., *American Bandstand: Dick Clark and the Making of a Rock and Roll Empire*, 1997.

Coffin, Charles Albert

(December 30, 1844–July 14, 1926)
Manufacturer

Charles Albert Coffin was the first president of the General Electric Company. Although Coffin was not technically oriented, he was a genius at organization, pragmatic in financial matters, and a key reason for the phenomenal early growth of General Electric.

Born on December 30, 1844, in Fairfield, Maine, Coffin was the son of the Quakers Albert and Anstrus Coffin. After graduating from the Bloomfield Academy in 1862, Coffin moved to Lynn, Massachusetts, to live with his uncle Charles and attend commercial school. But instead of doing as planned, Coffin became involved in the shoe-manufacturing business of his uncles' father-in-law, Micajah C. Pratt.

After several years of introducing new shoe patterns and designs in Pratt's company, Coffin was given the opportunity to move to sales. Though his eye for design was good, his talent at sales was exceptional. Coffin expanded the business by making extended trips to the West, and

he proved valuable in shaping company policies. Though his uncle Charles inherited the business upon Pratt's death, Coffin's influence in the company was significant, and he eventually took over the business. In 1873, a year after Coffin's marriage to Caroline Russel, the company changed its name to Charles A. Coffin and Company. Coffin was equal partners with Pratt's grandson, Micajah P. Clough.

Coffin, by now quite successful, became interested in new ventures. In 1883, he joined the Lynn Syndicate, a financial group of shoe manufacturers formed to purchase the American Electric Company of New Britain, Connecticut. In February of that year, the syndicate completed the purchase, reorganized the company as the Thomson-Houston Electric Company, and moved it to Lynn.

Though Coffin knew little about electrical matters, he was adept at organization. His skill was supplemented by his faith in the electrical prowess of inventors Elihu Thomson, Edwin J. Houston, and E. W. Rice. The early commercial success of the company came from sales of dynamos and arc lamps. Coffin, like his contemporary THOMAS EDISON, saw that the future of the business lay in centralized generation plants rather than sales to individuals for personal use.

To this end, Coffin made the decision to give up the shoe-manufacturing business and focus on the expansion of the Thomson-Houston Electric Company. He expanded the sale of stock in the company, but took care to sell only to those making a substantial investment. Though his philosophy on investing excluded smaller investors and personal acquaintances, the resulting strength of the stock earned him great respect from his partners and employees.

The move to centralize electricity generators was complicated. At this time, Coffin had to make training and equipment available to the local electric companies in order to be able to provide them with service. Understanding that his company's success rested on the success of these local businesses, he made the innovative decision to sell equipment in exchange for partial cash payments and the balance in the stock of the local company.

Coffin also invested in the development of the electric railway and electrification of railroad cars. Another step he took toward being able to offer complete electrical services was the purchase of controlling stock in the Brush Company. The Brush Company held a number of patents that made it difficult for competitors, including Coffin, to develop new products.

By 1888, the Thomson-Houston business volume had grown from $300,000 to $3.5 million. The acquisition of the Brush patents pushed them into yet another league, the playing field of the Edison Company.

By this time, the Edison Company was incorporated at a value of $15 million, reporting over $10 million in gross annual income. The Thomson-Houston Company was not far behind in any respect. A consolidation of Edison (with its success in incandescent lighting) and Thomson-Houston (with its focus on the alternating current system) was inevitable. In 1892, the two companies combined to form the General Electric Company, with Coffin at the helm as president and Edison serving on the board of directors.

Coffin's leadership of General Electric propelled the business from $12 million of income a year in 1873 to almost $1 million per day by 1920. The growth, however, was not always steady. The company endured erratic finances during the period surrounding the financial Panic of 1873. This period, described later by Coffin as "months that seemed like scalding centuries," caused Coffin to develop an obsessive drive to protect the company in subsequent years.

Coffin, for all his financial devotion to expanding the bottom line, believed that the reason to do business was the customer. Providing courteous and efficient service was the only acceptable course for his employees. Though he was seen as a kind and patient man, he was also distant, shunning interviews, publicity, and any public attention. Even the company records have only one picture of him—a candid shot taken without his knowledge.

Coffin worked to encourage the research efforts at General Electric. He endorsed practical inventions, as well as science for its own sake. Under Coffin, the General Electric Research Laboratories developed the Curtis Steam Engine, a product critical to the advancement of power-generation plants. He was also something of a visionary, understanding that just as electricity had helped to urbanize society, it would play a critical role in decentralization. Foreseeing the rise of suburbs, the telecommunication age, and the development of moving pictures, Coffin held that electricity was "social and democratic, and the greatest force in the world because it is everybody's servant."

While Coffin was extremely involved in his work, he also pursued other obligations and interests. During World War I, he created the War Relief Clearing House, an organization that would later be consolidated with the Red Cross. His work with the Red Cross, and other war efforts, earned him the rank of officer of the French Legion of Honor. An advocate of education, he funded a number of national and international scholarships. The Charles A. Coffin Foundation awards research fellowships to college graduates.

As Coffin shunned public attention, little has been noted of his personal life beyond his enjoyment of reading and gardening. He died on July 14, 1926.

BIBLIOGRAPHY

Cox, James A., *A Century of Light*, 1979; *Dictionary of American Biography*, vol. II, 1964; *Electrical Record*, August 1926; *Engineering News-Record*, July 22 and 29, 1926; Whyte, Adam Gowans, *Forty Years of Electrical Progress: The Story of the G.E.C.*, 1930; Wilson, Charles E., *Charles A. Coffin (1844–1926): Pioneer Genius of the General Electric Company*, 1946.

Cohen, Ben

(1951–)
Manufacturer

When Ben Cohen and JERRY GREENFIELD founded Ben & Jerry's Ice Cream, they began more than a company—they established a socially responsible organization that was intended to give to society as much as it received.

Born in Brooklyn, New York, in 1951, Cohen grew up and went to school in Merrick, Long Island, where he met Greenfield. They both graduated from Calhoun High School and followed a course that exuded 1960s countercultural values, with their distrust of big business and commitment to social reform.

Cohen enrolled at Colgate University but dropped out and returned to a job he had held during his senior year in high school—driving an ice-cream truck. He then attended Skidmore College and enrolled in the alternative University Without Walls, but he never received a degree. Instead, he moved to New York City, studied pottery, and held various odd jobs, including delivering pottery wheels and driving a taxicab. In 1974, he moved to Paradox, a town in upstate New York, and taught crafts at the Highland Community School, a small residential facility for emotionally disturbed adolescents. There, he later claimed, he began experimenting with ice cream, serving it to the students.

Three years later, he decided to go into the food business with Greenfield. They considered making bagels, but opted instead for ice cream, with Cohen fondly remembering his ice-cream truck days and how his father used to eat an entire half-gallon at the dinner table, spooning it directly from the carton. The two friends decided that a college town would be best for their shop, and, with a $12,000 investment, in 1978 they renovated a gas station on a busy street corner in Burlington, Vermont, and opened for business. They concocted their own rich, unusual flavors and gained a reputation not only for the creamy taste of their ice cream but also for the fun events they held, such as a free outdoor movie festival each fall.

The business grew rapidly, and in the 1980s they opened a plant in Waterbury, Vermont, and began making and packaging Ben & Jerry's Ice Cream for sale in grocery stores. The bearded, jeans-clad Cohen worked as a truck driver, salesperson, director of marketing, president, and CEO. He and Greenfield worried, however, that the business would develop into an uncaring impersonal corporation. To prevent this, they donated 7.5 percent of their pretax profits to nonprofit organizations through the Ben & Jerry's Foundation, which compared favorably to the average corporate giving rate of 2 percent. In 1988, they received a Corporate Giving Award for their contributions.

They also established an unusual workplace environment where they placed limits on the gap between the lowest- and highest-paid employees, solicited opinions from the workers through frequent surveys, and paid a minimum wage well above the federal one. The lowest salary at Ben & Jerry's—$22,000 in the early 1990s—exceeded the per capita income level in Vermont. In addition, they offered stock priced low enough so that many everyday people could buy it, resulting in one of every 10 Vermonters holding a share in the company.

At Ben & Jerry's in the early 1990s, 40 percent of the workforce was female and three of its six managers were women. Said one employee: "When you've been treated so well, it's hard not to appreciate it. And I'm not the only one—that's the best part about it. They do it for everyone. They really do go out of their way."

Ben & Jerry's frequently exerted itself to make a social difference. For example, it purchased brownies, an ingredient in an ice-cream flavor, from a nonprofit bakery in New York that trained and employed disadvantaged workers. And the company bought nuts from impoverished natives in Brazil. A writer for *Fortune* magazine claimed that such practices made raw ingredients more expensive. "Operating a business is tough enough," he said. "Once you add social goals to the demands of serving customers, making a profit, and returning value to shareholders, you tie yourself up in knots."

By Vermont standards, Ben & Jerry's was large in size—400 workers in 1991, with annual sales topping $100 million. The company ranked among the state's top 10 employers. As Ben & Jerry's Ice Cream spread across the nation, consumers recognized it for its often unusual flavors with such strange names as Cherry Garcia. By the mid-1990s, Ben & Jerry's distributed ice cream to grocery stores in all 50 states and franchised scoop shops in 20 of them.

Amid a drop in profits in 1994 and fatigue over the job, Cohen decided to retire as CEO, and he and Greenfield left the business but not until a search resulted in finding a leader who would maintain the company's commitment to social concerns. That person resigned in 1996, and another CEO was hired.

BIBLIOGRAPHY

Taylor, Alex, III, "Yo Ben! Yo Jerry! It's Just Ice Cream!," *Fortune*, April 28, 1997; Wierzynski, Casimir, "Changing the World with Ice Cream," *The Tech*, February 24, 1989.

Coker, James Lide

(January 3, 1837–June 25, 1918)
Manufacturer

James Lide Coker, a paper manufacturer, mill owner, and businessman, amassed one of the largest fortunes in the history of South Carolina. He was also a generous philanthropist and the founder of Coker College.

Coker, the son of Caleb and Hannah Lide Coker, was born on January 3, 1837, on a plantation near Society Hill, South Carolina. As a child, Coker demonstrated an early affinity for agriculture, an activity that later occupied much of his time and interest.

Coker attended the South Carolina Military Institute of Charleston prior to transferring to Harvard University in 1857. At Harvard, he studied soil analysis and plant development. Though he enjoyed his courses, Coker left school to get practical farming experience when his father gave him a large piece of property in the Hartsville region of South Carolina.

On March 28, 1860, Coker married Susan Stout, whose family was from Alabama. When the Civil War broke out, he volunteered for the Confederate army, serving as a captain. After several years in Virginia, he was transferred to Tennessee, where he was wounded and then promoted to major. Later during the war, he was captured briefly, and upon his release returned to his plantation in Hartsville. Though Coker toyed briefly with a career in public office, he rejected that path, instead resuming his farming and business ventures after the war.

In farming, Coker was extremely successful; remarkably, he did not experience one unsuccessful season in the 50 years that he farmed after the war. In 1866, he opened J. L. Coker and Company, a small store that would one day become one of the largest department stores in South Carolina. He also became a partner in Norwood & Coker, dealing in cotton as well as supplies for the U.S. Navy.

Coker consistently sought out new business ventures. In 1884, he established the Darlington National Bank. In 1889, he built a railroad that extended from Darlington to Hartsville. Later that year, Coker and his son James Jr. established the Carolina Fiber Company, a business that was the first to use the ubiquitous pinewood for wood pulp on a large scale. This venture was followed by the organization of the Southern Novelty Company, which made cones and tubes used for the shipping of yarn.

The decade of the 1890s was no less productive or successful for Coker. He established, in rapid succession, the Hartsville Cotton Mill, the Hartsville Cotton-Seed Oil Mill, and the Bank of Hartsville. He also entered into an experimental project for seed testing and plant development with his other son, David.

Though Coker had been virtually penniless at the end of the war, his businesses had proven so successful that he became one of the richest people in the history of South Carolina. As Coker's wealth increased, he became increasingly involved with social welfare and educational issues and provided funding for the establishment of a women's college. The institution, eventually known as Coker College, was a continued recipient of his generosity. By the time of his death on June 25, 1918, Coker was considered to be one of the most notable philanthropists of his generation.

BIBLIOGRAPHY

Cook, H. T., and J. W. Norwood, "Major James Lide Coker," in *Rambles in the Pee Dee Basin*, 1926; *Dictionary of American Biography*, vol. II, 1964; Simpson, George Lee, *The Cokers of Carolina: A Social Biography of a Family*, 1956.

Colgate, William

(January 25, 1783–March 25, 1857)
Manufacturer

William Colgate literally lived by the phrase "cleanliness is next to godliness." A deeply religious man, he created the world's largest soap company while adhering to the belief that he should give his heart to Christ.

William was born on January 25, 1783, in Hollingbourn, Kent, England, to Robert and Sarah (Bowles) Colgate. After his father immigrated to America in order to escape the authorities who wanted to arrest him for his views in support of the French Revolution, William lived in Baltimore, Maryland. He obtained limited schooling, and in 1798 began working as a tallow chandler—using solid animal fat to make candles, a common practice at that time.

In 1804, William moved to New York City, where he made candles for Slidell and Company. Three years later, in partnership with Francis Smith, he began making tallow candles and soap at his own shop on Dutch Street. This was hot, hard work—in that day, making soap required boiling water in kettles and stirring the mixture by hand. The soap came out in large chunks and then had to be cut into smaller pieces with a knife. Colgate added an extra touch: personally delivering the soap to his customers. "The delivery of this cake of soap may have cost me double my profit on the first sale," he said. "But . . . I won a good customer. . . ."

Soap had been around since biblical times, and soap making employing tallow was common in Italy and Spain dating back to at least the eighth century. Tallow, however, produced a coarse soap, and Colgate at first mainly made laundry detergent. Gradually, though, he took advantage of a new French process—known as saponification—that yielded soap and glycerin from different types of tallow and oils, usually combined, making it possible to produce varieties of soap. Colgate soon advertised in a New York newspaper as a maker of "Soap, Mould, & Dipt Candles of the first quality." In 1847, several years after he had gained full ownership of his business and then brought his son Samuel in as a partner, he moved his factory to New Jersey (where he had been making starch) and installed a soap-building pan whose capacity surpassed all others—43,000 pounds.

Through these years, Colgate remained committed to his religious convictions. He had married Mary Gilbert in 1811 and about that time joined the Baptist Church. He always considered his work in business as a part of God's will and believed he should serve the Lord. Wanting to put the Bible in as many

William Colgate (North Wind Picture Archives)

hands as possible, in 1816 he helped organize the American Bible Society. Beginning in the 1820s, he gave considerable money to a Baptist college, Madison University in Hamilton, New York—renamed Colgate University in 1890. Over time, however, he changed his religious views and withdrew from the Baptist Church in 1838 after concluding that all religious sects hindered the spread of Christianity. He helped organize a nondenominational Tabernacle society.

Colgate remained active in his business until 1856. After he died in New York City on March 25, 1857, his son Samuel continued to develop the company. He introduced perfumed soap in 1866 and began manufacturing perfumes and essences. In 1873, the Colgate Company produced its first toothpaste and sold it in jars before packaging it in collapsible tubes similar to those used today.

BIBLIOGRAPHY

Hardin, Shields T., *The Colgate Story*, 1959.

Colt, Samuel

(July 19, 1814–January 10, 1862)
Manufacturer

As a boy, Samuel Colt took an interest in guns—according to legend, at age seven he took one apart. As an adult, he amassed enormous wealth manufacturing the Colt revolver.

Born on July 19, 1814, in Hartford, Connecticut, to Christopher Colt and Sarah (Caldwell) Colt, Samuel moved in 1824 to Ware, Massachusetts, to work in his father's new dyeing and bleaching factory. At age 13, he attended a prep school but was expelled for disciplinary reasons after three years and traveled as a seaman to India. By 1832, he was back in the United States, working in his father's factory, and intensifying his interest in explosives and firearms. He especially worked on perfecting a revolving barrel firearm and later that year sent his idea to the U.S. Patent Office.

He obtained his patent for the revolving pistol in 1836, and with $200,000 that he borrowed, founded the Patent Arms Manufacturing Company in Paterson, New Jersey. Colt broke with tradition when he made his guns using machine-made rather than handmade parts. Soldiers who used his five-shot Paterson pistol in the era's Indian wars praised it. Nevertheless, in 1842, Colt's factory went bankrupt.

Soon after, the Texas Rangers adopted Colt's pistol and placed a large order for it. Colt began producing the weapons again with the help of another Connecticut gun maker and inventor, Eli Whitney. This time, Colt made a six-shot pistol, called a "Walker," after the captain of the Rangers who ordered them.

As production increased, Colt opened a factory on Pearl Street in Hartford. His Colt Patent Fire Arms Manufacturing Company sold thousands of pistols during the 1849 California gold rush. In the 1850s, Colt became a millionaire and in 1855 opened a new factory, his huge armory on 250 acres in Hartford along the banks of the Connecticut River. By 1857, his plant was producing 250 guns a day at $24 each. During this time, he married Elizabeth Jarvis, and within a few years, they had a son.

As the nation moved toward civil war, Colt's business increased some more, but his reputation took a beating when Northerners criticized him for sending guns to the South. Three days after the first shots were fired at Fort Sumter to begin the war, Colt secretly shipped 500 guns—in crates labeled "hardware"—to Richmond, Virginia. He seemed willing to sell his weapons to anyone who would pay for them.

Colt's health failed during the Civil War, and he died on January 10, 1862. He left an estate valued at $15 million. Colt Manufacturing moved from its armory to a more modern facility in 1994.

BIBLIOGRAPHY

Hosley, William N., *Colt: The Making of an American Legend*, 1996; Rohan, Jack, *Yankee Arms Maker: The Incredible Saga of Samuel Colt*, 1935; Rywell, Martin, *Samuel Colt: A Man and an Epoch*, 1952.

Cooke, Jay

(August 10, 1821–February 16, 1905)
Banker

As a result of his banking acumen, Jay Cooke earned a reputation as "the man who financed the Civil War."

Cooke was born on August 10, 1821, in Sandusky, Ohio. His parents, Eleutheros Cooke, a lawyer, and Martha (Carswell) Cooke, struggled to raise their family on what was then the frontier. After limited schooling, Cooke worked in the mid-1830s at various stores as a clerk. In 1837, he moved to Philadelphia, where he clerked on a shipping line that carried passengers, freight, and mail along canals. Two years later, he obtained a clerk's job at a bank, E. W. Clark & Company. From then on, he engaged in banking and investments. As the company expanded, Cooke advanced, and at age 21 became a partner. The following year, he married Dorothea Elizabeth Allen; they subsequently had eight children.

Clark & Company made handsome profits from its investments in the expanding economy of the 1840s and early 1850s, and Cooke emerged as the firm's leader. He specialized in financing railroad construction and other transportation. Although he lost money in the Panic of 1857, over the next two years, he replenished his capital with additional railroad investments.

Cooke left Clark & Company in 1860 and on January 1, 1861, established Jay Cooke & Company in Philadelphia. He did this despite the impending Civil War, for he had faith in a Union victory and knew that, for bankers, war could be lucrative. Indeed, Cooke worked closely with Secretary of the Treasury Salmon P.

Jay Cooke (North Wind Picture Archives)

Chase and, after the Battle of Bull Run in July 1861, rallied Philadelphia's banks to buy treasury notes. A few days later, Cooke assisted in getting bankers in New York City to advance the government $50 million, to be repaid through the sales of bonds.

In 1862, Cooke opened an office in Washington, D.C., to handle the government's need for money. Where Chase had difficulty finding subscribers to government loans, Cooke had none. Chase appointed Cooke a treasury agent to dispose of bonds, and the banker got citizens in all walks of life to buy them. When the government faced financial straits in 1865, Cooke sold $600 million of securities in less than six months.

After the war, Cooke expanded his bank, opening branches in New York City and London. He invested in the Northern Pacific Railroad, but in 1873 its continuing drain on finances and a general bad money market brought insolvency, and Jay Cooke & Company folded. The closure of such a prominent banking house sparked a general financial panic, spurred on by massive and widespread overspeculation in the booming post–Civil War economy. The Panic of 1873, as it came to be called, marked the beginning of a nationwide financial depression that lasted throughout much of the 1870s. According to historian Henrietta Larson, this ended the era when "speculative promotion of railroads" exceeded any "reasonable expectation of returns under the drive of post-war conditions."

Although Cooke never returned to banking, he invested to recoup his losses, primarily in silver mines. He once again built a substantial estate, a development applauded by many who appreciated his role in helping to save the Union during the Civil War. He died on February 16, 1905.

BIBLIOGRAPHY

Larson, Henrietta M., *Jay Cooke: Private Banker*, 1936.

Coors, Adolph

(February 4, 1847–June 5, 1929)
Brewer

The name Coors is instantly recognizable for its place in the beer industry and its association with the Colorado Rocky Mountains. Adolph Herman Joseph Coors founded the ale company, attained great wealth despite the outlawing of alcohol during Prohibition, and passed on his great success to future generations of the Coors family. His ingenuity led to success in such diverse enterprises as beer brewing, porcelain manufacturing, and the sale of malted milk products.

The son of Joseph and Helena Hein Coors, Coors was born in Barmen, Prussia (present-day Germany), on February 4, 1847. The family's poverty led Coors to begin working at the age of 13. After becoming an orphan at age 15, Coors began an apprenticeship at the Henry Wenker Brewery. As he was expected to pay for this opportunity to learn a trade, he also served as a bookkeeper for the brewery. After several years of work, Coors immigrated to the United States.

Arriving in Maryland in 1868 as a penniless stowaway, Coors pursued work wherever possible. By 1869, he had become the foreman of John Stenger's brewery in Naperville, Illinois. On January 22, 1872, Coors left Illinois and worked his way westward. By late spring of that year, he had arrived in Denver, where he worked as a gardener until he was able to purchase a partnership in the bottling company of John Staderman in

May. By the end of the year, Coors had bought out his partner's interest and assumed control of the company.

In 1873, Coors entered into a new partnership with Jacob Schueler, a confectioner. Coors's years of experience in the brewing industry helped persuade Schueler to join Coors in launching a new brewery. The two chose Golden, Colorado, as the site of the new company, based largely on Coors's belief that the hill country with the natural springs of Clear Creek was an ideal location for the brewing of quality beer. On November 15, 1873, the Golden Brewery opened. With Coors's energetic leadership, and Schueler's capital investment, the brewery reached a capacity of 100 kegs of beer produced daily long before the end of the first year of operation.

The next few years were categorized by vigorous growth. Coors maintained a strict policy of expansion based on the company's profits rather than seeking outside investment. With the assistance of an expanding system of railroads, Golden Brewery increased its sales influence to most of the western territories, Kansas, and New Mexico.

Coors added a malt house and bottling plant, created an ice dam over Clear Creek, and began to make improvements on a scenic area of the property, Golden Grove. As Golden Brewery prospered, the city and residents of Golden reaped many benefits, from increased employment to additional financial support of the local barley farmers. Coors also utilized the ice dam to provide ice service to customers within Golden.

Coors and his brewery played a large role in Golden community affairs. Coors added bathhouses to the Golden Grove, supplied the lake with boats, and leveled the area for landscaping. A playground, dance floor, picnic area, and outdoor bowling alley were erected. The Grove was the central spot in Golden for lodge meetings, community and church picnics, tourists, and school events.

In addition to his contribution to the physical setting, Coors served on a number of committees for the planning of community events. He also donated funds toward the establishment of several educational institutions.

By the end of 1879, the Golden Brewery was booming. It annually produced 2,000 barrels of bottled beer and 2,000 barrels of keg beer. Coors had also earned a reputation for high-quality ale. On May 1, 1880, Coors bought out Schueler's investment, and the company launched into a period of great expansion. The resulting increase in business caused Coors to cease public operation of the popular Golden Grove, feeling that it diverted attention necessary to run the company.

The end of the nineteenth century and the beginning of the twentieth were fraught with national tensions over the issue of Prohibition, the movement to outlaw the drinking of alcoholic beverages. In June 1881, Coors met with a number of other citizens and businessmen to form the Citizen's Protective Union of Colorado, one of the first antitemperance organizations in Colorado.

During these last decades before Prohibition, the Coors Golden Brewery experienced great growth despite the increasingly loud rumblings of the temperance movement. Though Coors, known by now as "the millionaire brewer," faced a great number of competitors, his product continued to receive acclaim. He also continued to diversify his business interests and remained active in community activities. The last decade of the century initiated a period of increased marketing and advertising of the Coors products.

On June 12, 1913, the company incorporated as the Adolph Coors Brewing and Manufacturing Company, with Adolph Coors as president and treasurer and Adolph Coors Jr. as vice president and secretary. When Colorado enacted Prohibition in 1916, the Coors Company was forced to dump over 17,000 gallons of beer into Clear Creek. Coors's long-term insistence on diversity, however, enabled the company to survive the Prohibition years. Coors began to manufacture "near beer," separating out the alcohol after the fermentation process and selling it legally to drug companies and hospitals. He also established the Coors Porcelain Company, to manufacture industrial and scientific porcelain. The porcelain division still exists and remains a leader in its field. Another highly successful endeavor involved the selling of malted milk.

In addition to his enthusiasm for business, Coors is remembered as a dedicated family man. Coors had six children by his wife, Louisa M. Weber, whom he had married in 1879. He also collected art and traveled widely. Coors died on June 5, 1929, after accidentally falling from a hotel window while on vacation in Virginia Beach.

BIBLIOGRAPHY

Ferrill, Will C., ed., *Sketches of Colorado*, 1911; "Goode Goodies No. 8—The Adolph Coors Story," http://www.users.visi.net/~cwt/goodie8.html; Kostka, William, *The Pre-Prohibition History of Adolph Coors Company, 1873–1933*, 1973; Vickers, W. B., ed., *History of Clear Creek and Boulder Valleys*, 1880; "Wealthy Colorado Manufacturer, 82, is Killed in Fall," *The Virginian-Pilot*, June 6, 1929.

Corliss, George

(June 2, 1817–February 2, 1888)
Manufacturer

With his inventions involving steam engines and his thriving manufacturing plant that produced them, George Corliss helped propel America's industrial development.

Born on June 2, 1817, in Easton, New York, to Hiram Corliss and Susan (Sheldon) Corliss, George moved at age 8 with his family to Greenwich, New York, where in school he showed a talent for mathematics and mechanics. At age 14, he worked in a general store and four years later enrolled at Castleton Academy in Vermont. George left the academy in 1837 and opened his own general store in Greenwich. When customers began complaining that the stitching in shoes he sold fell apart too easily, Corliss went to work on an invention that would solve the problem. He developed a machine that sewed boots by using needles and thread to create a cross-stitching.

After he obtained a patent for his invention in 1842, Corliss went to Providence, Rhode Island, where he tried to market it. The firm of Fairbanks, Bancroft & Company, which made steam engines, recognized Corliss's genius and hired him as a draftsman. He moved to Providence with his wife, Phoebe Frost, whom he had married in 1839, and his two children and in short order began making modifications to steam engines that revolutionized their operation.

Corliss left Fairbanks, Bancroft & Company in 1848 and joined two partners to form Corliss, Nightingale & Company. He then built the first steam engines that used his plans. The Corliss engines had rotary valves and valves that were cylindrical in shape, which equalized pressure and minimized friction, thus increasing efficiency. Corliss's work, alongside that of James Watt, proved to be monumental in the development of steam engines.

After his wife died, Corliss married Emily Shaw in 1866. Meanwhile, his company continued to grow through the 1870s and employed more than 1,000 workers. In addition to his work with steam engines, Corliss obtained patents for a gear-cutting machine, an improved boiler, and a pumping engine used at wa-

George Corliss (Library of Congress)

terworks. He served briefly in the Rhode Island legislature and, in 1876, as a Republican presidential elector. Corliss died on February 2, 1888.

BIBLIOGRAPHY

Corliss, Mary, *The Life and Work of George H. Corliss*, 1930.

Cornell, Ezra

(January 11, 1807–December 9, 1874)
Communications Executive

Ezra Cornell, the wealthy founder of Cornell University in Ithaca, New York, was a communications innovator who was among the first to recognize the potential of the telegraph. Cornell worked with Samuel F. B. Morse, the inventor of the magnetic telegraph, to refine the machine and devise means of building and improving the physical infrastructure of telegraph lines. Cornell's vision of connecting the nation by telegraph was realized in the creation of Western Union Telegraph Company, a highly successful firm that remains a significant member of the communications industry. His ideas on the advancement of education shaped the institution of Cornell University, while his generosity and lobbying efforts helped build it.

Ezra, the son of New England Quakers Elijah and Eunice Barnard Cornell, was born at Westchester Landing, New York, on January 11, 1807. In addition to his studies at the village school in De Ruyter, New York, Ezra learned farming and earthenware manufacturing from his father and pursued an interest in carpentry. Ezra left home at age 18 and obtained work as a mechanic and laborer in Syracuse and Homer, New York.

Even as a youth, Cornell was tenacious and alert to new opportunities. On hearing that Ithaca was a growing commercial town, he moved there in 1828 to work as a carpenter and millwright. He quickly demonstrated managerial skill and was designated the general manager of the flour and plaster mills owned by J. S. Beebe.

On March 19, 1831, Cornell married Mary Ann Wood, the daughter of an old friend of Cornell's father. Though his family approved of the cheerful, industrious girl, the De Ruyter Society of Friends excommunicated Cornell for marrying a non-Quaker. Though unrepentant and wholly pleased with his marriage, Cornell considered himself throughout his life to be a "well-wisher of the Society." Of the five children eventually born to the couple, two died in infancy. One of their surviving sons, Alonzo B. Cornell, would eventually become the governor of New York.

Cornell's tenure at the mill in Ithaca was characterized by both his managerial acumen and his ingenuity in designing a number of mechanical improvements. Although Cornell was well respected, he was forced to leave the job in 1841 when the decision was made to convert the mills into a woolen factory and cut back on personnel.

While working at a temporary job in Maine, Cornell happened to meet F. O. J. Smith, a member of the U.S. House of Representatives who was working to persuade the House to appropriate $30,000 for the development of Morse's magnetic telegraph invention. Having successfully secured the funds, Smith contracted Morse to lay pipe to carry wires between Washington, D.C., and Baltimore, and he appealed to Cornell to devise a machine to aid in the laying of the pipes. Though the mechanically adept Cornell was able to do so, he found that insulating the underground wires would not be feasible.

Fearing the loss of the contract, Morse and Cornell decided to buy time by destroying the pipe-laying machine to devise a better system of wires. Cornell designed a means of insulating wires on poles and supervised the building of an aboveground line between Washington and Baltimore.

The experience, which Cornell had embarked upon from the perspective of a mechanic, inflamed his entrepreneurial spirit. Excited by the commercial prospects of the telegraph, Cornell threw himself into the task of demonstrating its potential, raising investment capital, and building new lines. Within a few years, his energetic work had made him the principal figure in the budding industry. His Magnetic Telegraph Company connected New York and Washington, and in 1845 the line from the Hudson River in New York to Philadelphia was completed. By the time Cornell began work on the New York-Albany line, he began making large profits, which he used to continue the expansion. In 1847, turning his attention to the Great Lakes region, he launched the Erie & Michigan Telegraph Company, which ultimately linked Buffalo, Cleveland, and Detroit. The area of service continued to expand, and for a time the telegraph preceded the advent of the railroad in many midwestern towns.

As the infrastructure and popularity of the telegraph exploded, numerous rival companies emerged to challenge Cornell's network. In 1855, after several years of cutthroat competition, Cornell and other leading owners banded together to form the Western Union Telegraph Company, a consolidation of over seven disparate systems. The company rapidly expanded across the United States and Canada. Cornell served for 20 years as a director on Western Union's board and was the company's largest stockholder for 15 years.

With the enormous success of the company and the achievement of great personal wealth, Cornell became interested in public affairs. He established a public library in Ithaca, was active in the state agricultural society, and served in the New York legislature from 1861 to 1867.

Cornell became increasingly involved with the drive for a new educational institution devoted to liberal and mechanical arts. Working with Andrew D. White, a member of the state senate who espoused the need for expanded university facilities, Cornell pledged $500,000 for the acquisition of a site for a new university.

Cornell University, which received its first class in 1868, came into being through Cornell's diligence in enlisting political support and his generosity in funding the initial costs. Moreover, the spirit of the university was shaped by his ideals of freedom from religious ties, his belief in coeducational facilities, his emphasis on engineering and agricultural training, and his dedication to providing for poor students. He was also instrumental in the choice of Andrew White as the university's first president. Cornell's lean figure, in stovepipe hat and frock coat, was a fixture around campus until his death on December 9, 1874.

BIBLIOGRAPHY

Cornell, Alonzo B., *"True and Firm": Biography of Ezra Cornell, Founder of the Cornell University: A Filial Tribute*, 1884; Dorf, Philip, *The Builder: A Biography of Ezra Cornell*, 1952; Marshall, Walter P., *Ezra Cornell, 1807–1874: His Contributions to*

Western Union and to Cornell University, 1951; Smith, Albert William, *Ezra Cornell: A Character Study,* 1934; White, Andrew Dickson, *My Reminiscences of Ezra: An Address Delivered before the Cornell University on Founder's Day, January 11th, 1890,* 1890.

Corning, Erastus

(December 17, 1794–April 9, 1872)
Merchant

Beginning his career in hardware, Erastus Corning quickly became a successful merchant and businessman. He then moved into the manufacturing of iron and began investing in railroads. These interrelated endeavors proved very successful and made Corning one of the richest men in New York State, and helped him to become a prominent local politician.

Erastus was born to Bliss and Lucinda Smith Corning in Norwich, Connecticut, on December 17, 1794. At the age of 2, he fell from his crib, permanently injuring his hip to an extent that required him to use crutches for most of his life. In 1803, he was selected to attend a private school for outstanding students run by Yale graduate Pelatiah Perit. He also held an apprenticeship as a clerk in an uncle's hardware store in Troy, New York, beginning at age 13.

In March 1814, Corning left his uncle's employ and moved to Albany, New York, to begin working for the hardware firm of John Spencer and Company. Two years later, he bought a partnership in the business with the $500 he had saved. Spencer died in 1829, and Corning became sole owner by purchasing Spencer's share from his heirs. Corning married Harriet Weld, the daughter of another hardware merchant, on March 10, 1819. The couple subsequently had five sons, but only two survived to adulthood.

Corning became successful as a hardware merchant by taking calculated risks and making speculative investments. By 1826, he was ready to move from being a middleman to being a manufacturer. He purchased an iron mill just south of Troy and renamed it the Albany Iron Works. The plant produced rolled iron, which was initially used for making small iron pieces such as nails and rods. This began to change when Corning started investing in early railroad lines and recognized that there would eventually be a huge demand for iron rails as the railroads spread across the country. In the early 1830s, he helped finance the Mohawk and Hudson Railroad, serving as the company's president until 1853. During this time, he was also a financier and executive of the Utica and Schenectady Railroad.

During the same period of his life, Corning's political career blossomed. He was first elected mayor of Albany in 1834 and won reelection to the post three more times. He served as a New York State senator from 1842 to 1845 and was

Erastus Corning (UPI/Corbis-Bettmann)

elected to the U.S. Congress in 1857 and again in 1861.

In 1844, Corning made a key investment by purchasing the Mount Savage Ironworks in Maryland. This acquisition greatly expanded his production capabil-

ities, and by 1850 the plant was churning out 1,000 tons of rails per year. Corning, a staunch Democrat, was initially opposed to the Civil War and criticized President Abraham Lincoln; however, not wanting to miss a fabulous opportunity for profit, he privately sent agents to Washington, D.C., to secure lucrative military contracts for the manufacture of cannons, railway hardware, and iron plates for ships.

In 1853, Corning delved more deeply into the burgeoning railway business by creating the New York Central Railroad. To accomplish this task, he raised $23 million in capital and pulled together 10 minor railway lines throughout New York State, making the company into the largest corporation in the country at that time. Corning was elected founding president of the railroad and held the position for 12 years until he resigned in 1864 at age 70 due to both his failing health and pressure from a labor strike.

Corning was active in Albany civic affairs throughout his career. He directed the leveling of several of Albany's precipitously steep streets and the filling of some dangerous ravines, which allowed the addition of cross streets. In 1850, Corning headed Albany's first water commission, which established a reservoir system for the city's drinking water. At the time of his death on April 9, 1872, his estimated worth was $12 million, an extraordinary sum for the time.

BIBLIOGRAPHY

Atherton, Lewis E., *The Pioneer Merchant in Mid-America*, 1939; Grondahl, Paul, *Mayor Corning: Albany Icon, Albany Enigma*, 1997; Neu, Irene D., *Erastus Corning, Merchant and Financier*, 1960.

Crane, Richard Teller

(May 15, 1832–January 8, 1912)
Manufacturer

Richard Teller Crane started a small brass foundry that became one of the largest manufacturers of plumbing supplies and piping in the world. Crane's company also controlled 95 percent of the elevator manufacturing business in his day. An autocratic disciplinarian, Crane was highly respected by his employees and associates for his straightforward manner and belief in quality work.

Richard, the descendant of a family that had arrived in New England in 1655, was born on May 15, 1832, in Paterson, New Jersey, to Timothy Batchford and Maria Ryerson Crane. Due to his father's financial losses, Crane began working as the operator of a cotton mill at the young age of nine.

Crane switched jobs frequently during his youth. In 1847, he was hired by John Benson to work in a Brooklyn brass and bell foundry. Though Crane learned much in this job that would become useful in his later career, he soon moved on, obtaining work with a number of different press manufacturers before moving to Chicago in 1854.

Crane's uncle, Martin Ryerson, allowed Crane to set up shop in his lumberyard. The brass foundry that started from such humble beginnings would one day become the largest of its kind in the world. Crane initially specialized in making brass couplings and the copper points needed for lightning rods. Early in the venture, Crane was joined by his brother Charles S. Crane, who remained with the firm until 1871. R. T. Crane and Brother was incorporated as the Northwestern Manufacturing Company in 1865, though the name was changed to Crane Brothers Manufacturing Company in 1872.

Crane decided early on to expand the product line to include wrought iron pipes and fittings. Eventually, the company delved into the business of manufacturing elevator parts and selling shafting equipment, steam engines and pumps, and finished elevators. This specialty business, which was eventually run as a subsidiary, the Crane Elevator Company, at one time controlled 95 percent of the American elevator business. Around the turn of the twentieth century, Crane began to lose interest and sold the Crane Elevator Company to the Otis Elevator Company, a decision that freed up one of the firm's foundries for other purposes. Within a short time, the space was used in the service of new orders for various fittings for South African mining companies.

Over time, the Crane Company (as the business was renamed in 1890) developed a strong reputation for innovations in high-pressure piping that emerged largely from an intuitive and hardworking team of engineers and metallurgists kept on staff. By this time, the use of steel was gradually replacing the iron and brass fittings that had been the company's original basis.

Crane, known to his employees as the "Old Man," was a large man with a domineering personality. Considered by social acquaintances to be a genial host, in the workplace he was autocratic, with a fierce temper and iron resolve. Though a strict disciplinarian, Crane was widely respected by his employees. In the later years of his life, Crane instituted a profit-sharing program whereby employees annually received gifts of 5–10 percent of their annual earnings.

Crane was married to three different women over the course of his life: first, to Mary Josephine Prentice, in 1857, followed in 1889 by his marriage to her sister, Eliza Ann Prentice, and finally to Emily Sprague Hutchins in 1903. Crane had nine children, one of whom, Charles Richard Crane, succeeded Crane as president of Crane Company. Charles joined the company in 1896 after graduating from Yale, becoming president upon his father's death on January 8, 1912.

BIBLIOGRAPHY

Berryman, John B., *An Old Man Looks Back: Reminiscences of Forty-Seven Years, 1895–1942, in the General Offices of Crane Co.*, 1943; Ingham, John N., ed., *Biographical Dictionary of American Business Leaders*, 1983; Moskowitz, Milton, et al., eds., *Everybody's Business*, 1980.

Crow, Fred Trammel

(1914–)
Real Estate Developer

Homefurnishings Mart, Embarcadero Center, Peachtree Center—all came from Fred Trammel Crow's first foray into real estate, his decision to provide Ray-O-Vac batteries with a warehouse. By the 1980s, Crow had emerged as the nation's biggest real estate developer and among its wealthiest.

Crow came from a humble background. He was born in 1914 in Dallas, Texas, to Jefferson and Mary Crow. His father worked as a bookkeeper but had more interest in religion than in business and constantly impressed on his family the need to follow the Lord. When the elder Crow lost his job during the Great Depression, young Crow was forced to find work. While in high school, he made money plucking chickens. After he graduated, he held other odd jobs and attended night school at Southern Methodist University, where he studied accounting. Soon after he got his degree, Crow joined Ernst & Ernst, an accounting firm. In 1940, he left that firm for Smith, Morrison, and Salois, the leading accountants in Dallas. World War II then intervened, and in 1941 Crow joined the navy and audited defense contracts for them.

After the war, Crow returned to Dallas and married Margaret Doggett, who came from a wealthy family. Crow worked for Doggett Grain, a company that operated grain elevators, and quickly realized that the business was declining. As a result, he decided to diversify by leasing a Doggett warehouse to the Ray-O-Vac battery company. When Ray-O-Vac soon announced it would have to move because it needed more space, Crow convinced the firm to let him build a warehouse and lease it to them. This maneuver marked Crow's entry into real estate development and could not have come at a more opportunistic time since a postwar boom was stoking the American economy, and manufacturing companies needed more storage space. Building warehouses lacked glamour but meant money.

While he was employed at Doggett, Crow began developing properties. For capital, he at first relied on his wife's credit. He also established a close working relationship with John Stemmons, a wealthy Dallas investor. The Trammell Crow Company, as Crow called his firm, built several more warehouses in the early 1950s, and by the end of the decade, Crow owned several million square feet of warehouse space, making him the largest such developer. Often he took financial risks that others criticized. But Crow said, "Action is what counts. Too often businessmen are petrified by fears, await the unrolling of developments as though some inner logic will dictate the correct decision. I've never been impressed by such behavior. There is as much risk—even more—in doing nothing than in doing something."

Crow diversified after he visited the Chicago Merchandise Mart, a structure that had been built in Chicago's downtown district many years earlier. Crow believed that he could develop a more attractive, specialized mart in an accessible location outside of Dallas' downtown area. In July 1957, he opened the first stage of his 434,000-square-foot Homefur-

Fred Trammel Crow (UPI/Corbis-Bettmann)

nishings Mart in Dallas. Wholesale furniture dealers displayed their wares—in fact, so many businesses wanted to be at the mart that Crow opened a second stage in January 1958, with 90 percent of the space leased. By developing his project in stages and thus waiting to see if the initial construction succeeded before moving ahead, Crow limited his risks.

Crow followed this success with the construction of the Apparel Mart, also built in Dallas, and specialty trade marts constructed in several American cities and in Europe. In 1961, Crow and architect-developer John Portman built the Peachtree Center in Atlanta, the first suburban-style shopping mall in an urban downtown. The center housed shops,

hotels, and restaurants and rejuvenated Atlanta's downtown.

Crow's next big project was the Embarcadero Center, built in San Francisco in the early 1970s with the help of the Chase Manhattan Bank as part of an urban redevelopment program. By that time, Crow and his family held an interest in about 650 corporations or partnerships. (Crow has three sons and a daughter.) An economic recession in the mid-1970s, however, drove him to the brink of bankruptcy before the Chase Manhattan Bank bailed him out, and he brought in J. McDonald "Don" Williams to provide order to what had long been a chaotic operation.

Williams, in turn, attracted bright graduates from prestigious colleges. Between Williams's management expertise and Crow's continued deals, Trammel Crow Company dominated real estate development in Dallas, Houston, San Francisco, and Chicago. In the 1980s, Crow managed the 20-story New York Trade Mart at Times Square. He continued to erect trade and shopping centers, office and industrial buildings, warehouses, hotels, and housing that, as he put it, made his firm "the first truly national real estate developing company" and "the largest and most successful."

Crow's personal wealth neared $1 billion in the 1990s, but he seldom flaunted it. Unlike other real estate tycoons, such as DONALD TRUMP, he neither named his buildings after himself nor called much attention to his activities. As a result, to many Americans the name Trammel Crow remains obscure despite the real estate empire he had built.

BIBLIOGRAPHY

Sobel, Robert, *Trammel Crow, Master Builder: The Story of America's Largest Real Estate Empire*, 1989.

Cudahy, Michael

(December 7, 1841–November 27, 1910)
Meat Packer

By expanding refrigeration and developing new outlets for livestock, Michael Cudahy contributed to the emergence of the modern meatpacking industry.

Michael was born on December 7, 1841, in Callan, County Kilkenny, Ireland, to Patrick Cudahy and Elizabeth (Shaw) Cudahy. He immigrated to the United States with his parents in 1849 and lived in Milwaukee, Wisconsin.

Cudahy involved himself in meatpacking while still a kid, when he left school at age 14 and began working for the firm of Layton & Plankinton. He held various positions with them, including that of meat inspector in 1866. Cudahy's considerable talent resulted in the company—since reorganized as Plankinton & Armour—making him superintendent of its Milwaukee packinghouse in 1869. Six years later, Armour & Company made him a partner, and he supervised the firm's operations at the Union Stockyard in Chicago. About the same time, he married Catherine Sullivan.

A vicious field, replete with underhanded deals, cleaver-sharp competition, and unrepentant opposition to unions, America's meatpacking industry sought expansive outlets. Cudahy made his first notable contribution to this pursuit when he took GUSTAVUS SWIFT'S work on refrigerated railroad cars and applied that technology to the plant site. He put refrigeration units, or coolers, in his company's packing plants, thus changing the industry from largely seasonal, winter-only to year-round. Consumers now had a ready supply of meat, and packers could engage in more flexible marketing.

In 1887, Cudahy formed a partnership with his brother Edward Cudahy and the meatpacking tycoon PHILIP DANFORTH ARMOUR to buy a small plant in Omaha, Nebraska, under the name Armour-Cudahy Packing Company. Here, he made his second notable contribution to the industry when he developed outlets within the United States for the nation's expanding supplies of livestock, especially hogs.

Cudahy purchased Armour's interest in the firm in 1890, and it became the Cudahy Packing Company. He served as its president until his death on November 27, 1910.

BIBLIOGRAPHY

Clemen, Rudolf A., *American Livestock and Meat Industry*, 1923; Leech, Harper, and John Charles Carroll, *Armour and His Times*, 1938.

Cunningham, Harry

(1907–)
Merchant

Although not the first to open a discount store, Harry Cunningham applied the concept on a much larger scale than had others before him and founded Kmart, a discount merchandising industry leader.

Cunningham was born in 1907 in Home Camp, Pennsylvania, and grew up on his family's farm. He attended Miami University in Ohio, but after two years, financial difficulties forced him to quit. In 1928, he went to work at a Kresge store in Lynchburg, Virginia. Kresge's had been founded in 1899 by SEBASTIAN KRESGE and had grown into a large five-and-dime store chain. Cunningham worked long hours in the stockroom and then progressed through the company ranks as store manager, superintendent of stores, and assistant sales manager.

As an assistant sales manager, Cunningham discovered a disturbing trend: with its stores located in downtown districts, Kresge was losing out to competitors who were building in the rapidly expanding suburbs. He decided to investigate a new store, Korvette's, which was opened on Long Island by Eugene Ferkhauf. Korvette's had located in a shopping center with plentiful parking and offered discounts on all its items, even brand-name ones.

After Cunningham became Kresge's sales director in 1953, he developed a plan to copy Korvette's. He put the plan into action after he became president in 1959, committing $80 million to opening 60 discount stores. To break with the increasingly negative name recognition attached to Kresge, he called the stores Kmart. Each Kmart offered discount prices, extensive parking, and locations in the suburbs. The first Kmart opened in Detroit, Michigan, in March 1962, and its success—as well as that of other Kmarts—boosted Kresge ahead of its long-standing rival, Woolworth.

Cunningham opened Kmarts at the rate of 150 stores per year. Even after he resigned in the mid-1970s, the company, which changed its name from Kresge to the Kmart Corporation, continued to follow his formula: discounts in stores that offered few frills and emphasized self-service.

As Kmart neared the top of retail chains in sales, it faced stiff competition from a new discount company, Wal-Mart, founded by SAM WALTON. In addition, like Wal-Mart, Kmart had its critics who accused it of undercutting and destroying smaller community stores and of inundating America with look-alike buildings, sterile in spirit and harmful in fostering strip development and traffic congestion.

BIBLIOGRAPHY

Moskowitz, Milton, et al., eds., *Everybody's Business*, 1980.

Daly, Marcus

(December 5, 1841–November 12, 1900)
Mining Executive

"His training in Nevada and Utah...gave him the intelligent idea of mining which led him to purchase and develop the Alice [Mine]," said a newspaper about Marcus Daly, a giant figure in Western copper mining during the region's frontier era.

Marcus Daly (Baldwin H. Ward/Corbis-Bettmann)

"Its [the mine's] success has been one of the most important factors in the... prosperity that has dawned upon Montana Territory. When the better days of Montana are written up, let due honor and credit be given to Marcus Daly."

Marcus, born on December 5, 1841, to Luke and Mary Daly in County Cavan, Ireland, grew up in poverty and obtained little formal education before immigrating to the United States at age 15. He worked for several years on the docks in New York City—a bustling environment where ships carried news about mining adventures in the West and big money to be made. Daly heard these stories, and in 1861 journeyed to California, where he worked as a pick-and-shovel laborer in the mines.

In 1865, Daly began working at the Comstock Mine in Nevada. He studied mining diligently and learned how to identify potential ore deposits. He saved his money, and, in 1876—four years after he married Margaret Evans, the daughter of a Utah miner—he and several partners purchased the Alice Silver Mine in Butte, Montana. In 1880, he resigned as superintendent and sold his interest for $100,000.

After explorations near Butte, Daly believed that he had uncovered another large silver deposit, this one at the Anaconda Mine, but his estimate contradicted that held by many experts, making it difficult for him to find financial backers. He discovered one, however, in J. B. Haggin, a San Francisco lawyer and friend of WILLIAM RANDOLPH HEARST. Daly's mine produced 8,000 tons of silver, but this production soon petered out. In mining the silver, however, Daly discovered copper, and he convinced Haggin, Hearst, and others to join him in forming the Anaconda Copper Mining Company.

Daly's enormous copper discovery fed America's rapid industrialization. He built a smelter 26 miles west of Butte—in what became the town of Anaconda—that began operating in 1885, a railroad that snaked around the mountains from Anaconda to Butte, power plants, and an irrigation system. He founded a newspaper, the *Anaconda Standard* and, in order to get fuel for his operations, began a lumber company that scoured the hills. At one point, the government accused him of illegally chopping down millions of acres, but political deals allowed him to escape prosecution. All these businesses made Daly a millionaire. He lived on a spacious ranch in the Upper Bitter Root Valley and raced horses at the nation's prominent tracks.

A large man with a jocular face, Daly's outgoing manner won him many friends and, with his money, considerable influence. As an activist in the Democratic Party he had, from the late 1880s onward, a running feud with a fellow Democrat, William A. Clark. The two men vied for control of the Butte copper mines, and until 1900, Daly thwarted Clark's every attempt to win political office. Their fight produced sensational headlines.

Daly paid higher wages than most mining companies and remembered his friends from his early years, when he worked with pick and shovel. He brought several of them to Butte and helped them make fortunes.

In 1899, when 6,000 tons of ore a day ran through his smelter, Daly made a deal with Eastern financiers to combine his mining and lumber companies with others to form the Amalgamated Copper Company. He sold his holdings for $39 million but obtained shares in Amalgamated and served as company president. He died in New York City on November 12, 1900.

BIBLIOGRAPHY

Glasscock, Carl B., *War of the Copper Kings*, 1966; Shoebotham, H. Minar, *Anaconda: Life of Marcus Daly*, 1956.

Daniel, Jack

(1850–1911)
Manufacturer

Jasper Newton "Jack" Daniel walked a straight line from childhood to adulthood, owning a still at age 13 and creating a legendary whiskey.

Born in 1850 in Lynchburg, Tennessee, Daniel obtained little formal schooling, was raised by a family friend, and at age seven was hired out to Dan Call, a man with a peculiar combination of interests:

a Lutheran minister, he owned a whiskey still on the Louse River. In making his whiskey, Call mellowed it by running it through hard maple charcoal. Although some other Tennessee whiskey makers also used that process, many more avoided it as too time-consuming.

Call taught his method to the young Jack Daniel, and in 1863, when Call's congregation convinced him to give up whiskey making, he sold the still to Daniel, who was then just 13 years old. Three years later, Daniel made his still legal by registering it with the federal government.

Daniel's whiskey gained a reputation for its smoothness. He located his distillery in the Lynchburg Hollow at Cave Spring to take advantage of its cool iron-free limestone water. (Iron interferes with the taste of whiskey.) To make whiskey, he added the water to a mix of corn, rye, and barley malt, creating "mash." He then cooked the mash, let it ferment in huge vats, and distilled it in copper stills, producing a crystal-clear, 140-proof spirit. This was followed by the charcoal mellowing that lowered the whiskey to 110 proof. He then let it age in charred white-oak barrels, giving it a dark amber color.

The diminutive Daniel—five feet, two inches tall—dressed every day in a formal knee-length frock coat and broad-rimmed planter's hat, making himself a conspicuous figure in Lynchburg. He exhibited his whiskey at the 1904 World's Fair in St. Louis, Missouri, where it was awarded a gold medal as the world's best.

Around 1905, angry that he could not open the safe in his office, he kicked it and broke his toe. An infection set in, and several years later, in 1911, he died from blood poisoning. He never married, and so deeded his distillery to his nephew, Lem Motlow. Jack Daniel's whiskey continues as a renowned product—the "Old No. 7" made just as the company's founder had made it.

BIBLIOGRAPHY

Getz, Oscar, *Whiskey: An American Pictorial History*, 1978.

Davis, Arthur Vining

(May 30, 1867–November 17, 1962)
Manufacturer

From pots and pans to aircraft, Arthur Vining Davis brought aluminum into American society on a large scale through a company he helped found, Alcoa.

Arthur was born on May 30, 1867, in Sharon, Massachusetts, to Derley B. Davis, a minister, and Mary (Vining) Davis. After graduating from Amherst College in 1888, he joined the Pittsburgh Reduction Company, then being organized by Charles M. Hall to manufacture aluminum. Two years earlier, Hall, influenced by metallurgical experiments in Europe, had discovered a cheap and practical way to produce aluminum by extracting it from its ores, thus making it commercially feasible.

At the time Davis joined Hall in Pittsburgh, the business was struggling to produce substantial amounts of the metal. "Everybody is convinced of the success of the scheme—although we are not making sixty pounds a day," Hall reported. Davis worked in the factory amid dirt and soot to develop the business. He purchased stock in the company in 1891 and during that decade became general manager. The company needed financial help from banks, and ANDREW MELLON pumped money into the firm, eventually controlling one-third of its stock.

The Pittsburgh Reduction Company changed its name to the Aluminum Company of America (Alcoa) in 1908, while Davis pursued uses for aluminum that included airplanes—accelerated by World War I, when the Liberty V-12 engine used the material—and household utensils. Ball Brothers, led by FRANK BALL, showed early on how aluminum could be applied to the consumer market when they bought the metal to make seals for the Mason jars they produced.

Alcoa's dominance in the aluminum industry led to several investigations by the federal government to determine whether the company restrained trade. As president of Alcoa beginning in 1910, Davis had to confront these charges and turned aside the government challenge. In the 1920s, for example, the Federal Trade Commission (FTC) complained that cooking utensil manufacturers had been subjected to unfair competition when Alcoa sold aluminum sheets and handled scrap metal in a way that gave the company a monopoly. The FTC dropped all charges, however, in 1930.

That decision did not end the legal challenges. Under Davis, Alcoa stockholders formed the Aluminum Company, Ltd. of Canada, and although it operated semiautonomously from Alcoa, its existence stirred concerns about a corporate behemoth. In 1937, the Department of Justice filed suit charging Alcoa with monopolistic practices and asserted that the company should be dissolved. Alcoa, the government said, had engaged in illegal practices in the domestic market and conspired with foreign producers to control prices through the Canadian company. At the ensuing trial that began in 1938, Davis testified for six weeks. The legal battle in this case and others that followed resulted in Alcoa proving to the courts that it had acted lawfully.

Davis worked closely with the government during World War II to assure an adequate aluminum supply for the military. He held the post of chairman and director of Alcoa until 1957, when he resigned at age 90. He remained active in business, however, pursuing real estate investments in Florida. He purchased vast tracts of land in Dade County and contributed substantially to the region's postwar economic boom.

In other endeavors, he developed a resort in the Bahamas, owned an airline, and bought the Boca Raton Hotel and Club in Florida for over $22 million. Davis, who had married Florence Holman in 1896 and, after her death, Elizabeth Hawkins Weiman in 1908 (she lived until 1933), died on November 17, 1962.

BIBLIOGRAPHY

Carr, Charles C., *Alcoa: An American Enterprise*, 1952.

Davis, Marvin

(August 28, 1925–)
Oil Industrialist, Entertainment Executive

A big, burly man, Marvin Davis moved boldly across the business landscape making money through the Davis Oil Company and through Twentieth Century-Fox.

Born in Newark, New Jersey, on August 28, 1925, Davis graduated from New York University in 1947 with a degree in engineering. He then moved to Denver, Colorado, where his father, an ex-boxer who founded the Davis Oil Company, had recently opened an office. There he guided Davis Oil in purchasing oil leases that other companies considered worthless. Marvin Davis inherited the oil firm in the 1960s, and by the early 1970s—as he persuaded investors to take all the risk in his initial drilling—he owned an interest in more than 600 wells, which he kept expanding by about 250 per year. During that same decade, oil prices skyrocketed and, as a result, so did Davis's wealth.

Davis invested his money in Denver real estate, including four office towers, and operated the Metro Bank. In a move that displayed his financial prescience, he sold half of his oil properties in 1981, just before the boom went bust, and much of his real estate just before that market collapsed.

A few months later, Davis and his associate, Mark Rich, bought a movie studio, Twentieth Century-Fox, perhaps as much for the glamour as for the profit, since Fox had recently racked up losses. Davis and Rich paid $720 million for the studio, but by using shrewd banking arrangements, they put out little of their own money. They then shifted Fox assets to a holding company, sold a large number of

Marvin Davis (Lee/Archive Photos)

Fox-owned businesses, and reaped a profit exceeding $500 million. After Rich fled the United States in 1981 as the federal government pursued him for failing to pay income taxes on oil leases, Davis gained full control of Fox. Others said about Davis: "Now he's Mr. Twentieth Century-Fox. As a Denver oilman he was nobody. Now he can get into any restaurant he wants."

With his transactions at Fox and his sale of oil property, Davis became a billionaire in 1985. The following year, he bought the Beverly Hills Hotel and tried, but failed, to buy the Columbia Broadcasting System, the television network owned by Larry Tisch.

When, under Davis's control, Fox continued to decline, he sold it to Australian mogul Rupert Murdoch. In 1988, Davis obtained 50 percent ownership of Sports Club/LA, a chain of coed gyms, but sold his interest after the health craze flattened. Davis, married with five children, continued to invest his money in the 1990s, although with less zeal than he had previously. He obtained a small interest in MESA, Incorporated, a troubled oil company that he later sold for a loss, and obtained a license to operate a casino at Atlantic City, New Jersey, but did nothing to open it.

BIBLIOGRAPHY

McClintock, David, *Indecent Exposure*, 1983.

DeBartolo, Edward

(May 17, 1909–December 19, 1994)
Real Estate Developer

Prior to World War II, urbanites shopped downtown. Edward J. DeBartolo helped change that when, from the 1940s into the 1990s, he built shopping centers and malls that attracted consumers and complemented America's suburban sprawl. "Stay out in the country," he once said. "That's the new downtown."

DeBartolo was born Anthony Paonessa on May 17, 1909, in Youngstown, Ohio. Shortly after his father, Anthony Paonessa Sr., an Italian immigrant, died in 1909, his mother, Rose (Villani) Paonessa, married Michael DeBartolo, who owned and operated a construction firm. Anthony began working at his stepfather's business at age 13 and changed his name to honor the man who raised him.

Edward DeBartolo loved construction work and never doubted he would pursue it as a career. After graduating from South High School in Youngstown, he enrolled at the University of Notre Dame and studied civil engineering. He obtained his bachelor's degree in 1932 and then returned to Youngstown to work for his stepfather.

DeBartolo started his own business in 1937, when he began building single-family houses in Youngstown. He served in the army during World War II, obtaining the rank of second lieutenant in the Corps of Engineers, and married Marie Patricia Montani in 1943.

After the war, DeBartolo founded the Edward J. DeBartolo Corporation in Youngstown. He astutely realized the potential profit in the suburban growth then under way—after all, where would people shop now that they lived far from downtown? He started by building strip shopping centers—100 of them by 1965—and his first mall, in Youngstown in 1948. Critics said these structures would not work, and they condemned them for promoting sprawl and ugliness. On the first point, at least, they were wrong. Consumers flocked to the stores that leased space in DeBartolo's buildings.

DeBartolo diversified in the late 1960s: office towers, industrial parks, hotels, and condominiums. During the 1980s, he expanded into the retail market and bought department stores. He also bought professional sports teams—the San Francisco 49ers in football, the Pittsburgh Penguins in hockey, among others—and he bought horse racing tracks—Louisiana Downs, Remington Park in Oklahoma, and Thistledown in Ohio.

The late 1980s, however, brought crisis—overextension, a bad loan to Federated Department Stores, and a slump in real estate left his company struggling with a $4 billion debt. He reacted by selling several holdings, including the Pittsburgh Penguins and shopping centers, renegotiating his debt, and offering stock in his company. DeBartolo's business, while still owing millions, recovered, and in 1990 he acquired 10 percent of Battery One-Stop, a Canadian company that sold batteries at kiosks in malls.

In all, DeBartolo built more than 200 malls in 20 states, and in the mid-1990s his company ranked as the fourth largest owner of shopping and retail space in the nation. His own net worth exceeded $800 million, and he gave $33 million to the University of Notre Dame to construct a classroom building (dedicated in 1992).

DeBartolo died on December 19, 1994. A business commentator called him "One of the most influential forces to shape America's retail development during the last five decades." DeBartolo's son, Edward J. DeBartolo Jr., subsequently directed the company's holdings, including the San Francisco 49ers.

BIBLIOGRAPHY

Adams, David, and Stuart Drown, "DeBartolo's Legacy Seen in Malls, Healthy REIT," *Akron Beacon Journal*, December 25, 1994; Bryant, Adam, "Edward J. DeBartolo," *New York Times*, December 20, 1994; Noer, Michael, "Last Laugh?," *Forbes*, April 11, 1994; Zweig, Jason, "Energized," *Forbes*, July 9, 1990.

DeBow, James

(July 10, 1820–February 27, 1867)
Publisher

An ardent Southern nationalist, James Dunwoody Brownson DeBow published a widely read antebellum magazine, *DeBow's Review*, in which he expressed and popularized ideas that moved America toward civil war.

DeBow was born on July 10, 1820, in Charleston, South Carolina, and at a young age was left an orphan. He graduated from the College of Charleston in 1843 at the head of his class, after having endured poverty during his college years that sometimes left him with little to eat.

After a dalliance in studying law, DeBow began writing for the *Southern Quarterly Review*. By that time, economic controversies gripped the South as the region expanded behind cotton agriculture, but found itself subservient to Northerners who handled cotton exports and financed Southern development. Several commercial conventions appeared in the South, at which the region's political and economic leaders discussed issues such as the tariff, internal improvements, agricultural diversification, and slave labor.

In that atmosphere, DeBow founded a monthly magazine devoted to social and business topics, the *Commercial Review of the South and Southwest*, or, as it was more popularly known, *DeBow's Review*, which first appeared in January 1846. The publication struggled financially, however, and folded in August 1847.

DeBow's Review then experienced a revival when Maunsel White, a wealthy sugar planter, provided funds for it to resume publication. Nevertheless, limited readership meant that for two years DeBow and an assistant struggled with barely enough money to survive. Finally, their work paid off, and by 1850 the magazine prospered with the largest circulation of any in the South.

DeBow strongly promoted Southern nationalism. He wanted his region to diversify its economy so it could rid itself of Northern domination. He advocated manufacturing, railroads, colleges, direct trade with Europe, a canal through Central America, and more commercial conventions, which he compared to the glory of ancient Greece when citizens united to form common goals. He believed any economic development should support rather than threaten slavery, an institution he praised. "The Negro was created

James DeBow (Library of Congress)

essentially to be a slave," he said, "and finds his highest development and destiny in that condition."

DeBow sought to form a political alliance between the South and the West, and as tension mounted with the North in the late 1850s, he promoted the idea of secession. He said about the impending civil war:

That written thing we call a constitution is a mere treaty, league, compact, or articles of partnership. It is not a law, like the state constitutions, for the union is not a nation.

The Federal government has been called a government of opinion, of consent, of agreement. That is no government at all.

The "irrepressible conflict" is the struggle of nature to return when man has expelled her. The natural organism of society . . . its historical and God-ordained organism, has been disturbed, and almost destroyed, by the

North. The "irrepressible conflict" is socialism, unconsciously struggling to restore the natural constitution of society.

He suspended *DeBow's Review* during the Civil War and served as the Confederate government's agent for the purchase and sale of cotton. After the war, he again revived his magazine. DeBow died on February 27, 1867, from pleurisy. He was survived by his second wife, Martha E. Johns, whom he had married in 1860, and three children.

BIBLIOGRAPHY

McMillen, James A., *The Works of J. D. B. DeBow*, 1940; Skipper, Ottis C., *J. D. B. DeBow: Magazinist of the Old South*, 1958.

Deere, John

(February 7, 1804–May 17, 1886)
Manufacturer

The heavy Western soil stuck to traditional plows like mud to a shovel. Something had to be done, and John Deere met the challenge by developing a steel plow that opened the region's bounty.

Born on February 7, 1804, in Rutland, Vermont, to William Rinold Deere, a tailor, and Sarah (Yates) Deere, John received only modest schooling before serving a 4-year apprenticeship at a blacksmith's shop in nearby Middlebury from 1821 to 1825. After his apprenticeship, John worked for 12 years as a blacksmith at various locations in Vermont, selling hay forks and shovels. In 1827, he married Damaris Lamb. Two fires that destroyed his shops, coupled with hard economic times, caused him to sink into debt, and in 1837 he decided to move from the town of Hancock to Grand Detour, Illinois, where, like many other Vermonters before him, he could start anew in the burgeoning West.

Legend has it that Deere arrived in Illinois with $73.73 in his pocket. Whatever the case, he and a partner opened a small blacksmith shop (26 x 31 feet) and set to work shoeing horses and making pots, pans, skillets, and farm implements, including plows. He had from the start a thriving business and quickly learned the problems facing farmers in trying to use plows that had been designed for the sandy soil back east. The existing plows failed to scour, resulting in the heavy soil caking and sticking to the plowshare. Deere began experimenting with different plow designs and later in 1837 took a broken saw blade, polished it, and used its smooth surface for the plowshare and moldboard. He gave a new shape to the moldboard, too, and these changes produced a plow that could scour, thus allowing farmers to plant considerably more acreage.

According to his own account, Deere took his steel plow and placed it on a dry-goods box by the side of his shop door.

"A few days later," he said, "a farmer from across the river drove up. Seeing the plow, he asked: 'Who made that plow?'"

"'I did, such as it is, wood work and all.'"
"'Well,'" said the farmer, "'Let me take it home and try it, and if it works all right, I will keep it and pay you for it. If not I will return it.'"

"'Take it,'" said I, "'and give it a thorough trial.'"

About two weeks later, the farmer drove up to the shop, without the plow, paid for it, and said: "'Now get a move on you, and make me two more plows just like the other one.'"

Deere made 3 plows in all that year, 10 in 1839, and 40 in 1840. He was not the first person to use steel in a plow, however, nor the only one to produce them. Deere likely pirated his idea from others, and others in turn copied him—a widespread practice in the Midwest. In fact, in a case involving trademarks, the Illinois Supreme Court declared that Deere had not invented any part of the plow, although he had shown ability in adopting and modifying techniques already in use.

Deere refined the curvature of the moldboard and, over the years, made additional improvements to his plow as he worked long, hard hours. "[He was] hammering in the morning," noted a friend who slept in the shop, "when I was in the store in bed at four o'clock, and at ten o'clock at night; he had such indomitable determination to do and work out what he had in his mind."

Deere found Grand Detour too limited for distributing his plows, however, and in 1846 moved to another Illinois town, Moline. In seeking to acquire high-quality steel in greater quantities, he got the Jones & Quigg steelworks in Pittsburgh to make the plates he needed, resulting in the first manufacturing of cast-plow steel in the United States. By 1851, Deere, who had entered into a partnership, reported lucrative business, with his shop making 75 plows per week. Just five years later, his production neared 15,000 plows per year.

Unlike other blacksmiths, Deere did not wait for orders before making his plows; instead he manufactured them and then took them into the country to sell them. Additionally, he used extensive advertising, known for its attention-grabbing headlines, to get customers and exhibited his plows at agricultural fairs, where he won numerous awards. In 1858, he made his son Charles a partner (an older son had recently died). His son-in-law joined the firm in 1863, and in 1868, one year after marrying Lucinda Lamb, his first wife's younger sister, the business incorporated as Deere & Company.

Through the 1860s, Charles gained more authority—although John Deere remained the active head until 1874—and the product line expanded to include cultivators. In 1918, well after John Deere's death on May 17, 1886, the firm took over the Waterloo Gasoline Traction Engine Company and began manufacturing tractors. Financial difficulties in the 1980s threatened Deere's existence, but by the 1990s the company appeared to have weathered the crisis.

BIBLIOGRAPHY

Broehl, Wayne G., Jr., *John Deere's Company: A History of Deere & Company and Its Times*, 1984.

Dell, Michael

(1965–)
Manufacturer

When Michael Dell's parents announced they would be visiting him at his college dorm, he rushed about, collected the computers he had scattered around his room, and hid them. Dell did not want them to know about his business selling the machines, but they found out, and much to his relief, agreed he could continue. Before long, while he was still in his twienties, he had built a giant among computer companies with the establishment of Dell Computers.

Dell was born in Houston, Texas, in 1965. His father, Alexander Dell, an orthodontist, and mother, Lorraine Dell, a stockbroker, raised him within a comfortable family setting. Dell displayed his business drive early, when at age 13, he auctioned stamps through mail order and made about $2,000. Three years later, he used his first computer to generate letters offering free trial subscriptions to the *Houston Post*. Within a year, he had made $18,000 and bought a BMW.

After high school, Dell enrolled at the University of Texas in Austin where he planned to study medicine. Books bored him, however, and he once again resorted to business. He bought an IBM personal computer (PC) and began selling disk-drive kits and random access memory chips at computer-user meetings. More profit ensued when he convinced IBM dealers to sell him their excess stock. He then resold the units at cut-rate prices. As a college freshman, he grossed $80,000 a month in sales and quit school.

By late 1984, Dell was making his own IBM cloned computers and selling them

Michael Dell (Reuters/Peter Morgan/Archive Photos)

at computer fairs. The following year, he shipped thousands of his machines (at prices well below those charged by IBM), incorporated his business as Dell Computers, and leased office space in Austin. He developed an innovative strategy when he allowed customers to order computers by phone and specify the features they wanted. By assembling computers only after they were ordered, Dell kept his overhead low. He observed: "There's no great mystery to building a PC—the parts all come from the same few suppliers. I simply identified a market segment that was having to pay too much money for what they were getting, and found an efficient way to reach that segment."

In order to expand, Dell recruited E. Lee Walker, an Austin venture capitalist, as a consultant. Walker—who later served as the firm's president and CEO—raised much-needed money and guided Dell Computers in going public in 1987, when it sold 3.5 million shares of stock for $30 million.

Yet Dell had to weather a difficult time in 1989 when he bought too many chips. When they plunged in price, it cost him millions of dollars. Company revenues rebounded in 1991, however, to $54 million with earnings of $27 million.

Dell expanded his phone lines for sales and improved customer service. Heavily reliant on corporate and education accounts, he reached out to individuals. His computers ranked high in customer-satisfaction polls, and by 1998 the company had greatly eroded the commanding sales position held by its rivals, IBM and Compaq.

Dell, who had married Susan Lieberman in 1989, had two children, and worked 16-hour days, once observed, "One of the things I benefited from when I started this business was that I didn't know anything. It was just instinct with no preconceived notions. This enabled me to learn and change quickly without having to worry about maintaining any kind of status quo, like some of my bigger competitors."

BIBLIOGRAPHY

Angrist, Stanley W., "Entrepreneur in Short Pants," *Forbes*, March 7, 1988; Banning, Kent L., "An Instinct for Computer Success," *Nation's Business*, April 1991; McGraw, Dan, "The Kid Bytes Back," *U.S. News & World Report*, December 12, 1994; Poole, Claire, "The Kid Who Turned Computers into Commodities," *Fortune*, October 21, 1991.

DeLuca, Fred

(1948–)
Merchant

At the young age of 17, Fred DeLuca opened a sandwich shop in an out-of-the-way location. From that one store, he built what might today be the most successful franchise ever—Subway Sandwiches.

Born in 1948 in Bridgeport, Connecticut, DeLuca delivered newspapers as an adolescent and worked in a hardware store. When high school graduation neared, he contemplated how he could make enough money to attend the University of Bridgeport and discussed his plight with a family friend, Peter Buck, a nuclear physicist. Buck told DeLuca about how, during his boyhood in Maine, he enjoyed the hoagies served at a local sandwich shop. He suggested that DeLuca could make money opening a similar shop, and he agreed to help finance it with $1,000 in starting capital.

DeLuca liked the idea, and in 1965 he opened Pete's Super Submarines in a building near the hardware store where he worked. The shop prospered at first, and then, as winter came, business plunged. DeLuca and Buck held many a crisis meeting over pasta at the DeLuca home. They considered closing the shop but then decided they needed more advertising and that the best form of advertising would be to open a second shop. They did so, and it too struggled. This time, they concluded that poor locations had hurt them, so they forged ahead with a third shop in a better spot. Unlike the first two, it prospered.

Of the initial challenge and the turning point in his business, DeLuca said:

> We opened the first store in Bridgeport, Connecticut, and on the first day it did wonderfully. But . . . as the weeks passed, volumes got lower and lower. And by the time six months had passed we were losing a lot of money. . . . The sandwich quality wasn't that good, our customer service wasn't good, our pricing wasn't as good as it could have been. . . . We had a meeting to discuss what we should do. We sat down and wrote down our options, and the first option was basically lock the door and throw away the key. But we concluded if we quit and went out of business, we'd never achieve our goal, our dreams would be dashed, and we'd be failures. . . . If you have a lot of stores opening you have more visibility, which is indeed a form of advertising. So the idea of having wide distribution certainly builds on the foundation that you have.

While DeLuca completed a bachelor's degree in psychology at the University of Bridgeport in 1971, he expanded his sub shops. He opted for a more manageable and attractive business name, too, and chose Subway, with a bright yellow logo.

As McDonald's and other fast-food restaurants went into franchising, DeLuca decided to enter the field, and the first Subway franchise opened in Wallingford, Connecticut, in 1974. DeLuca expanded so rapidly that a mere four years later he opened store number 100 and in 1987 store number 1,000. From that point into the 1990s, DeLuca opened about 1,000 Subway shops a year. By 1989, he had about 3,800 stores, while his nearest competitor, Blimpie's, had only 350. At the same time, he developed a bread-making machine that Subway shops could use to bake their own bread and promoted the idea of freshness as opposed to the stale heating-lamp food found at other fast-food stores.

Subway's main appeal came from its quick service and limited menu. In addition, many health-conscious customers considered its sandwiches better than the higher-fat meals found at hamburger shops.

The eleven thousandth Subway store opened in 1995 as the chain grew not only in the United States but also overseas. "It is kind of my baby," the enormously rich DeLuca said about Subway. "I have no thoughts about selling the company."

BIBLIOGRAPHY

"It Started with a Loan and Turned into a Gold Mine," *Grand Forks (SD) Herald*, August 24, 1996; "Subway Sinks Competition: Franchise Sandwich Shops Raking in Record Profits," *Miami Herald*, October 5, 1989.

DeVos, Richard

(March 4, 1926–)
Merchant

Everything short of a hallelujah chorus runs through an Amway seminar with its revival-like atmosphere. As a multibillion-dollar company, Amway sells household products through a distribution system critics call a pyramid scheme, but its founders, Richard Marvin DeVos and JAY VAN ANDEL, along with its supporters, hail as an exemplar of the American dream.

The lives of DeVos and Van Andel parallel each other so closely that one leading magazine has called them "Amway's Dutch Twins." The two have been lifelong friends, from their childhoods in Grand Rapids, Michigan, through their success with Amway.

DeVos was born on March 4, 1926, in Grand Rapids, Michigan, where his father worked as an electrical contractor. He became friends with Van Andel in high school, and during World War II, they joined the U.S. Army Air Corps. They briefly attended Calvin College before deciding to enter business together.

In 1947, they purchased the Wolverine Air Service that operated a flying school and chartered planes from its base at Comstock Park Air Field near Grand Rapids. Although the business made money and expanded to 12 airplanes, DeVos and Van Andel tired of it and sold the air service in 1948.

The following year, they formed the Ja-Ri Corporation and through it distributed Nutrilite Products, a food supplement marketed in capsules. Soon, they embarked on direct sales. Under this system, they sold Nutrilite to customers in their homes and offices and recruited distributors, each of whom had a territory in which they sold the product. By 1955, some 5,000 independent salesmen worked for them within a large distribution network.

Four years later, however, poor relations with Nutrilite caused DeVos and Van Andel to break with the company, and in November 1959 they formed the Amway Sales Corporation to obtain such household products as laundry detergents, sell them to their distributors, and operate a marketing plan.

While DeVos and Van Andel both married women from the Grand Rapids Dutch community, had four children, and became active in the La Grave Christian Church, they developed a system of Amway distributorships that sparked controversy. Although distributors made some money selling an expanding line of products, big profits required sponsoring or bringing new recruits into the organization. One analyst explained: "The real money is made, not by what he and she personally sell, but by what their people sell. And so new distributors going into the Amway line will be encouraged to make a list of everyone they know. . . ." Thus developed a system akin to pyramid sales, although in 1979 a judge with the Federal Trade Commission ruled that Amway had not established a true pyramid system.

By the mid-1970s, Amway was selling about 150 products, and in the early 1980s some distributors reached incomes of between $200,000 and $350,000 a year. Amway held more than 200 seminars annually in about 80 cities throughout the United States and Canada. Enthusiastic, largely white participants listened to spellbinding sermons and patriotic music, and chanted in unison. One critic likened Amway to a religious cult and said, "What the revival meeting is to evangelical Christianity, the Seminar and Rally is to the world of Amway . . . a mighty coming together of the chosen to celebrate their salvation."

The Amway headquarters and plant site in Ada, Michigan, had expanded by the 1980s to 300 acres, and its laboratories and manufacturing facility exceeded 1 million square feet. Amway had an affiliate in Canada and subsidiaries around the world with more than 300,000 distributors. Later that decade, however, DeVos and Van Andel encountered problems when the Canadian government claimed Amway had avoided taxes by lying about the market value of its products. Amway had to pay more than $25 million in fines.

At the same time, the company obtained a bad reputation for trying to recruit through such deceptive tactics as when distributors invited prospects to meetings under the guise of friendly neighborhood socials. Also, some distributors developed blatant pyramid schemes. As a result, DeVos and Van Andel undertook reforms.

In politics, the two men enthusiastically supported Ronald Reagan's presidency and contributed large amounts of money to the Republican Party, believing it to be the best protector of "free enterprise."

Amway continued to grow in the 1990s when it had, by its own account, 2.5 million distributors. In 1997, the company's retail sales reached an estimated $7 billion. Troubles still bothered Amway, though. *Consumer Reports* magazine rated several Amway products as either more expensive or less effective than those of competitors. In 1997, Procter & Gamble sued Amway for operating an "illegal pyramid scheme" that had damaged its sales. In addition, Amway's distributors, perhaps cognizant of the firm's negative reputation, typically went after prospects with sales pitches that failed to mention the name Amway until late in the presentation or not until the prospect inquired. Amway refuted Procter & Gamble's charges and continued to emphasize its role in providing quality products and prosperity to distributors willing to work hard and follow its plan.

BIBLIOGRAPHY

Butterfield, Stephen, *Amway: The Cult of Free Enterprise*, 1985; Conn, Charles Paul, *The Possible Dream*, 1977.

Dillon, Sidney

(May 7, 1812–June 9, 1892)
Railroad Executive

The nineteenth century was a booming era of railroad construction in the United States, with thousands of miles of tracks laid down all across the North American continent. Sidney Dillon played a key role in building many of these railroads, particularly a portion of the nation's first transcontinental railway, the Union Pacific Railroad.

Sidney Dillon was born on May 7, 1812, in Northampton, New York. His father, Timothy Dillon, was a poor farmer and unable to provide Sidney with much of an education. At the early age of seven, Sidney decided to leave the family farm to find work.

Dillon began his railroad career as a "water boy" for the crew constructing the Albany and Schenectady portion of the Mohawk and Hudson Railroad. Several similar jobs followed over the next decade, including one with the Rensselaer and Saratoga Railroad.

As Dillon grew older, he gradually attained more responsible positions, acting as an overseer and then a foreman on a number of different construction projects. After some years, he was ready to start his own business. Despite lacking seed money, Dillon bid on and won a contract to build a section of the Boston & Albany Railroad. By 1840, construction of the new line had been completed, and Dillon's business was poised for success.

These were also promising times in Dillon's personal life. In 1841, he married Hannah Smith, whose family was from Amherst, Massachusetts. The couple eventually had two daughters.

Over the next 30 years, Dillon was involved in building thousands of miles of railroad. He had a hand in the Rutland & Burlington Railroad, the Central Railroad of New Jersey, the Philadelphia & Erie Railroad, the Pennsylvania Railroad, the New Orleans, Mobile & Chattanooga Railroad, and the Canada Southern Railroad. In addition to these successful projects, this period between 1841 and 1865 was lucrative because of a contract with CORNELIUS VANDERBILT to build the tunnel that runs between Grand Central Station in New York City to the Harlem River.

Dillon, a heavyset, active man over six feet tall, was known for his direct manner and decisiveness. Though he was cautious in undertaking new projects, he carried them out with energy and diligence. These characteristics stood him in good stead and were extremely useful in securing the most significant contract of his career—the construction of the Union Pacific Railroad as it extended west from Omaha, Nebraska, to meet the Central Pacific Railroad expanding east from Sacramento, California. When the two lines met, they formed America's first transcontinental railroad (in conjunction with several lines that ran from Omaha to the Eastern seaboard).

Initially involved in the Union Pacific as an investor, Dillon became one of the principal contractors in 1865. He also directed and organized the subsidiary contractors. In addition to managing the project, he was active in its construction, repeatedly traveling the line and assisting with problems and preparations.

Dillon served as the director of the Union Pacific Railroad Company from 1864 through 1892. He was also the company's president twice: from March 11, 1874, to June 19, 1884, and again from November 26, 1890, to April 27, 1892.

In addition, Dillon served as director of the Manhattan Elevated Railroad Company, the Missouri Pacific Railroad, and a number of other transportation organizations. In 1870, he received the honor of Fellow of the American Society of Civil Engineers. In addition to his railroad work, Dillon served as a director of the Western Union Telegraph Company.

By the 1870s, Dillon's interests had shifted to finance and investing. His great ownership of railroad stocks came largely from the many years in which he had accepted securities as partial payment.

By this time, he had amassed a large estate and much of his time was occupied in managing this wealth.

On June 9, 1892, after a three-month illness, Dillon died at his home in New York City.

BIBLIOGRAPHY

Bailey, William Francis, *The Story of the First Trans-Continental Railroad: Its Projectors, Construction and History*, 1906; Dillon, Sidney, "Historic Moments: Driving the Last Spike of the Union Pacific," *Scribner's Magazine*, August 1892; *Harper's Weekly*, Obituary, June 18, 1892; *New York Times*, Obituary, June 10, 1892; Sabin, E. L., *Building the Pacific Railway*, 1895; Trottman, N., *History of the Union Pacific*, 1923.

Disney, Walt

(December 5, 1901–December 14, 1966)
Entertainment Executive

From Oswald the Lucky Rabbit to Mickey Mouse, from a garage workplace to a major studio complemented by theme parks and a vast array of promotional items, Walter Elias Disney Jr. built an entertainment empire geared to children and the child in adults.

Born to Elias Disney and Flora (Call) Disney on December 5, 1901, in Chicago, Illinois, Walt spent his early childhood on his family's farm near Marceline, Missouri. In 1909, Elias moved the family to Kansas City, Missouri. While attending school there, Walt delivered newspapers and produced his first commercial art when he drew sketches for a local barber who, in return, gave him free haircuts. In 1918, Elias moved again, this time back to Chicago, where he owned a jelly company. Walt studied nights at the Chicago Academy of Fine Art and continued his secondary schooling at McKinley High School but never graduated; instead he served as a Red Cross ambulance driver in Europe as World War I came to an end.

Upon his return to the United States in 1919, Disney applied for a job as cartoonist at the *Kansas City Star* but the newspaper rejected him. He then obtained work at an advertising agency, where he

Walt Disney (Library of Congress)

drew farm equipment. The following year, the Kansas City Film Ad Company hired him at $40 per week. He drew stick figures for cartoon advertisements used in a new industry—motion pictures. These advertisements were shown in theaters before the main feature and enticed audiences that had recently been enraptured by Felix the Cat cartoons. Through this work, Disney learned about animated pictures.

Disney soon decided to form his own company to compete with Kansas City Film Ad and in 1922 founded Laugh-O-Grams. With the help of cartoonist Ub Iwerks, Disney worked in his garage, where he produced movies that combined slides with news headlines and shots of Kansas City. Although the movies proved popular in the local area, high costs and contracts with distributors who went out of business caused Laugh-

O-Grams to collapse in 1923, and Disney headed west to start anew.

That fall—with $85, a $500 loan, and $200 from his brother Roy—Disney founded Disney Brothers in Los Angeles, set up another garage studio, and began making cartoons. In fact, over the years, Roy handled nearly all of the financial aspects of the Disney enterprises and made the important decisions regarding contracts. Disney's first movie, *Alice's Day at Sea* (which was one-third animation and the rest live action) earned him $1,500. He followed this with other Alice shorts, feeding his profits into his fledgling company.

In July 1925, Disney married Lillian Bounds (the couple eventually had two daughters) and shortly after renamed his company Walt Disney Studio. He constructed a studio building, and early in 1927 Universal Pictures released the first of his "Oswald the Lucky Rabbit" cartoons, a short called *Trolley Troubles*. Audiences loved Oswald, but during a visit with executives in New York City, Disney had a falling out with the distributor.

On board a train headed back to California in February 1928, Disney thought of a new idea. He remembered his days in Kansas City: "Mice gathered in my wastebasket when I worked late at night," he later said. "I lifted them out and kept them in little cages on my desk. One of them was my particular friend." With this thought in mind, he decided to create a cartoon mouse named Mortimer. When he told his wife, she criticized the name as "too sissy" and advised him to change it to Mickey. He agreed and during the train ride created Mickey's image on paper and developed a plot for the first cartoon.

Later that year, Mickey Mouse appeared in two cartoons rejected by distributors. Then Disney produced *Steamboat Willie*, the first cartoon to use sound. The movie received a rave review from *Variety*, and the *New York Times* hailed it as creative fun. Walt Disney Studio had arrived.

In these projects, Disney relied on his friend Ub Iwerks to draw Mickey; in fact, from that time on, Disney did little drawing, partly because he had limited artistic talent and partly because he wanted to concentrate on developing stories and other ventures.

Over the next decade, Mickey Mouse, who underwent several changes in appearance, starred in over 100 cartoons, joined by Minnie Mouse, Pluto, and Donald Duck, who proved so popular that Disney began a Donald Duck cartoon series. At the same time, Disney produced "Silly Symphony" cartoons that included *Flowers and Trees*, released in 1932 as the first Technicolor animation, an improvement over earlier color movies and an innovation that Disney purposefully adopted as a means to boost his studio's reputation. The movie rewarded Disney financially and with an Oscar for Best Short Subject.

Disney's *Three Little Pigs*, a Brothers Grimm fairy tale, appeared in 1933, embellished by Disney's idea to have the pigs sing "Who's Afraid of the Big Bad Wolf?" Written by Frank Churchill and Ted Sears, it hit the Top Ten, and the movie's theme of perseverance found a receptive audience during the challenge of the Great Depression. The nation idolized Disney, and *Parents* magazine even presented him with a medal for his distinguished service to children. The cartoon grossed more than $250,000, and money flowed in from another source, integral to Disney's later efforts: merchandise, in this case, linked to the *Three Little Pigs*.

In 1937, Disney finished *Snow White and the Seven Dwarfs* (based on the classic fairy tale), which was Hollywood's first feature-length cartoon. Children flocked to see it, and the movie, which was eventually distributed in 46 countries, grossed more money than any other to that time. In 1939, Walt and Roy Disney officially incorporated as Walt Disney Productions and issued stock. The corporation included Walt Disney Enterprises that licensed cartoon characters and the Liled Realty and Investment Company.

After a grueling work schedule that pushed his cartoonists to the limit, in 1940 Disney completed another hit, *Pinocchio*, a retelling of a classic Italian children's story. The movie cost so much to make, however, that it put his studio deeply in debt and delayed work on two other projects, *Fantasia* and *Bambi*. Disney shot *Fantasia* to classical music, using mainly that of dead composers so he could avoid paying royalties, and considered it a sophisticated artistic accomplishment. The movie received generally good reviews but fared poorly at the box office.

At this time, relations between Disney and his cartoonists exploded into acrimony. Long discontent with low pay and with Disney taking full credit for every achievement, the cartoonists wanted recognition for their union, the Cartoonists Guild. Disney adamantly refused, and when he fired those who tried to organize, a strike ensued. Angered by Communist influence in the union movement (which was minimal, as it turned out), he publicly accused the guild of participating in a Communist conspiracy. In September, however, his brother Roy reached an agreement that recognized the guild, hired back those workers who had been fired, and adjusted pay scales.

At about the same time, Walt Disney enrolled as an official Hollywood spy for the FBI and began filing numerous reports about supposedly subversive activities. In 1944, he helped found and served as vice president of the Motion Picture Alliance for American Ideals, a virulent anti-Communist group.

During World War II, within weeks after Disney had completed another box-office failure, *Bambi*, the U.S. government took over his studio, and he began making propaganda films for the military. When this work caused a financial crisis, he reissued *Snow White*. The motion picture brought in needed money and gave Disney the idea to reissue his hit movies in seven-year cycles.

After the war ended in 1945, Disney returned to making motion pictures, among them *Song of the South*. That same year, he resigned as president of Walt Disney Productions, a post assumed by his brother Roy, but continued as chairman. Disney wanted to lessen his administrative burden. He pursued other studio projects while continuing a crusade against communism that included testifying before the House Un-American Activities Committee, where he repeated his charges that communism permeated the union movement. He created a stir when he called the staid League of Women Voters a Communist front.

With his desire to pursue new projects and with money flowing in from the highly popular *Cinderella*, Disney began making nature films. *The Living Desert* proved popular with audiences and won

an Academy Award for Best Documentary Feature in 1953. He also began talking of a bold project he called Disneylandia and established a privately held corporation, WED Enterprises, to handle it. In preparation, he traveled to amusement parks and studied them closely. His project went ahead after he reached an agreement with ABC television under which he produced a weekly show for the network, and ABC paid him money and secured bank loans for Disneylandia. Pursuing another avenue, he approved the shooting of movies in a new widescreen format, called CinemaScope, among them *Lady and the Tramp* (an animated feature) and *20,000 Leagues under the Sea* (a live-action one).

On July 17, 1955, soon after Disney scored yet another hit with his television saga *Davy Crockett* (which caused youngsters to buy coonskin caps), his Disneylandia opened in Anaheim, California, as Disneyland. In October, *The Mickey Mouse Club* premiered on ABC, and children across America sang along to M-I-C-K-E-Y M-O-U-S-E, five days a week. Disney soon sold some 25,000 mouse ear sets per day.

Disney's live-action movie *Old Yeller* received critical and popular praise in 1957, as did a feature-length cartoon, *101 Dalmatians*, four years later. In 1961, Disney moved his TV show *Walt Disney Presents* to the NBC network as *Walt Disney's Wonderful World of Color*. He felt too removed from filmmaking, however, which he had turned over to subordinates, and so searched for a project he could control. He found it with the combined live-action, animated movie *Mary Poppins*. Disney oversaw its every detail and worked at it day and night. The film, which starred Julie Andrews, premiered in August 1964 and generated rave reviews and a big profit by grossing more than $45 million.

Acting from a desire to pass his cartoonist legacy on to young artists, Disney merged an art school he controlled (Chouinard's) with the California Institute of the Arts (Cal-Arts). He provided it with money from *Mary Poppins* and gave it 778 acres for a new campus near Los Angeles.

Late in 1964, Disney began secretly buying land in Orlando, Florida, for a bigger, grander Disneyland. He acquired 27,500 acres, mostly swampland, with an intent to create not just an amusement park but an experimental community, a futuristic, livable "tomorrowland."

He never saw its completion. In November 1966, he entered St. Joseph's Hospital in Burbank. He died on December 14, 1966, at night, while looking from his elevated bed out the hospital window to his lighted studio in the distance.

In his career, Disney had received over 700 citations, awards, and honorary degrees, including Oscars, Emmys, and the Presidential Freedom Medal. The *New York Times* said he had "a gift of imagination that was somehow in tune with everyone's imagination, and a dogged determination to succeed," qualities that made him "one of Hollywood's master entrepreneurs and one of the world's greatest entertainers."

Roy Disney continued to lead the Disney empire, and in October 1971 Walt Disney World opened in Orlando. Two months later, Roy Disney died. Amid continued expansion, in 1984 the board of directors of Walt Disney Productions chose MICHAEL EISNER to head the corporation.

BIBLIOGRAPHY

Eliot, Marc, *Walt Disney: Hollywood's Dark Prince*, 1993.

Dodge, William

(September 4, 1805–February 9, 1883)
Mining Executive, Investor

William E. Dodge used his connections through marriage to develop copper mines and several other enterprises linked to America's newly industrializing economy, and he also played a prominent role in politics and reform.

Born on September 4, 1805, in Hartford, Connecticut, to David Low Dodge and Sarah (Cleveland) Dodge, William grew up in several different towns in the Northeast as his father moved about. After teaching school for a while, the elder Dodge worked at various times as a shopkeeper and became a partner in a large mercantile firm. He held strong pacifist beliefs, and this, along with his involvement in business, influenced William at an early age.

With his family's frequent moves, young Dodge had a sporadic schooling, and at age 13 his formal education ended.

He went to work first in a wholesale dry-goods store in New York City and then in a country store connected to his father's most recent endeavor, a factory that he managed in Connecticut.

Soon after the Dodge family moved to New York City in 1825, Dodge met Melissa Phelps, daughter of ANSON PHELPS, who had earned a fortune in the metals trade. Dodge married Melissa in 1828, and five years later, he and his father-in-law organized Phelps, Dodge & Company primarily to buy and sell copper, sheet iron, zinc, and other metals, although it also traded in cotton.

Dodge involved himself in active management only through the 1850s, when the firm's annual profits approached $500,000. During the Civil War, the company made higher profits, from which Dodge reaped additional wealth.

Dodge invested in other businesses, too—especially railroads that heralded a modernizing nation tied to industry. He served on the boards of five railroads and was the largest single shareholder of the Cayuga & Susquehanna. He was so heavily involved that he once said about his activities: "How often the question has been asked, sometimes in joke, but none the less embarrassing on that account, 'For which company are you speaking?'"

At the same time, he helped organize the Young Men's Christian Association and joined the temperance movement. He won election in 1865 to the presidency of the National Temperance Society (a post he held until his death).

Dodge was opposed to the Civil War and often criticized it. His position reflected, in part, the economic interests of Phelps, Dodge & Company, which was involved in the cotton trade and closely tied to Southern business leaders. But it reflected, too, his long-standing pacifism.

In 1864, he asked: "Is [President Lincoln] so fully committed to the entire abolition of slavery as a condition of peace that he will use all the power of the Government to continue the war till either the South is destroyed or they consent to give up the slaves?" To avoid that possibility, he called on Lincoln to offer terms to the South that would allow each state to decide whether to continue slavery.

When the war ended, Dodge favored a quick reconciliation between North and South, and he promoted this program in Congress when he was elected to that body as a Republican from New York City. Although he won the position in 1864, a dispute involving the close vote delayed his being seated until 1866. Once in office, he opposed a tax on cotton, while favoring one on liquor. He refused nomination to a second term.

Dodge remained active to the end and he continued meetings, speeches, and letters connected to his reform activities. He died on February 9, 1883, in New York City.

BIBLIOGRAPHY

Lowitt, Richard, *A Merchant Prince of the Nineteenth Century: William E. Dodge*, 1954.

Dorrance, John

(November 11, 1873–September 21, 1930)
Manufacturer

Though the name John Thompson Dorrance is unfamiliar to many, his business, the Campbell Soup Company, is a household name that evokes impressions of the distinctive red and white can immortalized in the paintings of pop culture artist Andy Warhol. Dorrance developed the modern technique for condensing soup, created a product famous for taste and value, and single-handedly made soup a common part of the American diet. Combining chemistry with a love of cooking, an insistence on quality, a flair for marketing, and an intense love for his work, Dorrance became one of the richest men in the United States.

Dorrance, the son of John and Eleanor Grillingham Thompson Dorrance, was born on November 11, 1873, in Bristol, Pennsylvania. His parents were wealthy timber and flour brokers who provided him with a solid education. Dorrance's privileged upbringing distinguishes him from many other notable industrial entrepreneurs of his generation who enjoyed a "rags-to-riches" rise in fortune.

The young Dorrance, who would remain known throughout his life as a shy and intellectual figure, received a B.A. in chemistry from the Massachusetts Institute of Technology in 1895. He then worked diligently to obtain a doctorate in organic chemistry from the University of Göttingen in Germany after only one year of study.

Though Dorrance received a number of teaching offers at prestigious academic institutions, he decided to move to Camden, New Jersey, to work for his uncle, who was part owner of the Joseph Campbell Preserve Company and eventually gained full control of the canning company upon the death of Joseph Campbell in 1900.

Dorrance's career decision confused many; despite his education and family connections, he was paid a meager $7.50 per week to conduct product research. Dorrance, however, relished the flexibility the job afforded for devising new products. While still in Europe, he had gained an appreciation for gourmet cooking, and he found his chemistry background to be an exciting complement to his interest in food preparation.

Dorrance's legacy to food preparation was built on a simple, yet ingenious concept. At this time, very few soups were sold commercially. The French had developed "bouillon cubes," blocks of condensed soup stock that when combined with water yielded only a weak broth. The Franco-American Company sold several ready-to-serve soups that were packaged in large containers that were costly to ship and thus too expensive to be in high demand. Much of the problem with producing and selling processed foods lay in protracted efforts to remove the water after the cooking process. Dorrance's simple idea was to add less water to begin with, thus creating a lighter, easier to ship, less expensive product.

In his first year with the company, Dorrance efficiently set about the task of developing nutritious, tasty soups. Though the soups would quickly gain enormous popularity, Dorrance was initially faced with the great challenge of creating a demand for the product. In the United States, during the late nineteenth century, soup was not a part of the average diet. It was time-consuming and costly to prepare and was not viewed by a "meat-and-potatoes" culture as a meal unto itself. Dorrance's skillful marketing and adherence to a low-cost, high-quality product revolutionized Americans' eating habits.

Once Dorrance was comfortable with the quality and diversity of the soup line, he vigorously market-tested his products. In reminiscing about this time period, Dorrance remembered being embarrassed while demonstrating the soups to grocers in Boston, his college town, while "interested friends encouraged me by rapping on the windows."

The soups, which sported a distinctive red-and-white label, quickly became the rage. Dorrance's next product success, pork and beans, emerged from his trademark emphasis on efficiency. As the preparation of soup stock was a time-consuming process, he developed the new product to fill the time that workers spent waiting for the soup to finish cooking.

When Dorrance started in 1897, the company had posted a loss of $60,000 the previous year. It would be the last unprofitable year for the Joseph Campbell Preserve Company. Though the company profits increased immensely from Dorrance's condensed soup, he did not immediately share in the good fortune. After his third year, he had only increased his salary to $12.50 per week. Despite the low wages, he was promoted during this period from lab technician to vice president. Dorrance, a meticulous planner, made a habit of saving money and purchasing additional company stock.

Dorrance's emphasis on advertising quickly enabled Campbell's to achieve brand loyalty. The "Campbell Kids," a series of illustrated children that appeared in all the advertisements, was a popular and ubiquitous marketing image. Dorrance's insistence on prime advertising position in magazines was so consistent that even today, the space he preferred is still called by advertising agencies the "Campbell Soup position."

On August 18, 1906, Dorrance married Ethel Mallinckrodt, a Baltimore socialite with whom he eventually had four daughters and one son. In 1911, the year that Dorrance became Campbell's general manager, the couple moved from Camden to a large home on a 176-acre farm in Cinnaminson, New Jersey.

Dorrance was involved in all aspects of the company. He stressed accurate record keeping and continued, after his purchase of controlling stock in 1915, to audit the books himself every month. On December 5, 1921, Dorrance formally dissolved the Joseph Campbell Company (by then the fourth iteration of the company name) and dubbed his new corporation the Campbell Soup Company. The company continued to be successful, eventually diversifying to include product lines such as Pepperidge Farm baked goods, Prego tomato sauce, and Godiva chocolates.

In addition to his manufacturing interests, Dorrance served at various times as a director of the Prudential Life Insurance Company and of the Guaranty Trust Company of New York. Dorrance, who died on September 21, 1930, at his Cinnaminson farm, left his estate of almost $115 million to his family.

BIBLIOGRAPHY

"Campbell's Community Center," http://www.campbellsoup.com/center/history/1900.html; Collins, Douglas, *America's* *Favorite Soup: The Story of Campbell Soup Company*, 1994; "Rob Campbell's Home Page," http://www.stetson.edu/~rcampbel/Campbell's.html/.

Doubleday, Frank

(January 8, 1862–January 30, 1934)
Publisher

Frank Nelson Doubleday established one of the nation's leading publishing houses, while working closely with authors and forming lasting friendships with them.

Born on January 8, 1862, in Brooklyn, New York, to William Edwards Doubleday, a merchant, and Ellen (Dickinson) Doubleday, Frank attended the Brooklyn Polytechnic Institute but left at age 15 to

Neltje and Frank Doubleday (Library of Congress)

join the publishing firm Charles Scribner's Sons. He remained there 20 years, during which time he edited *The Book Buyer* and managed *Scribner's Magazine*. In 1886, he married Neltje De Graff, who wrote several books about birds, flowers, and gardening, and who later influenced his publishing of books on the outdoors. (After she died in 1918, he married Florence Van Wyck.)

In 1897, Doubleday joined Samuel Sidney McClure to form the publishing company Doubleday & McClure. Two years later, he took in other partners, forming Doubleday, Page & Company, a name the firm retained until 1927, when it absorbed the George H. Doran Company to form Doubleday, Doran & Company. Doubleday served as president until 1927 and thereafter as chairman of the board.

While heading the company, Doubleday moved the headquarters to Garden City, Long Island, and established several subsidiaries, including the Garden City Publishing Company, Doran Book Shops, the Crime Club, and the Sun Dial Press. He also acquired the William Heinemann Company of London, a prestigious British publisher.

Doubleday published books by some of the world's most influential writers: Henry George, Rudyard Kipling, Joseph Conrad, O. Henry, Booth Tarkington, Sinclair Lewis, Ellen Glasgow, Edna Ferber, and Kathleen Norris. He loved books and enjoyed working with writers, a combination that earned him much acclaim in the publishing and literary worlds.

Doubleday died on January 30, 1934, while at his winter home near Miami, Florida. He was survived by a daughter and a son.

BIBLIOGRAPHY

Doubleday, Frank, *A Few Indiscreet Recollections*, 1928; Doubleday, Frank, *The Memoirs of a Publisher*, 1972.

Douglas, Donald

(April 6, 1892–February 1, 1981)
Manufacturer

As a gifted designer and innovator in the field of large-scale aviation, Donald Wills Douglas was one of the central figures in the creation of a global air transportation network. An engineer at heart, he relentlessly studied the principles of flight in order to improve the speed, range, and efficiency of the aircraft built by the Douglas Aircraft Company, making it the world leader in both commercial and military aircraft manufacturing.

Donald, the second son of William Edward and Dorothy Locker Douglas, was born on April 6, 1892, in Brooklyn, New York. After completing grade school in Brooklyn, Douglas enrolled at the Trinity Chapel School, a college preparatory school in Manhattan. Douglas's two main childhood interests were sailing and aviation. He loved reading about the early experiments in flying by the Wright brothers and enthusiastically built his own wooden model airplanes.

Upon graduating from Trinity Chapel in 1909, Douglas decided that the best way to pursue his sailing and flying interests was to continue his education at the U.S. Naval Academy in Annapolis, Maryland. After witnessing Orville Wright's demonstration of the Wright Flyer to the U.S. Army on July 30, 1909, aviation became his consuming passion. After three years at the Naval Academy, Douglas, frustrated with the academy's lack of interest in the military potential of aviation, left to attend the Massachusetts Institute of Technology (MIT). Although it was the leading engineering college in the country, MIT did not have an aeronautical engineering program, so Douglas completed a bachelor of science degree in mechanical engineering in just two years.

After graduating in 1914, Douglas stayed at MIT to work as an assistant to Professor Jerome C. Hunsaker in the aerodynamics department, and the two men built one of the early wind tunnels. One year later, he was briefly employed at the Connecticut Aircraft Company and then joined the Glenn L. Martin Company as chief engineer in Los Angeles, California. By 1920, he had risen to the vice presidency of the business. On June 5, 1916, Douglas married Charlotte Marguerite Ogg, with whom he would have four sons and one daughter.

At age 28, with $600 in assets, Douglas decided to create his own aircraft business. He convinced a wealthy Los Angeles sportsman, David R. Davis, to join him as a partner in forming the Davis-Douglas Company in 1920. Working from

Donald Douglas (Archive Photos)

a tiny office and warehouse in Santa Monica, Douglas began constructing his streamlined "Cloudster" prototype. Soon after, Davis sold his share in the company to Douglas. Having secured an order from the U.S. Navy for three of the Cloudsters for $120,000, Douglas raised capital from a group of Los Angeles businessmen to begin construction. Other government contracts followed, including one from the U.S. Post Office after airmail service was begun in 1925. The company grew quickly, and in 1928 it was reincorporated as the Douglas Aircraft Company with Douglas as president and eventually as chairman of the board.

In 1932, Douglas began manufacturing the DC (Douglas Commercial) series of aircraft for commercial flights after winning a contract from Transcontinental and Western Airlines. The DC-2 represented a major advancement in domestic air travel by achieving speeds of 180 miles per hour with a range of 1,000 miles. By 1939, the company had grown to employ 8,000 workers, and as war loomed on the horizon, Douglas once again turned his attention to building military aircraft. During World War II, the Douglas Aircraft Company expanded rapidly, employing 160,000 people by 1944. The DC-3 model was converted to the C-47 for transport purposes, and the B series of bombers and the A series of small attack planes were also developed. During the war, Douglas produced about 30,000 aircraft, representing over 10 percent of the total airpower of the United States.

As the war drew to a close, Douglas drastically scaled back his workforce and production capacity. Even so, the company remained about four times larger than its prewar size. As the number of commercial airline companies and routes increased, so did the orders for Douglas aircraft. In 1953, the DC-7 model became the first commercial plane to fly nonstop across the United States. In the late 1950s, Douglas was designing the company's first jet airplane, the DC-8, but the Seattle-based Boeing Company had a huge lead in the development of jet aircraft. The Boeing 707 was finished in 1959 and was snatched up by all the major airlines. Even when the DC-8 was finished, the Douglas Company could not keep up with its own orders. This failure left the Douglas Aircraft Company in poor financial shape and with little choice but to accept a merger with another aircraft manufacturer, the McDonnell Company, in 1967.

In 1957, Douglas was succeeded by his son Donald Douglas Jr. as president of the company, but the elder Douglas remained active in decision-making. In his spare time, Douglas enjoyed quiet evenings reading at home and, being of Scottish descent, took pride in his skill at playing the bagpipes. He was a Republican and a member of the Episcopalian Church. A few years after retiring to a home in Pacific Palisades, he died on February 1, 1981.

BIBLIOGRAPHY

Cunningham, F., *Sky Master: The Story of Donald Douglas*, 1943; Forbes, B. C., *America's Fifty Foremost Business Leaders*, 1948; Morrison, Wilbur H., *Donald W. Douglas: A Heart with Wings*, 1991.

Dow, Clarence

(November 6, 1851–December 4, 1902)
Publisher

Today the *Wall Street Journal* is renowned for its business news and stands as a giant in the communications industry with several other publications under its ownership—a long way from when Clarence Henry Dow cofounded the paper using shorthand notes written on his shirt cuffs.

Dow was born on November 6, 1851, in Sterling, Connecticut, and in his twenties took up journalism. In 1880, he moved to New York City, where he worked as a financial reporter on Wall Street. Two years later, he teamed with another reporter, Edward Jones, to form a financial news service called Dow, Jones & Company.

The partners worked from behind a soda fountain in a basement on Wall Street, pulling together notes and turning them into news copy. Dow oftentimes recorded the news by making shorthand notes on his shirt cuffs. A third partner, Charles Bergstresser, also worked as a reporter. Jones edited the stories and dictated them to clerks who handwrote them on sheets that they reproduced by carbon copy. Messenger boys then delivered the news—called "flimsies"—to clients.

Dow, Jones & Company prospered, and in 1883 the partners began publishing their news bulletins as the *Customer's Afternoon Letter*. The following year, Dow began compiling the first average of selected stock prices, which would later become known as the Dow Jones averages.

In 1889, Dow, Jones & Company had 50 employees and converted the *Letter* into a newspaper titled the *Wall Street Journal*. Dow served as its editor and provided market analysis while a member of the New York Stock Exchange and a partner in the brokerage firm of Goodbody, Glyn & Dow. Jones retired in 1899, and Dow and Bergstresser sold their interest in the company in 1902 to Clarence Barron. Dow died later that year, on December 4 in Brooklyn, New York.

BIBLIOGRAPHY

Moskowitz, Milton, et al., eds., *Everybody's Business*, 1980.

Dow, Herbert

(February 26, 1866–October 15, 1930)
Manufacturer

Herbert H. Dow developed chemicals from brine that made his Dow Chemical Company a leader in its field.

Herbert was born on February 26, 1866, in Belleville, Ontario, Canada, to Joseph Henry Dow and Sarah (Bunnell) Dow. Soon after Herbert's birth, the family moved to Derby, Connecticut, and then to Cleveland, Ohio, where the elder Dow worked as a master mechanic. Herbert earned his bachelor of science degree in 1888 from the Case School of Applied Science (present-day Case Western Reserve University) and as a senior wrote a thesis that discussed brines (water saturated with salt). He analyzed brines from several sites and discovered that those in Canton, Ohio, and Midland, Michigan were rich in bromine—a volatile, corrosive, nonmetallic liquid known for its highly irritating vapor.

Later in 1888, Dow taught at the Homeopathic Hospital College of Cleveland and patented a method for obtaining bromine using electrolyzed brine. In 1890, Dow founded the Midland Chemical Company that employed his method, which was notable for using little fuel and for avoiding a heavy salt by-product that would have been cumbersome to dispose. Dow then electrolyzed brine to produce chlorine, and in 1897 he formed the Dow Chemical Company, which soon absorbed Midland Chemical and manufactured bleached powder.

Dow's work with brines produced new chemical compounds, and his chlorine process led to the making of insecticides. Dow also took the magnesium chloride made from brine and used it as an oxychloride in stucco. In 1918, his electrolysis of magnesium chloride produced magnesium metal. From this development came the production of alloys he named Dowmetal, which was a light metal useful in industry.

An important breakthrough occurred in the 1920s when Dow extracted iodine from Louisiana brines—the first time iodine had been made in the United States. In all, Dow obtained 65 patents covering different chemical processes, and Dow Chemical emerged as one of the leading manufacturers of chemicals in the nation.

Dow, who had married Grace A. Ball in the 1890s and had three sons and four daughters, died on October 15, 1930, in Rochester, Minnesota, following an operation.

BIBLIOGRAPHY

Dow, R. P., *The Book of Dow*, 1929.

Drew, Daniel

(July 29, 1797–September 18, 1879)
Financier

Illiterate and unscrupulous, Daniel Drew went from cattle drover to stock manipulator and precipitated a titanic financial battle in America's early business history, the Erie War.

Born on July 29, 1797, at Carmel, New York, where he grew up on his father's farm and received little formal schooling, Drew served briefly in the War of 1812 and then worked as a cattle drover and horse trader. This led to his buying cattle, and with his profits, in 1829 he opened Bull's Head Tavern at Third Avenue and 24th Street in New York City—complete with cattle yards—where drovers met to make cattle deals.

In 1834, Drew entered the steamboat business and ran a connection between Albany and New York. He later began a profitable steamboat service on Lake Champlain. With his newly acquired capital, in 1844 he founded Drew, Robinson & Company, a stock brokerage and bank. His dealings earned him money and infamy as an untrustworthy speculator and manipulator.

Drew's biggest business battle erupted in 1866, amid surging northern industrialization. Previously, CORNELIUS VANDERBILT had invested in the Erie Railroad—a poorly managed and nearly bankrupt line. Vanderbilt reached an agreement whereby Drew, also an investor, served as treasurer and agreed to cooperate in various stock dealings. Instead, Drew manipulated the stock for his own benefit and sought to link the railroad with one that would hurt Vanderbilt's interests. Vanderbilt reacted by deciding to buy majority control of the Erie, whereupon Drew, along with fellow investors JIM FISK and JAY GOULD, issued more stock, draining millions from Vanderbilt. When Vanderbilt challenged the stock issuance, Gould used money and leverage to get the state legislature to certify his actions as legal. When the battle ended, Vanderbilt had lost, but so too had the Erie, which was plundered and shaken. The public read about the financial war and recoiled in disgust, more so when bad conditions on the railroad caused a train wreck in 1868 that cost many lives.

Drew, along with Gould and Fisk, used the profits from the war to engage in stock maneuvers and misrepresentations that ruined thousands of investors. Drew, though, soon lost money in his own bad investments and in March 1876 declared bankruptcy. He lived his last few months shunned and despised by most, although

Daniel Drew (Library of Congress)

well remembered by those to whom he had donated money, among them the Drew Theological Seminary in Madison, New Jersey. Drew, whose wife Roxana Mead had died before his death on September 18, 1879, left an estate valued at $148.22.

BIBLIOGRAPHY

Browder, Clifford, *The Money Game in Old New York: Daniel Drew and His Times*, 1986.

Drexel, Anthony

(September 13, 1826–June 30, 1893)
Banker

Anthony Joseph Drexel inherited an investment house and made it one of the greatest brokerages in the nation.

Anthony was born on September 13, 1826, in Philadelphia, Pennsylvania, to Francis Martin Drexel and Catherine (Hookey) Drexel. His father owned a recently opened brokerage office that had proven successful. The elder Drexel educated Anthony at home, training him in business and teaching him music, English, and foreign languages. In 1847, Anthony's father made him a member of the firm Drexel & Company. At about the same time, Anthony married Ellen Rozet, the daughter of a Philadelphia merchant.

After the elder Drexel died in 1863, Anthony became the head of Drexel & Company. Although the Civil War was then under way, Drexel's ascension occurred at a propitious time. The Northern economy was expanding, and after the war ended, industrial and governmental growth required new financing. With Drexel's experience in this field, his firm handled investment securities covering national and local debts, mining, and the building of factories. Known for his sound and cautious judgment, Drexel disliked speculation and refused to get involved in the risky investments prevalent in the railroad industry.

Drexel built a new bank and office building in Philadelphia during the 1880s, an impressive structure noted for its architecture and symbolic of the firm's expansion. He also diversified his business interests and invested heavily in the city's real estate, making a considerable profit. He entered the newspaper field when he became partial owner of the *Public Ledger.*

Drexel developed an extensive philanthropy, giving money to hospitals, churches, and charities. He founded the Childs-Drexel Home for Aged Printers in Colorado Springs, Colorado, and he promoted industrial education by founding the Drexel Institute in Philadelphia, to which he gave $3 million. The institute, which opened in 1892, emphasized technology—and thus Drexel's faith in the industrializing nation—and earned a reputation for innovation with its free scholarships, low tuition, and admission policies that placed no restrictions to entry based on religion, race, sex, or social class.

Drexel died on June 30, 1893, in Carlsbad, Germany, while on a trip intended to help him recover from an illness. He was remembered for his crucial role in funding America's industrial expansion.

BIBLIOGRAPHY

Creese, James, *A. J. Drexel, 1826–1893, and His Industrial University,* 1949.

Dreyfus, Camille

(November 11, 1878–September 27, 1956)
Manufacturer

Camille Edouard Dreyfus, a chemist and inventor from Switzerland, is responsible for the scientific and commercial development of cellulose acetate, the material used to create the first man-made fibers for fabrics. The Celanese Corporation, under his direction, contributed substantially to the modern chemical industry and revolutionized the fashion industry by creating fabrics that were high quality but inexpensive.

Camille, one of six children of banker Abraham Dreyfus and his wife Henritte Wahl, was born on November 11, 1878, in Basel, Switzerland. From an early age, Camille expressed an interest in chemistry, conducting research with his brother Henry in their father's garden shed. After earning an M.A. and a Ph.D. from the University of Basel in 1902, Camille studied at the Sorbonne in Paris for four years. In 1910, he established a laboratory in Basel with his brother Henry, who by this time had also earned his advanced degree. Their factory was called the Cellonit-Gesellschaft Dreyfus & Cie.

One of the brothers' first achievements was the development of synthetic indigo dyes, an appropriate research area given that Basel was a center of the dye industry. Early in their research, Camille and Henry began the manufacture of cellulose acetate, produced by the chemical reaction of cellulose (which is a fiber derived from either wood pulp or cotton) and acetic acid. This combination resulted in the first nonflammable variety of celluloid. As such, it yielded a number of practical applications such as serving as the raw material for plastics and film for motion picture cameras.

After 1913, Camille and Henry began working extensively on a process to create acetate continuous filament yarn. The research had to be put on hold because of the outbreak of World War I. During the war, the brothers developed a solution of the nonflammable cellulose acetate for military applications, primarily the coating of the fabric that covered the wings and fuselage of aircraft. The utility of the solution for this purpose was instantly recognized, and in 1914 Camille was asked to establish a plant in Great Britain to produce cellulose acetate for the war effort. The British Cellulose & Chemical Manufacturing Company would shortly be followed by an Italian plant and a French factory established for the same purpose.

When the United States became involved in World War I, Camille was once again asked for his services. At the request of the secretary of war, Camille incorporated the American Cellulose & Chemical Manufacturing Company in 1918 in Cumberland, Maryland. By the time the plant opened, however, the war had ended and the military market had evaporated.

By the end of the war, the British branch of the company had finished the first commercially viable acetate textile yarn. Introduced as "artificial silk," and selling at half the price of real silk, the yarn sold well but had many flaws. Its primary use was for crocheting and special trim effects. Among additional problems, the artificial yarn could not be colored with commercially available dyes, and traditional textile machinery was not adapted for use with chemical fibers.

Over the next six years, Camille worked on perfecting the yarn and standardizing production methods. By 1923, the brothers Dreyfus, working with other chemists, devised a dyeing technology for use with the man-made fiber. In December 1924, the yarn, called "Celanese," began production at the Maryland branch. By the following year, the company was incorporated under the new name Celanese Corporation of America with Camille as president. The financier, J. P. MORGAN SR., also came on board to underwrite the stock issues.

As business of the American firm (and its foreign counterparts) took off, Camille began to commission silk mills to weave fabrics made from acetate yarn, in part to familiarize mills with the new fiber, as well as to show the high quality of the finished product. Before the development of the Celanese man-made fiber, almost all high-quality dresses were made from silk. Within 20 years of the introduction of the acetate, less than 5 percent were made from silk. It was discovered early that the blending of silk, acetate, and cotton was a wonderful combination for creating fabrics and carpets that were durable, yet soft, and inexpensive to produce.

On September 18, 1931, Dreyfus married a singer, Jean Tennyson. The early years of the 1930s were a heady time for him. He began experimenting in 1932 to try to produce acetic acid so that the company would not have to purchase it from other firms. Every year after 1925,

the Celanese Corporation showed a profit, experiencing its first exceptional year in 1939. The company continued to grow rapidly.

In 1944, Dreyfus incorporated Celanese Mexicana, S.A., a Mexican affiliate. The following year, Dreyfus relinquished his role as president of Celanese Corporation of America to Harold Blancke, though he continued to be the executive head and chairman of the board until his death. By 1948, eager to close the production cycle even further, Celanese obtained lumber rights in British Columbia, Canada, in order to supply its own raw material for the production of cellulose. Celanese continued to produce fabrics from acetate fiber. The fabrics had the virtue of drying quickly, remaining virtually free of wrinkles, and being inexpensive to produce.

Throughout his career, Dreyfus was active in professional organizations such as the American Chemical Society, the American Association for the Advancement of Science, and the National Association of Manufacturers. In 1946, in memory of his brother Henry who had died in 1944, Dreyfus established the Camille and Henry Dreyfus Foundation for the advancement of chemical science and engineering. Dreyfus died on September 27, 1956, at the age of 78.

BIBLIOGRAPHY

Blancke, Harold, *Celanese Corporation of America: The Founders and the Early Years*, 1952; "The Camille & Henry Dreyfus Foundation, Inc.," http://www.dreyfus.org/ history.html; *Current Biography*, 1955; *Fortune*, May 1948.

Dryden, John

(August 7, 1839–November 24, 1911)
Insurance Executive

Often called "the father of industrial insurance in America," John Dryden founded the Prudential Life Insurance Company.

John was born on August 7, 1839, near Farmington, Maine, to John Dryden and Elizabeth (Butterfield) Dryden. He grew up on his family's farm, and in 1861 entered Yale University. Illness, however, forced him to leave college before graduating.

Dryden developed an interest in life insurance and studied the success of the Prudential Assurance Company of London, which wrote industrial insurance policies. These policies were sold to factory workers, who could afford to pay only small premiums. In 1873, Dryden moved to Newark, New Jersey, and joined several investors to form the Prudential Friendly Society, the first company in the United States to make life insurance available to working-class people.

John Dryden (Archive Photos)

He wrote the firm's initial insurance policy in 1875 while serving as secretary, and by the end of the year, Prudential had sold nearly 300 policies. The firm changed its name in 1878 to the Prudential Insurance Company, and three years later, Dryden became its president.

Dryden guided Prudential in writing industrial insurance. Under his system, copied from that used in England, each company agent was responsible for a certain number of blocks in a working-class neighborhood and within those blocks sold life insurance door-to-door. The workers were allowed to pay for the policies through a small weekly premium, generally 10 cents, but sometimes as few as 3. The agent had to collect the premium—in fact, Dryden considered this crucial to the system since the workers might otherwise not keep up with their payments. Although the cost of the policies sounded low, the workers paid more for them than they would have paid for regular life insurance, the type purchased by wealthier Americans.

By 1899, Prudential's receipts exceeded $17 million, and the company played an important role in the growth of the life insurance industry, from covering 2 percent of the population in 1875 to over 17 percent at century's end. By 1900, Prudential had written nearly $450 million worth of industrial life insurance.

In addition to his work with Prudential, Dryden served as vice president of Fidelity Trust of Newark and as director of both the Merchants National Bank and, in New York City, the U.S Casualty Company. He served one term in the U.S. Senate from 1902 to 1907 as a Republican. Dryden died on November 24, 1911.

In 1996, Prudential had the largest capital base—$12.1 billion—of any life insurer in North America.

BIBLIOGRAPHY

Douglass, Elisha P., *The Coming of Age of American Business*, 1971.

Du Pont, Pierre

(January 15, 1870–April 5, 1954)
Manufacturer

An explosives and chemical manufacturer who built the Du Pont Company into a modern corporation, Pierre Samuel Du Pont described the day his cousins proposed that he join them in buying the business: "Would I do it? This was the most important far-reaching decision of my life; no position, salary or interest . . . was offered but the three minute allowance of a telephone conversation was quite long enough for me to receive the account of the proposition placed before me, and to make up my mind and give my reply in one word, *yes.*"

For all practical purposes, when Du Pont, came into this world on January 15, 1870, in New Castle County, Delaware, he was born into his career. His parents, Lammot Du Pont and Mary (Belin) Du Pont lived in a mansion called Nemours on the west bank of Brandywine Creek. Lammot worked as a chemist in the family's explosives manufactory. This business dated back to the early 1800s when Pierre's great-grandfather, Eleuthere Irenee Du Pont, began making gunpowder at what had been a cotton mill near Wilmington, Delaware. Lammot had changed the company's direction when, in 1857, he devised a means to substitute nitrates for saltpeter, resulting in "B" Blasting Powder—which was cheaper and more powerful than any previously made and soon became the leading explosive for blasting.

A shy child who preferred books to athletics, Pierre spent part of his boyhood in New Jersey after his father opened a manufacturing plant there, the Repauno Chemical Company, to make nitroglycerin powders. Pierre attended the Quaker-run William Penn Charter School in Philadelphia, during which tragedy struck when, in 1884, his father died in an accidental explosion at the plant. His uncle, Alfred I. Du Pont, became his guardian. The young man entered the Massachusetts Institute of Technology and after his graduation from there in 1890, joined the family business in Wilmington. Initially, he dried samples of powder. At the same time, he invested in the

Johnson Company (a steel manufacturer) and learned about finances.

Soon after Pierre transferred to the Smokeless Powder factory at Carney's Point, New Jersey, he discovered a way to make the dangerous product, also called guncotton, safe for use in shotguns. Irritated by the way his cousin ran the plant, he left the family business in 1899 and accepted an offer to lead the then financially troubled Johnson Company as its president. Three years later, his cousins Alfred and Coleman proposed they buy the DuPont Company, to which Pierre agreed and served as treasurer.

Pierre and his cousins, helped by JOHN RASKOB, soon acquired for the DuPont Company a competitor, Laflin & Rand, that held stocks in other powder companies, thus making DuPont the dominant firm and allowing it to integrate its dynamite and powder holdings.

As president, Pierre centralized the administrative structure; developed vertical integration that, for example, brought Chilean nitrate beds and shipping firms under DuPont's control; opened a modern laboratory to develop new products; and invented accounting methods that later became standard throughout American industry.

When World War I erupted, DuPont provided ammunition for the Allied powders and, later, the United States—in all, some 1.5 billion pounds of explosives. This greatly expanded DuPont's business, carefully crafted by Pierre, who made sure that prices covered the costs of factory expansion should the war end with construction still under way. Pierre invested his war profits in General Motors (GM) and through other investments positioned DuPont to manufacture new chemical products after the war. The

Pierre Du Pont (Library of Congress)

company made plastics, cellophane, neoprene synthetic rubber, and nylon to the point that the manufacture of explosives fell to a secondary position within the company.

At about the same time, in 1915, he married Alice Belin, while on the business front he bought Coleman's shares in DuPont. The move left Alfred powerless and led to a bitter dispute between him and Pierre, involving a highly publicized lawsuit.

Pierre had held the DuPont presidency since 1909 and retired from it in 1919, but the following year brought an unexpected development when GM, which was close to bankruptcy, asked him to be its president. He agreed and served in that position until 1923 and as chairman of the board until 1929. With the help of ALFRED SLOAN, he reorganized GM so that each auto division sold cars in a different price class, and his leadership produced growth that exceeded all other auto-makers.

Amid the Great Depression, in 1933 he served on the advisory board of President Franklin Roosevelt's National Recovery Administration and on the Labor Relations Board. Discontented with the New Deal, however, he broke with Roosevelt in 1934 and founded the American Liberty League to oppose the president's economic policies. During that same decade, the Nye Committee, formed by Congress, investigated events surrounding World War I, and angered Pierre by suggesting that DuPont and other munitions manufacturers had exploited the war for profit.

Pierre remained active in DuPont as a member of its finance committee until his death on April 5, 1954. He had mastered the intricacies that made DuPont a leader among modern corporations.

BIBLIOGRAPHY

Chandler, Alfred, Jr., and Stephen Salsbury, *Pierre S. Du Pont and the Making of the Modern Corporation*, 1971.

Duer, William

(March 18, 1747–May 7, 1799)
Financier, Merchant

William Duer, a prominent eighteenth-century merchant and financier, was an energetic, daring businessman who consistently muddied the distinction between political and business activities. Many of his commercial enterprises involved government contracts, and he used his influence as an elected official to engage in speculative stock and real estate dealings. He was also known for his role in the founding of the Bank of New York and his involvement in the Sciotto Speculation, a plan that allowed Duer and others to purchase large western tracts of land to sell to foreign investors. While Duer was wealthy for much of his life, his financial risk taking eventually precipitated his impoverishment and subsequent arrest for failure to pay his debts.

William Duer, the son of John Duer and Francis Frye Duer, was born in Devonshire, England, on March 18, 1747. His father was the wealthy owner of plantations in Antigua and Dominica. After being educated at Eton, William became an ensign in the British army, serving in 1764 as an aide-de-camp for Lord Clive, the governor of Bengal in India. Soon after his return to England, Duer inherited a share in the family plantations.

Duer moved to the West Indies to take a more active role in managing his inheritance. In 1768, on a visit from the West Indies to New York, where he supplied goods for the British navy, Duer purchased a large tract of timberland in the Saratoga area. In 1773, Duer returned to New York to make it his home.

Despite his British origins, Duer quickly became involved politically with the opposition to the British government's rule in North America. In 1775, Duer was appointed deputy adjutant general of the New York patriot forces. That same year, Duer served as a delegate to New York's provincial congress, followed by his appointment in 1776 as a delegate to the New York constitutional convention. In this capacity, he helped draft the state constitution, receiving praise for his analytical skill and energy.

Between 1777 and 1786, Duer received appointments to various public offices. He served as a New York delegate to the Continental Congress and was a member of the Board of War. He was also one of the signers of the Articles of Confederation.

In 1779, Duer married Catherine Alexander (nicknamed "Lady Kitty"), who was the daughter of Maj. Gen. William Alexander. Alexander, also known as Lord Stirling, was the colorful son of wealthy merchants James and MARY SPRATT PROVOOST ALEXANDER.

In January of that same year, Duer resigned from Congress, but by July 1780 was appointed commissioner for conspiracies, a position that allowed him to become involved in many commercial projects. He secured some of the largest government supply contracts and became quite wealthy. Duer was also active in influencing the founding of the Bank of New York in 1786. Later that same year, he moved to New York City to become the secretary of the Board of Treasury and a member of the New York Assembly.

In 1787, Duer joined with associates to influence the government to sell land in the western states. Known as the Sciotto Speculation, Duer's intention was to sell the land primarily to capitalists in Holland and France. This venture was one of the prime examples of Duer's tendency to use public office for personal gain. He was instrumental in influencing his associates in the deal to alter their proposal to Congress. Duer would then, through his public role, convince Congress that it was a sound deal. When he proved successful in influencing Congress, he reaped the financial benefits along with his associates.

Duer was also interested in the establishment of an international bank, which he believed could commercially and financially rival the dominant Dutch banks. But his reputation as a planner with interesting ideas was tempered by his inattention to detail and lack of ability to carry plans from conception through implementation.

In 1789, Duer spent six months at the newly established Treasury Department under the direction of Alexander Hamilton. After resigning, he threw himself into his business activities. His business dealings were frequently under scrutiny, with the criticism often raised that he used his political influence to advance his financial projects. Over the next few years, he engaged in many speculative real estate purchases. After becoming heavily involved with risky stock ventures, he found himself mired in government charges related to his earlier activities while secretary of the New York Board of Treasury.

Duer's unsuccessful stock dealings left him unable to pay off his debtors. On March 23, 1782, he was arrested and imprisoned for failure to make good on his debts. As Duer's schemes had attracted many investors over the years, his insolvency and arrest resulted in New York City's first financial panic.

Though freed temporarily in 1797, Duer remained in prison until 1799. In March of that year, on the basis of his failing health, Hamilton interceded on Duer's behalf and arranged for his release. Duer died on May 7, 1799, apparently of yellow fever.

BIBLIOGRAPHY

Davis, J. S., *Essays in the Early History of American Corporations*, 1917; Duer, William Alexander, *Reminiscences of an Old Yorker*, 1867; "The Duers," *New York Evening Post*, April 27, 1901; Jones, Robert Francis, *The King of the Alley: William Duer, Politician, Entrepreneur, and Speculator, 1768–1799*, 1992; Jones, Thomas, *History of New York during the Revolutionary War*, 1879; *New York Monthly Magazine*, August 1852.

Duke, James Buchanan

(December 23, 1856–October 10, 1925)
Manufacturer

Tough and hard as granite, James Buchanan "Buck" Duke combined determination with illegalities to form the nation's largest tobacco manufacturer.

Buck was born on December 23, 1856, to Washington Duke and Artelia (Roney) Duke on his father's small farm near Durham, North Carolina. Two years later, his mother died from typhoid fever. As the Civil War engulfed the nation, Buck received a rudimentary education at a log schoolhouse where his aunt taught him.

The war destroyed Washington Duke's farm, but the elder Duke soon renewed his growing of tobacco—a laborious, backbreaking chore that convinced him to work more as a factor or middleman than as a farmer. He built a small log-and-chink 20-x-30-foot factory and granulated and packed local bright tobacco into tobacco plugs he called Pro Bono Publico. Buck labeled burlap sacks, oiled the plug

pressing and grinding machines, and delivered the finished product to country stores.

By this time, William T. Blackwell and JULIAN SHAKESPEARE CARR had organized the nation's largest tobacco company, Bull Durham, in Durham, North Carolina. In 1873, Washington Duke decided to build a small factory there to take advantage of the bright leaf tobacco being marketed in the town. He sent Buck to Poughkeepsie, New York, where the young man completed a course at the Eastman National School of Business in just six months. The following year, Washington Duke made his two sons Buck and Brodie partners in his company, thus beginning W. Duke & Sons. Buck worked long hours keeping the books and, in the mornings, buying tobacco at warehouse auctions and driving bargains.

Clearly the force in the company, Buck decided to lead W. Duke & Sons into a new field and manufacture cigarettes. Few Americans smoked them at the time, and those who did had to roll their own or buy hand-rolled brands. When he first began making cigarettes in 1881, Buck relied on Russian immigrants to hand roll them. He stimulated sales by launching an extensive advertising campaign and by slashing the price for his cigarettes after he learned, in 1883, that Congress intended to lower revenue taxes.

At the same time, Buck Duke paid royalties that enabled him to replace his immigrant laborers with a cigarette-rolling machine developed by James Bonsack. After helping to perfect the machine, Duke put it to work making 200 cigarettes a minute. This output boosted his sales and emboldened him to enter the New York City market. He opened a factory there in 1884, and by the following year, W. Duke & Sons had sales nearing $600,000 annually. Three years later, his company produced half the total number of cigarettes made in America.

After a "tobacco war" among cigarette manufacturers cut into profits, Duke convinced his competitors to join him in 1889 and form a combination, the American Tobacco Company. He, in turn, served as its president.

In the 1890s, Duke strove to eliminate all competition. First, he obtained exclusive rights to the Bonsack machine. Then, he used his cigarette profits to launch the "plug tobacco war," and in 1898 forced his competitors to form the Continental Tobacco Company, a chewing-tobacco combination under his control. In 1900, he put together another combination, the American Snuff Company, and through it controlled 80 percent of that market. Duke formed the American Cigar Company in 1901, followed by the

American Stogie Company, and then directly entered retail trade with the United Cigar Stores Company. He organized the Consolidated Tobacco Company as a holding business for all these firms.

Duke diversified beyond tobacco when, in 1904, he formed the Southern Power Company. Factories in the Piedmont of North and South Carolina relied on Southern, and it grew into a highly profitable industrial giant. That same year, he married Lillian McCredy, but they divorced in 1905, and two years later he married a widow, Nanaline Holt Inman. They had one daughter.

Duke turned aside several challenges to his tobacco empire. When public opposition arose to cigarette smoking, he used his money to buy lawyers, lobbyists, and politicians to assure that no restrictions would be allowed. When, in 1904, the Supreme Court ruled holding companies illegal, he disbanded Consolidated, but reorganized the American Tobacco Company to continue his drive toward monopoly. By 1906, American controlled four-fifths of the domestic tobacco industry, excluding cigars. He tried to penetrate the British market, but an ensuing war with tobacco manufacturers there resulted in an agreement by which he withdrew from England, and the English companies agreed to stay out of the United States. The agreement established the British-American Company to handle world trade, with Duke and his interests holding two-thirds of the stock and English interests holding the remaining one-third.

Duke's expansion provided hardships for laborers and farmers. He vehemently opposed unions, paid low wages, and mechanized operations in every way he could. His company dictated lower tobacco prices, an oppressive measure that caused some farmers to resort to violence and burn down several of Duke's warehouses. One historian states that during such a raid on Hopkinsville, Kentucky, in 1907, a building "was expertly and quickly put to the torch and . . . the aroma of flaming tobacco filled the air."

Under President Theodore Roosevelt, the federal government sued to get the American Tobacco Company broken up as a trust in restraint of trade, and in 1911 the case reached the Supreme Court. Duke denied that he had acquired companies as a way to crush them. But letters written by his vice presidents and used by the government as evidence revealed otherwise: a national spy system, hidden rebates, dummy companies founded with funds from American Tobacco, secret control of seemingly independent corporations—in short, a host of duplicitous and illegal acts. Consequently, the Supreme Court ordered American Tobacco divided into competing units.

Duke did more than survive this decision—he prospered from it. President William Howard Taft allowed him to direct the creation of four new companies, and he chose the leaders of each. These companies turned out to be even more profitable than the old trust.

In his later years, Duke contributed some of his vast fortune to public causes. He gave money to hospitals, orphanages, and churches, and provided the funds that created Duke University in North Carolina. About his wealth, shortly before his death on October 10, 1925, he said: "One million mixed with other millions is like people in a crowd: you lose sight of the individual in the jam."

BIBLIOGRAPHY

Cunningham, Bill, *On Bended Knees: The Night Rider Story*, 1983; Winkler, John K., *Tobacco Tycoon: The Story of James Buchanan Duke*, 1942.

Dunlap, Al

(July 26, 1937–)
Corporate Executive

He goes by the nickname "Chainsaw Al." When Albert Dunlap gains control of an ailing corporation, he boosts profits by firing workers—often indiscriminately and never with remorse. That's what he did at Scott Paper, and that's what he was doing at Sunbeam until the chainsaw backfired.

Born on July 26, 1937, in Hoboken, New Jersey, to Albert Joseph Dunlap and Mildred Veronica (O'Toole) Dunlap, Al grew up in a blue-collar environment, with his father working in a shipyard and his family living in a basement apartment under a beauty parlor. In 1956, Al was accepted into West Point and in 1960 graduated 537th out of a cadet class of 550. He then served as an army officer until 1963, married a New York model, had a son, got divorced, and at age 29 began running a small Wisconsin company, Sterling Pulp & Paper. Two years later, in 1968, he married Judy Stringer.

Dunlap gained a reputation for "making over" corporations by trimming fat—or at least what he considered to be fat—which usually meant firing lots of workers, abruptly and coldly. He was an executive at companies ranging from American Can (where he served as senior vice president for corporate management from 1977 to 1982) to the Australian National Industries (where he served as CEO from 1992 to 1994), but he gained his first widespread attention at Scott Paper, the company founded by EDWARD SCOTT, where, from 1994 to 1996, he served as CEO. "Business is damn tough," he observed. "There shouldn't be an Al Dunlap. There is because someone else has made a horrible mess." To which one observer retorted: "There is no excuse for treating employees as if they are disposable pieces of equipment."

Dunlap fired 11,200 workers at Scott—35 percent of the company's labor force. He told executives to quit doing community service, canceled $3 million in pledges to charities, and moved the corporate headquarters from Philadelphia to Florida. The chief of staff told Philadelphia's mayor: "Virtually all other companies in Philadelphia have figured out a way to strike some sort of balance between community responsibility and responsibility to shareholders. I don't think he has a social conscience."

Shareholders, however, applauded Dunlap. He paid off Scott's huge $2.5 billion debt and boosted its stock value. He successfully merged the company with Kimberly-Clark and in the process received $100 million in salary and stock. "Most

Al Dunlap (Reuters/Sunbeam Corp./Archive Photos)

CEOs are ridiculously overpaid," he said, "but I deserved the $100 million."

In July 1996, Dunlap left Scott Paper for another ailing company, the Sunbeam Corporation, which was primarily an appliance manufacturer. He promised its stockholders higher earnings on their shares and 20 percent gains in annual sales and profits in an industry that was growing at the rate of only 3 percent a year.

Dunlap again seemed to be working his aggressive magic. For Sunbeam, he acquired the Coleman Company, manufacturers of camping equipment, and the companies that made Mr. Coffee and First Alert fire alarms. Stock prices rose, sales surged in late 1997, and Dunlap declared Sunbeam "fixed."

To achieve his needed sales boost, however, Dunlap resorted to devious tactics, making the numbers look good by shipping too many products to stores. Overstocked, the stores cut their orders in 1998. In addition, he offered sharp discounts and delayed-payment terms to Wal-Mart and Kmart so they could buy Sunbeam grills during the winter months. They did and then refused to order more when the traditional spring buying season arrived. Dunlap's legerdemain resulted in $58 million in grill sales in December 1997 that helped the company post an 18 percent surge in overall sales for that year. Sunbeam could not sustain that rate, however, and in 1998 sales and share prices dropped.

In June 1998, Sunbeam's board of directors rebelled and fired Dunlap. Angry with his tactics, they threatened to withhold his severance pay. Few observers thought the board would be able to enforce the threat, given the legalities of the situation and the pervasive practice in America that even failed corporate executives depart from their jobs loaded with money. For Chainsaw Al the severance package could total $35 million.

BIBLIOGRAPHY

Canedy, Dana, "Sunbeam Board, in Revolt, Ousts Job-Cutting Chairman," *New York Times*, June 16, 1998; Dunlap, Al, *Mean Business*, 1997; Sider, Don, "The Terminator," *Time*, November 25, 1996.

Durant, William

(December 8, 1861–March 18, 1947)
Manufacturer

A founder of the American automobile industry, William Crapo Durant took his method for making horse-drawn vehicles and applied it to building a giant corporation, General Motors.

William, nicknamed "Billy," was born on December 8, 1861, in Boston, Massachusetts, to William Durant and Rebecca (Crapo) Durant. Little is known about his father, who probably worked as a clerk. Durant's mother came from a wealthy family that had made its money in whaling and lumber. William never finished high school; instead he worked at odd jobs and at age 20 managed the waterworks in Flint, Michigan. In 1885, he bought the patent rights to a two-wheeled cart for a mere $50 and formed a partnership with J. Dallas Dort to begin making the horse-drawn vehicle. The Durant-Dort Carriage Company used a technique that Durant later applied to his auto business: the various parts such as wheels and axles were made at separate plants and then assembled at the main factory in Flint.

Durant entered the emerging automobile industry in 1904, when he bought out the Buick Motor Car Company. With his talent as a dynamic promoter and administrator he soon built Buick into the largest car manufacturer at a time when many small companies were making "horseless carriages." As his profits grew, Durant, perhaps at the suggestion of auto manufacturer Benjamin Briscoe, tried to buy three main competitors, Maxwell-Briscoe, Reo, and Ford, and thus consolidate production. Durant, however, was unable to meet Ford's demands for $3 million in cash.

Instead, Durant incorporated the General Motors Company (GM), under whose umbrella he included several car manufacturers, among them Buick, Cadillac, and Oldsmobile. By 1910, Durant was making one-fifth of the nation's automobiles, and his profits neared $10 million. He had expanded much too quickly, however, and when his capital grew short, a group of bankers forced him out and took over GM.

Durant lost no time in organizing yet another firm with the mechanic Louis Chevrolet, and in 1911 the Chevrolet Motor Car Company sold so many automobiles that Durant, flush with profits, exchanged stock in Chevrolet for stock in GM and regained control of the latter company. Shortly thereafter, JOHN RASKOB and PIERRE DU PONT invested heavily in GM. When Durant organized the United Motors Corporation in 1916 to control the Hyatt Roller Bearing Company and the Dayton Engineering Laboratories Company (Delco), he brought ALFRED SLOAN and CHARLES KETTERING into GM.

Under Durant, GM acquired the Fisher Body Company in 1919 and began the General Motors Acceptance Corporation to provide financing for auto dealers. But a saturated market for cars and an economic slump in 1920 hurt GM and enabled the Du Ponts to wrest control of the corporation from Durant. Only after Durant left did GM, under Sloan and Du Pont, develop a plan that established a modern administrative structure.

The following year, Durant raised enough capital to found Durant Motors. With weak sales, the company faltered, and the stock market crash of 1929 destroyed it. Durant filed for bankruptcy in 1933, but neither that action nor the Great Depression ended his business career. In 1936, he opened a supermarket in Asbury Park, New Jersey, and in 1940 he returned to Flint with the intention of opening a chain of bowling alleys, a plan disrupted by the outbreak of World War II. Durant died in New York City on March 18, 1947, after having guided the beginning of the American automobile industry and, in particular, General Motors.

BIBLIOGRAPHY

Gustin, Lawrence R., *Billy Durant: Creator of General Motors*, 1973; Sloan, Alfred P., Jr., *My Years with General Motors*, 1964.

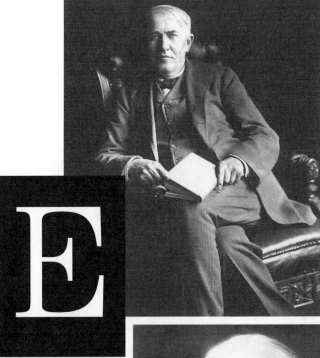

E

Eastman, George

(July 12, 1854–March 14, 1932)
Manufacturer

As a young man, George Eastman could often be seen working alone in his shop, his head silhouetted in a window where lights burned deep into the night as he pursued his dream to change photography. Indeed, with his innovations in filmmaking and processing, and in the production of cameras, he brought picture taking to America's middle class.

George Eastman (Library of Congress)

George was born on July 12, 1854, in Waterville, New York, to George Washington Eastman and Maria (Kilbourn) Eastman. In 1842, his father founded the first commercial college in Rochester and lived half the year in that city and

half in Waterville, before moving his family in 1860 to live near the school. Two years later, the elder George Eastman died, and Maria took in boarders to keep the family financially afloat.

Young Eastman attended public school for seven years and then worked in an insurance office. In 1874, the Rochester Savings Bank made him a junior bookkeeper, and, through his diligence, he advanced rapidly.

Attracted to photography, Eastman spent $49.58 on equipment in 1877 and learned the prevailing "wet-plate" system, a difficult and time-consuming procedure that involved taking heavy panes of glass and coating them with chemicals just before exposing film. Never one to idly pursue a hobby, Eastman searched for a way to make money from his new interest. When he read about an innovative "dry-plate" emulsion formula through which the size and weight of outdoor photographic equipment could be reduced, he began experimenting in his mother's kitchen. By 1879, he obtained patents in England and the United States for a dry-plate coating machine and was ready to enter business. He then left the bank and with Henry A. Strong founded the Eastman Dry Plate Company.

While other inventors were working on ways to replace the cumbersome glass plates with film stored on rolls, so did Eastman. He perfected a paper-backed film in 1884 that fit on a wooden spool and could be used in existing cameras. (Another inventor had, three years earlier, patented the first camera to use film on a roll.) That same year, he reorganized his business as the Eastman Dry Plate and Film Company.

To improve his product, Eastman hired a chemist, Henry A. Reichenbach, who discovered a way to eliminate the paper used as backing on Eastman's film. In 1888, Eastman began placing film rolls inside box cameras. Consumers could buy a leather-covered camera complete with carrying case and shoulder strap for $25 and send the entire camera (along with $10) to Eastman for processing. He would then return the camera with a new roll of film inside. Eastman called the camera a Kodak—his first use of the name, chosen because it had a strong sound to it.

Commentators offered differing assessments about Eastman's pursuit:

> As a fad, [photography] is well nigh on its last legs, thanks principally to the bicycle craze.

> The craze is spreading fearfully. Chicago has had many fads whose careers have been brilliant but brief. But when amateur photography came, it came to stay.

> Beware the Kodak. The sedate citizen can't indulge in any hilariousness without the risk of being caught in the act and having his photograph passed around among his Sunday School children.

While the Kodak democratized photography by making it more easily available to the middle class, Eastman went further when he developed the idea, and Frank Brownell worked out the details, for a $1 camera intended to be used by children as a way to get them interested in taking pictures. Eastman called the camera a Brownie—named after illustrated characters then popular in magazines. About this time, he coined his famous advertising slogan: "You press the button, we do the rest."

Eastman opened a new plant in the 1890s, called Kodak Park, and avoided labor disputes by developing an industrial welfare program. He established an employee benefit fund of $500,000 in 1911 and founded a medical department and provided lunchroom facilities. In 1919, he sold 10,000 shares of Eastman stock at par to older employees—a gift worth $5 million. A few years later, he began a plan of retirement annuities, life insurance, and disability payments.

By World War I, Eastman had a virtual monopoly of the home photography industry and made an average profit of 171 percent on products sold. In 1915, a federal district court declared that the company had violated the Sherman Antitrust Act. Eastman, however, began selling some subsidiaries, and another court dismissed the case on appeal. Despite this collision with the federal government, Eastman firmly supported America's entry into World War I and provided plant space and staff for the effort. He refused excessive wartime profits and, as a result, returned more than $300,000 to the government.

In his later years, Eastman gave vast sums to various institutions, making him among the nation's top five philanthropists. His gifts included $50 million to the University of Rochester and $20 million to the Massachusetts Institute of Technology. Since he admired Booker T. Washington for advocating African-American self-education, he gave substantial sums to Hampton and Tuskegee Institutes. He founded the Eastman School of Music and the School of Medicine and Dentistry—both attached to the University of Rochester—and built the Eastman Theater, a state-of-the-art site for showing movies. In all, he gave over $100 million to society.

A private man who refused even company-sponsored biographies, Eastman had many friends and, although he never married, several romantic relationships. In his last months, however, he lived in seclusion. Overtaken by a degenerative condition of the spine, he committed suicide on March 14, 1932.

BIBLIOGRAPHY

Brayer, Elizabeth, *George Eastman: A Biography*, 1996.

Eaton, Cyrus

(December 27, 1883–May 9, 1979)
Financier

Cyrus Stephen Eaton built a multimillion-dollar empire that included railroads, utilities, and mining and steel corporations before losing most of his fortune in 1933. He gradually rebuilt his assets by again investing in mining and railroad operations through his investment banking firm, Otis and Company. While remaining a strong defender of the capitalist system, he devoted the latter part of his career to improving business relations between the United States and Communist bloc countries in Eastern Europe.

Descended from John Eaton who settled in Massachusetts in about 1640, Cyrus was born to Joseph Howe and Mary Adelle Eaton on December 27, 1883, in Pugwash, Nova Scotia. Cyrus studied at the Amherst Academy and then Woodstock College. At age 17, his desire to join the Baptist ministry led him to visit an uncle who was a minister in Cleveland, Ohio. His uncle arranged a clerical job for Cyrus at the estate of JOHN D. ROCKEFELLER, the wealthy oil magnate and Baptist parishioner. Cyrus later returned to Canada to attend McMaster University in Toronto and completed his B.A. degree in 1905.

After graduating, Eaton moved back to Ohio and began working as an adjuster for the East Ohio Gas Company. The financial Panic of 1907 wiped out many utility companies, and Eaton seized this opportunity to buy a small franchise and build a power plant with capital that he raised. That same year, he married Margaret House, eventually fathering seven children by her.

In 1912, he began an aggressive acquisition campaign to consolidate many electric and gas companies throughout the United States and Canada. This endeavor ultimately resulted in the formation of the Continental Gas and Electric Company of which Eaton was the chairman of the board of directors. In 1916, he became a partner in Otis and Company, a Cleveland investment bank, and continued to engineer mergers, including the formation of the United Light and Power Company in 1923, which combined the Continental Gas and Electric Company with three other utilities. In 1926, Eaton incorporated Continental Shares, a holding company, for his substantial investments in United Light and Power as well as his interests in rubber and steel companies.

His interest in the steel industry continued to grow in the late 1920s after he invested $18 million in the weakened Trumbull Steel Company. This company was merged with other steel acquisitions under the newly formed Republic Steel Corporation in 1930. Eaton joined with his fellow Cleveland financier W. G. Mather in 1929 to form the Cliffs Iron Corporation, which held six subsidiary iron and steel companies.

While forming his own conglomerates, Eaton contested a merger by two of his biggest competitors, Bethlehem Steel and Youngstown Sheet and Tube. He won the cause when the merger was declared illegal by the courts in 1931, but in the process, he lost most of his personal fortune, which he had pledged as collateral to Chase Manhattan Bank during the proceedings for his expenses.

In the next few years, Eaton began rebuilding his finances through his investment banking firm, Otis and Company. By 1942, Eaton was once again able to make an ambitious purchase. He paid $20,000 for the Steep Rock Iron Mines, which had enormous proven iron reserves under a deep lake in Canada. Since iron was in high demand during World War II, Eaton was able to secure a $5 million loan to drain the lake and begin mining the iron ore. The investment paid off handsomely as he had secured long-term agreements for the sale of the ore.

In 1945, under Eaton's direction, Otis and Company sponsored a $17 million stock offering for the Kaiser-Frazer Automobile Company. Eaton, however, withdrew any further financial support of a subsequent proposed stock offering in 1948 after one of the automobile company's main stockholders filed suit against it. This in turn led to a lawsuit for breach of contract by Kaiser-Frazer against Otis and Company. After a lengthy legal battle, which included an extensive investigation by the Securities and Exchange Commission, the matter was finally dropped due to lack of evidence and conflicts of interest within the commission.

As the cold war grew more serious in the 1950s, Eaton became an advocate of maintaining normal trade relations between the West and the Communist bloc countries of Eastern Europe. Beginning in the late 1950s, he frequently met with Communist Party officials, including Soviet Premier Nikita Khrushchev. For his efforts, Eaton was awarded the Lenin Peace Prize in 1960. Beginning in 1955, Eaton sponsored a series of annual conferences, called the Pugwash Conferences, to bring together scholars, scientists, and business leaders of the United States and the Soviet Union. He died at his home on Acadia Farm in Northfield, Ohio, on May 9, 1979.

BIBLIOGRAPHY

Business Week, June 15, 1946, and March 1, 1947; Gibson, M. Allen, *Beautiful upon the Mountains: A Portrait of Cyrus Eaton*, 1977; Gleisser, Marcus, *The World of Cyrus Eaton*, 1965.

Edison, Thomas

(February 11, 1847–October 18, 1931)
Inventor, Manufacturer

Known more as an inventor than a business leader, Thomas Alva Edison nonetheless used his laboratory to make practical inventions and turn a profit, and he formed numerous companies that made his work available to the public.

Born on February 11, 1847, in Milan, Ohio, the son of Samuel Edison and Nancy (Elliott) Edison, Thomas moved with his family to Port Huron, Michigan, in 1854, where his father owned various businesses, sold real estate and timber, operated a grocery store, and developed a prosperous truck farm. Thomas attended school only briefly—he disliked math and appeared in general to be a slow learner. He suffered, however, from a variable hearing loss, most likely a result of fluid retention in his inner ear, and this may have caused an attention deficit disorder. In any event, his mother educated him at home.

In his adolescence, Edison established a steady business selling newspapers, magazines, and candy on trains, while pursuing his interest in chemical experiments, even setting up a chemical laboratory in a baggage car. He read extensively and already showed the traits that characterized his later life: boundless energy with little need for sleep, an inquisitive mind, a concern with practicality, and an ability to engage in several projects at the same time.

In 1863, Edison worked as a telegraph operator while traveling through the Midwest, and his earliest inventions concerned telegraphy. Five years later, he joined the Western Union Telegraph

Thomas Edison (Library of Congress)

Company in Boston, Massachusetts, and in 1868 patented his first invention, a vote recorder that he tried, and failed, to get adopted by the U.S. House of Representatives. The following year, he moved to New York City and gained notice when he repaired a stock ticker for Laws's Gold Indicator Company. A short time later, he formed a partnership to create Edison & Company, described as an electrical engineering firm particularly dedicated to building telegraphic equipment.

After the Gold & Stock Telegraph Company bought Edison out in 1870, he used the $40,000 he had made from the deal to start his own laboratory and manufacturing business in Newark, New Jersey. He employed 50 workers, and they made perforators, transmitters, ink recorders, and typewriters designed for automatic telegraphy. In 1871, he met and married Mary Stillwell, a 16-year-old worker in his company; they subsequently had three children.

In 1874, Edison made quadruplex telegraphy possible, which allowed the sending of four messages simultaneously over the same wire. He also developed a telephonic transmitter that was capable of increased volume and a clearer sound, which improved on Alexander Graham Bell's telephone.

After establishing a new laboratory in Menlo Park, New Jersey, Edison invented in 1877 what many consider to be his finest piece of work, the phonograph. *Scientific American* declared:

A WONDERFUL INVENTION—SPEECH CAPABLE OF INDEFINITE REPETITION FROM AUTOMATIC RECORDS

Edison's phonograph used a tinfoil cylinder to reproduce sound, the harshness of which necessitated improvements that took 10 years to complete.

Next to the phonograph—and some observers say exceeding it in importance—was the incandescent lamp. Other inventors had previously worked with incandescent lamps, and many historians consider an Englishman to have been its inventor. Edison, however, applied numerous improvements that made it possible to produce the lamp cheaply and by 1882 was lighting his lamps from a power plant he had designed in New York City.

In 1887, Edison moved his laboratory from Menlo Park to West Orange, New Jersey, and in 1891 invented a kinetoscope camera, a "peep show" that produced moving pictures but without screen projection, which later came from an invention by Thomas Armat. Edison secured the patent for Armat's machine in 1895, made improvements to it, and promoted what he called Edison Vitascope. The latter move was a business one intended to meet growing competition in the market and make money. In fact, from the 1890s on, Edison established several commercial companies, although he always showed more interest in inventions. These companies were later consolidated into the Edison General Electric Company, forerunner to the General Electric Company.

By synchronizing his phonograph to moving pictures in 1913, Edison produced the first talking movie. Other inventions followed over the years, including a phonograph that used a disk rather than a cylinder, an electric pen, and a mimeograph machine. Edison invented by trial and error, and the businesses that he founded he set in motion and then left in the hands of others to manage.

Edison died on October 18, 1931, survived by his second wife Mina Miller (Mary Stilwell had died in 1884 and Edison remarried in 1886) and his three children. In describing his success, he once said: "The first step is intuition, and comes with a burst. It has been just so in all of my inventions."

BIBLIOGRAPHY

Baldwin, Neil, *Edison: Inventing the Century*, 1995; Clark, Ronald William, *Edison: The Man Who Made the Future*, 1977; Friedel, Robert D., *Edison's Electric Light: Biography of an Invention*, 1986; Josephson, Matthew, *Edison: A Biography*, 1959; Phillips, Ray, *Edison's Kinetoscope and Its Films: A History to 1896*, 1997; Wachhorst, Wyn, *Thomas Alva Edison: An American Myth*, 1981.

Eisner, Michael

(March 7, 1942–)
Entertainment Executive

After gaining a reputation for programming high-rated shows at ABC television and for developing hit movies at Paramount Pictures, Michael Eisner took a moribund Disney studios and created an enormously profitable company instrumental in shaping popular culture.

Michael was born on March 7, 1942, in Mt. Kisco, New York, to Lester Eisner and Margaret (Dammann) Eisner. His father had amassed a fortune as a lawyer and investor, and as a child, Eisner lived in a luxurious apartment in New York City. Soon after graduating from Denison College in Granville, Ohio, in 1964 (where he majored in English and theater), Eisner obtained a job in the mail room at NBC television. There followed several low-level jobs until he applied to Barry Diller (programmer at ABC television), who hired him as assistant to the national programming director in New York City. Known for his uncanny instinct in choosing television shows, Eisner advanced quickly and by 1968 worked as director of specials and talent. He revamped ABC's Saturday programming for children by introducing shows that featured animated versions of two popular singing groups, the Jackson Five and the Osmonds.

Under Fred Silverman (ABC's chief programmer), the network went from last place to first—a startling development owing to Eisner's work. He brought two hit daytime soap operas to ABC, *All My Children* and *One Life to Live*, and programmed several prime-time series that drew large audiences, notably *Hap-*

Michael Eisner (Saga/Archive Photos)

py Days, Welcome Back Kotter, Barney Miller, and *Starsky and Hutch.*

After Diller moved to Paramount Pictures in 1976 as its chairman, he hired Eisner as president. Together they emphasized producing movies at Paramount rather than making them elsewhere, as had been the case, and they analyzed scripts for their mass appeal. As a result, Paramount produced *Grease* and *Raiders of the Lost Ark*, both box-office hits, and the company's earnings climbed markedly.

In 1980, Eisner took a chance on *Airport!*, which spoofed disaster movies but had been rejected by several other studios. *Airport!* cost $6 million to make and earned $83 million. He followed this with *Footloose*, a box-office surprise in 1984.

That same year, Diller left Paramount, and Eisner stunned Hollywood when he, too, departed the studio and became chairman and CEO at the Walt Disney Company. Disney needed a boost—it had fallen on hard times as children deserted its movies for such action-oriented films as *Star Wars*, and its theme parks had stagnated. Eisner—a family man who was married to Jane Breckenridge and had three sons—wanted to return to his work with children's shows. His success at Paramount, where he had a reputation for enthusiasm, creativity, and demands, allowed him to join Disney as the highest-paid executive in the movie industry with an annual salary of $750,000, along with bonuses and stock options.

A year after his arrival, Eisner boosted Disney's net earnings by 75 percent—accomplished by reviving the company's movie and TV production. Under Eisner, Disney, for the first time, made movies intended primarily for adults, such as *Down and Out in Beverly Hills*; produced *Golden Girls* for television, along with two Saturday-morning cartoon series; and released old films and cartoons on videocassettes. There followed other R-rated movies, including *Ruthless People* and *The Color of Money* (which won for Paul Newman his first Academy Award).

Eisner also brought Disney's theme parks back to life, with a three-dimensional Michael Jackson video at Walt Disney World, along with a $300 million movie studio and a 50-acre water park.

As Disney prospered and its stock values soared, Eisner reaped considerable wealth. Movie hits in the 1990s such as *The Lion King*, *Pocahontas*, and *The Mighty Ducks*, along with *Home Improvement* on television, made Disney a $10 billion giant. One magazine declared: "If Disney is today an icon of American culture, a lion king's share of the credit goes to Eisner."

In 1994, however, Eisner suffered a heart attack and underwent triple bypass surgery. His illness sent Disney into turmoil and raised questions as to whether he would return. He did—and with renewed energy put the Euro Disney theme park in the black by cutting costs and attracting additional investors. Then, in 1995, he surprised many when Disney bought Capital Cities/ABC for $25.8 billion, a move that created one of the largest entertainment and information companies in the world. Eisner told a reporter: "Finding a partner was like shopping for a house. All of a sudden you come upon the place that just makes sense."

In 1997, Eisner optioned stocks that brought him $131 million after taxes. Many Disney shareholders, meanwhile, balked at his new 10-year contract worth several hundred million dollars. The complainants called it extravagant, but Eisner's defenders said he deserved the money for having made Disney a financial and cultural giant.

BIBLIOGRAPHY

Taylor, John, *Storming the Magic Kingdom*, 1987.

Fairbanks, Erastus

(October 28, 1792–November 20, 1864)
Manufacturer

A manufacturer of farm implements and equipment, Erastus Fairbanks is chiefly known for his business expertise in the marketing and manufacture of his brother's invention of a highly popular platform scale. He is also notable for his tenure as governor of Vermont in the 1850s.

Erastus Fairbanks, the oldest son of Maj. Joseph and Phebe Paddock Fairbanks, was born in Brimfield, Massachusetts, on October 28, 1792. In 1815, Erastus moved to St. Johnsbury, Vermont, with his parents and two brothers. All three boys had a mechanical aptitude that proved useful to their father when he opened a saw and grist mill. Shortly thereafter, Erastus and brothers, Thaddeus and Joseph, built a foundry and wheelwright shop.

After the move to Vermont, Erastus married Lois C. Crossman, with whom he had eight children. The business flourished, and the wheelwright shop expanded to include the manufacture of stoves, plows, and agricultural devices. By 1823, Erastus and Thaddeus had founded E. T. Fairbanks and Company. While Joseph continued to work with his brothers, the company, as reflected by the name, was formed on the strength of the business acumen of Erastus and the mechanical ingenuity of Thaddeus.

The firm began to build machinery used by the hemp industry. After observing that there was no mechanism for weighing the wagon loads of raw material brought into town, Thaddeus invented a device to lift the wagon and thus determine the approximate weight of the load.

Though this method was an improvement over previous weighing practices, it was still imprecise. By 1830, Thaddeus had devised a more accurate design for a simple platform scale.

After Thaddeus secured a patent, Erastus, as chief executive of the firm, applied himself to the task of marketing their new device. The respective skills of the Fairbanks brothers boded well for success. Thaddeus was eventually awarded 32 patents for different types of scales. The original platform scale was extremely popular, and through Erastus Fairbanks's astute sales abilities, became known worldwide. Under Erastus's direction, the volume of the company's business doubled every year between 1842 and 1857.

Growth slowed after 1857 as the country suffered an industrial depression, but picked up rapidly again during the Civil War. The firm continued to grow and was run as a family partnership until 1874, when the Fairbanks brothers incorporated it as the Fairbanks Scale Company.

Erastus was an active man outside of his business interests. He was a devout member of the Congregational Church and a generous benefactor of the city of St. Johnsbury. His primary outside interest, however, was politics. After holding several elected positions, including a term as a representative in the Vermont legislature, Erastus was elected governor of Vermont in 1852 as a member of the newly formed Republican Party.

As governor, Erastus's priorities were education and social welfare, including temperance. His fervent support for a state prohibition law, in contrast to the sentiments of most of Vermont's citizenry, resulted in the failure of his reelection bid for a second term. In 1856, he ran for governor again under the banner of the Republican Party and was elected in a landslide vote. During his second term, he organized Vermont's support for the Union cause in the Civil War and even pledged the credit of his company for the purchase of militia equipment.

Fairbanks was a hard worker, devoting long hours to public office and his business. He died on November 20, 1864.

BIBLIOGRAPHY

Dictionary of American Biography, vol. III, 1964; Fairbanks, E. T., *The Town of St. Johnsbury, Vt.*, 1914; Fairbanks, L. S., *Genealogy of the Fairbanks Family in America*, 1897; Goodell, C. L., *Congressional Quarterly*, 1867.

Faneuil, Peter

(June 20, 1700–March 3, 1743)
Merchant

With money inherited from his uncle, Peter Faneuil accumulated a fortune as a leading early American merchant.

Peter Faneuil (Archive Photos)

Peter was born on June 20, 1700, in New Rochelle, New York, to Benjamin Faneuil and Anne (Bureau) Faneuil. When his father died in 1718, Peter moved to Boston, where his uncle Andrew had prospered as a merchant. Peter worked for his uncle and made his own investments. Andrew, a childless widower, promised that upon his death Peter would inherit his fortune—provided the young man never marry. Peter abided by this request, and when Andrew died in 1738, Peter inherited one of the largest fortunes in the North American colonies.

Faneuil continued as a merchant and owned several ships. He believed that Boston needed a public market place and offered to donate one to the town. Bostonians, divided on the issue, debated the proposal before accepting it by a margin of just seven votes at a town meeting in July 1740. Faneuil died on March 3, 1743, shortly before the building was completed. Since then Faneuil Hall—nearly totally destroyed by fire in 1763 and then re-built—has maintained a prominent place in history as the site of meetings leading to the American Revolution.

BIBLIOGRAPHY

Brown, A. E., *Faneuil Hall and Faneuil Market*, 1900.

Field, Cyrus

(November 30, 1819–July 12, 1892)
Merchant, Communications Executive

Doubters scoffed at Cyrus Field. How, in the 1850s, could he possibly lay a cable across the Atlantic Ocean from Newfoundland to Ireland? But Field did, and made rapid communication between two continents possible.

Born on November 30, 1819, in Stockbridge, Massachusetts, to Dudley Field and Submit (Dickinson) Field, Cyrus was raised in a family still attached to Puritan values. At age 15, he got permission from his father to leave Stockbridge for New York City. There he worked as an errand boy in a dry-goods store. In 1837, he quit the store and returned to Massachusetts, where he assisted his brother as a paper manufacturer before opening his own papermaking company in the town of Westfield. Soon after, he joined E. Root & Company, wholesale paper dealers in New York City, as a partner. He married Mary Bryan Stone in 1840, and over the years, they had several children.

Disaster struck, however, when in 1841 E. Root & Company failed, and the collapse left Field heavily in debt. With a partner, he founded Cyrus W. Field & Company and worked hard to pay his creditors. Finally, in 1849, he accumulated enough wealth to retire from his business.

The always energetic Field, however, sought new outlets, and after a Canadian engineer told him of plans to install a telegraph line across Newfoundland, he took the idea further and proposed laying a line from Newfoundland to Ireland. Others had previously raised the possibility, but Field took action and obtained capital from New York business leaders, particularly the wealthy banker Moses Taylor. The American and British governments both helped Field by providing ships for the project.

Workers started laying the cable in 1857, but on several occasions it broke. Finally, the cable was completed in August 1858, and Britain's Queen Victoria used it to send a message to U.S. President James Buchanan. Then, suddenly, the cable failed, perhaps due to poor insulation. Field's critics pilloried him, but he renewed his project the following year. After several more failures, Field achieved success in 1866, and in 1867 Congress voted him a commemorative gold medal.

Field invested in several other enterprises, among then the New York City elevated railway system. His financial support enabled the city to complete the

Cyrus Field (Library of Congress)

system. In his later years, however, he suffered severe financial reverses. Field died on July 12, 1892.

BIBLIOGRAPHY

McDonald, Philip B., *A Saga of the Seas: The Story of Cyrus W. Field and the Laying of the First Atlantic Cable*, 1937.

Field, Marshall

(August 18, 1834–January 16, 1906)
Merchant

Marshall Field, a merchant, built what one observer called the "Cathedral of All the Stores"— a magnificent structure dedicated to providing quality goods and courteous service. One day, while walking through his dry-goods store, Field encountered an employee arguing with a female customer. Perturbed, Field asked him, "What are you doing here?" "I am settling a complaint," was the reply. "No you're not," responded Field. "Give the lady what she wants."

Born on August 18, 1834, to John and Fidelia (Nash) Field on the family farm near Conway, Massachusetts, Marshall left school at age 17 to clerk at a dry-goods store in nearby Pittsfield. For five years, he worked 10 hours a day, six days a week, and earned a reputation for courteous behavior, especially toward women. In his diligence, he went so far as to keep a notebook that listed his customers' preferences.

Attracted by the expansive West, in 1856 he moved to Chicago, where he clerked at Cooley, Wadsworth & Company, the city's largest dry-goods store. He earned $400 per year, of which he saved half by sleeping at the store and keeping his expenses minimal. From time to time, Field traveled as a salesman and in this line perceived opportunities for business expansion. Before long, he earned junior partnership in what was then called Cooley & Farwell and ascended to full partnership in 1861. Cooley soon withdrew from the business, and Field took in Levi Leiter as a partner. Field's personal life underwent change in 1863, when he married Nannie Scott.

Marshall Field (Library of Congress)

At this point, POTTER PALMER shaped Field's direction. Palmer had opened a dry-goods store in Chicago noted for its appeal to women through a pleasant atmosphere in which he sold shawls, laces, cloaks, and similar items. In 1865, he decided to sell his store to Field while maintaining an interest in it, thus creating Field, Palmer & Leiter. This arrangement continued until 1867, when Palmer withdrew and Field brought in his brothers, Henry and Joseph, as junior partners.

The firm, now called Field, Leiter & Company, grew as Field appealed primarily to women by offering quality merchandise at a reasonable price, coupled with courteous service. He said, "The best way to show a lady the merchandise she purchased is worth the dollar she paid for it is to give her the dollar in return." His goods-on-approval policy guaranteed that a customer could bring back any item for nearly any reason and obtain a full refund.

In 1868, Field opened a store on State Street—a massive, marble structure whose first floor had walnut counters and frescoed walls, and housed, among other items, silks, satins, and sable-trimmed cloaks. Around 1870, he opened offices overseas to buy the best goods available.

Tragedy struck in 1871, however, when the Chicago fire destroyed Field's store. Convinced that he must be the first to meet what he expected to be a strong postfire demand for goods, Fields quickly reopened in a renovated brick barn. By 1872, he had moved again to State Street, but misfortune repeated itself when another fire burned down the store. Once more he used temporary quarters and then in 1879 opened a new store. Fields expanded his policy of buying goods first and creating a demand later—a move that allowed him to undersell his competitors who usually waited for demand to build and then had to buy items at higher prices. Additionally, he began manufacturing many of the items sold in his store.

Leiter left the firm in 1881 over policy differences with Field, and the business carried the name Marshall Field & Company. Field maintained his policy of paying low wages while providing customers with rich surroundings, but he opened a bargain basement as well. Once again focussing on his largest clientele, the ladies, Fields also opened a tearoom.

Always aloof, Field participated in few community activities, but he gave 10 acres of land as a site for the new University of Chicago, and donated money to the school. In addition, he built a library for his hometown of Conway. His wife having died in 1896, Field married Delia Spencer Canton in 1905. He died from pneumonia on January 16, 1906. Most of his considerable estate, valued between $100 and $150 million, was held in trust for his grandchildren, although he provided $8 million in his will for the Field Museum of Natural History, built in Grant Park.

Today, Marshall Field & Company carries the name Marshall Field's, part of the Department Store Division of the Dayton Hudson Corporation, the nation's fourth largest general merchandise retailer. Marshall Field's stores are located in Illinois, Ohio, Wisconsin, and Texas.

BIBLIOGRAPHY

Tebbel, John William, *The Marshall Fields: A Study in Wealth*, 1947; Wendt, Lloyd, *Give the Lady What She Wants! . . . The Story of Marshall Field & Company*, 1952.

Fields, Debbi

(August 18, 1956–)
Manufacturer

"Someday it might happen that you'll find yourself in a shopping mall somewhere, strolling by a Mrs. Fields Cookies store, and there you may observe . . . a funny little group of people singing away," said Debbi Fields. "That odd group will include me . . . plus the staff of the store . . . and we'll all be wearing red aprons, and we'll be singing at the top of our lungs: Chippity doo-dah, chippity-ay, My, oh my, what a wonderful day. . . . I'm not teaching everybody in the group how to sing. . . . I'm teaching them that you *can* make excitement. . . ." On this feel-good philosophy, Fields founded a cookie store chain ubiquitous in the shopping malls that dominated modern suburban America.

Fields was born Debra Jane Sivyer on August 18, 1956, in East Oakland, California. She grew up in a working-class environment—her father worked as a welder at the U.S. naval base in Alameda, and she attended parochial school and Alameda High School. As a teenager, Fields held various odd jobs, including ball girl for the Oakland Athletics baseball team, a clerk at a department store, and a water-skier at Marine World amusement park.

After graduating from high school, she took a few classes at a community college but felt adrift until she met Randy Fields, who owned a financial management business. They married in 1975, and Debbi settled in as a housewife. Among her activities, she enjoyed making chocolate-chip cookies for her husband and their guests, all of whom raved about them. She had been baking cook-

ies ever since she was a girl, like many Americans using the Toll House recipe that Ruth Wakefield had developed in 1930. Debbi, however, used ingredients different from those used by other bakers (such as butter in place of margarine), made the cookies bigger than standard-sized ones, and made them chewy rather than crispy.

In 1977, Fields asked her husband to support her in opening a cookie store. She reached this decision, she said, after grappling with the question of what to do with her life. She claimed: "I needed to share something of myself with the world. I wanted to give, to be a part of things. . . . And what I happened to have available for giving was a pretty darn good chocolate-chip cookie."

She opened her first store as Mrs. Fields Chocolate Chippery on August 13, 1977, at Liddicoat's Market, an old grocery store in Palo Alto recently converted into an arcade. Many predicted her failure—either insisting that consumers preferred crisp to soft cookies or declaring that a cookie store could never turn enough profit to make the effort worthwhile. On the first day, it seemed as if the critics were right. She had no customers in the morning, and the few who came in the afternoon did so because she had stood outside on the street, giving away free samples. That tactic, however, proved a boon, and word spread quickly about her great-tasting cookies.

With the success of her first store, Fields decided in 1978 to open a second one, and from there, a chain developed. She insisted on using the best available ingredients, even if it meant a higher-priced product, and trained her employees to realize they were selling more than a cookie—they were selling a good feeling. Randy Fields's financial acumen played a crucial role in her success (he served as the chairman of the board), as did his development of a computer system to closely monitor each store's volume, a practice that enabled the managers to know with precision the quantity of cookies that needed to be baked each day.

As the business expanded, Debbi Fields developed 14 different cookies, including pecan whites, milk chocolate, oatmeal raisin nut, raisin spice, and royal pecan. She introduced brownies to the product line, along with ice cream and candy. In 1990, she began franchising her stores.

By 1997, Mrs. Fields Cookies had more than 650 stores in the United States, located largely in or near malls to take advantage of upscale customers willing to enliven their shopping by spending more for a cookie than they would, say, in a grocery store. In this way Fields capitalized on the widespread desire for items that reminded people of simpler times, and she reflected the "mallization" of America with its emphasis on convenience and trendiness over price.

BIBLIOGRAPHY

Fields, Debbi, *One Smart Cookie*, 1987.

Firestone, Harvey

(December 20, 1868–February 6, 1938)
Manufacturer

At the time America changed from horse-drawn carriages to automobiles, Harvey Firestone developed rubber tires needed to make the new transportation more comfortable and safer.

Harvey was born on December 20, 1868, to Benjamin Firestone and Catherine (Flickinger) Firestone on a farm near Columbiana, Ohio. His father had a prosperous, 148-acre spread, where he raised sheep and grew some wheat. Harvey worked on the farm and attended Columbiana High School. After he graduated in 1887, he enrolled in a three-month bookkeeping and penmanship course at Spencerian Business College in Cleveland.

Several jobs followed. In January 1888, Firestone began work as a bookkeeper at a coal company in Columbus, earning $30 a month. He wanted to get into sales, however, and so that fall, he traveled from town to town hawking patent medicines and notions. When the company he worked for failed, he returned to Columbus and worked in his cousin's buggy shop. At first he kept the books, but then he sold buggies and discovered that customers liked one whose rubber-padded wheels cushioned the ride.

This company, too, went out of business, and in 1896 Firestone decided he wanted his own firm, where he could make and sell the rubber tires he admired. At this time, several companies made rubber tires for bicycles, but few produced them for buggies. In a partnership with others, he bought an old rubber tire shop in Chicago that in January 1898 he renamed the Firestone Company. In a few short months, he sold out to a competitor for a substantial profit.

Firestone longed to resume his business career, however, and explored possibilities in Akron, a town already called Rubber City. By this time, B. F. GOODRICH and the Diamond Company were making rubber tires in small quantities for a new invention: the automobile. Firestone moved with his family—he had married Idabelle Smith in 1895—to Akron in 1900 and arranged for the Whitman & Barnes Company to manufacture his type of rubber tire on a royalty basis.

Firestone then visited James A. Swinehart, who had invented an improved tire, one that held firmly to the rim by using steel rods embedded crosswise at intervals and wire hoops that sprung inside the rim's edges. Firestone liked what he saw, and the two men reached an agreement that, on August 3, 1900, began the Firestone Tire & Rubber Company. At first, Firestone bought the finished rubber that he used in his product from suppliers. In January 1903, however, the small factory on Sweitzer Avenue began making its tires from scratch for both light and heavy vehicles.

Firestone obtained orders from many concerns, including cab and delivery truck companies in Chicago, fire departments in New York City, and Anheuser-Busch Brewery in St. Louis, which used his tires on its five-ton beer trucks. In 1905, HENRY FORD catapulted Firestone forward when he ordered 2,000 sets of tires for the cars made in his factory.

Harvey Firestone (Library of Congress)

By 1906, Firestone's sales reached the million-dollar mark. In the 1930s, Firestone waged a successful legal battle to prevent U.S. Rubber from collecting royalties on a production process used by his company.

By the time Firestone died on February 6, 1938, Firestone Tire had 40,000 employees, 32 subsidiaries, and owned large rubber plantations in Liberia. Firestone Tire made supplies for the U.S. military during World War II, and after the war, Harvey Firestone Jr. (the company's president and, later, chairman) oversaw Firestone Tire's enormous retail store expansion.

BIBLIOGRAPHY

Lief, Alfred, *Harvey Firestone: Free Man of Enterprise*, 1951.

Fisher, Donald

(1928–)
Merchant

With his Gap and Banana Republic stores, Donald Fisher set the jeans and clothing industry on end, forcing staid department stores to change their consumer appeal.

Born in San Francisco, California, in 1928, Fisher graduated from the University of California, Berkeley, in 1950 with a degree in business and finance, and over the years operated several different enterprises. He worked as a building contractor and real estate developer, and also owned a franchise that sold ice to gas stations. According to Fisher's account, the idea for the Gap developed in the late 1960s, when he searched in vain for a pair of jeans that could fit him. He had a common frame: 6-foot, 1-inch tall with a 34-inch waist, but the department stores that he visited were poorly stocked and disorganized. He told his wife, Doris (Feigenbaum) Fisher, about his problem, and together they started a store that sold mainly jeans and records, with a wide selection of jean sizes, all neatly arranged. (They stopped selling records after three months.)

The Gap began in California and by the early 1970s had expanded to other states and offered a wider variety of clothes. Fisher faced a challenge, however, when jeans sales proliferated in department stores and other specialty shops. He then recruited Millard S. Drexler, known as an outstanding merchandiser, to help. Drexler put the entire product line except Levi's jeans under the Gap label.

By 1983, Fisher had 550 Gap stores, and that same year, he acquired Banana Republic, a two-store chain with a popular catalog business. He diversified the store's line of travel and safari wear, and added private-label items. Three years later, after Drexler on a family outing found it difficult to buy comfortable children's clothing, Fisher opened his first GapKids store. In 1987, he opened the first Gap outside the United States, in London, leading to the formation of the Gap International division. In 1994, the Gap began its newest division, the Old Navy Clothing Company, a value-priced outlet.

Although Fisher, who has three children, became a billionaire, he neither acted pretentious nor flaunted his wealth. In 1995, he and other business leaders founded the San Francisco Partnership to attract businesses to that city. In 1997, the Gap, with more than 1,750 stores, reported an increase of 23 percent in sales from the preceding year, with net earnings up 18 percent to nearly $554 million.

BIBLIOGRAPHY

Smith, Sarah, "The Supermen of Specialty Stores," *Fortune*, October 12, 1987.

Fisher, Herman

(November 2, 1898–September 26, 1975)
Manufacturer

Ducks quacked and beaks moved —toy ducks that Herman Guy Fisher made from ponderosa pine delighted kids and contributed to the growth of Fisher-Price as a company known for its ingenious, durable products.

Fisher was born on November 2, 1898, in Unionville, Pennsylvania, graduated from the University of Pennsylvania in 1921, and then worked for a bond company in New York City and later in Rochester, New York. By 1926, he so disliked dealing with bonds that he went into advertising for Alderman-Richardson, a company that made paper boxes and a few toys. The latter intrigued him, and he decided to make his career in toys. He worked for a while as vice president of All Fair, a toy and game manufacturer, and then met Irving Price, who served on the school board at East Aurora, New York, and was trying to attract new businesses to the town.

With Price's help and with that of Helen Schelle (the former operator of a toy store), Fisher founded the Fisher-Price Toy Company in 1930 amid the Great Depression. Fisher and his two partners had little money, and the economic hard times made their enterprise a struggle. They raised funds, however, from local businesses and paid workers in stock shares that they said would eventually turn a profit.

Fisher insisted on making his toys from solid ponderosa pine so that they would not splinter. He also insisted on making action toys that kids would find fun, and he aimed them at toddlers and those slightly older, who he believed would benefit from manipulating the toys. Rolling push toys, for example, encouraged toddlers to walk and to use their leg and arm muscles.

Fisher-Price struggled for several years and made little money but gradually earned a reputation for producing quality toys that amused, educated, and engaged children. Then, in 1938, the company designed Snoopy Sniffer, a floppy-eared spotted dog toy that, when pulled, wagged its tail and went woof. Snoopy Sniffer sold so well it made Fisher-Price a major toy company.

Fisher followed Snoopy Sniffer with Timmy Turtle, a Teddy Bear that played a xylophone, and a mama duck that waddled with three ducklings alongside her. Fisher obtained the rights to make toys using Disney characters, and by World War II, the company's annual sales topped $1.5 million.

After the war, Fisher-Price benefited from a baby boom and economic prosperity. As sales expanded, the company decided to replace ponderosa pine with plastic, but in keeping with its concern for quality, it used only high-impact plastic that would resist breakage. In 1957, Fisher-Price bought Trimold, the company that made the plastic.

Soon after Price retired from the company in 1965, Fisher relinquished the presidency but continued to serve as chairman of the board. He hired Henry Coords as the new president and CEO, and in 1968 they opened a nursery school in the firm's research and development building, enabling them to study how children reacted to toys. About Fisher-

Price, one analyst commented, "If children discard a toy after one session of play, it is not right. Before a new toy is put in the market, it must have demonstrated high and persistent entertainment value."

The company kept its focus on toys for preschoolers and in doing so aimed most of its advertisements at parents, all the while stressing enrichment and quality. The tact differed markedly from other toy companies that appealed directly to the kids and usually considered any mention of enrichment or education a sure way to lose sales. Only Playskool, owned by MILTON BRADLEY, offered Fisher-Price any serious competition in preschool toys.

Quaker Oats (the cereal company) bought Fisher-Price in 1969, at which time Fisher retired from the firm. He died on September 26, 1975. With the massive advertising budget provided by Quaker Oats and by deciding to leave electronic and video games to other companies while sticking to its niche, Fisher-Price enjoyed explosive growth. In the mid-1980s, annual sales reached $353 million. In 1993, Fisher-Price became a division of Mattel, the toy company founded by ELLIOT HANDLER.

BIBLIOGRAPHY

Fucini, Joseph J., and Suzy Fucini, *Entrepreneurs: The Men and Women behind Famous Brand Names and How They Made It*, 1965; McClintock, Inez, and Marshall McClintock, *Toys in America*, 1961.

Fisk, Jim

(April 1, 1834–January 7, 1872)
Financier

James Fisk swaggered across America's industrial landscape as a daring and unscrupulous speculator who laid to waste anything that did not contribute to his wealth.

Born in Bennington, Vermont, on April 1, 1834, to James Fisk and Love (Ryan) Fisk, Jim received little schooling and held numerous odd jobs—as a waiter, a ticket seller at a circus, and as a salesman for his father's "traveling emporium." He moved to Boston in 1860 and worked for Jordan & Marsh, a merchant company, first in its wholesale department and then as manager of its Civil War contracts, which he handled on a commission basis. He later worked for a Boston syndicate and bought cotton from planters in the South's occupied zones. Fisk made enough money from that venture to begin his own business as a dry-goods jobber (buying products from manufacturers and selling them to retailers) and to open his own brokerage office in New York City. A postwar depression, however, ruined him.

Seeking to recoup his losses, Fisk teamed with DANIEL DREW and, with the latter's backing, opened a new brokerage house in 1866. By this time, America stood ready for industrial expansion, a development that relied on the growth of railroads, the iron skeleton that brought shape and life to the era. The brash Fisk was determined to exploit the railroads, indeed the entire economy, to become wealthy. He, Drew, and JAY GOULD, known as the "Erie Gang," acquired the Erie Railroad in New York and through stock manipulations defeated an attempt by CORNELIUS VANDERBILT to control the line. Fisk and Gould subsequently dominated the Erie, and issued and sold more stock in it. From their proceeds, they made some improvements to the railroad, but they used their profits largely to engage in speculation.

In 1869, the Erie Gang tried to corner the market on gold by buying up reserves and trying to force its price up. Although President Ulysses S. Grant foiled them when he ordered the federal treasury to sell government gold deposits, the speculators exited the market before it plunged downward. Others, however, failed to do so, and the Erie Gang's escapade ruined many investors while damaging the national economy. Without a doubt, many people hated Fisk after the financial debacle that became known as Black Friday.

Nothing stopped Fisk's lavish spending, however, and he bought an opera house in New York City and launched the *James Fisk*, the largest ferryboat to ply

Jim Fisk (Corbis)

the Hudson River—a floating monument to his wealth. Although Fisk had married Lucy D. Moore in 1855, he had several mistresses, and a quarrel with Edward Stokes over one of them, the actress Josie Mansfield, resulted in Stokes shooting him on January 6, 1872. Fisk died the next day.

BIBLIOGRAPHY

Ackerman, Kenneth D., *The Gold Ring: Jim Fisk, Jay Gould and Black Friday, 1869*, 1988; Swanberg, W. A., *Jim Fisk: The Career of an Impossible Rascal*, 1959.

Fitzhugh, William

(ca. January 10, 1651–October 1701)
Planter

William Fitzhugh, an Englishman by birth, was one of the foremost businessmen in Virginia in the seventeenth century. He was a successful merchant, planter, and lawyer, and was active in colonial militia and legislative activities.

The son of Henry Fitzhugh, a barrister-at-law, William Fitzhugh was born in Bedford, England. The exact date of his birth is not known, but according to parish records, he was baptized on January 10, 1651. Details regarding his early life in England remain obscure, but it is likely that the young Fitzhugh received a quality education, probably receiving his training in law in his father's offices.

In 1670, Fitzhugh moved to Stafford County, Virginia, where he purchased property and established himself as a planter and exporter. He proved to have an aptitude for both activities, becoming a successful merchant and maintaining high agricultural yields.

Fitzhugh also quickly gained prominence as a lawyer. In 1682, he was the defense counsel for a notable legal case of the era. Maj. Robert Beverley, who served as the clerk for the Virginia House of Burgesses, had been arrested after incurring the wrath of the governor by refusing to provide him with copies of legislative journals without the permission of the members of the House. Though Fitzhugh was unable to acquit his client, his writings on Beverley's behalf demonstrate an astute knowledge of law that is in keeping with his reputation.

On May 1, 1674, Fitzhugh married Sarah Tucker. While there is little information available about the couple's children, it is known that his granddaughter Sarah became the wife of Edward Barradall, attorney general of Virginia in the eighteenth century.

Fitzhugh, active in the county militia, served in 1687 as lieutenant-colonel in command of a force that fought against the Seneca Indians. He continued to devote his extra time to addressing Virginia's legislative needs. In 1692, he sent a manuscript he had prepared of Virginia's laws to England for publication. He was unsuccessful in his aspirations, and the manuscript has not survived.

Though little is known about Fitzhugh's personality or family life, his prolific correspondence reveals that his mercantile and agricultural interests and success were central to his life. He died in Stafford County, Virginia, sometime in October 1701.

BIBLIOGRAPHY

Fitzhugh, William, *Letters of William Fitzhugh, 1679–99*, 1899; "The Fitzhugh Family," *Virginia Magazine of History and Biography*, October 1899; MacIlwaine, H. R., ed., *Journals of the House of Burgesses of Virginia*, 1659–1693.

Flagler, Henry

(January 2, 1830–May 20, 1913)
Real Estate Developer, Railroad Executive

From the oil that seeped through rocks, Henry Flagler built an industry; from the palmettos that dotted the Florida peninsula, he built a state.

Born in Hopewell, New York, on January 2, 1830, to Isaac Flagler, an itinerant Presbyterian minister, and Elizabeth (Morrison) Flagler, Henry grew up in poverty. At age 14, he left school, struck out on his own, and obtained a job at a country store in Republic, Ohio, where he worked for $5 a month plus board and earned a reputation for salesmanship. After a brief residency in Fostoria, Ohio, Henry moved to Bellevue and began his own business as a grain merchant. He made a fortuitous acquaintance there when he sold some grain through another business neophyte, JOHN D. ROCKEFELLER. After accumulating $50,000, Flagler moved to Saginaw, Michigan, in 1863 and began a salt manufactory, Flagler & York. At first, the business prospered, but when the Civil War ended in 1865 and salt prices collapsed, so too did the company.

With this setback and with little money in his pocket, Flagler moved to Cleveland, Ohio, and once again worked as a grain merchant. Rockefeller had preceded Flagler to the city and had recently entered the oil industry. Oil had for many years seeped through the earth's surface and into springs and streams in the area. Farmers considered it a nuisance for ruining water and land. After the Civil War, however, America's burgeoning industries demanded oil as a lubricant and later as a fuel. Rockefeller met the demand by establishing a refining company, Rockefeller & Andrews.

After one of Rockefeller's leading investors insisted that Flagler be brought in, the company changed its name to Rockefeller, Andrews & Flagler. Flagler, a quiet man known for his ruthless strategies, stood second only to Rockefeller in power and led the firm in its remarkable expansion. By 1869, the company's refineries had the largest capacity in the world at 1,500 barrels per day. The following year, it incorporated as the Standard Oil Company, and by the end of the decade, it controlled nearly the entire oil business.

Flagler, however, had tired of the business, and at the same time his wife, Mary Harkness, whom he had married in 1853 and by whom he had three children, fell seriously ill. Doctors advised that Flagler take Mary to Florida for sunshine and warmth, and in 1883 they headed south. He found the most primitive state in the nation. Florida had few hotels and no decent transportation; cypress, pine, live-oak, palmetto, and exotic wildlife dominated the peninsula, where the interior remained devoid of white settlers; and the coasts and adjacent sea supported only a scattering of fishing villages.

Although his wife soon died, Flagler grew enchanted with Florida and began investing heavily—partly to make money but partly to distance himself from Standard Oil. Thus, while he remained vice president of Standard until 1908 and served on its board until 1911, his projects in Florida absorbed him. Flagler bought the Jacksonville, St. Augustine &

Halifax River Railroad in 1886, combined it with several smaller lines, improved them, and created the Florida East Coast Railway (FEC). In 1892, he began extending his railroad southward and in 1896 reached Miami—then only a clearing. Along the line, he built such palatial hotels as the Ponce de Leon and Alcazar in St. Augustine, the Breakers and the Royal Poinciana (the world's largest wooden building with 1,150 rooms) in Palm Beach, and the Royal Palm in Miami—all of which served as winter refuges for the wealthy.

Flagler then undertook a daring extension, taking the FEC to Key West. Over 4,000 workers labored at laying track through the Everglades and for 106 miles across the string of islands known as the Florida Keys—filling in shallow water and building viaducts, bridges, and drawbridges. One bridge extended 7 miles. The obstacles and difficulties seemed incredible, and the sites stunning. "The mosquitoes on this key are almost unbearable," said one participant, "and the problem is to persuade the laborers not to run away, for it means certain death as there is no possible outlet to the mainland."

While construction continued, a stunning development unsettled Flagler's personal life when his second wife, Ida A. Shourds, went insane. After obtaining a divorce from her in 1901, he married Mary Lily Kenan.

Flagler's railroad reached Key West in 1913 and shortened travel to Cuba, since ferries could take freight cars to there. A massive hurricane destroyed the Keys extension in 1935, although it was later rebuilt.

All told, Flagler, who died on May 20, 1913, invested more than $40 million in Florida and laid the foundation for the state to develop into a tourist mecca. He built schools, churches, and hospitals—requesting that his donations remain anonymous—and helped the needy when severe freezes damaged the state's citrus crop. A powerful man, he considered Florida his domain, and many there considered him their savior. One of his biographers claimed that "No one in American history, with the possible exception of Brigham Young, has been so singly responsible for the creation of a state."

BIBLIOGRAPHY

Akin, Edward N., *Flagler: Rockefeller Partner and Florida Baron*, 1992; Chandler, David, *Henry Flagler: The Astonishing Life and Times of the Visionary Robber Baron Who Founded Florida*, 1986.

Flint, Charles

(January 24, 1850–February 12, 1934)
Financier

The style of Charles Ranlett Flint, an enthusiastic and energetic financier, seemed to bear a closer resemblance to the corporate raiders of the 1980s and 1990s than Flint's entrepreneurial contemporaries who epitomized the late nineteenth and early twentieth centuries. Dubbed the "Father of Trusts," Flint's business focus was to facilitate the merger of industrial units into larger conglomerates. His role of intermediary played out, to varying degrees of success, in such diverse arenas as the supply of munitions and transport equipment to foreign governments and the union of various crude rubber producers and merchants. Flint was also an avid participant in the politics of Latin America, serving as the representative in the United States of the governments of Chile, Nicaragua, and Costa Rica.

Born in Thomaston, Maine, on January 24, 1850, Charles was the son of Benjamin Flint, a shipbuilder, and Sarah Tobey Flint. In 1856, three years after Sarah's death, Benjamin moved the family to Brooklyn, New York, where he became a partner at Chapman & Flint, a shipping firm. Though Charles was young when he relocated from rural Maine to the bustling town of Brooklyn, he had developed an enduring love of the wilderness and would remain an avid outdoorsman all his life. At the Brooklyn Polytechnic Institute, from which he graduated in 1868, Charles acquired a new love— engineering.

This pursuit proved to be short-lived; Flint's childhood amid sailors and shipbuilders had left an impression, and for his first job Flint went to work as a clerk for the New York City docks. In 1871, Flint became a partner in the Gilchrist, Flint & Company ship chandlery. A year later, he was a new partner of W. R. Grave & Company, a prominent commission firm that dealt in South American trade. He remained a partner in both ventures until 1879.

Flint was an extremely active and ambitious man, always engaged in diverse activities that sometimes appeared to conflict. For instance, from 1876 until 1879, he served as the Chilean consul in New York, during which time his mercantile company was a financial agent for the government of Peru. This became complicated in 1879 when Peru and Chile engaged in war. Flint resigned his consulship, but actively continued to supply military equipment to Peru.

After 1879, Flint decided to shed partnership affiliations and become a freelance business agent. By 1880, he had become the president of the United States Electric Company, where he attempted to use his authority to arrange for the merger of the light and power interests of THOMAS EDISON and C. F. Brush. Flint believed his failure in this endeavor could be attributed to his being directly vested in the outcome rather than acting as, in his words, a "disinterested intermediary." Amid this turbulent phase of his business career, Flint was married on November 21, 1883, to a musician, Emma Kate Simmons. The two never had children but enjoyed a long, companionable marriage during which they traveled together frequently.

In 1885, Flint's career as both merchant and negotiator of business deals began in earnest. He joined Flint & Company, a commission firm that was an offshoot of his father's shipbuilding company, Chapman & Flint. By this time, Chapman & Flint had diversified to include foreign trade and merchant banking. In 1894, the foreign trade was delegated to Flint, Eddy & Company. In 1899, Flint, Dearborn & Company took over the fleet of sailboats. Flint himself worked on behalf of each of these subsidiaries. Because of his activities, Flint, Dearborn & Company gained a reputation for supplying foreign governments with munitions and military transport vehicles. Flint's firm provided war vessels to Japan in 1895 for use against China, it provided Brazil with an entire fleet of war vessels, and it aided the Russian government during its war against Japan in 1905. The company was also an agent for the sale of Wright airplanes and the submarines designed by Simon Lake.

While active in foreign dealings, Flint also participated in a number of significant domestic deals. He was dubbed the "Rubber King" for his importation of Brazilian rubber and for his efforts to consolidate a number of intensely competitive rubber boot and shoe manufacturers into one organization. The United States Rubber Company, consolidated in 1892, was the result of his efforts. Flint was dubbed by Chicago journalists the "Father of Trusts" in 1900, the year after he completed the consolidations of, respectively, the American Woolen Company, the Sloss Sheffield Company, the American Chicle Company, and the United States Bobbin Company. Flint never strayed from the conviction that larger business units created greater stability and profits that would benefit both owners and workers. He understood well that his own strength lay in the ability to get all the players to the table to talk about a deal.

In 1926, Flint's wife died. A year later, on July 28, he married Charlotte Reeves. Though he attempted to retire in 1928, he found retired life boring and resumed work in 1931. Throughout his life, he maintained an interest in Latin American affairs. In addition to his consulship for Chile, Flint also acted at one time as a consul for Nicaragua and as consul general for Costa Rica. Though intrigued by foreign politics, international commerce was his first love. He died in Washington, D.C., on February 12, 1934.

BIBLIOGRAPHY

Bridge, J. H., *The Trust: Its Book*, 1902; Eaton, Cyrus, *Hist. of Thomaston, Rockland and South Thomaston, Me.*, 1865; Flint, Charles Ranlett, *Memories of an Active Life; Men, and Ships, and Sealing Wax*, 1923.

Forbes, Malcolm

(August 19, 1919–February 24, 1990)
Publisher

After Malcolm Forbes inherited his father's publishing business, he earned a reputation for business accomplishments in his own right and for an active, flamboyant life that included lavish parties, hot-air balloon rides, and motorcycle races.

Malcolm was born on August 19, 1919, in Englewood, New Jersey, to B. C. "Bertie" Forbes and Adelaide (Stevens) Forbes. His father, a Scottish immigrant, used his success as a Wall Street columnist to found *Forbes* in 1917, a business magazine that quickly gained a wide readership. Malcolm graduated from Princeton University in 1941 and two days after re-

ceiving his degree began his own weekly newspaper, the *Fairfield Times*, in Lancaster, Ohio. He founded a second newspaper the following year, and then entered the U.S. Army, where he served in Europe during World War II as a staff sergeant of a heavy machine-gun unit.

After the war, Forbes joined the family business and was soon named vice president of Forbes, Incorporated and associate publisher of the magazine. He married Roberta Remsen Laidlaw in 1946, and they had five children. Three years later, Forbes plunged into politics when he won election to the borough council in Bernardsville, New Jersey. He ran for

Malcolm Forbes (Archive Photos)

the New Jersey Senate in 1951 as a Republican and won by a large margin. Forbes left the Senate in 1957 to seek the governorship and campaigned with the promise of no state income tax and no state sales tax. He lost, however, and then concentrated on his job as editor and publisher of *Forbes* magazine, a position he had assumed in 1954 after his father died.

Forbes became president of Forbes, Incorporated in 1964 and then diversified his holdings and activities. In the 1960s, he bought a 170,000-acre ranch in Colorado and purchased Hank Siegers Company to form Siegers & Forbes, the largest motorcycle dealership on the East Coast. He also wrote several books including a best-seller, *They Went That-a-Way*.

Forbes momentarily traded his office for a gondola in 1973 and became the first person to fly across America, coast to coast, in a hot-air balloon. He entered motorcycle races with his Harley-Davidson bike and gained a reputation for, as one newspaper stated, "capitalist machismo."

Forbes collected art and precious objects designed by the Russian jeweler Faberge. He owned houses in New Jersey, Colorado, Tangiers, and the South Pacific. His lavish parties included a $2 million extravaganza in Morocco to honor his own seventieth birthday. His 1,000 guests included some of the world's most prominent businesspeople and celebrities—including Fiat chairman Govanni Agnelli, Australian publishing mogul Rupert Murdoch, television newscaster Walter Cronkite, opera singer Beverly Sills, the former kings of Greece and Bulgaria, and his then-companion, actress Elizabeth Taylor.

By 1990, *Forbes* magazine reached a circulation of 720,000 and was valued at $600 million. In addition, Forbes's *American Heritage* magazine and his newspaper and real estate holdings were valued at over $100 million, while his own worth neared $1 billion.

Forbes died from a heart attack on February 24, 1990, at his home in Far Hills, New Jersey. More than 2,500 people turned out for his funeral—from Taylor and former President Richard Nixon to columnist Ann Landers and 50 Hell's Angels. Publicity surrounded Forbes even in death as numerous reports revealed that the publisher, who had divorced in 1985, had been a homosexual. Forbes's friends, however, most remembered him for his spirited life and his exceptional business acumen.

BIBLIOGRAPHY

Forbes, Malcolm, *Further Sayings of Chairman Malcolm*, 1986; Forbes, Malcolm, *They Went That-a-Way*, 1988; Winans, Christopher, Malcolm Forbes: *The Man Who Had Everything*, 1990.

Ford, Henry

(July 30, 1863–April 7, 1947)
Manufacturer

Some historians assert that in perfecting assembly-line production and making a car for the masses, Henry Ford did more to change American society in the first half of the twentieth century than any other single person.

Born on July 30, 1863, in a farmhouse in Greenfield (now Dearborn), Michigan, to William Ford and Mary (Litogot) Ford, Henry assimilated the individualism then prevalent in rural America and instilled in him by his mother. He found farm life confining, however, and after completing his formal education in a rural school in 1879, he went to Detroit, where he worked as an apprentice in a machine shop during the day and repaired watches for a jeweler at night. His arrival coincided with that city's industrialization and the increasing use of steam and gasoline-powered engines.

As a road agent of the Westinghouse Engine Company in 1882, he serviced steam traction engines for farmers—work that strengthened his desire to avoid the drudgery of farm labor. In 1886, Ford accepted from his father the use of a wooded tract in Dearborn. Whereas the elder Ford expected his son to farm the land, Ford built a workshop on it and tinkered with engines, all the while making a living repairing them for others. In 1888, he married Clara Bryant.

At that time, several inventors worked to produce automobiles. Gottlieb Daimler and Karl Benz built self-propelled gasoline vehicles in Europe, and in 1891 the French firm Panhard et Levassor began making automobiles commercially. Starting in 1893, Ford experimented to find a

Henry Ford (Ford Motor Company)

gasoline engine that could propel a vehicle and intensified his work after he witnessed the test of a horseless carriage by Charles King in Detroit in 1896. Ford made his own car later that year, but it provided no improvements over others. Nevertheless, unlike many other inventors, he had confidence in the automobile as a vehicle for the masses, not just one for the wealthy.

Between 1897 and 1902, Ford involved himself in two failed automotive businesses, and in mid-1902, he began designing an automobile model that could compete with the increasingly popular Oldsmobile, then being manufactured in Detroit for mass distribution. The following year, Ford founded the Ford Motor

Company after obtaining capital from bankers.

Ford produced his first Model T in 1908, a car with a price low enough to make the vehicle widely affordable. Although he did not invent interchangeable parts or originate assembly-line production, he advanced both with production of the Model T. By making the Model T a basic car and by making each one look the same, his assembly lines operated quickly, and the price for the vehicle eventually dropped to $350. The Model T had many faults, but wherever it went, "curious groups gathered to gaze and confident owners paused to point out its advantages." Year after year, he produced the Model T, year after year it looked the same, and year after year people bought it.

Ford the businessman was also popular, and in 1918 the Republican Party nominated him for U.S. senator from Michigan. He lost the election, however, although he remained influential in Republican circles. The following year, he built the Henry Ford Hospital in Detroit for $7.5 million.

In 1919, he began publishing the *Dearborn Independent*, a weekly newspaper that he required every Ford car dealership to carry. He used the newspaper as a mouthpiece for his virulent anti-Semitism. One American traveler in Europe was surprised to discover that the *Independent* was a favorite publication of an aspiring German politician, Adolph Hitler. Although Ford later apologized for his anti-Semitic articles, many believed that he held to those ideas throughout his life.

Ford sold some 15 million Model Ts until 1927. Then the market for them collapsed as other automakers pulled ahead of Ford by making cars with more options, such as different colors, and by introducing new models nearly every year. Although Ford retooled his factory and made a new model that sold well, his company never regained its number one position.

In the late 1920s, Ford experienced labor problems. He had startled industrialists in 1914 by raising wages at his factory to $5 a day. He expected the then-high wage to lower the turnover rate at his factory (which had been substantial as workers tired of the monotonous assembly-line labor) and to enable workers to buy Model Ts. A few years later, he established the five-day workweek. His policies had earned him the admiration of many workers who considered him the friend of the common man.

Several of Ford's practices, however, changed opinions of him. Ford insisted on saddling workers with his own morality, a puritanical standard that forbade such activities as modern dancing. He posted security guards in his factory to enforce a rule against talking, and he sped up production by making workers move faster and faster.

With increased competition, Ford at times had to cut work hours. Then when the Great Depression hit, he had to close his plant. At the same time, he blamed the economic collapse on workers in general, saying they were lazy. Meanwhile, he lavished hundreds of thousands of dollars in presents on his children.

Among all the major automobile manufacturers in Detroit in the late 1930s, Ford was the only one that refused to recognize a labor union for its employees. The National Labor Relations Board found Ford guilty of repeated violations of the National Labor Relations Act.

Finally, after a damaging strike in 1941, Ford negotiated a labor contract.

That same year, he obtained government contracts to manufacture parts for bombers and, later, to produce entire airplanes. He built a huge plant at Willow Run, Michigan, which by the end of World War II had manufactured over 8,000 planes.

Ford retired from active direction of the Ford Motor Company in 1945 and died in Dearborn on April 7, 1947. He left a personal fortune estimated at $500 million to $700 million and bequeathed most of his holdings in the company to the Ford Foundation, a nonprofit organization.

"I will build a motor car for the multitude," said Ford, "so low in price that the man of moderate means may own one and enjoy with his family the blessings of happy hours spent in God's great open spaces." Through his business leadership, America stood transformed.

BIBLIOGRAPHY

Batchelor, Ray, *Henry Ford: Mass Production, Modernism and Design*, 1994; Bryan, Ford R., *Beyond the Model T: The Other Ventures of Henry Ford*, 1990; Ford, Henry, *My Life and Work*, 1922; Herndon, Booton, *Ford: An Unconventional Biography of the Men and Their Times*, 1969; Jardim, Anne, *The First Henry Ford: A Study in Personality and Business Leadership*, 1970; Lee, Albert, *Henry Ford and the Jews*, 1980; Nevins, Allan, *Ford*, 3 vols., 1954–1963; Nevins, Allan, *Ford: Decline and Rebirth, 1933–1962*, 1963; Sward, Keith, *The Legend of Henry Ford*, 1948.

Forten, James

(September 2, 1766–March 4, 1842)
Merchant

One of the foremost African Americans of his time, James Forten built a very successful business in sail making and ship supplies in Philadelphia. He was one of the early proponents of equal rights for African Americans and women and was widely respected in Philadelphia for both his business acumen and his philanthropic spirit.

James Forten, the grandson of a slave, was born in Pennsylvania on September 2, 1766. He attended a school founded by Anthony Benezet, a Quaker abolitionist. His father, Thomas Forten, died when the young James was only 7 years old, and he subsequently left school in 1775 at the age of 9 to help his mother by working. Forten joined the colonial navy during the American Revolution when he reached the age of 14. He was aboard a colonial ship, which was captured by the British ship *Amphion*, but he was fortunate enough to be spared from forcible enlistment in the British navy or being sold into slavery in the West Indies. He was taken to a prison ship moored in New York harbor, where he remained until prisoners were exchanged.

After returning to Philadelphia, Forten became an apprentice to the veteran sail maker, Robert Bridges. By the age of 20, he was the foreman of the sailmaking crew and soon became owner of the entire sail loft. In this period of his life, Forten married; he and his wife (whose name has been lost to posterity) would ultimately have eight children. The sailing supply business would remain very profitable throughout his life, and Forten acquired considerable wealth from it. By 1832, Forten's fortune was estimated at over $100,000, an enormous amount at that time.

In addition to his success in business, Forten was an outstanding citizen. In 1814, he helped organize over 2,000 African-American volunteers to protect the city of Philadelphia from the British during the War of 1812. His courage and selflessness were noteworthy. On seven different occasions, Forten rescued people drowning in the water near his business establishment.

Forten was intensely interested in the plight of his fellow African Americans. In 1817, he presided over a meeting called to oppose the actions of the newly formed American Colonization Society, which had been created with the mission of sending free African Americans to colonies in Africa, as an alternative to emancipation in the United States. The society was harshly discredited by Forten and other abolitionists, including William Lloyd Garrison, as merely a scheme formulated by slaveholders to recapture escaped slaves once they returned to Africa. Forten also opposed slavery through his business by refusing to sell any supplies or riggings to shipowners who employed slave crews on their vessels. It is a testament to his character and to his business skills that he was able to be selective in choosing his customers, but still prosper financially.

Later in life, Forten became an ally of temperance societies and a defender of women's rights. He was highly respected for his good deeds and generous personality. After Forten's death in Philadelphia on March 4, 1842, large crowds of admirers attended his funeral.

BIBLIOGRAPHY

Child, L. Maria, *The Freedmen's Book*, 1865; Douty, Esther Morris, *Forten, the Sailmaker: Pioneer Champion of Negro Rights*, 1968; Johnston, Brenda A., *Between the Devil and the Sea: The Life of James Forten*, 1974; Purvis, Robert, *Remarks on the Life and Character of James Forten*, 1842; Washington, Booker T., *The Story of the Negro*, 1909.

Franklin, Benjamin

(January 17, 1706–April 17, 1790)
Printer

When people think of Benjamin Franklin, they often associate him with the American Revolution and the writing of the Constitution, or perhaps they remember the aphorisms stated in his almanac. They often overlook his shrewd and aggressive work as a business leader.

Benjamin was born on January 17, 1706, in Boston, Massachusetts, to Josiah Franklin and Abiah (Folger) Franklin. His father, a tallow chandler and soap boiler, taught Benjamin to read at an early age and sent him to school. The youngster, however, ended his formal education at age 10 and entered his father's business.

Benjamin disliked the trade, though, and in a short while began working for his half brother, James, who operated a printing shop. Benjamin read extensively and improved his writing, at one point composing an essay that he signed as Silence Dogood and left under the shop door, not revealing to James who really wrote it. James printed the essay, and it proved so popular that Benjamin followed it with 14 additional ones.

A quarrel with James, however, caused Benjamin to leave Boston for Philadelphia in 1723. There he obtained a job in a printing shop owned by Samuel Keimer and displayed his already impressive talent. With the help of the colonial governor, young Franklin sailed for London in 1724 and worked at a leading printing house. He returned to Pennsylvania in 1726, and after again working for Keimer, formed a partnership in 1728 with Hugh Meredith. The two men bought the *Phila-*

Benjamin Franklin (Library of Congress)

delphia Gazette in 1729, and the following year, Franklin began operating the printing shop and newspaper on his own.

In 1730, Franklin took Deborah Read as his common-law wife, and they subsequently had two children. He also had two illegitimate children, one of whom, William Franklin, later served as governor of New Jersey.

For the next 18 years, from 1730 to 1748, Franklin applied himself to his business. He preached and practiced industriousness and frugality and in that way reflected his roots in New England Puritanism while displaying the qualities of an emergent secular, materialistic society. He said: "I was seen at no places of idle diversion. I never went out fishing or shooting; a book, indeed, sometimes debauched me from my work, but that was seldom, snug, and gave no scandal."

His ease at making friends and his knack for self-promotion contributed greatly to his business accomplishments. Perhaps no more prominent example of promotion existed in early America than Franklin's *Poor Richard's Almanack*. His aphorisms deposited middle-class ideas in quantity:

> He that hath a trade hath an estate.

> There are no gains without pains.

> At the working man's house hunger looks in, but dares not enter.

The *Almanack*, printed from 1732 to 1757, made Franklin famous throughout the colonies and in England and France, where many people read it. He also earned considerable money from its publication.

All the while, Franklin engaged in extensive philanthropy that helped Philadelphia. In 1731, he founded the first circulating library in America, in 1743 the American Philosophical Society, in 1751 a city hospital, and, that same year, an academy that later became the University of Pennsylvania. He held public office, too, as a member of the Pennsylvania Assembly and as deputy postmaster at Philadelphia and postmaster general for the colonies. He made the post office a financial success.

In addition, the indefatigable Franklin pursued science, or "natural philosophy." The field appealed to him so strongly that, at age 42, he decided to leave business, thus beginning a new phase in his life devoted to intellect and politics. He turned his printing shop over to his fore-man, David Hall, in 1748, who agreed to pay Franklin an annual amount that, along with returns from real estate, allowed him to live well.

Franklin conducted his famous kite experiment in 1752 and showed the connection between lightning and electricity. In 1754, he represented Pennsylvania in the Albany Congress, which adopted his proposal for intercolonial union, although the plan was never adopted by the colonies as a whole.

Despite his retreat from business, Franklin still promoted material success. In 1757, he issued his essay "The Way to Wealth," in which he advised:

> It would be thought a hard government that should tax its people one tenth part of their time. . . . But idleness taxes many of us much more, if we reckon all that is spent in absolute sloth, or doing of nothing.

> Sloth, by bringing on diseases, absolutely shortens life. Sloth, like rust, consumes faster than labor wears, while the used key is always bright.

> How much more than is necessary do we spend in sleep, forgetting that the sleeping fox catches no poultry, and that there will be sleeping enough in the grave.

> Drive thy business, let not that drive thee; and early to bed and early to rise makes a man healthy, wealthy and wise.

Franklin served in England during the 1760s as agent for Pennsylvania, during which time Parliament began levying taxes on the colonies. He opposed the taxes but, at first, advised the colonists to accept them. The outrage in the colonies over Parliament's action forced Franklin to reconsider, and in 1766 he presented 174 questions to Parliament that showed how the taxes violated custom.

Controversy surrounded Franklin in 1772 when, while an agent for Massachusetts, he obtained letters from that colony's royal governor, Thomas Hutchinson, in which the governor asserted "there must be an abridgment of what are called English liberties." When Franklin sent the letters to Massachusetts, radicals printed them to show that British officials wanted to crush liberty. The episode hastened the American Revolution, while, back in England, the British government vilified Franklin for his act.

In May 1775, shortly after he returned to Philadelphia, Franklin was chosen as a member of the second Continental Congress, which in July 1776 declared American independence from Britain. He served during the American Revolution as an American representative to the French government, and while overseas won not only the accolades of Parisian society but also negotiated in 1778 an alliance with France that proved crucial in the ultimate American victory.

In 1781, Franklin was named one of the commissioners to negotiate peace with Britain. His mission accomplished, he returned to Philadelphia in September 1785 and served as president of the state executive council and as a member of the 1787 Constitutional Convention that created a new national government. His compromise proposal regarding representation in Congress did much to make the Constitution a reality.

During the last five years of his life, Franklin lived with his daughter and grandchildren (his wife had died in 1774) and worked on several inventions, including a tool for lifting books from high shelves. Shortly after appealing to Congress to abolish slavery, he died on April 17, 1790. At his funeral, 20,000 mourners honored the leader who combined middle-class business values with republican ideals. Scholars have since praised Franklin for his many accomplishments in an extremely active life and criticized him for his base appeal to materialism.

BIBLIOGRAPHY

Becker, Carl Lotus, *Benjamin Franklin: A Biographical Sketch*, 1946; Crane, Verner Winslow, *Benjamin Franklin and a Rising People*, 1954; Franklin, Benjamin, *The Autobiography of Benjamin Franklin*, 1993; Van Doren, Carl, *Benjamin Franklin*, 1938.

Frick, Henry C.

(December 19, 1849–December 2, 1919)
Manufacturer

An unceasing drive for power and money and a fanatical hatred of unions—these propelled Henry Clay Frick in his building a major coke company and commanding Carnegie Steel.

Frick was born on December 19, 1849, near Connellsville, Pennsylvania, where

Henry C. Frick (Library of Congress)

his father and grandfather owned farms. His father, John Frick, came from a Swiss family, and his mother, Elizabeth (Overholt) Frick, came from a German one. Clay, as his parents called him, admired his grandfather, who operated a highly profitable farm and at an early age set his sights on exceeding the older man's wealth.

A frail and sickly boy, Frick attended West Overton Independent School. He began his higher education at Otterbein College in Westerville, Ohio, but left there to clerk in a store owned by his uncle. He later worked at a department store in Carlisle, where he excelled at sales. Typhoid fever, however, struck him down, and after his recovery, he worked as the chief bookkeeper at his grandfather's distillery. In 1870, opportunity appeared when a cousin, Abraham Tintsman, asked him to help manage some coal lands.

By this time, a few years after the Civil War, America stood poised for great industrial development, and Frick perceived this. He knew that large coal deposits around Connellsville could be profitably exploited.

Frick joined his cousin, borrowed money to buy desired coal lands, and started a new business incorporated as the Henry C. Frick Coke Company. Over the next few years, he obtained additional capital through a mortgage on his father's farm, and by convincing a prominent judge, Thomas Mellon, to invest $10,000, thus beginning a long association between the Mellon family and Frick.

Frick used the proven method of making coke by taking soft coal and placing it in ovens under tremendous heat. This removed the sulphur and phosphorous and produced a coal cake, called coke for short. Mixed with lime in a blast furnace, coke removed unwanted elements from iron ore, leaving molten iron. All iron and steel mills needed coke, and Frick provided it.

By 1873, Frick was selling all the coke his ovens could produce. Then a severe depression hurt his business. Rather than retrench, however, Frick expanded, buying out his competitors at favorable prices. When the economy revived in 1877, Frick's business prospered, and by 1880, with nearly 1,000 ovens at work, he made his first million dollars, a cherished goal that, when reached, caused him to break out a cigar and smoke it.

A few days after his marriage to Adelaide Childs on December 15, 1881, Frick dined with ANDREW CARNEGIE, the iron and steel tycoon and an important customer. Carnegie invited Frick into his company, Carnegie Brothers. The two men had a mutual interest: Carnegie needed a reliable source of coke at a steady price, and Frick needed capital to expand his company. Their agreement led to reorganizing the Frick Coke Company in 1882, and by the end of 1883 Carnegie and his partners owned over 50 percent of the business. Carnegie kept Frick in charge of operations—he considered him a management genius.

In January 1887, Carnegie sold 2 percent of Carnegie Brothers to Frick without requiring him to put up any money. He wanted to move Frick closer to the steel operation by giving him a greater financial stake in it. That same year, though, friction developed between the two men over a labor dispute. After coke workers in Connellsville went out on strike, Frick formed an alliance with rival coke companies in the area to destroy the union. When Carnegie heard about this, he ordered Frick to retreat and meet the union's demands. This infuriated Frick and he resigned, but Carnegie brought him back into the company.

In January 1889, Carnegie made Frick chairman of Carnegie Brothers. In that position, he acquired the Duquesne Steel Works for $1 million in bonds, and, under his leadership, the company's profits reached $4.5 million by 1892, surprising even Carnegie. That same year, Carnegie Brothers became the Carnegie Steel Company with Frick as president.

Frick wanted to reduce labor costs, and Carnegie wholeheartedly agreed. An obstacle confronted them, however: the Amalgamated Association, the union representing skilled workers at Carnegie's modern Homestead plant. Carnegie and Frick nevertheless determined to change the pay scales at Homestead and thus lower the wages for most workers. Moreover, they wanted to permanently break the power of the union.

As a result, with Carnegie away in Scotland, Frick refused to offer the union anything near a compromise in contract negotiations. At the same time, he built a wall around the Homestead plant, an ominous declaration, pounded together from boards and containing holes to fit gun barrels. He secretly arranged to have Pinkerton guards secure the complex. As tension mounted, a strike began on June 30, 1892, and the workers occupied Homestead before Frick could finish securing it. A few days later, Frick sent in the Pinkertons who, under the cover of night, drifted on barges down the Monongahela

River. After a worker spotted the guards, sirens and bells sounded an alarm, and everyone at the plant and thousands from the nearby town rallied to stop Frick's assault. A 12-hour gun battle raged on July 6, resulting in a victory for the workers. That soon changed: the governor ordered in the state militia, and, facing such massive force, the workers surrendered. Frick had won the war and busted the union.

In this violent atmosphere, on July 23, an anarchist, Alexander Berkman, entered Frick's office and shot him twice at close range. Showing amazing fortitude, Frick struggled with his assailant, who pulled out a knife and stabbed him. At this point, a sheriff wrestled Berkman to the ground and captured him. Frick called a doctor to his office, and, after the bullets were removed from his body, went back to work on a deal for a loan.

Publicly, Carnegie praised Frick for his stand in the Homestead strike. Privately, he had doubts, for the violence had heaped nearly universal condemnation on Carnegie and Frick. The two men grew distant, and in 1900 Frick resigned in a dispute over the price Carnegie Steel would pay for coke from the Frick Coke Company.

Frick remained active in business, though. He played a role in the negotiations that led to the founding of the United States Steel Company, formed in 1901 when J. P. MORGAN SR. purchased Carnegie Steel. Frick served as a director in the new corporation.

In an ostentatious display, Frick built a mansion on Fifth Avenue in New York City and collected valuable art. Shortly after his death on December 2, 1919, the mansion was converted into a museum with a $15 million endowment from Frick. His wife survived him, as did a daughter and son. Frick had built an industry, made a fortune, destroyed a union, and won the title "coke king."

BIBLIOGRAPHY

Schreiner, Samuel Agnew, *Henry Frick: The Gospel of Greed*, 1995; Warren, Kenneth, *Triumphant Capitalism: Henry Clay Frick and the Industrial Transformation of America*, 1996.

G

Gallo, Ernest

(1910–)
Wine Maker

Along with his brother JULIO GALLO, Ernest Gallo built the nation's largest winery, famous for products from low-cost wine coolers to more expensive premium brands.

Ernest was born in 1910 near Modesto, California. His father, Joseph Gallo, was an immigrant from northwestern Italy who grew and shipped grapes, primarily for use in making wine. This business prospered—despite Prohibition in the 1920s—until the Great Depression hit and nearly destroyed him financially. The pressure placed on him may have been the reason why, in 1933, he went berserk, shot his wife, and then killed himself.

Shortly after the catastrophe, Ernest and his younger brother Julio decided to switch from growing grapes to making wine. Using instructions from a library book, they learned the trade, and Ernest, who was more outgoing than Julio, took charge of sales. At one point, he flew to Chicago and sold a dealer 6,000 gallons of wine at 50 cents a gallon. After selling wine in bulk for several years, the Gallos started to bottle their own in 1938 under the family name.

When in the 1950s they first sold lemon-flavored Thunderbird (a port wine), the E. & J. Gallo Winery earned a reputation for producing low-priced, low-end products—a reputation the firm would never completely shake. In the 1960s, the Gallos signed long-term contracts with grape growers and acquired 95 percent of their grapes through them rather than by operating their own vineyards as most wine companies did. To grape growers, the arrangement brought a mixed result.

On the one hand, they had a large customer ready to buy most of their grapes; on the other hand, Ernest often drove hard bargains that caused some grape growers to complain about low prices received for their crops.

With its ready supply of grapes and with Ernest's aggressive marketing, Gallo wine bested its competition and dominated the lower-end wine market. Ernest promoted Gallo as grown not by some snobby vintager but by a winery concerned with popular tastes, which led him to market Ripple along with Boone's Farm, a carbonated "pop wine." And in the 1980s, after he saw a small company sell "California" wine coolers with great success, he introduced Bartle's & Jaymes, backed it with heavy promotion, and knocked the "California" brand from its leading position. By that time, Gallo produced one out of every four bottles of wine sold in the nation, bought 30 percent of California's annual wine-grape harvest, and sold more champagne, brandy, sherry, vermouth, and port than anyone else. Sales hovered around $1 billion annually, compared to $350 million for the closest competitor, Seagram's. At the same time, Gallo owned the Fairbanks Trucking Company, California's largest trucker, and the Midcal Aluminum Company, which made screw tops for bottles.

In the 1990s, Ernest also entered the premium wine market. Expanding on a foray begun two decades earlier, Gallo introduced premium wines under the brand names Anapamu, Zabaco, and Ecco Domani. Ernest remained active in Gallo in the late 1990s, and the company's revenues ranked it among the 200 largest businesses in the nation.

BIBLIOGRAPHY

Adams, Leon, *The Wines of America*, 1973.

Gallo, Julio

(1911–1993)
Wine Maker

In building the E. & J. Gallo Winery in Modesto, California, with his brother ERNEST GALLO, Julio Gallo established a production system that made the company the nation's leader in making wine.

Julio was born in 1911 near Modesto, California. His father, Joseph Gallo, was an immigrant from northwestern Italy who began growing and shipping grapes, primarily for use in making wine, shortly after his arrival in the United States. His business prospered until the Great Depression hit and nearly destroyed him financially. In 1933, probably as a result of the economic pressure, he went berserk, shot his wife, and then killed himself.

Shortly after the catastrophe, Julio and Ernest decided to switch from growing grapes to making wine. They learned the trade by reading wine-making instructions in a library book, and Ernest, who was more outgoing than Julio, took charge of sales. In fact, Ernest remained the company's driving force, a dour, ruthless perfectionist who remained the opposite of Julio's gregarious, easygoing personality.

When in the 1950s they sold lemon-flavored Thunderbird (a port wine), the E. & J. Gallo Winery earned a reputation for producing low-priced, low-end products. In the 1960s, the Gallos signed long-term contracts with grape growers and acquired 95 percent of their grapes through them rather than by operating their own vineyards as most wine companies did.

In operating the company, Julio and Ernest divided the duties. Julio served as president and oversaw production, while Ernest served as chairman and directed marketing, sales, and distribution. Together, they developed wines that appealed to popular tastes, most notably Ripple and Boone's Farm (a carbonated "pop wine"). In the 1980s, after they saw a small company sell wine coolers with great success, they introduced Bartle's & Jaymes, backed it with heavy promotion, and soon became the nation's leading seller of wine coolers.

In the 1990s, Gallo also entered the premium wine market, although in a limited way until after Julio's death in 1993. By that time, Gallo controlled nearly one-third of the national wine market.

BIBLIOGRAPHY

Adams, Leon, *The Wines of America*, 1973.

Galvin, Paul

(June 29, 1895–November 5, 1959)
Manufacturer

After two business failures trying to make batteries, Paul Galvin turned his idea for manufacturing car radios into the creation of Motorola, which soon became one of the most prominent electronics companies in the country.

Born in Harvard, Illinois, on June 29, 1895, Galvin got his first job stripping stems in a local tobacco factory. After graduating from Harvard High School, he attended the University of Illinois, where he studied business administration for two years before entering the U.S. Army in 1917. Galvin served in Europe during World War I and returned to the United Sates in 1919.

After leaving the military, Galvin worked at the D & G Storage Battery Company in Chicago. In 1921, he and a friend, Edward Stewart, founded the Stewart Battery Company in Marshfield, Wisconsin. Intense competition from other battery companies, along with a national economic downturn, caused the firm to collapse in 1923, and for the next three years, Galvin sold candy for the Brach Candy Company.

In 1926, Galvin and Stewart tried again to make batteries, but within a short time they went bankrupt. Galvin tried yet a third time when he founded the Galvin Manufacturing Corporation in 1928. One year later, the Great Depression began, and Galvin realized he needed a different idea to survive, so he decided to make car radios. The automobile had emerged as a popular consumer item only a few years before, and few cars had radios. Galvin hired an inventor who made a pro-

totype, and by the early 1930s Galvin's radios outsold all others. He used the name Motorola for his new product. Later in the decade, Motorola radios were the first to feature push-button tuning, fine tuning, and tone controls.

During the 1930s, Galvin added police radios to his product line and, for the U.S. Army, his chief engineer invented a two-way portable radio called the "Handie-Talkie," the size of which was reduced during World War II, resulting in a walkie-talkie. Galvin produced radar equipment, too, during the war, and the military contracts caused his company's profits to soar.

After the war, Galvin needed to diversify, and in 1945 he changed the company name to Motorola while bringing his son ROBERT GALVIN into the firm. Together, they manufactured the first practical television set, which, priced at under $200, boosted company sales to over $47 million.

In the mid-1950s, Motorola developed transistors at its research laboratory in Phoenix, Arizona, and entered the expanding field of semiconductors. By now a giant in the electronics industry, Motorola's annual sales reached $277 million in 1956, and Paul Galvin moved up to chairman of the board while Robert Galvin served as president.

At that time, Motorola struggled in the consumer market with its televisions. In order to sell more televisions, the company had compromised quality for lower prices and had entered the color television field unprepared. The strategy backfired, and television sales declined. On

November 5, 1959, Paul Galvin died from leukemia. A revival for Motorola would come about under Robert Galvin's leadership.

BIBLIOGRAPHY

Petrakis, Harry M., *The Founder's Touch: The Life of Paul Galvin of Motorola*, 1965.

Galvin, Robert

(October 9, 1922–)
Manufacturer

After inheriting the huge Motorola company from his father, Robert Galvin took the firm in a new direction, from concentrating on consumer products to emphasizing semiconductors and communications equipment.

Galvin was born on October 9, 1922, in Marshfield, Wisconsin. His father, PAUL GALVIN, had founded Motorola in the 1920s (then the Galvin Manufacturing Corporation) to make car radios. After graduating from high school in Evanston, Illinois, to where his family had moved, Robert Galvin attended the University of Chicago and the University of Notre Dame. Before receiving a degree, he entered the family business as a laborer in the stockroom. He served in the U.S. Army Signal Corps during World War II, and in 1945 was named director of Motorola.

Galvin worked with his father to reverse the company's sagging sales after the war by having Motorola make the first practical television set. The set sold for under $200, and its popularity boosted annual sales to over $47 million.

After Paul Galvin died from leukemia in 1959, Galvin struggled to correct the company's losses from its declining sales of televisions and its disastrous entry into color television. He decentralized the corporate structure and moved into making semiconductors. Following a fitful start, Motorola became the nation's second largest semiconductor manufacturer by the mid-1960s.

Consumers still considered Motorola's products outdated, and, to counteract this, Galvin marketed an all-transistor television (featuring a pullout drawer that contained its electronic parts) and a space-age name—Quasar. Motorola, however, continued to struggle in the consumer market, and in 1974 Galvin sold the Quasar division to the Japanese firm Matsushita. That same year, Motorola introduced its first microprocessor, which contained 4,000 transistors. In 1977, Galvin bought Codex (a manufacturer of systems for data communications networks) and Universal Data Systems (a maker of data communications equipment).

By the mid-1980s, Galvin had made Motorola a world-class semiconductor manufacturer, selling $2.5 billion worth of the product. He moved the company into making pagers and in 1987 joined with the Japanese firm Toshiba to establish the Tohoku Semiconductor Company.

In the late 1980s, Galvin helped formulate the United States-Japan semiconductor trade agreement, under which Japan agreed to increase its purchases of semiconductors from the United States and to stop dumping computer chips onto the U.S. market. In return, the United States agreed to forego antidumping duties against Japan.

Motorola made its last car radio in 1987, and in 1990 Galvin retired from his chairmanship of the company but agreed to head the executive committee. His son, Christopher Galvin, was elected president in 1991.

BIBLIOGRAPHY

Okimoto, Daniel I., et al., *Competitive Edge: The Semiconductor Industry in the U.S. and Japan*, 1984; Petrakis, Harry M., *The Founder's Touch: The Life of Paul Galvin of Motorola*, 1965.

Gannett, Frank

(September 15, 1876–December 3, 1957)
Publisher

From partial ownership of a small-town daily, Frank Gannett built a newspaper chain that extended into dozens of medium-sized cities.

Frank was born on September 15, 1876, near the town of Bristol, New York, to Joseph Gannett and Maria (Brooks) Gannett. His father owned a farm but was forced to sell it after a long illness. Gannett Sr. subsequently worked as a tenant farmer and as part owner of a hotel, which required the family to make several different moves. As a result, young Frank attended a number of schools.

Gannett eventually graduated from high school in Bolivar, New York, and worked for a short time as a bookkeeper, after which he enrolled at Cornell University. There, he got his first journalistic experience when he worked on the college newspaper. Gannett graduated from Cornell in 1898, and a few weeks later, the president of the university recruited the young man to accompany him on a political mission to the Philippine Islands, recently acquired by the United States in the Spanish-American War.

Gannett's experience in the distant land convinced him to oppose imperialism, and he later took that position in his editorials. Gannett returned to the United States in 1900 and worked as city editor of the *Ithaca Daily News*. He eventually moved up to business manager, but in 1905 he left the *Daily News* and bought a half-interest in another New York newspaper, the *Elmira Gazette*. From that point forward, he quickly expanded his newspaper investments. In 1907, he bought the *Elmira Star* and merged it with the *Gazette*.

Gannett bought the *Ithaca Journal* in 1912, and six years later, with the help of two partners, he added the *Rochester Union and Advertiser* and the *Rochester Evening Times*, which he merged to form the *Times-Union*. He married

Frank Gannett (UPI/Corbis-Bettmann)

Caroline Werner in 1920, and they later had two children.

Gannett purchased two Albany newspapers in 1929 by obtaining a loan from the president of International Paper and using shares of stock in the Gannett business as collateral. He lived in Rochester, and by 1924 had enough money—$2 million—to buy out his partners. By the mid-1940s, he controlled 21 newspapers in 16 midsize cities. Gannett much preferred these markets to large urban ones and, in fact, his single foray into a big city, when he bought a daily in Brooklyn, New York, ended in failure. He achieved success once again, however, with the founding of the Gannett National News Service in 1943.

Gannett established a policy that governed his newspapers long after his death: each editor should have independence in stating opinions. Only the

Times-Union expressed Gannett's views. He embraced new technology, too, when he invested money to develop a teletype setter, used shortwave radio sets to speed the reporting of news, and purchased radio stations.

The newspaper magnate entered politics in 1940 when he sought the Republican Party presidential nomination. President Franklin D. Roosevelt branded Gannett as an isolationist, but the publisher denied the charge and said he only wanted a cautious foreign policy to prevent the United States from entering World War II. Gannett lost his bid for the nomination, but remained influential within the party and in 1944 served as an adviser to presidential nominee Thomas Dewey.

Gannett formed the Frank E. Gannett Newspaper Foundation, a philanthropy intended to help charities and schools. By requiring a majority of the foundation's members to be editors who worked for his company, Gannett sought to attach the newspapers to community programs.

When Gannett died on December 3, 1957, he was president emeritus of the Gannett Company. The corporation continued to grow, especially in the 1970s and 1980s under AL NEUHARTH, and earned praise and criticism when it began a national newspaper, *USA Today*. In 1997, the Gannett Company achieved revenues of $4.7 billion and a profit of $712 million; with a daily circulation of 6.7 million, it ranked as the nation's largest newspaper publisher.

BIBLIOGRAPHY

Williamson, S. T., *Frank Gannett: A Biography*, 1940.

Gardner, Edward

(February 15, 1925–)
Manufacturer

Recognizing that white cosmetics companies ignored African Americans, Edward Gardner began Soft Sheen, a hair-care business that provided products for blacks and also developed black pride.

Gardner was born on February 15, 1925, in the area of Chicago, Illinois, called the Black Metropolis. In the early 1940s, he obtained a bachelor's degree from Chicago Teachers College and in 1945 worked as an assistant principal at an elementary school. He continued his education and received a master's degree from the University of Chicago.

In the 1950s, Gardner began making beauty products from the basement of his home, and, with his wife Bettiann, founded the E. G. Gardner Beauty Products Company. Several other small black-owned businesses also produced beauty products, largely because white corporations ignored the market, and in 1954 George Johnson provided a model for Gardner and others when he founded Johnson Products to make Afro Sheen, a hair-care product.

Around 1960, Gardner worked for a black beauty supply company, and when it went bankrupt, he began selling his own products to its customers. He started a new company, Soft Sheen Products, whose name emphasized the preference of African-American women for shiny hair. Through the 1960s, Soft Sheen remained a small company, well behind Johnson Products in sales. During the following decade, however, the Afro hairstyle that Johnson Products had recently catered to lost its appeal, and Gardner

guided Soft Sheen to a larger market. Then, in 1979, when a loose-perm look called the curl appeared—popularized by singer Michael Jackson—Gardner struck it big with his product Care Free Curl. Soft Sheen soon surpassed Johnson Products, and by 1987 its annual sales exceeded $81 million.

Yet at that time a threat loomed: white-owned Revlon announced its intention to take over the African-American beauty products industry. By 1988, white-owned businesses had grabbed 50 percent of the ethnic hair-care market.

Gardner and his fellow African-American business leaders launched a counterattack, and with the help of civil rights activist Jesse Jackson, they sponsored a boycott of Revlon products while black magazines such as *Jet* and *Ebony* refused to carry Revlon advertisements. In addition, Gardner, along with George Johnson and nine other leaders of black-owned hair-care companies, rallied the American Health and Beauty Aids Institute (AHBAI), which they had formed in 1981, to lead a $3 million advertising campaign that encouraged blacks to buy black-made products. AHBAI developed a "proud lady" logo, and many African Americans supported the cause.

Gardner diversified in the late 1980s. He established Brainstorm Communications that advertised Soft Sheen products, Bottlewerks that packaged Soft Sheen products, and *Shoptalk* (a trade magazine). He also bought Dyke and Dryden, a black-owned business that made and distributed hair-care products in Britain and Africa.

By 1990, Gardner had relinquished management of Soft Sheen to his son Gary, while at the same time contributing his time and money to projects in Chicago's black South Side, including renovating the historic Regal Theater. In 1997, Terri Gardner, Edward and Bettiann Gardner's daughter, became president and CEO of Soft Sheen. She eliminated unprofitable products while maintaining an ethnic hair-care line that included Mizani, Wave Nouveau, Optimum Care, Tender Care, Care Free Curl, Sportin' Waves, and Baby Love. Annual sales surpassed $90 million, and the company called itself the "global leader in ethnic hair-care products."

BIBLIOGRAPHY

Dunn, Carolyn, "The Ethnic Hair Care Market," *Happi*, April 1997.

Gates, Bill

(October 28, 1955–)
Manufacturer

William H. Gates III founded the world's leading software firm, Microsoft, and became a billionaire at age 31—the youngest person to ever reach that level.

Born on October 28, 1955, in Seattle, Washington, son of William Henry Gates Jr. and Mary (Maxwell) Gates, Bill grew up in an affluent family. His father was a partner in a leading Seattle law firm, and his mother served on the University of Washington board of regents and on the boards of several corporations. Gates first showed an interest in computers in the late 1960s, when he and three friends began the Lakeside Programming Group and programmed a class schedule for Lakeside School, which they attended. Later, they developed a computerized payroll system for the school and founded Traf-O-Data, a computerized traffic-counting system that they sold to local governments. Although they earned more than $20,000 from the business, many potential customers distrusted them because they were still in high school.

Gates worked as a congressional page during the summer of 1972 and displayed his instinct for making money in a deal involving campaign buttons. After presidential candidate George McGovern announced he was dropping his running mate Thomas Eagleton from the ticket, Gates started buying McGovern-Eagleton campaign buttons for a nickel, speculating they would soon be worth much more. He was right; people wanted them as collector's items, and he sold the buttons for $25 each.

After graduating from Lakeside School in 1973, Gates entered Harvard as a prelaw major. Two years later, a friend of his, Paul Allen, read about the world's first microcomputer, the Altair 8800, manufactured by MITS in New Mexico. The computer, Allen pointed out, had no software, and he proposed that he and Gates write a program for it. Gates agreed, and they adapted a computer language called BASIC, used on large models, to the Altair and then sold it to the company. Soon an industry standard, their program dominated the software market for several years.

With that success, Gates left college, and in the summer of 1975 he and Allen founded Microsoft in Albuquerque, New Mexico, to produce their BASIC program for MITS. Although MITS went bankrupt, Gates had signed up such other companies as Apple and Commodore as customers for his software. Microsoft prospered and received another boost when in 1977 the Tandy Corporation, makers of Radio Shack computers, hired Gates and Allen to make software for them.

Two years later, Gates relocated Microsoft's headquarters to Bellevue, Washington, near Seattle, and Microsoft surged ahead of its competition when, in 1980, International Business Machines (IBM) signed a contract with the company to devise an operating system for a new personal computer. Since Gates lacked the time to develop a system from scratch, he and Allen bought one, called 86-DOS, from a small firm, Seattle Computer. Gates then improved the system for IBM and renamed it MS-DOS, which stood for Microsoft Disk Operating System.

To this day, controversy surrounds the making of MS-DOS. Gary Kildall, the owner of a competing company, accused Microsoft of stealing codes from his own operating system. Kildall said: "I have grown up in this industry with Gates. He is divisive. He is manipulative. He is a user. He has taken much from me and the industry."

Soon after developing MS-DOS, Gates persuaded IBM to make public the design specifications for its personal computer so that software companies could more

Bill Gates (Archive Photos)

easily make programs for it. IBM agreed, and computer companies began making IBM-compatible machines. As they did, they bought MS-DOS from Microsoft.

By 1981, Microsoft had 125 employees and annual sales of $16 million. Gates obtained contracts to make software for Apple computers and for Radio Shack's Model 100. Dominant in producing operating systems, Gates expanded in the mid-1980s to making applications software—programs for such specific tasks as word processing or composing spreadsheets. Within a short while, Microsoft dominated that market as well. In 1985, Microsoft's sales topped $140 million, and in 1986 the company moved its 1,200 employees to a new 29-acre campuslike facility in Redmond, Washington, a suburb of Seattle. That same year, Gates went public and for the first time offered stock in Microsoft.

When in March 1987 Microsoft reached $90.75 a share, Gates became a billionaire. Two years later, he took on another competitor, Lotus, then dominant in making spreadsheet software. He introduced his Excel program at a greatly reduced price and substantially cut into Lotus's market share.

With growth came controversy, and by the early 1990s competitors were complaining that Gates had unfairly placed hidden "calls," or programming codes, into his operating systems that would allow Excel or Microsoft Word, the company's word-processing software, to run well, but make it difficult for competing software to do so. Gates denied the charge, until a book published in 1992 substantiated it, at which point Microsoft admitted it had implanted at least 16 calls into its operating system, called Windows.

Known as fiercely competitive and as a workaholic given to temper tantrums, Gates could also be humorous and inspirational. On January 1, 1994, he married Melinda French at a wedding ceremony in Hawaii that cost $1 million. (The couple had a child in 1996.) Shortly before, he completed building a 37,000-square-foot house on the shore of Lake Washington that included a movie theater, underground parking, and a pavilion that had seating for 100 dinner guests.

Microsoft continued to enjoy record profits and revenues, largely from the sale of its operating systems DOS and Windows, the latter an easy-to-use system that for commanding a computer required nothing more than clicking a mouse pointed on symbols. In 1996, Microsoft stock rose 90 percent, and Gates's personal wealth neared $24 billion, by far the greatest fortune in America and probably the greatest in the world.

At about that time, Gates began engaging in philanthropy and established a foundation with a contribution of $100 million. He gave $15 million to Harvard and $19 million to the University of Washington law school. He also contributed to the Seattle Symphony and a Seattle children's hospital.

Critics claimed that Gates wanted to do more than defeat competitors—he wanted to crush them. For his part, Gates saw Microsoft battling in a risky industry, one in which the next technological innovation could make a company fall from first-rate to second-rate or disappear altogether. Thus, survival and prosperity required a fierce, uncompromising competitiveness.

In August 1997, Gates and STEVEN JOBS (founder and head of Apple computers) stunned the business world when they formed a partnership under which Microsoft invested $150 million in Apple and agreed to let Apple remain largely autonomous. Gates's motivation was unclear, but he may have feared that if Apple collapsed, Microsoft would be accused of operating a monopoly and thus would face legal action.

Whatever the case, Microsoft failed to avoid a legal challenge. In October 1997, the Justice Department filed an antitrust suit against the corporation, charging that it had restrained trade when it required computer makers who wanted to install Microsoft Windows 95 (the world's most popular operating system) to also install Microsoft Internet Explorer. In July 1998, a federal appeals court ruled that Microsoft could legally package its products that way, but the Justice Department vowed it would continue with its suit. The *New York Times* commented:

What makes the . . . antitrust fight particularly significant is that the World Wide Web is emerging as the next new platform for global commerce, research, and entertainment. Not since the government took on the likes of AT&T and IBM more than a generation ago has the antitrust division issued such a challenge to a corporate titan.

Despite Microsoft's complicated legal battles with the federal government, Gates's personal fortune continued to grow. By 1998, he had become the richest man in the world with an estimated worth of $62 billion.

BIBLIOGRAPHY

Eller, Marlin, *Barbarians Led by Bill Gates: How the World's Richest Corporation Wields Its Power*, 1998; Gates, Bill, *The Road Ahead*, 1995; Ichbiah, Daniel, *The Making of Microsoft: How Bill Gates and His Team Created the World's Most Successful Software Company*, 1991; Manes, Stephen, *Gates: How Microsoft's Mogul Reinvented an Industry and Made Himself the Richest Man in America*, 1994; Wallace, James, *Overdrive: Bill Gates and the Race to Control Cyberspace*, 1997.

Geneen, Harold

(January 22, 1910–November 22, 1997)
Communications Executive

Hailed as "the twentieth century's greatest manager-industrialist," Harold Geneen led the International Telephone and Telegraph Company (ITT) in pursuit of his idea that a conglomerate could profitably invest in any business while rejecting allegiance to any one nation.

Born on January 22, 1910, in Bournemouth, England, to S. Alexander Geneen, a concert manager, and Aida (DeCruciani) Geneen, Harold was brought to the United States a year later by his parents. He spent his childhood largely in exclusive boarding schools and summer camps in the Northeast. In 1934, he earned a B.S. degree from New York University and joined the accounting firm of Lybrand and Ross Brothers & Montgomery in New York City as an accountant. Ambitious, he advanced through the ranks of corporate America, as chief accountant at the American Can Company from 1942 to 1946; as comptroller of the Bell and Howell Company from 1946 to 1950; and as vice president and comptroller of the Jones and Laughlin Steel Company from 1950 to 1956.

In the latter year, Geneen joined the Raytheon Manufacturing Company in Waltham, Massachusetts, as its executive vice president, a position that gave him substantial managerial power. There he developed the system he would later apply to ITT: dividing the company into semiautonomous divisions but making the head of each division strictly accountable to top management.

Under Geneen, Raytheon's profits soared, but he chafed at restrictions and in 1959 left the company to accept the presidency at ITT. He headed an international corporation of telephone companies that suffered from loose organization and had earned nowhere near its potential. To correct this, Geneen tightened ship by making all divisions accountable to him. He summoned division heads to annual meetings infamous for his penetrating questions and frequent browbeating.

Geneen pursued as well his belief that sound financial management could be applied to any business, and so he determined to increase ITT's profits by acquiring a host of companies. In the 1960s, he bought, among others, General Controls (a manufacturer of thermostatic equipment), Levitt and Sons (a large construction business), the Hamilton Management Company (a mutual funds firm), and the Sheraton Corporation (owner of hotels). In 1970, he purchased the Hartford Fire Insurance Company, a lucrative addition, and, soon after, Continental Baking, makers of Wonder Bread.

Geneen said he operated according to "the old-fashioned virtues of hard work, honesty, and risk-taking." Honesty took a beating, however, when, in the 1970s, scandal rocked ITT. First, evidence indicated that ITT had funneled money to the Republican Party during the presidency of Richard Nixon in order to get favorable treatment from the federal government in an antitrust suit aimed at the firm. Then newspapers reported that ITT had provided money to help overthrow the president of Chile, Salvador Allende, who had nationalized an ITT subsidiary in his country. The successful coup resulted in Allende's death and the establishment of a right-wing dictatorship. Although the charges were not conclusively proved, a hail of criticism descended on Geneen and ITT, for the Chilean episode revealed a multinational corporation that acted like a sovereign country in making foreign policy.

Geneen forged ahead, however, and under him ITT's sales grew from $700 million early in his reign to about $17 billion in the late 1970s. ITT managed some 250 companies in about 60 countries. Geneen relinquished the presidency in 1972 to serve as CEO and chairman of the board, and left ITT in 1979 to pursue his own investments. After his departure, ITT concluded that it had acquired too many bloated companies and relinquished many of its holdings.

An incessant worker who, after a divorce in 1946 married June Elizabeth Hjelm in 1949, Geneen professed to have no time to raise a family, and so the couple had no children. In offering advice, Geneen stated:

> The worst disease which can afflict executives in their work is not, as popularly supposed, alcoholism; it's egotism.

> Do you want my one-word secret of happiness? It's growth—mental, financial, you name it.

> You lead people a little—you push them a bit, and you're the catalyst. You hold people to high standards for their own good. Much better than holding their hands.

Geneen wrote a book, *The Synergy Myth*, in 1997, in which he criticized such recent business concepts as networking and excessive compensation for CEOs, and called for a return to traditional values. He died in New York City on November 22, 1997, from a heart attack.

BIBLIOGRAPHY

Geneen, Harold, *The Synergy Myth*, 1997;
Sampson, Anthony, *The Sovereign State of ITT*, 1973.

Gerber, Daniel

(May 6, 1898–March 16, 1974)
Manufacturer

The emergence of Gerber as the world's leading manufacturer of baby food began inadvertently when Daniel Gerber had an argument with his wife. Gerber, late for a social engagement, grew impatient waiting for Dorothy Gerber to strain the peas for their baby daughter's meal. Perturbed, Dorothy handed the green mush and the strainer to Dan and told him to finish the job. After Dan experienced the tedious chore, Dorothy suggested that he manufacture strained baby food, and he immediately went to work on the project.

Manufacturing had been in the Gerber family for years. His father, Frank Gerber, had founded the Fremont Canning Company, which canned peas and later beans and small fruits from area farms. By 1917, the company reached $1 million in sales.

Daniel was born on May 6, 1898, in Fremont, California, and graduated from St. John's Military Academy in Delafield, Wisconsin, in 1916. He then joined the U.S. Army, serving as a sergeant during World War I. While in fighting in the war, he received France's highest military honor, the Croix de Guerre. After he returned to the United States, Daniel spent one year taking courses at a business school before joining his father in the family's cannery. He married Dorothy Marion Scott in 1923, and they eventually had five children.

In 1927, soon after the episode with his wife and the partially strained peas, Gerber employed market research—a newly emergent technique attached to modern consumerism—and investigated the demand for baby food. He knew that many mothers believed babies should be restricted to liquid diets in their first year and that other companies already made strained baby food. They sold it only through druggists, however, and at high prices. Instead, Gerber wanted to mass-produce it.

Toward this end, he and his father developed strained fruit and vegetable recipes, and tested their mixtures on his baby daughter, Sally, and on other local babies. The babies seemed pleased, the market reports appeared favorable, and in 1928 the Gerbers launched an advertising campaign in three magazines, where they offered six cans for $1 through the mail—provided the customers send them coupons that included the names and addresses of their grocers. With this information in hand, the Gerbers convinced wholesalers that a market existed, and, by the end of the year, customers could buy their baby food in grocery stores as opposed to drugstores.

By the end of 1929, the Fremont Canning Company had sold nearly 600,000 cans of baby food, and despite the Great Depression and competition from more than 60 baby-food manufacturers, the Gerbers expanded their sales as they expanded their product line and offered a greater variety of fruits and vegetables. While their success had much to do with what was in the cans, it had equally to do with shrewd marketing. For example, the Gerbers asked artists to send them illustrations of a happy baby for promotional use. From the many submissions, they picked an unfinished charcoal sketch by Dorothy Hope Smith, one they liked for its innocence, as the Gerber baby. In another instance, the Gerbers used Austin cars for a promotion gimmick, sending the jaunty vehicles into towns and cities with each Austin displaying a picture of the Gerber baby in its rear window and sounding a horn that played "Rock-a-Bye-Baby." In addition, they won the loyalty of young mothers by publishing baby-care pamphlets and answering the many questions about babies that flooded their company's office. In the early 1940s, the Gerbers ceased canning adult foods and changed the name of their business to the Gerber Products Company.

The post–World War II baby boom created a Gerber empire, with sales reaching 7 million cans per day by 1947. After his father died on October 7, 1952, Gerber developed advertising for television and sponsored the children's show *Captain Kangaroo*—a smart move that solidified Gerber's identification with family values. In the 1960s, Gerber added nonfood baby products to the company's line, including such items as plastic panties, lotions, vaporizers, and toys.

Gerber contributed to community programs and served on the boards of the Nutrition Foundation of New York and the United Negro College Fund. At the time of his death on March 16, 1974, no other company could compare to Gerber's sales in baby food.

BIBLIOGRAPHY

Fucini, Joseph J., and Suzy Fucini, *Entrepreneurs: The Men and Women behind Famous Brand Names and How They Made It*, 1965.

Getty, J. Paul

(December 15, 1892–June 6, 1976)
Oil Industrialist

Intensely driven to make money and acquire power, Jean Paul Getty parlayed his success in the oil industry to become, at one point, the wealthiest man in the world.

Jean was born in Minneapolis, Minnesota, on December 15, 1892, to George Franklin Getty and Sarah McPherson Risher Getty. His father, an insurance lawyer, bought 1,100 acres in Oklahoma in 1903, soon after oil had been discovered in that state. The following year, George Getty struck oil on his land, and he moved his family to Bartlesville, a nearby town.

At age 11, Jean began acquiring knowledge of the business world when, with money from his father, he invested in the elder Getty's Minnehoma Oil Company. In 1906, George Getty moved his family to California. Five years later, Jean entered the University of California, Berkeley, but the following year withdrew and enrolled at Oxford University in England. He showed little interest in his studies and instead toured Europe. Although he claimed to have received a diploma from Oxford in 1914, the record remains in dispute.

Whatever the case, Getty returned home, and in 1916 obtained an oil lease to the Nancy Taylor farm in Oklahoma. There he struck oil and then sold the lease and made an $11,000 profit. This accomplishment impressed his father, who made him a director of the Minnehoma Oil Company. Getty lived in Tulsa, where he quickly parlayed oil deals into his first million dollars. He later said that after his experiences in Tulsa he "knew all the nuts and bolts of the oil industry."

J. Paul Getty (Archive Photos)

A shrewd businessman—critics said he frequently lied to get his way—Getty worked indefatigably in building his fortune. He married three times between 1923 and 1928, and in 1930 began an adulterous relationship with an office clerk he met in Berlin, Germany. His marriages, divorces, and unfaithfulness so angered his father that when the elder Getty died in 1930 he left nearly his entire fortune, $10 million, to his wife, Sarah. Jean Paul Getty got $500,000.

When the Great Depression hit in 1929 and sent the nation's economy reeling, Getty reacted differently from most other investors: rather than sell stocks, he bought them. Confident that in the long run his stocks would rise in value, he used the purchases to bring oil companies under his control. Between 1930 and 1936, while president of George F. Getty, Incorporated, he gained majority interest in Pacific Western, the largest oil company in California.

At the same time, Getty aimed at a bigger target: Tidewater Associated Oil Company. He bought stock in it for under $3 per share but encountered stiff resistance from Standard Oil, who controlled Tidewater through the Mission Company. Consequently, Getty pursued Mission, and by 1936 acquired 40 percent of its shares. This investment allowed him to dominate the Mission board of directors, although he failed to gain control of Tidewater until the early 1950s.

While Getty expanded his investments in the late 1930s, he traveled frequently to Europe, where he socialized with Hitler's aides and expressed admiration for the dictator. After the United States entered World War II, he applied for a naval commission, but the government harbored doubts about his loyalty and rejected him.

Nevertheless, Getty personally supervised war production at Spartan Aircraft, a company he owned, and made sure it turned out reliable planes for the U.S. military. He took great pride in this accomplishment.

In 1949, Getty gambled in oil. He paid the king of Saudi Arabia $8 million as a down payment for a 60-year lease on land near Kuwait. Although oil had been discovered in the Middle East, there was no guarantee it would be found on this tract, and the first 4 years of exploration, which cost $30 million, resulted in dry wells. In February 1953, however, Getty struck it big, and the oil and profits flowed.

In 1956, after Getty became president of the Mission Company, he changed the name of Pacific Western to the Getty Oil Company and placed it atop his corporate pyramid. Through interlocking share holdings, Getty Oil, and thus Getty himself, controlled Tidewater, Mission, and Skelly Oil, and owned several high-rise buildings (among them the Getty Building in New York City), and Spartan, the company that once made aircraft but now made mobile homes.

Throughout the 1950s, Getty invested heavily: $207 million for the first supertankers to carry crude oil, $120 million to expand Tidewater gas stations, and $200 million for a new refinery in Delaware. His net worth at decade's end vacillated between $700 million and $1 billion, making him the world's richest man.

Getty had, since the 1930s, collected art, and in 1953 founded the J. Paul Getty Museum in Malibu, California. He endowed it with $2 billion, making it the richest museum in the world. Today, it houses many valuable collections, including paintings by Vincent van Gogh and Rembrandt.

Getty married five times and had five sons, one of whom died in childhood, another who as an adult committed suicide. A difficult man, known for his miserly ways (he once installed a pay phone at his palatial house in England and required guests to use it to make calls) and for his demanding attitude, he had no lasting intimate relationships. He lived his last years at his home in England and died of prostate cancer on June 6, 1976.

Perhaps Getty desired more than a business legacy. "I never enjoyed making money, never started out to make a lot of it," he once said. "Money doesn't necessarily have any connection with happiness. Maybe with unhappiness."

BIBLIOGRAPHY

Lenzner, Robert, *The Great Getty: The Life and Loves of J. Paul Getty, Richest Man in the World*, 1985; Miller, Russell, *The House of Getty*, 1985.

Giannini, Amadeo

(May 6, 1870–June 3, 1949)
Banker

Amadeo Giannini changed American banking by establishing branch banks, a practice scorned by most in the industry. From a single, modest community bank, he built the mammoth Bank of America.

Amadeo was born on May 6, 1870, in San Jose, California, to Luigi Giannini and Virginia (Demartini) Giannini, Italian immigrant farmers from Genoa. Luigi Giannini was killed in 1877, and several months later, Virginia married Lorenzo Scatena. Scatena moved the family to San Francisco in 1882 and within a year opened a wholesale produce business that soon prospered. Amadeo left school after the eighth grade, obtained some additional education at Heald's Business College, and then applied himself to his stepfather's company. He traveled with horse and wagon to farms in the nearby valleys and as far south as Los Angeles, buying fruits and vegetables and finding new customers. His success led to his stepfather making him a partner in 1889. Three years later, Giannini married Clarinda Agnes Cuneo, daughter of a wealthy Italian immigrant who had made money in real estate.

With profits from his partnership and from his own real estate investments, Giannini retired from the produce business in 1901. The following year, his father-in-law died, and the family appointed him to manage the estate and to a seat on the board of a small bank, the Columbus Savings & Loan Society, located in San Francisco's immigrant North Beach district.

Giannini wanted the bank to attract more small borrowers, and when the directors opposed him, he quit and founded the Bank of Italy with four friends in October 1904. Located in a former North Beach saloon, the bank served merchants, farmers, and workers, primarily Italian immigrants. It gained a reputation for making small loans needed by persons with limited finances and for making them at reasonable rates—many called it "the little fellow's bank."

Giannini raised the ire of other bankers with a high-profile campaign to attract customers. First, he went into the streets, mingled with the immigrants, and convinced them to trust his bank. Then, he placed advertisements in newspapers, an unusual step for a banker in that era.

Giannini gained a reputation for reliability when, during San Francisco's great earthquake and fire in 1906, he moved his bank's deposits to a suburb to protect them before returning to the city, opening for business on the street, and making loans and dispensing funds to his many anxious depositors. He earned their confidence again in 1907 when, amid a financial panic, he refused to place a limit on withdrawals.

Giannini's greatest contribution to banking, though, occurred when he opened branch banks. He adopted the concept from elsewhere but popularized it at a time when most banks considered it dangerous. He opened the first Bank of Italy branch in 1909 in San Jose, just weeks after a law permitting the practice had passed the California legislature. By the end of 1918, he had 24 branches with more than $93 million in funds—the first statewide branch banking system in the nation. The system allowed the Bank of Italy to meet local needs by drawing on the strength of all its banks. For example, if a crisis hit one part of the state, as it did farm districts with bean growers in 1919, the bank in the hard-hit location could make loans at lower interest rates than its competitors by using funds from other branches.

Giannini had another goal, however, one driven in part by his hostility toward the domination of finances by eastern banks: he wanted to develop a worldwide banking system. Toward that end, in 1919, he organized the Bancitaly Corporation, a holding company that bought the East River National Bank in New York City and several banks in Italy. In 1924, Giannini retired from the presidency of the Bank of Italy while continuing as president of Bancitaly. In 1928, he acquired a new branch banking system in California and renamed it the Bank of America, while Bancitaly—the holding company—was renamed the Transamerica Corporation. In 1928, he merged the Bank of America with the Bank of Italy to form the Bank of America National Trust and Savings Association.

During the Great Depression of the 1930s, Giannini ousted Elisha Walker, who had succeeded him as president and chairman of Transamerica and had sold off bank properties. Giannini cut costs, acquired new accounts, and led Transamerica and the Bank of America through the depression. The Bank of America's resources grew, and by the mid-1930s, it had become the world's largest commercial bank with 493 branches in California and assets exceeding $5 billion.

Giannini's Bank of America played a major role in helping California survive the Great Depression (although it also foreclosed on numerous small businesses and farms) and in building industries during World War II. "The West has all the money to finance whatever it wants to," Giannini said right after the war. "We no longer have to go to New York for financing and we're not at its mercy." Giannini, who had resigned as chairman at the Bank of America in 1934, continued as chairman at Transamerica. By 1948, Transamerica controlled 645 bank branches in California, Oregon, Nevada, Arizona, and Washington, along with insurance companies, finance companies, and real estate interests.

Giannini died of a heart attack at his home in San Mateo on June 3, 1949. His son, Lawrence Mario Giannini, served as president of the Bank of America from 1936 until 1952. That year, the Federal Reserve Board ordered the separation of

Transamerica from the Bank of America. The BankAmerica Corporation (the firm's current name) was the fifth largest bank holding company in the nation in 1998 in terms of total assets, and had 1,796 branches in California, Washington, Texas, Arizona, Oregon, Nevada, New Mexico, Idaho, and Alaska.

BIBLIOGRAPHY

Bonadio, Felice, *A. P. Giannini: Banker of America*, 1994; Johnston, Moira, *Roller Coaster: The Bank of America and the Future of American Banking*, 1990; Nash, Gerald D., *Giannini and the Bank of America*, 1992.

Gibbons, Fred

(1949–)
Engineer

As the personal computer revolution overtook America in the late 1970s, particularly in businesses, Fred Gibbons decided to provide consumers with software that could increase productivity, and so founded the Software Publishing Company.

Gibbons was born in Boston, Massachusetts, in 1949, the son of a sea captain. He displayed an interest in business at an early age and while still in high school designed a canvas ski bag that sold in stores so well that the product paid for his college education. After graduating from the University of Michigan with a degree in computer science, he worked for a small computer company in Boston and, to improve his financial knowledge, enrolled at the Harvard Business School. He subsequently joined Hewlett-Packard and worked there six years in the marketing division. In 1979, he got the idea for software that would improve productivity for persons in business. He tried to sell it to his bosses at Hewlett-Packard, but they rejected it.

At that point, Gibbons and two co-workers founded their own company and, working out of a garage, wrote a database management program called *Pfs: file*. They began selling the software in 1980, calling themselves Software Publishing. Their product sold well, and Gibbons left Hewlett-Packard to concentrate on building his company. He convinced venture capitalist Jack Melchor to provide them with funds. *Pfs: file* sold more than 200,000 copies, and Software Publishing followed it with other successful programs. In 1994, its sales revenues reached $62 million, the year it released Harvard Graphics 3.0, a program that helped computer users create quick electronic presentations for meetings.

Gibbons served as president and chief executive officer of Software Publishing until early 1996, when he relinquished the former post. The company merged in December 1996 with Allegro New Media, and, shortly after, Gibbons left the firm.

BIBLIOGRAPHY

Silver, A. David, *Entrepreneurial Megabucks: The 100 Greatest Entrepreneurs of the Last Twenty-Five Years*, 1985.

Gillette, King

(January 5, 1855–July 9, 1932)
Manufacturer

King Camp Gillette gained renown for inventing and manufacturing the double-edged razor blade, but he wanted to be remembered most for his utopian vision, a plan for the entire world to be run as a single corporation.

King was born on January 5, 1855, in Fond du Lac, Wisconsin, to George Gillette and Fanny (Camp) Gillette. He grew up in Chicago, and when his family lost everything in the Chicago Fire of 1871, he went to work as a salesman for a hardware company and, later, a bottle-stopper company. In 1890, he married Alanta Ella Gaines, and they eventually had one son.

Gillette liked to tinker with inventions and ideas. In the latter realm, he wrote a ponderous treatise in 1894 called *The Human Drift* that represented his attempt to correct the abuses evident in an industrializing society. He proposed that the entire world be run as a single corporation, owned by the citizens, who would hold equal shares in the enterprise. Such an arrangement, he believed, would encourage maximum work while eliminating competition and its inhumane features. He wanted the center for the North American utopia to be near Niagara Falls, whose water power could generate electricity for a city of 60 million people housed in glass-domed, circular apartment towers.

Few read Gillette's work, but they took note of his invention intended to improve shaving. Gillette got the idea for a razor after his employer told him he should invent something useful but disposable—something people would buy over and over again. Gillette noticed the inefficiency in the use of straightedge razors, for they required sharpening or stropping, accomplished by stroking the blade for several minutes against a leather strap. Gillette's invention consisted of a disposable thin double-edged blade attached to a metal handle.

Shortly after 1900, Gillette, in partnership with machinist William Nickerson and backed by Boston investors, began manufacturing and selling his product from a small loft. His American Safety Razor Company (later the Gillette Company) encountered a problem, however, when it was unable to make enough razors to meet the demand. Help arrived when a local brewer, John Joyce, provided the company with $60,000 to buy equipment, in return for his receiving a controlling interest. In late 1904, Gillette sold 20,000 razor sets, consisting of the handle and 20 disposable blades, at $5 each.

Gillette served as spokesman for the company, and his picture appeared in many advertisements, including one that portrayed the Gillette razor as conquering the "harshest beard" and involving "no stropping, no honing." Gillette had numerous quarrels with Joyce, however, with each man considering the other arrogant. The two antagonists agreed in 1910 to a deal whereby Joyce bought most of Gillette's interest for $1 million. Although Gillette remained president of the company until 1931, he played only a small role in its operations.

Gillette's fortune allowed him to continue writing and presenting his utopian ideas. He persuaded writer and reformer Upton Sinclair to edit *The People's Corporation*, published in 1924. As with Gillette's other works, however, few people took notice.

While he continued to write, Gillette lived in Los Angeles, where he bought and sold real estate. He died on July 9, 1932, disappointed that his utopian vision had failed to reform the world or bring recognition to his abilities as a thinker. Today, the Gillette Company

King Gillette (Library of Congress)

makes more than razors—it produces a wide line of toiletries, among them Right Guard deodorant, and has acquired other companies, including Paper Mate pens.

BIBLIOGRAPHY

Adams, Russell, *King C. Gillette: The Man and His Wonderful Shaving Device*, 1978; Gillette, King, *The Human Drift*, 1894, reprt. 1976.

Gimbel, Bernard

(April 10, 1885–September 29, 1966)
Merchant

Bernard Feustman Gimbel expanded the successful chain of retail stores established by his grandfather and continued by his father and uncles. With his knack for sensing public tastes and his shrewd business practices, Gimbel transformed the company from a handful of stores into a retail empire with $600 million in sales by 1966, the year of his death.

On April 10, 1885, Bernard Gimbel was born to ISAAC GIMBEL and Rachel Feustman in Vincennes, Indiana. Bernard's grandfather, Adam Gimbel, had emigrated from Bavaria and established a store called the Palace of Trade in Vincennes in 1842. The store prospered, and Adam Gimbel left its management to his seven sons, one of whom was Bernard's father, Isaac.

The seven Gimbel brothers expanded the operation with a few branch stores and then moved to Milwaukee in 1887. The young Bernard was educated in the Milwaukee public school system until age nine, when his father moved the family to Philadelphia to manage a newly opened Gimbels branch store. Bernard continued his education at the William Penn Charter School, excelling in football and boxing, which he continued to enjoy throughout his life. In 1904, Gimbel went on to study economics at the Wharton School of Finance and Commerce at the University of Pennsylvania.

Like his father and uncles, Gimbel learned the retail business from the bottom up. He began working on the receiving platform at the Philadelphia Gimbels store in 1907 after finishing his B.S. degree at the Wharton School. He served in various other positions before becoming vice president at the end of that year. Gimbel eventually took over as president of the company after his father's retirement in 1927.

One of the early highlights of Gimbel's career was persuading his father and uncles to open a major branch store in New York City in 1910. The favorable location of the store, centrally positioned at the crossroads of two railroads and four subway lines, was one of the keys to the branch's impressive success. In a wise financial move, Gimbel soon swayed his father and uncles to purchase the store building for $9 million rather than continue to pay an annual rent of $655,000.

Gimbel married Alva Bernheimer on April 4, 1912. Alva bore him five children including two sets of twins, one set of girls and one set of identical boys. One son, Bruce, would eventually succeed his father as president of Gimbels. In the early 1920s, Gimbel moved the family to a 200-acre estate in Greenwich, Connecticut, where, with his love of athletics, travel, and moderate gambling, he earned a reputation as a member of the so-called "international sporting set."

In business matters, Gimbel was becoming respected within the family establishment. In 1922, on Gimbel's counsel, the business was incorporated as Gimbel Brothers. Having earned his elders' trust, he was given leeway that allowed him to engineer the purchase of two Saks Fifth Avenue stores in New York City in 1923, as well as Pittsburgh's Kaufmann and Baer retail stores in 1925.

Bernard Gimbel with his wife, Alva (Library of Congress)

Gimbel did not consider himself to be an outstanding retail merchant like his father, but after assuming the corporate presidency in 1927, he guided the company through the Great Depression, making the enterprise profitable again by 1934. At the beginning of World War II, Gimbel borrowed $21 million in order to stockpile items that he had astutely guessed would become scarce during the war. These items were then sold at sizable profits during the worst shortages in 1942 and 1943. His management success was due largely to his ability to ascertain the public's moods and tastes. During and after the war, he stressed a thrifty appearance for his stores to attract bargain hunters, but when Gimbel sensed the growing affluence of the country in the late 1940s, he refurbished his New York store in 1949 to appeal to a more fashionable clientele.

Gimbel was slow to join the exodus of department stores to the burgeoning suburban malls, holding out against the trend until 1953, the year he stepped down as president and delegated many management tasks. With the new direction of talented outsiders, the company expanded to include 27 Gimbels stores and 27 Saks stores, many of them in the new suburban malls. Gimbel, a dedicated Roosevelt Democrat, was widely liked, prompting the editorial comment in the New York *Herald-Tribune* that "Mr. Gimbel not only has more real friends than any other New Yorker but has them amongst the widest array of groups and classes."

Gimbel remained chief executive officer of the company until 1961 and then served as chairman of the board until his death in New York City on September 29, 1966.

BIBLIOGRAPHY

Fortune, July 1945; *Life*, December 12, 1949; *New York Times*, Obituary, September 30, 1966; *New York Times Magazine*, April 4, 1965; *Washington Post*, Obituary, September 30, 1966.

Gimbel, Isaac

(April 24, 1856–April 11, 1931)
Merchant

With the help of six brothers, Isaac Gimbel made Gimbels Department Store a leader in national merchandising.

Gimbel entered the merchant business by way of his father. Isaac was born on April 24, 1856, in Vincennes, Indiana, to Adam Gimbel and Fridolyn (Kahnweller) Gimbel. The elder Gimbel had begun a store in 1842 called The Palace of Trade. He ran this Vincennes establishment according to a principle: "If anything said or done in this store looks wrong or is wrong . . . we shall set it right as soon as it comes to our knowledge." By the time Isaac was born, such fair dealing had made Adam Gimbel prosperous, and he looked to Isaac and his other sons to continue and expand the business. Adam moved to Philadelphia in 1865 and left his eldest son, Jacob, in charge of the Vincennes store. Isaac began his mercantile career at age 13, working for Jacob.

The Gimbels opened branch stores in Danville, Illinois, and Washington, Indiana, in 1882, and five years later, they opened their first store under the name Gimbel Brothers in Milwaukee, Wisconsin.

Their success in Milwaukee caused the Gimbels in 1894 to buy Granville B. Haines & Company in Philadelphia, Pennsylvania, for $1 million and compete with one of the nation's most prominent merchants, JOHN WANAMAKER. They converted Haines & Company into another Gimbel Department Store. That same year, Isaac Gimbel took charge of Gimbel Brothers as president.

The prosperity of the Philadelphia store convinced Isaac to enter the nation's biggest mercantile market, New York City. In 1909, he built a large department store on Broadway between 32nd and 33rd Streets, and put his eldest son, BERNARD GIMBEL, in charge of it. When Gimbels opened in 1910, it went head-to-head with another big department store, Macy's (founded by ROWLAND MACY), located just one block away.

The Gimbels incorporated their company in 1922, with Isaac as president. He traveled the world to find new merchandise and developed innovative department store layouts and advertising campaigns. In 1923, Bernard arranged to buy a competitor, Saks & Company, whose two stores it continued to operate under that name, one on 34th Street and the other on Fifth Avenue (a new building that cost more than $4 million). In 1925, the Gimbels bought a 16-story building opposite their original store in New York City and added three more stories to create 27 acres of floor space.

Isaac became chairman of the board in 1927, while Bernard assumed the presidency. By 1930, the annual net sales at the seven Gimbels Department Stores reached $123 million, making it the largest department store business in the world.

Isaac died on April 11, 1931, but Gimbels continued to grow under Bernard's leadership. He served as president until 1953 and then as chairman of the board until his death in 1966. Gimbels went into a sharp decline after the 1960s, and the chain folded in September 1986 when it closed its flagship store on Broadway in New York City.

BIBLIOGRAPHY

Harris, Leon, *Merchant Princes: An Intimate History of Jewish Families Who Built Great Department Stores*, 1979.

Girard, Stephen

(May 20, 1750–December 26, 1831)
Financier

A merchant and banker, Stephen Girard amassed wealth few thought possible in early America and devoted considerable time and money to charitable and philanthropic causes.

From the moment Girard was born on May 20, 1750, the sea captured him. His hometown, Bordeaux, France (a port on the Garonne River), harbored many ships, and his father, Pierre Girard, worked as a ship's captain. At the time of Stephen's birth, Pierre owned several vessels.

Young Girard received little formal education. In 1762, his mother, Odette (Lafargue) Girard, died, and two years later, he went to sea as a cabin boy on a ship headed to the West Indies. Despite being blind in his right eye, Girard proved a worthy crewman and advanced rapidly. In 1773, he received official certification as a captain. The following year, he sailed for Haiti but suffered a setback when, unable to sell that part of the cargo owned by him, he lost money. Later that year, he made the first of several voyages for a merchant firm, Thomas Randall & Son, as a captain. He traded some goods for himself and earned enough money to buy half-interest in a ship, *La Jeune Babe*. Aboard this vessel in 1776, he made an emergency stop in Philadelphia as the city was moving toward revolution. Just five weeks after his arrival, the Americans declared their independence from Britain.

Girard never joined the American military, but he supported the revolution and in 1777 commanded a merchant ship that evaded a British blockade and brought in supplies needed by civilians and the military. From this and other voyages, he earned a substantial profit. Later that year, he married Mary Lum, the penniless daughter of a shipbuilder. At that point, Girard decided to settle in Philadelphia and establish himself as a merchant. He never again commanded a ship.

Girard set a work and investment regimen that brought great success. His biographer, George Wilson, claims that Girard made millions in maritime trade "by being flexible, resourceful, and opportunistic, by constantly buying and selling ships (or fractional interests in ships), building ships, leasing ships, and renting cargo space on ships he did not own. He put his eggs in many baskets. He maintained a healthy mix of calculated risk and thoughtful prudence." Girard watched costs closely and keenly studied market trends and political changes in other nations.

In 1785, tragedy struck when Girard's wife suddenly went insane, and he placed her in the Pennsylvania Hospital (where she died in 1815). He subsequently had two mistresses: Sally Bickham followed by Polly Kenton. Meanwhile, Girard developed an expanding merchant trade with Europe, despite the French Revolution that began in 1789 and the nearly constant warfare between Britain and France. His high profits allowed him to buy several ships—at one time, he owned six.

When a yellow fever epidemic swept Philadelphia in 1793, Girard, rather than flee as many prosperous merchants did, gave money and time to help those stricken and superintended the fever hospital at Bush Hill. For two months, while thousands died, he worked day and night caring for patients. He told a friend: "I only regret that my strength and ability have not fully seconded my good will." Throughout the 1790s, Girard contributed substantial sums to charities and public programs. And although he lived comfortably and owned a slave, he rejected opulence, refusing even to purchase the fancy carriages favored by the rich.

In business, Girard expanded into the China trade shortly after 1800, but he ranged beyond shipping and invested in real estate, insurance, and banking. Soon after the First Bank of the United States folded, Girard bought its building and other assets and started his own bank in 1812 with capital of $1.2 million. He played an important role during the War of 1812 when he lent money to the national treasury and, along with David Parish and JOHN JACOB ASTOR, obtained subscribers to a federal loan. He profited monetarily from these endeavors but at the same time provided funding to a financially strapped government.

After the war, Girard served as president of the commission appointed to supervise the founding of a new national bank. He firmly believed that the U.S. government should participate directly in banking. When no buyers came forward to subscribe to the bank's $3 million stock issue, Girard bought the shares. This made possible the start of the Second Bank of the United States, for which Girard served as a director. He soon disagreed with loan policies that he considered too liberal, however, and left his position and sold his stock.

In his later years, Girard mainly tended a farm he bought in south Philadel-

Stephen Girard (Library of Congress)

phia, but he continued to engage in shipping and finance. He resolutely opposed idleness and still reported to his banking house even after a serious accident in 1830, when he was run over by horses and a wagon. When he died on December 26, 1831, from pneumonia, newspapers reported a huge funeral and recounted his life with high praise. In his will, he bequeathed large land holdings in Louisiana to the cities of New Orleans and Philadelphia, and among other amounts, gave $500,000 to the city of Philadelphia and $6 million to found a boarding school for educating "poor white orphan males." This became Girard College. One contemporary said of Girard that his merits included "probity of the strictest kind, diligence unsurpassed, [and] perseverance in all pursuits."

BIBLIOGRAPHY

Adams, Donald R., *Finance and Enterprise in Early America: A Study of Stephen Girard's* Bank, 1812–1831, 1978; Wilson, George, *Stephen Girard: America's First Tycoon,* 1995.

Goizueta, Roberto

(November 18, 1931–October 18, 1997)
Merchant

Roberto Goizueta ascended to the leadership of Coca-Cola at a difficult time: the world-famous company, founded in its modern form by ASA CANDLER, had suffered an intense attack by its main competitor, Pepsi Cola, and, mired in tradition, had failed to respond effectively. Goizueta changed all that—

Roberto Goizueta (George Lange/The Coca-Cola Company)

dynamic and innovative, he brought Coke to new heights of popularity and profitability.

Goizueta had the distinction of losing nearly all his money in a Communist revolution. He was born in Havana, Cuba, on November 18, 1931, to a wealthy family. His father, an architect and sugar refinery owner, sent him to the exclusive Cheshire Academy in Connecticut, a prep school. From there, Goizueta enrolled at Yale University and in 1953 obtained a degree in chemical engineering. He returned to Havana and, after a few months in the family business, joined Coca-Cola as a quality-control chemist. In August 1960, however, Goizueta and his wife Olga, along with their three children, fled Cuba when Fidel Castro's Communist regime began confiscating property and nationalizing the economy. They left all their belongings behind, and Goizueta arrived in Miami with $40 in his pocket.

He still had his connection with Coca-Cola, however, and worked for the company's Latin American operations in the Bahamas. Goizueta moved to Coke's corporate headquarters in Atlanta in 1964 and earned a reputation for hard work and creativity. "Once you lose everything, what's the worst that's going to happen to you?" he said. "You develop a self-assurance."

Goizueta worked his way up from technical operations, all the while cultivating ROBERT WOODRUFF, the former head of Coke who still had considerable clout within the company. In 1979, Goizueta was promoted to a group of six vice chairmen, potential successors to the presidency. Few observers expected Goizueta to get the top post, but with Woodruff's blessing he did so in 1980, and the following year was named chairman of the board and CEO.

Woodruff and other leaders at Coke wanted a change—someone who could shake the entrenched bureaucratic structure and take on Pepsi-Cola. In the 1960s and 1970s, Pepsi had made serious inroads on Coke, first by portraying itself as the drink of young people, and then by creating its "Pepsi challenge" advertising campaign, which showed that in taste tests consumers preferred Pepsi to Coke.

Goizueta immediately threw his support to those within the company who wanted to develop a new drink, Diet Coke, to compete with Diet Pepsi. He considered the project essential in reviving Coke's profits and took a bold move when he launched Diet Coke in the New York market without first trying it out in a smaller area. The gamble paid off, as did a new advertising campaign with the slogan "Coke is it!"

At the same time, Goizueta decided Coke needed to enliven its image by diversifying into a glamour industry. He accomplished this by acquiring a Hollywood movie studio, Columbia Pictures, in 1982 for $750 million.

Another challenge appeared on the soft drink battlefield when Pepsi and Royal Crown began selling caffeine-free colas. Goizueta responded by providing caffeine-free versions of Coke, Diet Coke, and Tab. By 1983, Diet Coke emerged as the third best-selling soft drink in the country (surpassing Diet Pepsi) and *Ad-Week* magazine named Goizueta its marketer of the year.

Nevertheless, Pepsi continued to hold its taste tests and claim that consumers liked it the best. Younger people especially liked Pepsi's slightly sweeter taste. As a result, Goizueta made his most daring and controversial move: he decided to change the Coke mixture, to revamp the sacred, supersecret formula called Merchandise 7X. Coke tested the new, sweeter 7X100 formula with select groups of consumers in mid-1983, and they overwhelmingly preferred it. The company responded by marketing New Coke in 1985.

Disaster struck, however. Consumers rejected New Coke and demanded a return to the old formula, not so much out of taste as out of attachment to an American standard. Pepsi rejoiced in the New Coke fiasco, claiming that in producing the New Coke, Coca-Cola had at last admitted that Pepsi tasted better. Within weeks, Goizueta retreated and returned to making Merchandise 7X as Coca-Cola Classic. He declared: "There is a . . . group of consumers to whom we want to speak today and our message to this group is simple: We have heard you." Within a short time, New Coke disappeared from the scene.

The controversy may actually have served Coke well—it enhanced the image of Coca-Cola as something special, a soft drink above all other soft drinks. By 1985, sales of Coca-Cola's three sugared colas, including the new Cherry Coke, had topped sales from the previous year by 10 percent.

That same year, Goizueta acquired Embassy Communications, a leading television production company, and, in 1986, Merv Griffin Productions. *Business Week* called Goizueta "a bold agent of change in a once-stodgy corporation." Goizueta sold Columbia Pictures in 1989 for a large profit. After the Soviet Union collapsed in 1990, he expanded Coke into the former Communist-bloc nations, an ironic victory over the ideological system that had caused him to flee Cuba more than 30 years before.

Goizueta's aggressive tactics enriched Coke's shareholders and himself. The company's market value surged from $5 billion when he took command in 1981 to $150 billion in 1997. A $100 investment in Coca-Cola in 1981 increased in value to $6,500 in 1997. Coca-Cola compensated Goizueta in 1991 with stock worth over $59 million, and at the time of his death in Atlanta from lung cancer on October 18, 1997, his personal wealth had reached $1.3 billion.

BIBLIOGRAPHY

Louis, J. C., and Harvey Z. Yazijian, *The Cola Wars*, 1980; Oliver, Thomas, *The Real Coke, the Real Story*, 1986.

Goldenson, Leonard

(December 7, 1905–)
Entertainment Executive

In 1952, Leonard Goldenson, then the head of United Paramount Theaters, took a gamble: he bought the American Broadcasting Company (ABC), a fledgling radio and television network, for $25 million. Over succeeding years, he built it into a company that challenged the CBS and NBC networks for a national audience, and at times emerged as the ratings leader.

Born on December 7, 1905, in Scottdale, Pennsylvania, to Lee Goldenson and Esther (Broude) Goldenson, Leonard developed an interest in show business while still a boy, when his father, who owned a clothing shop, invested in two movie theaters. Despite his interest, after obtaining a B.S. degree from Harvard in 1927, Leonard Goldenson returned to the college and studied law.

Degree in hand, Goldenson joined a large law firm in 1930. By that time, the Great Depression had begun, and he learned from one of the firm's partners that Paramount Pictures was nearing collapse. Looking for help to reorganize its New England theaters, Paramount wanted a young, energetic lawyer—and turned to Goldenson. He did so well that in 1938 Paramount gave him full responsibility for its 1,700 movie theaters throughout the nation.

Paramount made Goldenson a vice president in 1942, and two years later a director and president of Paramount Theaters Service Corporation. In an antitrust action, however, the U.S. government ordered Paramount Pictures to divest itself of its movie theaters. Thus emerged United Paramount Theaters (UPT), with Goldenson as its president. Under a court ruling, he reduced the number of theaters owned by the company but increased profitability to the point that UPT sought a new investment.

Goldenson considered television a communications medium poised for tremendous growth, and in 1951 UPT announced that it would buy ABC, which had been founded in the 1940s. The Federal Communications Commission approved the merger in 1953, and Goldenson worked to convert ABC—clearly trailing the well-established CBS and NBC networks—into a broadcasting power. At that time, ABC controlled 5 TV stations and 12 radio stations, and through its affiliates had 81 TV outlets and 355 radio outlets. The network, though, had limited access to major urban markets.

ABC's emergence as a credible challenge to CBS and NBC occurred in 1954 when Goldenson signed a $2 million deal with WALT DISNEY to produce an evening show for the network. In addition, Disney provided Goldenson the following year with a tremendously successful children's show, the *Mickey Mouse Club*. Such programs as *Kukla, Fran and Ollie; Omnibus; the Lawrence Welk Show;* and *Wyatt Earp* added to ABC's ratings.

Goldenson expressed his business philosophy:

I think it's highly important that a network be held in the hands of broadcasters. You can't operate a network like you run a bank.

You've got to be in a position where creative people are given . . . the opportunity of expressing themselves, and to take chances.

Goldenson made sure that ABC aimed at an audience younger than that attracted by his competitors. He believed CBS and NBC were too rooted in their days as radio broadcasters and had too many older entertainers from that era. He insisted on fresh faces and shows with action.

Despite ABC's steady expansion, it remained behind the other two networks until the 1970s, when it finally achieved number one in the ratings. Critics said it did so by developing increasingly shallow adventure shows and situation comedies, such as *Three's Company.*

Goldenson also developed ABC's news division, which not only turned a profit but also gained a reputation for quality. He later traced its maturation to two events: the assassination of President John F. Kennedy in 1963, which showed viewers that the network could cover a crisis just as well as the news departments at CBS and NBC, and to the airing in 1967 of a regular half-hour evening news program. Over the years under Goldenson's tenure, ABC hired several prominent journalists, among them Bill Lawrence, John Scali, and Howard K. Smith.

Goldenson headed ABC until 1985, when he helped negotiate a deal that merged the network with Capital Cities Communication. He defended the merger as essential to deflect hostile bids. "We became prey to the specter of unfriendly takeover attempts," he said.

Goldenson continued his association with ABC as a director of Capital Cities/ABC, Inc., but by 1990 he had retired from all except an advisory status. Despite the merger with Capital Cities, Goldenson later warned that media ownership could fall into a few hands, a development that would threaten diversity and encourage blandness in programming.

BIBLIOGRAPHY

Goldenson, Leonard, *Beating the Odds: History of a Campaign That Succeeded*, 1991; "Mortgaging the Future," *Broadcasting*, April 7, 1986.

Goodrich, B. F.

(November 4, 1841–August 3, 1888)
Manufacturer

An industrializing America needed rubber—rubber hoses and rubber belts for its factories and machines—and Benjamin Franklin Goodrich provided it.

Benjamin was born on November 4, 1841, to Anson Goodrich and Susan (Dinsmore) Goodrich on the family farm near Ripley, a small town in upstate New York. His mother named him Benjamin Franklin after the famous early American whom she admired, and as it turned out, the young Goodrich replicated Franklin's assiduous commitment to business and success.

Goodrich's first interest, however, was in medicine, and in 1859, after studying under several doctors, he entered Cleveland Medical College. After he graduated in 1861, he opened a practice in Mayville, New York. The Civil War interrupted, however, and Goodrich served as a hospital steward to the Ninth New York Cavalry before being promoted to assistant surgeon. While on leave from 1862 to 1863, he studied surgery at the University of Pennsylvania and then served with the Army of the Potomac as an assistant surgeon and head of a small hospital.

After the war, Goodrich struggled with his medical career. He opened several practices, including one in Pit Hole, Pennsylvania, an oil boomtown. There he finally quit medicine and joined the Brown Brothers Oil Company that sent him to New York City to work in its shipping department.

In the metropolis, Goodrich and a friend, John P. Morris, invested in real estate and used their profits to buy stock in the Hudson River Rubber Company. When they discovered the company had deep financial problems, they bought more stock in an attempt to save it. With his interest, Goodrich became the company president, and to lower the firm's overhead, he moved the business to a rubber factory in Melrose, New York. At about the same time, in 1869, he married Mary M. Marvin. The couple subsequently had three children.

As Goodrich worked to right his company, which was then losing money, he read publicity issued by the city of Akron, Ohio. He particularly liked Akron's railroad connections, and he met with several of the city's business leaders who, after some smart selling on his part, promised him financial support if he moved his factory to their town. Goodrich agreed, and in February 1871 he and four partners opened a new plant in Akron. Unlike some of his competitors, Goodrich rejected specialization and instead manufactured a variety of rubber products, most prominently fire hoses and industrial belting.

Goodrich acquired raw rubber from brokers in New York City and then subjected it to a process whereby he soaked it in warm water, ran it through roller washers to remove the dirt, hung it dry for several weeks over a heater, mixed it with sulfur and other chemicals, and then ran it through heavy rollers to make thin layers. He then used these layers to make the final product.

The 1870s afforded Goodrich a rich market as America industrialized, but the decade had its economic problems, notably a severe depression that lasted over two years and nearly bankrupted Goodrich. Amid this crisis, in 1874, Goodrich reorganized his firm as B. F. Goodrich & Company. Six years later, in search of more capital, he incorporated as the B. F. Goodrich Company.

In 1883, Goodrich obtained a patent on improved industrial belting, a product made more flexible through a vulcanization process. Although Goodrich had problems with fluctuations in the price of rubber—nearly all rubber came from the Amazon River basin and the supply varied—his company prospered and in 1888 profits reached $107,000 on sales of $696,000.

Later that year, Goodrich's health declined from tuberculosis, and he died on August 3, 1888, in a sanitarium in Colorado. His successor as head of the firm, George T. Perkins, made B. F. Goodrich into a prosperous national company while expanding its product line to include golf balls, footwear, and tires.

BIBLIOGRAPHY

Blackford, Mansel G., and K. Austin Kerr, *B. F. Goodrich: Tradition and Transformation, 1870–1995*, 1996.

Gordy, Berry

(November 28, 1929–)
Producer

After owning a failed record store in Detroit, Michigan, Berry Gordy Jr. turned to writing and producing songs. He changed rhythm and blues into a commercialized rock 'n' roll that resulted in dozens of hit records for his company, Motown, and resulted in his status as one of America's most successful African-American business leaders.

Berry was born on November 28, 1929, in Detroit, Michigan, to Berry and Bertha Gordy. His father owned a plastering and carpentry service, a general store, and a printing business, and young Berry likely

Berry Gordy (Archive Photos/Lawrence Siskind)

got his entrepreneurial ambition from Berry Sr. At first, however, Berry pursued athletics and dropped out of high school in the eleventh grade in order to box. He fought as a featherweight and showed talent but earned little money. Then, in 1951, the U.S. Army inducted him into service.

Upon his discharge in 1953, Gordy, who that year married Thelma Louise Coleman, borrowed money from his father and opened a record store in Detroit. The 3D Record Mart, as he called it, sold jazz recordings, which had limited appeal among his black clientele. Gordy started hanging out in the Detroit jazz scene, but his store closed within two years, and he went to work as a chrome trimmer at a Ford assembly plant.

Gordy had begun writing songs, however, and in 1957 Jackie Wilson recorded "Reet Petite," cowritten with Gordy's sister, Gwen, and with Tyran Carlo. The song climbed the charts, and over the next two years, Gordy wrote three more hits for Wilson. Yet after the record labels and others took their cuts, he was left with little profit.

During that period, Gordy met Raynoma Lile, a trained musician (later his second wife), and she encouraged him to produce his own records. With $800 that he borrowed from his family, Gordy founded Motown in 1958, and for his base of operations used at first an apartment and then a bungalow on Detroit's Grand Boulevard. The following year, he issued Marv Johnson's "Come to Me" and Barret Strong's "Money (That's What I Want)" under the Tamla label, and the latter record reached the charts. He established the Motown label in 1960 and a second one, Gordy, in 1962.

At the same time, Gordy signed artists who proved crucial to his success: the Spinners, Junior Walker and the All Stars, Smokey Robinson and the Miracles, and Lamont Anthony, later known as Lamont Dozier, who was part of a phenomenal song-writing group at Motown—Holland, Dozier, and Holland.

Gordy wanted a record company that could appeal to whites. He developed Motown at a time when young people, and especially white suburban kids, had more money to spend on records. Many African Americans were also pursuing integration with white society through their involvement with the civil rights movement. Gordy determined, then, that Motown would take gospel and rhythm and blues influences and commercialize them. As one observer later noted: "Gordy had an uncanny feeling for the tinny-sounding car radio; he grasped that it was where most young people were first to hear new records. Motown records were always mixed to play well on car radios."

Amazingly, though, Gordy had no formal training in music and could neither read music nor play a musical instrument. He relied on an innate sense that enabled him to write hit songs, identify hit songs written by others, and recognize stage talent.

Four Motown singles made the Top 10 in 1962, followed by six more in 1963, with a new artist, Stevie Wonder, reaching number-one. Gordy produced four number-one hits in 1964, a feat that made the pop world take notice. His gifted writers turned out hit after hit in factory fashion—Gordy wanted only songs that had commercial appeal.

Of the early years at Motown, Gordy later said:

> [The young artists] could be channeled and directed, but they couldn't do things for themselves that much. So we did it for them; we taught them how to create.

> Of course, I didn't really know myself; I was just a competent, cocky kid who felt I knew a lot more than I did.

> I never thought about whether there was or wasn't talent in Detroit. I just felt everybody was talented. And at that time, I felt I could make a hit out of anybody.

> Every record we felt had to go Top 10. We'd always say, "No album cuts."

Of all the Motown artists in the 1960s, the Supremes, led by Diana Ross, scored the greatest hits, second only to the Beatles in national record sales. They displayed Gordy's penchant for sweet harmonies and upbeat tunes. When the Supremes faded in the early 1970s, Gordy found another hot group in the Jackson Five. At the same time, Gladys Knight and the Pips won several Grammy awards.

Gordy disappointed Detroit when, in 1972, he moved Motown to Los Angeles. From that location, he produced movies and television shows. *Lady Sings the Blues*, starring Diana Ross, premiered later that year and won critical acclaim, with Ross receiving an Academy Award nomination. She also starred in a film that Gordy directed in 1975, *Mahogany*. His 1978 movie *The Wiz*, however, flopped, and he did not make another movie until 1985, when *The Last Dragon* attracted large audiences. Meanwhile, he produced a TV special, "Motown 25—Yesterday, Today, and Forever," that received nine Emmy nominations and was the highest-rated variety special in TV history.

Gordy sold Motown Records to MCA, Incorporated in 1988 for $61 million. By that time, the label had passed its prime, and MCA sold the label to Polygram Records in 1993. In 1997, EMI Music Publishing bought a half-interest in Jobete, the publishing company that owns the rights to Motown's old songs. In the deal, EMI paid Gordy $132 million.

While the head of Motown, Gordy had his detractors. Many artists complained that he allowed them no freedom, and several of them, particularly Marvin Gaye, feuded with Gordy, while others, like the Jackson Five, left Motown. Yet Gordy had made many an unknown singer a star while mainstreaming black music. "The success of Motown," claimed one observer, "stands as the most shining hour of the American black in popular culture."

BIBLIOGRAPHY

Benjaminson, Peter, *The Story of Motown*, 1979; Early, Gerald, "One Nation under a Groove," *The New Republic*, July 15, 1991; Gordy, Berry, *To Be Loved: The Music, the Memories of Mowtown: An Autobiography*, 1994; Singleton, Raynoma Gordy, *Berry, Me, and Motown: The Untold Story*, 1990; White, Adam, "Gordy Speaks," *Billboard*, November 5, 1994.

Gould, Jay

(May 27, 1836–December 2, 1892)
Financier

Through unscrupulous deals mainly involving railroads, Jason "Jay" Gould amassed a fortune. His actions often shocked America, but in many ways Gould epitomized a striving, materialistic nation.

Jay was born on May 27, 1836, in Roxbury, New York, to John Gould and Mary (Moore) Gould. Since his father struggled at farming, Jay went to work at an early age as a blacksmith and a clerk in a general store. He obtained only a rudimentary education, but learned surveying and used this talent to make money. At about age 18, he helped map Ulster, Albany, and Delaware Counties in New York and other counties in Ohio and Michigan. By age 21, he had saved $5,000.

Gould used this money to join with another businessman in gaining control of a tannery in Pennsylvania. His maneuvering earned him a reputation for dishonesty. Gould soon sold the tannery, worked briefly as a leather merchant, and in 1860 moved to New York City, where he began speculating in railroads. By that time, he had married Helen Day Miller. (His eldest son, George Jay Gould, was later a prominent railroad owner.)

The railroad business had great potential, for the nation was experiencing rapid industrialization that was supported by the building of train lines. Almost completely unregulated by government, railroads allowed Gould and others like him to engage in underhanded deals. After buying bonds in some small lines, in 1867 Gould joined JIM FISK and DANIEL DREW to keep CORNELIUS VANDERBILT from gaining control of the Erie Railroad. Gould used fraudulent stock issues and bribed state legislators to win the "Erie War."

After ending Vanderbilt's challenge, Gould and Fisk together plundered the Erie through stock speculation. In 1869, they joined politicians William "Boss" Tweed and Peter Sweeney to corner the gold market by buying large amounts of the precious commodity. The U.S. Treasury defeated their effort by placing more specie on the market, but the entire affair disrupted investments and caused a financial panic, which in turn sparked a nationwide depression in the 1870s. Public outrage over this maneuver and over the Erie War forced Gould to relinquish control of the Erie in 1872, but his tactics

Jay Gould (Library of Congress)

differed only in degree from those used by other investors in an era known for its greed.

Gould had by that time amassed $25 million and had no intention of retreating from the money and power he extracted from business. By 1874, he gained control of the Union Pacific Railroad and became its director. He retained control until 1878, all the while gaining interests in other railroads. By 1880, he owned the Missouri Pacific, Texas & Pacific, St. Louis Southwestern, and the International & Great Northern—nearly 9,000 miles of railroad or one-half the total mileage in the Southwest.

Gould diversified his business interests and bought the Western Union Telegraph Company in 1881, after weakening it by having smaller telegraph companies that he owned engage in cutthroat competition with it. In addition, he owned the *New York World* newspaper from 1879 to 1883, and by 1886 he controlled New York City's elevated railways.

By the time Gould died of tuberculosis on December 2, 1892, he had acquired a fortune of about $77 million, along with a sullied reputation and a friendless existence.

BIBLIOGRAPHY

Hoyt, Edwin Palmer, *The Goulds: A Social History*, 1969; Oglivie, J. S., *Life and Death of Jay Gould*, 1981.

Graham, Katharine

(June 16, 1917–)
Publisher

Among journalists, some refer to Katharine Graham as "Katharine the Great." The reason: she took the *Washington Post* and, among newspapers, made it second only to the *New York Times* in prestige.

On June 16, 1917, Katharine was born in New York City to wealthy banker Eugene Meyer and author Agnes Elizabeth (Ernst) Meyer. Katharine later described her childhood in Washington, D.C., as privileged but lonely. Both parents had little to do with her, or any of their five children, as they pursued their business and literary worlds.

Graham attended Madeira School, a prep school, and worked on the student newspaper. In 1935, she entered Vassar College but transferred to the University of Chicago, which she found more intellectually stimulating. By that time, her father had bought the *Washington Post*, a financially troubled newspaper, and was spending millions of dollars to improve it. During her summer vacations, she worked at the *Post*, and after she received her B.A. degree in 1938, she took a job as a reporter with the *San Francisco News*.

The following year, at her father's insistence, she returned to the *Post* and worked in the circulation and editorial departments of the Sunday edition. On June 5, 1940, she wed Philip L. Graham, a Harvard law school graduate then clerking for Supreme Court Justice Felix Frankfurter, thus beginning a tumultuous and tragic marriage. After Philip returned from fighting in World War II, Eugene Meyer hired him as the *Post*'s associate publisher. Just six months later, in July 1946, he became publisher. In 1948, Meyer sold all his voting stock in the *Post* to the Grahams for $1.

Philip Graham then expanded the *Post* by acquiring a competitor, the *Washington Times-Herald*, in 1954 and by buying *Newsweek* magazine in 1961. The following year, he cooperated with the *Los Angeles Times* in founding an international news service. The *Post* also owned a radio station and two television stations.

Clearly, Philip had arrived in terms of money and power but that only worsened his relationship with his wife. He criticized Katharine and held her in contempt. She later said that he "gradually undermined my self-confidence almost entirely." Involved with another woman, he asked for a divorce and for Katharine's controlling interest in the newspaper. She had no problem with granting a divorce, but every problem with giving up the *Post* and refused to do it. She later recalled: "My bitterness was extreme, and my intention to dig in was total. . . . I was not about to give up the paper without a fight." Philip's behavior reflected in part a worsening manic depression, and in 1963 he shot himself to death.

The tragedy propelled Graham from the confines of her Georgetown townhouse, where she lived with her children, and back to the *Post*. She assumed the

Katharine Graham (Ron Sachs/CNP/Archive Photos)

presidency of the company in September 1963 and immediately shaped the newspaper in her own right. She determined that the *Post* would pursue truth for the public good and not simply be used to enrich its owner. A keen judge of talent, in 1965 she appointed Benjamin Bradlee, then Washington bureau chief for *Newsweek*, to managing editor of the *Post*. He, in turn, developed a renowned group of reporters.

Graham questioned editorial policies but refrained from dictating her own beliefs. She said she had no respect for anyone who would simply accept an edict from above. By 1966, the *Post* ranked third among the nation's newspapers in advertising lineage, while Graham greatly increased the editorial budget and raised salaries.

In 1971, the *Post* and the *New York Times* successfully fought an attempt by President Richard Nixon to prevent them from publishing the Pentagon Papers, a secret government document that revealed American duplicity in Vietnam. The *Post*'s most prominent and finest hour, however, came in the early 1970s when, alone among the nation's newspapers, it pursued a lead about a break-in by Nixon operatives into the Democratic National Headquarters at the Watergate Apartment Complex. The investigation, led by two of Bradlee's reporters, encouraged congressional hearings and the uncovering of illegal activities by the president that led to Nixon's resignation in 1974.

Graham withstood tremendous political pressure from Nixon and others during the Watergate hearings. She said about the crisis, "It was a feeling of vindication when the facts began to come out and the feeling that we were proved to have been right, which was very reassuring. But were we satisfied to have a President of the United States have to resign because of the Watergate stories? No. It proved that our democracy was very strong, that it could survive this, and that it could accept that this man had to go . . . that there wasn't any trauma that the country couldn't survive and live with. We mastered those difficulties, I think it was a great tribute to our kind of democracy."

Graham described herself as insecure when she took over the presidency of the *Post*. She has, over the years, gone well beyond that insecurity to create a corporation with diverse media investments, and a financially successful and critically acclaimed newspaper, among the most powerful in the nation. In April 1998, she won the Pulitzer Prize for her memoir published the previous year.

BIBLIOGRAPHY

Davis, Deborah, *Katharine the Great: Katharine Graham and Her Washington Post*, 1991; Felsenthal, Gary, *Power, Privilege, and the Post: The Katharine Graham Story*, 1993; Graham, Katharine, *Personal History*, 1997.

Graves, Earl

(January 9, 1935–)
Publisher

Earl Gilbert Graves Jr. founded *Black Enterprise*, the first magazine in the United States devoted to black-owned businesses, and has since been described as the nation's leading educator on African-American enterprises.

Earl was born on January 9, 1935, in Brooklyn, New York, to Earl Godwin Graves, a shipping clerk, and Winfred (Sealy) Graves. After graduating in 1958 with a B.A. in economics from Morgan State College in Baltimore, Maryland,

Earl joined the U.S. Army and achieved the rank of captain before leaving the service in 1962. During his tenure in the army, he married Barbara Kydd. They have three children.

Graves briefly sold real estate in 1962 and, that same year, joined the U.S. Justice Department as a narcotics agent. In 1968, he was hired by New York Senator Robert Kennedy as a staff assistant to plan and supervise events. After Kennedy's death in June 1968, Graves started his own business, Earl G. Graves Associates, a management consulting firm.

Then, in 1970, with $150,000 borrowed from the Manhattan Capital Corporation, Graves founded *Black Enterprise.* As publisher and editor, he directed the magazine to success from the start, partly by attracting such corporate advertisers as IBM—an impressive accomplishment given the failure rate for new periodicals. *Black Enterprise* offered advice on building minority businesses and provided a forum for expressing African-American views about economics and politics. "I feel that a large part of my role as publisher of *Black Enterprise,*" said Graves, "is to be a catalyst for black economic development in this country."

In 1975, Graves began presenting the *Black Enterprise* Achievement Awards to successful African-American entrepreneurs, and in 1982 he organized a board of economists to issue periodic reports on blacks in the economy. He diversified his economic interests as well and established five other businesses, including a development firm and a market research firm.

By 1990, *Black Enterprise* had a circulation of over 230,000 and revenues of more than $15 million. That year, Graves entered a highly publicized $60 million deal with basketball star Earvin "Magic" Johnson to purchase the Pepsi-Cola distribution franchise for Washington, D.C.

In 1996, the circulation of *Black Enterprise* reached 350,000. Through his magazine and his autobiography, *How to Succeed in Business without Being White* (published in 1998), Graves proclaimed the importance of African-American community in a white society that still practiced oppression. He also condemned recent attempts to roll back measures passed during the 1960s civil rights movement. "Affirmative action was intended to make opportunities available, not to guarantee success." He said, "anyone who has administered it otherwise has corrupted the intent. Anyone who says it is something else is wrong." And he observed, "I believe it is abundantly clear that the bottom line today is this: The vast majority of white America doesn't much care about whether you and I succeed in business, or even whether we make it home tonight. Nor should they, necessarily. But that leaves you and me with each other, and if I get mine and say the hell with you, that makes for two lost people."

BIBLIOGRAPHY

Davis, Tim, "Graves Gets Serious," *Beverage World,* October 1992; Graves, Earl G., *How to Succeed in Business without Being White,* 1998.

Greenfield, Jerry

(1951–)
Manufacturer

With his friend BEN COHEN, Jerry Greenfield founded an ice-cream shop that grew into Ben & Jerry's Ice Cream, a company known for its fanciful flavors and commitment to social programs.

Born in Brooklyn, New York, in 1951, the same year as Cohen, Greenfield went to school in Merrick, Long Island. There he met Cohen, and they both graduated from Calhoun High School. Greenfield received a National Merit Scholarship, enrolled as a premed student at Oberlin College in Ohio, and, after graduating from there, applied to medical school. Rejected, he worked as a lab technician in New York and in 1974 moved to North Carolina.

Three years later, Greenfield decided to enter the food business with Cohen, and they looked for a college town with a progressive environment. They settled on Burlington, Vermont, and, with a $12,000 investment, opened their shop in a renovated gas station on a busy street corner in May 1978. The two entrepreneurs concocted their own rich, unusual flavors and gained a reputation not only for the creamy taste of their ice cream but also for the fun events they held, such as a free outdoor movie festival each fall.

The business grew rapidly, and in the 1980s they opened a plant in Waterbury, Vermont, and began making and packaging Ben & Jerry's Ice Cream for sale in grocery stores. Greenfield left the business in the early 1980s to help his wife complete a Ph.D. program in Arizona, but he returned in 1985.

As the company grew, he and Cohen worried that the business would develop into an uncaring, impersonal corporation. To prevent this, they donated 7.5 percent of their pretax profits to nonprofit organizations through the Ben & Jerry's Foundation, which compared favorably to the average corporate giving rate of 2 percent. In 1988, they received a Corporate Giving Award for their contributions.

They also established an unusual workplace environment where they placed limits on the gap between the lowest- and highest-paid employees, solicited opinions from the workers through frequent surveys, and paid a minimum wage well above the federal one. The lowest salary at Ben & Jerry's, $22,000 in the early 1990s, exceeded the per capita income level in Vermont. In addition, they offered stock priced low enough so that many everyday people could buy it, resulting in one of every 10 Vermonters holding a share in the company.

At Ben & Jerry's in the early 1990s, 40 percent of the workforce was female and three of its six managers were women. Said one employee: "When you've been treated so well, it's hard not to appreciate it. And I'm not the only one—that's the best part about it. They do it for everyone. They really do go out of their way."

Ben & Jerry's frequently exerted itself to make a social difference. For example, it purchased brownies, an ingredient in an ice-cream flavor, from a nonprofit bakery in New York that trained and employed disadvantaged workers. In addition, the company bought nuts from impoverished natives in Brazil. A writer for *Fortune* magazine claimed that such practices often made raw ingredients more expensive. "Operating a business is tough enough," he said. "Once you add social goals to the demands of serving customers, making a profit, and returning value to shareholders, you tie yourself up in knots."

By Vermont standards, Ben & Jerry's was large in size—400 workers in 1991, with annual sales topping $100 million. The company ranked among the state's top 10 employers. As Ben & Jerry's Ice Cream spread across the nation, consumers recognized it for its often unusual flavors with strange names, such as Cherry Garcia. By the mid-1990s, Ben & Jerry's

distributed ice cream to grocery stores in all 50 states and franchised scoop shops in 20 of them.

Amid a drop in profits in 1994 and fatigue over the job, Greenfield, who had been chairman of the board since 1990, and Cohen, the CEO, decided to retire from the business, but not until a search resulted in finding a leader who would maintain the company's commitment to social concerns. That person resigned in 1996, and another CEO was hired.

BIBLIOGRAPHY

Taylor, Alex, III, "Yo Ben! Yo Jerry! It's Just Ice Cream!," *Fortune*, April 28, 1997; Wierzynski, Casimir, "Changing the World with Ice Cream," *The Tech*, February 24, 1989.

Gregg, William

(February 2, 1800–September 13, 1867)
Manufacturer

Holding a minority view in the antebellum South, William Gregg advocated that the region industrialize. Through his ideas and his own factory, he changed the Southern economy.

Born on February 2, 1800, near Carmichaels, Virginia (present-day West Virginia), to William Gregg and Elizabeth (Webb) Gregg, William was raised by his uncle, Jacob Gregg, a prosperous watchmaker and manufacturer of cotton-spinning equipment at Alexandria, Virginia. William had little, if any, schooling but learned about cotton manufacturing after his uncle founded a short-lived fac-

tory in Georgia. In addition, his uncle placed him with a friend, who taught Gregg watchmaking and silversmithing.

Gregg founded his own business in 1824 in Columbia, South Carolina, and by the 1830s he had earned considerable wealth, largely through trade. In 1829, he married Marina Jones.

Gregg moved to Charleston in 1838, where he joined a jewelry firm as a partner. Shortly after, he began advocating in a series of newspaper articles that the South develop industry, primarily cotton factories, as a way to ease its economic dependence on agriculture. Such factories, he believed, would employ poor whites who lost their jobs to black slaves, and make the region like the North with its cities and dynamic growth. Slave labor, he said, should be restricted to agriculture and the reclamation of swamps. Yet he realized that in severe cases blacks could be used to keep white factory workers in line. "Capital," he said, "will be able to control labor, even in manufactures with whites, for blacks can always be resorted to in case of need."

Dedicated to more than just talk, Gregg and several partners organized a company in 1845 to build a cotton factory at Graniteville, near Aiken, South Carolina. The mill had nearly 9,000 spindles and 300 looms and, abutting the plant, a village to provide housing for its workers.

Gregg insisted that, in addition to jobs, the factory provide decent living quarters, health care, and education. He built 85 Gothic-style cottages for the workers and required that his employees be sober and refrain from such "hedonistic activities" as dancing. He lived near the mill, supervised its operations, and maintained a generally warm relationship with his employees. The factory began operating in 1848 with some 300 poor whites as workers, mainly women and children. Gregg paid them $3 to $5 per week and rented the cottages for $16 to $25 per year.

After a brief period of difficulty, the factory prospered, and its success encouraged other capitalists to build plants elsewhere in the South. Gregg entered politics in 1856 and won two terms in the state legislature. In 1858, he advocated a tariff to protect industry from foreign competition. His stand angered many Southerners who considered such a position to be pro-Northern and damaging to their interests.

The Civil War, however, found Gregg supporting the South, and in December 1860 he signed the South Carolina ordinance of secession. Gregg kept operating his factory during the war, and after it ended, he traveled to Europe, where he bought new equipment. Tragedy struck, though, in 1867 when a milldam broke, and Gregg helped to repair it while standing in waist-deep water. He became ill and died on September 13, 1867.

BIBLIOGRAPHY

Mitchell, Broadus, *William Gregg: Factory Master of the Old South*, 1928.

Grove, Andrew

(1936–)
Manufacturer

An immigrant who fled communism, Andrew Grove helped establish the Intel Corporation, a leader in the development of computer technology.

Grove was born in 1936 in Budapest, Hungary, but left there in 1956 when a Communist regime began to tighten its grip on the country after an abortive uprising by freedom fighters. Grove immigrated to the United States, taught himself English, and entered college. In 1960, he graduated from the City College of New York with a bachelor's degree in chemical engineering. He continued his studies and in 1963 obtained his Ph.D. from the University of California, Berkeley.

With his outstanding background, Grove joined Fairchild Semiconductor in 1963 and four years later became the assistant director of research and development. At Fairchild, he met GORDON MOORE, inventor of the semiconductor, and when Moore left the company in 1968 to join ROBERT NOYCE in forming the Intel Corporation, he asked Grove to join him. Grove agreed, partly because he liked Moore and respected his work. Grove later said about the new business and his move: "I barely knew and cared very little what it was going to be. I was just going to go with Gordon. I hesitate to put it this way, but it was that simple."

Yet another factor influenced him: he saw the technological revolution that could be advanced. "Computer memory was originally built out of little doughnut-like magnetic cores—tiny little ones—that people strung on wires manually," he said. "It was very labor-intensive.... What

Andrew Grove (Courtesy: Intel Corporation)

Intel's technology offered to do was replace those things in the form of lots of transistors that are all fabricated using semiconductor technology—lots of them at the same time."

Grove helped guide Intel in its tremendous growth, making it a brand name in computer chips. He became president in 1979 and CEO in 1987. Intel survived a challenge from Japanese manufacturers and in the 1990s gained prominence as maker of the Pentium chip. His company adroitly handled a problem with the product's mathematical capabilities—one that could hinder some computer calculations—by recalling and replacing any defective chips, a move that quickly restored consumer confidence in Intel.

In addition to his management of Intel, Grove obtained several patents on semiconductor technology, taught graduate courses in physics at Berkeley, and lectured at Stanford University in the Graduate School of Business, teaching the topic "Strategy and Action in the Information Processing Industry."

Grove wrote four books, including *High Output Management*, which was translated into 11 languages, and *Only the Paranoid Survive*, published in 1996. He wrote also 40 technical papers and a column on management for *Working Woman* magazine. He received several honorary degrees and in 1994 was elected a Fellow of the Academy of Arts and Sciences.

Grove adhered to a business philosophy that the status quo must be fought and that fear had to be used advantageously. He claimed that it is only through fear that people do what is difficult, be it fear of change or some other fear. He said: "What you need to do is train people that the way to respond to fear is . . . by going forward, by taking charge of your destiny." Grove did exactly that in developing Intel.

BIBLIOGRAPHY

Grove, Andrew, *Only the Paranoid Survive*, 1996; Morgenson, Gretchen, ed., *Forbes: Great Minds of Business*, 1997.

Guccione, Robert

(December 17, 1930–)
Publisher

Robert Guccione appeared all vanity and self-importance—gold chains and medallions draped from his neck to his chest, exposed by the shirt unbuttoned nearly to his navel. So many people could not stand him, he once said, that he had to go into business for himself—and that he did, creating a soft-porn magazine, *Penthouse*, that tumbled *Playboy* from its previously unchallenged domination of men's magazines.

Guccione was born on December 17, 1930, in Brooklyn, New York, where his father worked as an accountant and amid the Great Depression was able to maintain his family's middle-class status. In his youth, Guccione served as an altar boy and spent three months in a Roman Catholic seminary. He decided the priesthood was not for him, however, and after graduating in 1948 from Blair Academy (a prep school), he went to Los Angeles, determined to pursue a career as a painter. After a brief marriage that produced a child, Guccione traveled to Europe. There he met Muriel Hudson, an Englishwoman, and in 1954 they married. Over the next few years, they had four children.

In the 1950s, Guccione held several different jobs while making no progress with his painting. In 1960, he moved to England and was appointed managing editor of a newspaper, the *London American*. He tried to keep the tiny publication solvent, but it failed. Nevertheless, his experience convinced him to pursue a publishing career, and after studying *Playboy*, an enormously successful magazine published by Hugh Hefner, that featured nude women, he decided to enter the field. While selling American girlie magazines in the mail, he fervently pursued financial backing to start his own publication. As he sank into debt and spent untold hours in his quest, his wife left him. Guccione's perseverance resulted in *Penthouse* magazine appearing in 1965 and selling 120,000 copies at British newsstands.

The magazine struggled, however, until Kathy Keeton, an exotic dancer in a London nightclub, met Guccione and began selling advertising space. He soon had enough advertisers to assure a substantial income, and Keeton and Guccione began living together.

Guccione decided to place more pressure on *Playboy* in England by going full frontal with nudity and showing pubic hair. The strategy boosted sales, and in 1969 he decided to challenge *Playboy* on its home turf, in the United States. His timing proved astute—a sexual revolution within America made *Playboy* seem tame, a larger young male population wanted its printed sex explicit, and *Playboy* itself had grown complacent from the lack of any serious competition.

Guccione boldly announced *Penthouse*'s arrival with a full-page advertisement in the *New York Times*, which showed the Playboy bunny in the crosshairs of a rifle sight and announced that the new publication was "going rabbit hunting." But his greatest appeal, after a modest start in the early issues, came in presenting a raunchy version of *Playboy* complete with explicit shots and letters from readers that discussed various sex practices and sexual devices in tantalizing tones.

Guccione also benefited by eschewing subscriptions and selling at newsstands where he could get full price for each issue, by undercutting *Playboy*'s price, and by offering wholesalers and retailers a more profitable deal. Although the first issue of *Penthouse* sold 235,000 copies, *Playboy*'s circulation remained in the millions, and Guccione faced a long fight to dislodge his competitor from its premier position.

Guccione appeared on radio and TV shows, promoting *Penthouse* with a flair. In 1971, he crossed another cultural divide when *Penthouse* printed photos showing two women in a lesbian love scene—an issue that generated the controversy he wanted. When local law enforcement in several cities removed *Penthouse* from the newsstands as an obscene magazine, Guccione reveled in the attention. In addition, the publicity got him customers—in 1972, *Penthouse*'s circulation was up 143 percent, while that of *Playboy* rose only 10 percent.

In the mid-1970s, Guccione went further by showing women fondling themselves, displaying their genitalia, and posing with men in graphic scenes. At the same time, he presented hard-hitting journalistic articles, including those revealing government mistreatment of Vietnam War veterans. In 1975, *Penthouse* outsold *Playboy* for the first time.

Guccione expanded his publishing business and issued *Penthouse Forum*,

Variations, and *Omni*, a science magazine. In his personal life, he married Kathy Keeton in 1988.

In the late 1980s, *Forbes* magazine estimated his worth at about $300 million. *Playboy* remained his toughest competition.

BIBLIOGRAPHY

Ramsey, Douglas K., *The Corporate Warriors*, 1987.

Guggenheim, Daniel

(July 9, 1856–September 28, 1930)
Mining Executive

B uilding on his father's wealth and benefiting from the talented help of his brothers, Daniel Guggenheim created a mining empire that spanned the globe.

Daniel was born on July 9, 1856, to Meyer Guggenheim and Barbara (Mayer) Guggenheim in Philadelphia, Pennsylvania. Meyer Guggenheim had an uncanny business sense and had accumulated a fortune through several different endeavors. Shortly before the Civil War, he operated a grocery store and a stove polish factory. During the war, he supplied the Union army with clothes and foodstuffs, and in the 1870s he imported fine laces and embroidery. That same decade, he sent Daniel to Switzerland, where the young man helped manage an embroidery factory. By 1880, Meyer had established a close working relationship with his five sons and founded M. Guggenheim's Sons. In this arrangement, Daniel worked hard and stood out as the leader.

Meyer Guggenheim earned his greatest fortune in the 1880s, when he invested $5,000 in silver mines in Leadville, Colorado, that struck rich deposits. In the late 1880s, Daniel, who had returned to the United States, closed the embroidery business and helped his father develop mines and smelters. When the federal government bought large quantities of silver after 1890, the Guggenheim fortune multiplied. A smelter built by the Guggenheims in Pueblo, Colorado, prospered, and Daniel and his brothers decided to lease mines in Mexico and build smelters there. Smelters at Monterrey and Aguascalientes made the Guggenheims the most powerful industrialists in Mexico.

Shortly after 1900, a large trust named the American Smelting and Refining Company (ASARCO) attempted to crush the Guggenheims, but the move backfired, and Daniel led his brothers in gaining control of ASARCO. With this expanded wealth and power, Daniel sought to become the dominant force in exploiting the world's minerals. Among his many projects, he developed a huge open-pit copper mine at Bingham Canyon, Utah, and another in Chile. In fact, he considered the cheap labor available in undeveloped countries essential in depressing wages and prices in the United

States, thus enabling ASARCO to earn greater profits and acquire competing companies.

In 1907, Daniel joined other financiers, among them J. P. MORGAN SR., and mined copper deposits near Kennecott Creek in Alaska. The enterprise required enormous sums of money and bold engineering feats—including a $25 million railroad to reach the remote mine—but it resulted in the mining of the lowest-priced copper in the world and in millions of dollars flowing to the Guggeheims and their newly formed Kennecott Copper Company. Daniel and his brothers controlled 80 percent of the international silver, copper, and lead markets, and ranked among the five richest families in America.

A heart condition forced Daniel to retire from ASARCO in 1919, and he devoted the remainder of his life to philanthropic work. In 1924, he and his wife Florence Sloss, whom he had married in 1894, founded the Daniel and Florence Guggenheim Foundation, which granted money to the American Woman's Association and various Jewish organizations. Since Daniel's death on September 28, 1930, the foundation has made hundreds of grants to organizations in the United States and overseas. Daniel had two sons and a daughter, but only one of his chil-

Daniel Guggenheim (Library of Congress)

dren, Harry, continued in the family business. Today, Kennecott owns enormous copper reserves in the United States, along with mines and smelters.

BIBLIOGRAPHY

Davis, John J., *The Guggenheims: An American Epic*, 1979; Hoyt, E. P., *The Guggenheims and the American Dream*, 1967; Lomask, Milton, *Seed Money: The Guggenheim Story*, 1964; O'Connor, Harvey, *The Guggenheims*, 1937.

H

Hall, Joyce

(August 29, 1891–October 19, 1982)
Manufacturer

From a cramped room at the Kansas City YMCA, Joyce Clyde Hall sold postcards that led him to develop the world's largest greeting card company, Hallmark.

Hall, born on August 29, 1891, in David City, Nebraska, had to begin working as a child, after his father (an itinerant Methodist preacher) deserted his family. In 1902, his older brothers bought a bookstore in nearby Norfolk, and Hall worked there for long hours, a routine that prevented him from finishing high school. He was minding the bookstore in 1905 when a salesman who represented a New York firm came in and tried to get the store to sell his postcards, which were larger than standard size and displayed lithographs that Hall liked. These cards were popular at the time—people collected them and sent them to friends and relatives at birthdays, although the pictures left little room for writing. Hall and his brothers agreed to sell the postcards wholesale, and to do this, they founded the Norfolk Post Card Company.

Hall decided to pursue a bigger market in 1910, and so moved to Kansas City, where he obtained his room at the YMCA. He mailed postcards in packages of 100 to businesses, requesting they sell them. Some returned them, but most sold the cards, and before long Hall made a good profit.

At the same time, greeting cards first appeared in stores, and Hall, convinced they would soon replace his postcards, began selling them as well. Subsequent adversity turned into an unexpected benefit when, in 1915, a fire destroyed the warehouse where Hall had his Valentine's Day cards stored. To recover quickly from the loss, he decided to make his own cards and had them printed in time for that winter's Christmas season. By 1916, he and his brothers were producing cards as the Hall Brothers, and they had introduced an innovation by placing Valentine's Day cards in envelopes, thus allowing buyers to send their greetings in private.

World War I boosted Hall's business when soldiers and their relatives began sending greeting cards to one another, a social custom that accelerated after the war. Hall developed the market with cards less formal than those produced by other companies, more colorfully illustrated, and aimed not just at holidays but at such everyday events as cards that expressed friendship. His card bearing the saying "I'd like to be the kind of friend you've been to me" sold widely.

Hall abandoned postcards by 1920 to focus on greeting cards, including fancy engraved cards for Christmas. On the whole, his cards sold particularly well with women and those who wanted a packaged message rather than one they would have to compose themselves. Hall realized he had a profitable market among people who felt too inarticulate or too embarrassed to write sentimental messages.

In 1923, one year after having married Elizabeth Dilday (they eventually had three children), Hall started using the name Hallmark on his cards, and three years later, he began selling gift wrap and ribbon, substitutes for the more common brown paper. Hallmark's famous slogan, "When you care enough to send the very best," appeared in 1944, and after World War II, the company expanded again, aided by Hall's decision to display his cards on racks rather than keep them in drawers, as had been the practice.

Hall officially changed the company name to Hallmark in 1954 and in 1958 began selling cards overseas. He remained active in the business until 1980, although his son, Donald Hall, had become president and CEO in 1966. By the time of Hall's death on October 19, 1982, in Leaward, Kentucky, Hallmark had 20,000 employees, with 6,000 at its headquarters in Kansas City. The company's annual sales approached $1.5 billion, and Hall-

mark controlled 70 percent of the greeting card market, although its closest competitor, American Greetings Corporation, had made inroads on this share.

Sensing that the domestic greeting card market held limited potential for future growth, Hallmark diversified in the mid-1980s and acquired other companies, among them the British card firm W. N. Sharpe, and the makers of Crayola crayons, Binney & Smith.

BIBLIOGRAPHY

Goldwasser, Thomas, *Family Pride: Profiles of Five of America's Best-Run Family Businesses*, 1986.

Hammer, Armand

(May 21, 1898–December 10, 1990)
Oil Industrialist

How could anyone know that beneath Armand Hammer the international industrialist and oil tycoon, the peace advocate and philanthropist, there lived Armand Hammer the Communist agent, the unscrupulous megalomaniac? For anyone who first met Armand Hammer, it stretched credulity to think he was any of these. "[He] does not look like the kind of man who dines with Moroccan princes or builds factories in the Soviet Union," said one observer. "Short, smiling, and comfortably upholstered, he goes about in an elderly camel's-hair coat and a limp Borsalino hat, chuckles disarmingly at his own

anecdotes, and might well be mistaken for an old-fashioned country doctor."

Armand was born on May 21, 1898, in New York City to Dr. Julius Hammer and Rose (Robinson) Hammer. His father practiced medicine and operated a wholesale pharmaceutical business, along with drugstores in the city. In a peculiar twist, while running his business, the elder Hammer worked for an anticapitalist Communist Party that had ties to Marxist dictator Vladimir Lenin.

Shortly before 1920, Julius Hammer's business faced financial problems, and Armand and his brothers worked to save it. Armand made money buying whiskey when Prohibition began and selling it as medicine—all this while he was enrolled in medical school at Columbia University. In fact, Armand made $1 million before he graduated.

In 1920, Hammer faced another crisis when his father was arrested for having killed a woman while performing an illegal abortion. Charged with manslaughter, a jury found Julius Hammer guilty, and he was sentenced to Sing Sing prison. Evidence indicates, however, that Armand Hammer had actually performed and botched the operation, and that his father took the blame.

Hammer remained in graduate school and obtained his medical degree in 1921. He never practiced medicine but instead pursued business as a means to make more money and accumulate power. That same year, he journeyed to his family's homeland, Russia. He intended to help Russians suffering in a famine area and toward that end set up a mobile medical hospital. But he mixed business with his humanitarian impulse, and self-promotion with his sincerity—character traits that reappeared often in his life—and met with Lenin to strike a deal whereby he provided grain for the Russians and, in return, obtained furs.

He soon obtained a concession from Lenin to operate an asbestos mine in the Ural Mountains, and his intimacy with the Russian government allowed him to handle trade arrangements for several leading companies, including Ford. Hammer bought a mansion in Russia and began collecting art for it—what critics called his trophies, which were intended, they said, to show he had arrived as a powerful insider. Hammer's collection came from Russia's czarist era, works criticized by Lenin as decadent and ones the Communist regime no longer wanted.

After Hammer lost his asbestos concession in 1925, he got another one to import pencils into the Soviet Union. In one year, he made more than $1 million. Unable to gain cooperation from the new Soviet leader, Joseph Stalin, Hammer returned to the United States in 1930, bringing his art collection with him. In the meantime, he and his brothers had opened the Hammer Galleries in New York City, and they displayed Russian art there, among them icons and Faberge Easter eggs. *Time* magazine praised the exhibition as "the largest collection . . . ever shown in the United States," and called Hammer and his brother Victor two of the art world's "most startling characters." As it turned out, startling to many since Hammer's collection included forgeries that he sold for millions of dollars.

Hammer's contacts with the Soviet regime stirred suspicion in the United States. He steadfastly denied any skullduggery, however, as he would throughout his life. Yet state documents released in Russia after his death showed he obtained money from the Soviets that he distributed to underground Communists in the United States and that he developed schemes to launder money for secret Communist activities, espionage among them. Like his father, Hammer had developed a strange mix of capitalist business pursuit and Communist activism.

Hammer saw another opportunity to expand his wealth and power during World War II, when grain shortages hampered the whiskey industry. He began buying half-rotten potatoes for as little as 10 cents per 100-pound sack and used them to make his own whiskey brand: Old Cooperage. Although he soon dropped the potatoes for traditional grain, he managed to best his competition when he sold J. W. Dant bourbon at a low price. Hammer controlled 11 distilleries before he decided to sell them for over $6 million.

Hammer moved to California in 1956, intending, he said, to retire. Retirement did not suit his ambition, however, and in 1957 he bought the Mutual Broadcasting System, which he soon sold for a profit. At the same time, using his wife's money, he bought an interest in the Occidental Petroleum Corporation. Hammer knew little about oil. He did know that Occidental had little money in the bank (less than $14,000), and he fully expected his investment to return a loss, which he could then use as a tax shelter.

Much to his surprise, the opposite happened. Occidental struck oil at two wells, and the company's fortunes changed. With a handsome profit in hand, Hammer moved quickly to control Occidental. He intended to make it a multinational corporation and in the 1960s reached this goal when he obtained an oil concession in Libya in a deal that involved bribe money paid to foreign officials. Hammer expanded Occidental's holdings and in the 1970s acquired Hooker Chemical Company and the Island Creek Coal Company (the third largest coal business in America) and merged them with Best Fertilizers, International Ore & Fertilizer, and Jefferson Lake Sulphur. With all these deals, investors questioned Occidental's soundness, and in 1971 the Securities and Exchange Commission charged the company with issuing misleading earnings reports and statements. Hammer agreed to sign a consent decree to stop the practices but refused to admit guilt.

Trouble appeared on the political front, too. Hammer frequently tried to ingratiate himself with presidents by contributing to their campaigns. His donation of $54,000 to Richard Nixon's campaign violated campaign laws, and, amid the Watergate scandal, the government prosecuted him. Found guilty, he received a light sentence—probation and a $3,000 fine—but the verdict rankled him. A decade later, he used his influence to get a pardon from President George Bush.

Throughout the 1970s, Hammer maintained close relations with Soviet leaders and exerted his influence in Soviet-American relations, which at that time were experiencing a thaw. In 1972, he reached a trade agreement involving oil and gas exploration in the Soviet Union, along with the shipment of phosphates to the Soviets, a stunning multibillion-dollar deal.

Despite his advanced age, Hammer continued to lead Occidental in the 1980s, maintaining his customary firm grip while pursuing mergers. He acquired the Cities Service Company (a large oil corporation based in Oklahoma) and then promptly slashed personnel. He also acquired MidCon, a natural gas pipeline company, for $43 billion, and in an unlikely link, purchased Iowa Beef Producers. Again he cut jobs, and his actions prompted a union leader to claim that Hammer obtained his financing by "the savage exploitation of workers."

When Hammer acquired Hooker Chemical, he inherited a major problem. Hooker had dumped thousands of gallons of carcinogenic chemicals into the Love Canal landfill site in New York. The chemicals contaminated houses built on the site and led to demands that Occidental compensate the homeowners and pay for the cleanup. Hammer at first opposed any payments, and his comment that no cause and effect had been proven between the chemicals and illnesses angered environmentalists and many others.

Hammer acted more speedily in 1986 when he sent doctors and medical equipment to help the Soviets deal with the disastrous nuclear power plant explosion at Chernobyl. Some distrusted him and called his effort self-promotion, but his admirers thought otherwise. "His accomplishments, his steadfast advocacy of East-West trade, his art exchanges, his aid to Chernobyl victims, and his role as a personal liaison between world leaders have merit independent of his motivations," said two authors. "Historians may someday conclude that Hammer had done the right things in Soviet-American relations for the wrong reasons. But his legacy of right things may remain long after the reasons have faded."

Also in the 1980s, Hammer obtained a contract from China to explore for oil in the South China Sea. In 1986, he began open-pit coal mining in that Communist country. While these deals generated publicity, they resulted in little profit.

In his last years, Hammer devoted a greater amount of his money to philanthropy. He gave millions to the medical school at Columbia University and to institutions elsewhere for cancer research at a time when President Ronald Reagan appointed him to chair the President's Cancer Panel. In the late 1980s, he founded the United World College in Montezuma, New Mexico. The school, one in a group of colleges in various nations, engaged in international cultural exchanges to pursue Hammer's dream of world peace.

Hammer unabashedly promoted himself for the Nobel Peace Prize, even providing Israel with $100 million in aid as a way to get that nation's prime minister, Menachem Begin, to intervene with the Nobel committee on his behalf. Begin did so, but the prize went to the Dali Lama.

Only a few weeks before Hammer's death on December 10, 1990, the Armand Hammer Museum of Art and Cultural Center opened in Los Angeles. Here appeared his vast collection, nearly all purchased with money from Occidental. The collection did not represent Hammer's interests or knowledge, for he knew little about art; rather it reflected his desire for exposure and his hope to assure himself some "immortality." Indeed, if he were to be remembered positively, it might likely have to come through his art collection or his philanthropy, for although at his death, Occidental ranked as the nation's sixteenth largest industrial corporation (and to the public at large Hammer seemed to possess a Midas touch), the company had lost billions in his deals. Repulsed by his secretive and dishonest methods, many soon distanced themselves from the Hammer legacy.

BIBLIOGRAPHY

Blumay, Carl, *The Dark Side of Power: The Real Armand Hammer*, 1992; Epstein, Edward Jay, *Dossier: The Secret History of Armand Hammer*, 1996; Weinberg, Steve, *Armand Hammer: The Untold Story*, 1989.

Hancock, John

(January 12, 1736–October 8, 1793)
Merchant

Most Americans identify the colonial merchant John Hancock with his bold signature that appears on the Declaration of Independence. Supporters say it symbolized his bravery; critics, his vanity.

As a child, Hancock had every financial advantage. He was born on January 12, 1736, in Braintree, Massachusetts (near Boston), to John Hancock, the preacher at the town church, and Mary (Hawke) Hancock. His father died, however, while Hancock was still a boy, and the youngster was adopted by his uncle, Thomas Hancock, a wealthy Boston merchant. Young Hancock attended Boston Latin School and then Harvard, from where he graduated in 1754. He then entered his uncle's merchant house, Thomas Hancock & Company. In 1763, he became a partner, and the following year, when his uncle died, he inherited both the business and considerable wealth.

Hancock failed to display extraordinary skills either as a merchant or as a political leader, but circumstances soon thrust him forward. In 1768, British customs agents seized his sloop, *Liberty*, for smuggling wine and thus avoiding what most colonials considered a hated import tax. The seizure sparked a riot on June 10, 1768, aimed at the British authorities, and resulted in Britain sending troops to Boston. The entire Liberty affair, as the episode came to be known, made Hancock a hero, and in 1769 he gained election to the Massachusetts General Court (the colony's legislative body). When in 1774 Massachusetts moved closer to revolution and the General Court declared itself a Provincial Congress, Hancock was elected its president. In an oration, he condemned the continued presence of British troops in Boston, claiming they sought "to deprive us of the enjoyment of our religious privileges, to vitiate our morals, and thereby render us deserving of destruction."

In 1775, the year he married Dorothy Quincy, Hancock was elected as a delegate from Massachusetts to the Second Continental Congress in Philadelphia. He arrived there in ostentatious splendor—a display many colleagues found offensive; nevertheless, they elected him congressional president. He expressed few political ideas—other than the widely held view that power threatened liberty and had to be kept in check by a representative government and vigilant public—yet his fame among the people made his support essential. He vigorously backed the revolutionaries and, in bold script, signed the Declaration of Independence on July 4, 1776, the only one to do so that day.

Hancock resigned the presidency in 1777 after what he perceived to be a slight against him and in 1778 gave a pedestrian performance in commanding Massachusetts troops in Rhode Island. While the war continued, he won election in 1780 as the first governor of Massachusetts. Illness forced him to resign in 1785, but he won election again in 1787—soon after the second of his two children had died—and played a role in getting the state to ratify the federal Constitution.

Despite his popularity, many knew Hancock as a vain man who lived lavishly, even amid the hardships brought by

John Hancock (Library of Congress)

war. This tendency for ostentation, along with mediocre talent as a merchant, may account for his losing much of his money (although he remained wealthy in land, with more than 3,000 acres in New England). Another factor must be considered, however, mainly that he expended substantial amounts supporting the revolution in its dire need and refused to exploit the war for profit. Hancock died in Boston on October 8, 1793, while serving his ninth term as governor.

BIBLIOGRAPHY

Fowler, William M., Jr., *The Baron of Beacon Hill: A Biography of John Hancock*, 1980.

Handler, Elliot

(1914–)
Manufacturer

Combine Elliot Handler's talent for design with his wife's sales ability, add to them a population boom together with unparalleled suburban prosperity and a new technology called television, and you have a toy company that reshaped American popular culture.

Handler was born in 1914 in Denver, Colorado, and as a young man aspired to be an artist. In the 1930s, he moved to California with his childhood sweetheart Ruth, and in 1938 they married. Over the years, they worked closely together in developing their business interests.

With a background in industrial design, Elliot joined with Harold Matson to make picture frames as Mattel Creations (MATT for Matson and EL for Elliot). After Matson sold out, Elliot brought Ruth into the business. Challenged by what to do with leftover wood scraps, he decided to make dollhouse furniture. Ruth set up the sales organization, and they were soon selling more than $100,000 worth of miniature furniture each year.

The Handlers' success coincided with a postwar baby boom and prosperity. As suburbia grew, middle-class parents lavished their children with clothes, bicycles, toys, and games. In the emerging highly competitive modern toy business, the Handlers realized that they needed to develop products that other manufacturers would find difficult to copy. As a result, in 1948, they produced an all-plastic toy piano, the first of its kind. After it sold well, they bought the rights to a music box that contained a band of rubber dotted with knobs that, when a child turned a crank, struck metal strips to produce a tune.

By 1955, Mattel's annual sales reached $6 million. Then came a daring decision: the Handlers decided to risk nearly all their capital by advertising on WALT DISNEY'S *Mickey Mouse Club*. The advertisements catapulted Mattel into unchallenged supremacy in the toy industry and ignited a new type of advertising that appealed directly to kids rather than to their parents. Critics condemned the advertisements as exploiting children, while many parents felt pressured to buy what the advertisements promoted.

Mattel's impact on popular culture climbed another notch when, in 1959, the Handlers introduced the Barbie doll. Unlike previous dolls, Barbie looked like a buxom teenager. Ruth later explained: "If a little girl was going to do role playing of what she would be like at age 16 or 17, it was a little stupid to play with a doll that had a flat chest. So I gave it beautiful breasts." Ruth and Elliot realized, too, that they could sell an entire wardrobe for Barbie and make yet more money—what Elliot called the razor and blade effect: if you buy one, you have to buy the other.

By 1967, revenues from Barbie—the toy originally retailed at $3—and its accessories hit $500 million. In the meantime, Mattel had manufactured spin-offs: Ken (a boyfriend to go along with Barbie) and several doll friends. *Barbie Magazine* ran stories about the Barbie clan, all to make her appear real.

Mattel produced such other hugely successful toys in the 1960s as Chatty Cathy (a talking doll) and Hot Wheels (miniature model cars that boys liked to race). The Handlers made most of the toys overseas, where they could use cheap labor, and with their profits, they diversified and bought other companies, including Ringling Brothers–Barnum & Bailey Circus.

The Handlers' empire seemed impregnable—until disaster struck. In 1970, the Mattel plant in Mexico burned, and in 1971 a shipping strike disrupted the flow of toys from the Far East. Sales for Hot Wheels dropped considerably, and as company profits declined, Ruth and Seymour Rosenberg (Mattel's executive vice president) juggled the books and lied to their stockholders. In 1973, the Securities and Exchange Commission sued Mattel, the Handlers, and Rosenberg. The following year, the company's bankers and creditors ousted the Handlers. In 1978, a federal district court fined Ruth and Rosenberg $57,000 each and gave them 41-year sentences, suspended in return for 500 hours of charitable work per year over 5 years. Mattel stock that had once sold for more than $52 a share dropped to $2 a share.

With the Handlers gone, Mattel, behind its competitor Hasbro in sales (a company founded by STEPHEN HASSENFELD), revived under Arthur Spear. In 1979, Mattel produced Intellivision, a video game that challenged Atari 2600. By 1984, however, the product had run into technical and marketing problems, and Mattel sold its rights in it to another company. In the 1990s, Mattel made CD-ROM software for Barbie and for other toys. Mattel tried but failed to buy Hasbro, which by that time Mattel had pushed into second place among toy makers. In 1997, Mattel bought Tyco Toys, Incorporated, the nation's third largest toy company and the maker of Martchbox cars and Sesame Street products, for $755 million.

BIBLIOGRAPHY

Boy, Billy, *Barbie: Her Life and Times*, 1987; Kay, Marvin, *The Story of Monopoly, Silly Putty, Bingo, Twister, Frisbee, Scrabble, Etc.*, 1973; McClintock, Inez, and Marshall McClintock, *Toys in America*, 1961.

Hanna, Marcus

(September 24, 1837–February 15, 1904)
Mining Executive, Transportation Executive

Parlaying wealth and power that he had obtained in his mining and transportation ventures, Marcus Alonzo Hanna emerged as one of the most important figures in late-nineteenth-century politics. Hanna made William McKinley president through a promotional strategy that came from the business world. "He . . . advertised McKinley," joked Theodore Roosevelt, "as if he were a patent medicine."

Marcus was born on September 24, 1837, in New Lisbon, a town in eastern Ohio, to Leonard and Samantha (Converse) Hanna. His mother was a former schoolteacher, and his father a former physician forced by an injury to leave medicine for business. In 1852, Leonard Hanna lost money in a canal project and moved his family to Cleveland. There young Hanna graduated from Central High School. He enrolled at Western Reserve University but left after the faculty suspended him for a prank he pulled on the junior class.

In 1858, Hanna entered his father's wholesale grocery business—Hanna, Garretson & Company—and labored in the warehouse. Soon he traveled as a salesman, peddling groceries in northern Ohio. When his father became ill in 1860, he assumed more responsibility in the business, and upon his father's death two years later, he headed the company.

Hanna served only briefly in the Civil War. As a member of the Perry Light Infantry, a company within the Ohio National Guard, he saw garrison duty near Washington, D.C., for a few weeks in 1864. Rather than engage in combat, he concentrated on developing his business and, that same year, married C. Augusta Rhodes. The couple had their first child in 1866.

After losing money on a transport boat that sank in the Great Lakes and on an oil refinery that burned, Hanna went into the iron and coal business in 1867 with Robert R. Rhodes. For Rhodes & Company—later M. A. Hanna & Company—he mined coal and sold it on commission. He also invested in transportation, especially in shipping iron ore on the Great Lakes. His Cleveland Transportation Company evolved from this venture, as did his Globe Shipping Company that built ships, including the first steel-keeled vessel on the Great Lakes.

Among his other business interests, Hanna acquired the *Cleveland Herald*,

Marcus Hanna (Library of Congress)

and in 1884 organized the Union National Bank and served as its president. Although Hanna took risks, he never speculated, and he earned a reputation for integrity by scrupulously fulfilling all contracts he signed. His biographer, Herbert Croly, wrote that Hanna's "salient characteristic in business was initiative. He was essentially, if not exclusively, an *entrepreneur.* He broke new ground. He started and developed enterprises."

Yet Hanna lived robustly. Seldom extravagant, he nonetheless rejected penury and the tight-fisted approach to money practiced by such businessmen as JOHN D. ROCKEFELLER.

From business, Hanna entered politics and wielded so much power in Ohio that people called him a "boss." His activism stirred in the mid-1870s, when he worked Cleveland's wards for the Republican Party. Then, in 1888, he managed Senator John Sherman's failed bid for the Republican presidential nomination. All along, he strove to unite the nation's emerging big corporations with the party. From them, he raised huge sums of money for campaigns. His successful effort in 1890 to get the McKinley Tariff passed by Congress resulted in the highest tariff to that time, one that protected businesses from foreign competition.

Hanna planned to make William McKinley president. In 1891, he managed McKinley's victorious campaign for the Ohio governorship. He then set his sites on the presidential race in 1896, and by the time the Republican delegates convened at that year's national convention in St. Louis, Hanna had secured enough votes for McKinley to secure the presidential nomination.

Under Hanna's leadership, McKinley sided with big business, and in his race against the Democratic nominee, William Jennings Bryan, took a strong position supporting the gold standard. Bryan and his largely rural supporters favored the coinage of more silver, but corporate, urban America believed this would devalue the currency and undermine big businesses and banks. Hanna sensed that he had the advantage on this issue—for the nation had shifted from farming to industry as its mainstay—and he advised McKinley to reject campaign travel, stay at home, and, from his front porch, present speeches filled with platitudes and vague promises about prosperity. The strategy, Bryan's inept campaign, and money raised by Hanna for advertising—as much as $7 million—propelled McKinley to victory.

In 1897, John Sherman resigned his senate seat to become secretary of state, and Ohio's governor appointed Hanna to the vacated office. In January 1898, he won election to the Senate (at that time state legislatures elected senators) and from that position developed a strong imperialist stance, advocating the United States acquire overseas colonies.

He remained McKinley's most important adviser, continued to forge an alliance between the Republicans and corporations, and often accepted money for the party from big businesses that wanted to exert influence in legally questionable ways. In 1900, he managed McKinley's reelection campaign, during which he obtained more financial support from Wall Street than ever before, and approved the selection of Theodore Roosevelt for the vice presidential nomination. McKinley won big, again over Bryan, and Hanna's influence seemed assured.

But in 1901, an assassin killed McKinley, and although, as president, Roosevelt listened to Hanna, the Ohioan had less influence in the White House than had been the case under McKinley. Hanna supported Roosevelt's effort to build the Panama Canal, and in 1902 helped the president resolve the anthracite coal strike, in which Hanna's contacts with corporate leaders proved essential in establishing an arbitration commission.

Hanna died in Washington, D.C., on February 15, 1904, from complications surrounding typhoid fever. His success at merging politics with corporations epitomized modern America where big business had gained primacy.

BIBLIOGRAPHY

Croly, Herbert, *Marcus Alonzo Hanna: His Life and Work*, 1912, reprt. 1965.

Harper, James

(April 13, 1795–March 27, 1869)
Publisher

James Harper, the originator of the popular periodical *Harper's Weekly Magazine*, was the eldest sibling in the family publishing partnership of Harper & Brothers. His drive for innovation in printing practices, combined with an industrious work ethic, helped establish Harper & Brothers as a well-respected firm that remains, under the name Harper & Row, a fixture of the publishing industry.

James, the eldest son of the six children of Joseph and Elizabeth Kolyer Harper, was born on April 13, 1795, in Newtown, a village on Long Island in New York State. As two of the Harper children had died in infancy, the remaining family members were an extremely close-knit and religious family. Though James attended a small, rural school, he developed a strong passion for reading. It was his interest in Benjamin Franklin's *Autobiography* that inspired him to pursue the career of printing.

At 16, James became an apprentice at a Methodist printing firm, Paul & Thomas, in New York City. An affable and industrious worker, he quickly made friends and earned respect. In 1817, James and his younger brother John, who had also recently completed a printing apprenticeship, established the small printing firm of J. & J. Harper. The brothers quickly gained a reputation for efficient service and quality workmanship. Despite the goodwill, business was slow, prompting the brothers in 1818 to venture into publishing. The first run was 200 copies of the Enlightenment philosopher John Locke's *Essay on the Human Understanding*.

Business increased, and by 1825 the remaining brothers, Joseph Wesley and Fletcher, had joined the organization. By 1830, the company was the biggest publisher in the country, releasing a title per week. The firm focused on several book series, launching Harper's Family Library, the Classical Library, and the Boys and Girls Library, which included the first American printing of the children's classic, *The Swiss Family Robinson.*

In 1833, the company adopted the name Harper & Brothers. In extolling the loyalty and participation of all the partners, James once remarked in an interview that "either one is the Harper, the rest are the brothers." Eventually, roles were delineated on the basis of preference and skills. John was principal proofreader as well as business manager, Joseph Wesley was the literary critic, and James employed his impressive mechanical skills by assuming charge of the presses. He was an innovator who liked to improve upon existing methods. Harper & Brothers became one of the first printers to use steam-run presses and pioneered the large-scale use of electrotyping.

Though James enjoyed his hands-on role with daily operations, he made important contributions to the business and editorial decisions of Harper & Brothers. It was James who in 1850 originated *Harper's New Monthly Magazine,* which quickly became one of the nation's most important literary journals. By 1853, Harper & Brothers was the largest publishing house in the world.

The success of Harper's earlier periodical was followed in 1857 with *Harper's Weekly,* a journal that carried the political cartoons of Thomas Nast and other political commentaries and features. In 1867, the brothers released *Harper's Bazaar,* a popular women's magazine now owned by the Hearst Corporation.

James was a well-rounded individual, well liked by his employees, and well versed in social and political events of the day. In 1844, he was elected mayor of New York City on a reform platform exhorting the need for a businesslike approach to running the city. He followed up on his campaign promises with several improvements in city policies. He was later encouraged to run for the governor's office, but declined.

Though the details have been lost to posterity, it is clear that James was married twice, initially to Maria Arcularius, with whom he had one son, and later to Julia Thorne, with whom he had a son and three daughters. On March 27, 1869, James Harper died from injuries incurred in a horse-riding accident.

BIBLIOGRAPHY

Derby, J. C., *Fifty Years among Authors, Books and Publishers,* 1886; Harper, J. H., *The House of Harper,* 1912; *Harper's Weekly,* April 10 and April 17, 1869; Muskowitz, Milton, et al., eds., *Everybody's Business,* 1980; Putnam, G. H., *George Palmer Putnam: A Memoir,* 1912.

Harriman, Edward

(February 20, 1848–September 9, 1909)
Railroad Executive, Financier

Edward Henry Harriman's ruthlessness complemented an era known for its unbridled economic development. In the late nineteenth century, when corporations first appeared on a large scale and smokestacks told of the nation's change from farms to factories, Harriman financed and built railroads, thus propelling the nation's industrialization and acquiring power and fortune.

Edward was born on February 20, 1848, in Hempstead, New York, to Orlando Harriman, an Episcopal clergyman, and Cornelia (Neilson) Harriman. He left school at age 14 and worked as a messenger on Wall Street. Enamored with making money, he borrowed $3,000 from a wealthy uncle, bought a seat on the New York Stock Exchange, and opened his own brokerage. He quickly displayed a keen ability to evaluate stocks, and his acumen attracted prominent investors, among them AUGUST BELMONT.

Harriman's greatest triumphs came in the railroad industry, however. He entered the railroad business in 1881, two years after marrying Mary Williamson Averell, the daughter of the president of a railroad. (The couple eventually had six children.) Harriman formed a syndicate, bought a bankrupt railroad in central New York, rebuilt it, and sold it for a considerable profit. He realized then that money could be made by improving weak lines and running them efficiently.

Harriman gained prominence in 1883, when he obtained a seat on the board of the Illinois Central. Four years later, he became vice president and worked closely with Stuyvesant Fish, a friend and president of the railroad, to expand it. Harriman used his financial genius in obtaining funds by marketing bonds at low interest. At the same time, he learned the details of railroad construction and closely supervised improvements.

Harriman entered the top ranks of the railroad industry when, in 1897, he headed a syndicate that for $58.4 million bought the dilapidated Union Pacific. Within a short time, he turned the railroad around—buying locomotives and cars, replacing rails, relocating stretches of road, and improving curves and grades. For the Union Pacific, he acquired the Oregon Short Line and the Oregon Railroad & Navigation Company, thus gaining an outlet to the Pacific Ocean at Portland. Union Pacific profits jumped from $14 million in 1899 to $20 million in 1900, and its stock rose from $25 a share in 1897 to $106 by 1906, ranking it among the most valued railroad properties in the world.

Harriman acted in 1901 to dominate traffic in the West by acquiring the Southern Pacific, whose founder, Collis P. Huntington, had recently died. Harriman's improvements included an amazing engineering feat, the building of a cutoff across Utah's Great Salt Lake.

A titanic struggle erupted when JAMES J. HILL used his control of the Great Northern and the Northern Pacific to challenge Harriman for control of the Chicago, Burlington & Quincy, a line crucial to dominating traffic from the West into Chicago. The warring sides decided in 1901 to organize the Northern Securities Company, a holding company for the stock of the Great Northern and the Northern Pacific that assured a cooperative arrangement with the Burlington. In 1903, Harriman became president of the Union Pacific. Northern Securities, meanwhile, imposed monopolistic rates that injured farmers, resulting in the U.S. Supreme Court declaring the company an illegal combination in restraint of trade in 1904.

Harriman subsequently sold his holdings in several railroads, making a profit of over $50 million. He used that money along with his earnings from the Union Pacific to purchase stocks in other lines. He went to the Far East in 1905 with plans to use steamships that he owned to help build a worldwide transportation system.

Harriman's railroad acquisitions caused the Interstate Commerce Commission (ICC) to investigate his companies in 1906. The hearings revealed the power Harriman had amassed in the railroad industry, and that he had turned the Union Pacific into an investment company, as much concerned with speculating in securities as in operating transportation. The ICC decided not to prosecute Harriman, even though his combinations defied antitrust laws as interpreted at that time. In all, the hearings sullied his reputation with the public.

Yet Harriman had a humanitarian side. He organized a scientific expedition to Alaska, formed a boys' club in New York City to help immigrant children, bought land in Orange County, New York, to pro-

Edward Harriman (Library of Congress)

tect it from timber harvesting, and helped victims of the great San Francisco earthquake. Harriman died on September 9, 1909, admired by business leaders who followed his financial strategies. "I never cared for money except as power for work," he once said. "What I most enjoy is the power of creation."

BIBLIOGRAPHY

Eckenrod, H. J., *E. H. Harriman: The Little Giant of Wall Street*, 1981; Kennan, George, *E. H. Harriman: A Biography*, 1922; Mercer, Lloyd, *E. H. Harriman: Master Railroader*, 1985.

Hartford, George

(September 5, 1833–August 20, 1917)
Merchant

Chinese pagodas, a green parrot, band music—all these decorated the store that George Huntington Hartford and a partner started and built into a retail giant, the Great Atlantic and Pacific Tea Company.

George was born on September 5, 1833, in Augusta, Maine, to J. Brackett Hartford, a farmer and small merchant, and Martha (Soren) Hartford. He moved to St. Louis, Missouri, around 1858, and two years later to New York City. At both locations, he worked for George F. Gilman, a leather merchant and fellow Maine native, first as a clerk and then as an associate. In 1862, he married Josephine Ludlum.

During the 1850s, Gilman used connections he had made through his father's shipping business to buy tea in great quantities, importing it directly from China and Japan without using layers of middlemen. He and Hartford opened a small shop on Vesey Street in New York City and gave it a grandiose name, the Great American Tea Company. Their buying scheme allowed them to sell tea at 30 cents a pound, while competitors were charging $1. In addition, they attracted customers with exotic displays and spectacular gimmicks—cashiers' cages shaped like Chinese pagodas, a green parrot in the center of the main floor, band music, premiums for lucky customers, and eight horses pulling an eye-catching red wagon through the city.

Less flamboyant than Gilman, Hartford kept the business on an even keel and in 1867 became the junior partner. Two years later, the entrepreneurs changed the firm's name to the Great Atlantic and Pacific Tea Company (A&P) while opening outlets in other cities. Each store displayed a distinctive red-and-gold facade, easily identified by the nation's burgeoning consumer population. By 1879, Gilman and Hartford had 67 stores and had expanded the products carried to spices, coffee, soap, baking powder, and other groceries. They emphasized small stores with a personal appeal. By that time, Hartford had also assumed active management of the company.

When Gilman died in 1901, Hartford, along with two of his sons, George Ludlum Hartford and JOHN HARTFORD, bought total ownership of A&P, which by that time consisted of 200 stores selling over $5 million worth of goods. The new owners began the practice of offering credit buying and delivery services to their customers. Despite its impressive growth, the firm's greatest expansion occurred under John Hartford, after the elder Hartford died on August 20, 1917.

BIBLIOGRAPHY

Adelman, M. A., *A&P: A Study in Price-Cost Behavior and Public Policy*, 1959; Hoyt, Edwin P., *That Wonderful A&P!*, 1969; Walsh, Will, *Rise and Decline of the Great Atlantic and Pacific Tea Company*, 1986.

Hartford, John

(February 10, 1872–September 20, 1951)
Merchant

Amid America's late-nineteenth-century industrialization and urbanization, John Augustine Hartford converted the grocery stores begun by his father into one of the nation's first retail chains.

John was born on February 10, 1872, in Orange, New Jersey, to GEORGE HARTFORD and Josephine (Ludlum) Hartford. His father and a partner, George F. Gilman, had founded the Great Atlantic and Pacific Tea Company (A&P), which, by the 1870s, comprised 67 stores selling tea, coffee, and various grocery items. John entered the firm at age 16, and in 1893 married Pauline Corwin. When Gilman died in 1901, John purchased ownership of the company with his father and his older brother, George Ludlum Hartford.

Hartford led A&P's rapid expansion beginning in 1912, when he decided to open "economy stores" as a way to return to the company's original emphasis on low prices and limited service. Over the next three years, he opened a new A&P store every three days, expanding the total number to 1,000 across the nation and creating one of the first chain-store operations.

After his father died in 1917, Hartford became company president and supervised the stores. He frequently visited A&P stores and established a paternalistic system in which he opposed unionization but fired or demoted long-time employees only as a last resort.

Hartford divorced his wife in 1923 and married Frances Bolger, a model. They divorced, however, within a few months,

and the following year, he remarried his first wife.

Meanwhile, Hartford continued to expand A&P, adding additional products to the store, including meat in 1925. In 1929, total revenues exceeded $1 billion, and by the following year, nearly 16,000 A&Ps dotted the landscape.

All through the 1920s, the appearance of more A&Ps led owners of general stores and small businesses to complain that the chain stores would swallow them up. In 1922, the National Association of Retail Grocers urged the states to pass laws that would inhibit the growth of chains, and several states responded by levying taxes on them.

During the following decade, Congress passed legislation aimed at prohibiting unfair pricing policies that allowed the chain stores to obtain items at discount prices and sell them cheaper than could smaller stores. "The chain stores are undermining the foundation of our entire local happiness and prosperity," claimed one congressman. Chain-store growth, however, continued apace, and Hartford defused the opposition by rallying farmer and consumer groups that benefited from the markets the chain stores had created. Still, in 1946, the federal government obtained a conviction against A&P for violating antitrust laws.

At the same time, A&P faced a strong challenge from a new type of store, the supermarket. These independent businesses provided a greater range of goods than found at A&P's smaller stores. Hartford responded by opening A&P supermarkets, and although this move reduced the total number of stores, it boosted overall sales.

Hartford died on September 20, 1951, in New York City. A&P continued to grow for several more years, and by 1971 the company had 4,358 stores and a sales volume of $5.5 billion. After that date, however, A&P slipped into decline as such competitors as Safeway eclipsed its sales in volume. In 1997, A&P operated 973 stores under the trade names of A&P, Waldbaum's, Food Emporium, Super Fresh, Farmer Jack, Kohl's, Dominion, and Food Basics.

BIBLIOGRAPHY

Adelman, M. A., *A&P: A Study in Price-Cost Behavior and Public Policy*, 1959; Hoyt, Edwin P., *That Wonderful A&P!*, 1969; Walsh, Will, *Rise and Decline of the Great Atlantic and Pacific Tea Company*, 1986.

Hassenfeld, Stephen

(January 19, 1942–June 25, 1989)
Merchant

Stephen David Hassenfeld, a third-generation toy maker, rescued his family company, Hasbro, from obscurity through deft management and a keen sense of the marketplace. Under his leadership, the company rocketed from a loss position of $2.5 million in 1978 to sales of over $800 million in the late 1980s. His skill at advertising was a pivotal factor in muddying the lines between television programming and commercialism. His drive and energy reinvigorated both his own company and the toy industry.

Stephen, the son of Merrill and Sylvia Hassenfeld, was born on January 19, 1942, in Providence, Rhode Island. His father's company, Hasbro (which stands for Hassenfeld Brothers), had been started in 1923 by his grandfather Henry and great-uncle Hillel. Hasbro began as a manufacturer of pencil boxes, progressed to include the manufacture of pencils themselves, and then branched into toys. By the time Stephen was born, the company consisted of two distinct divisions, Hasbro Toys (run by his father) and Empire Pencil (run by his uncle). The most notable product in the early years of Hasbro was Mr. Potato Head.

Stephen became fascinated by the toy industry at an early age and spent summers on the floor of the factory. After attending Moses Brown School, a private Quaker academy, he majored in political science at Johns Hopkins University with the idea of becoming a diplomat. Stephen left Johns Hopkins in 1962 when he realized that business held a greater appeal for him than diplomacy. Though he wanted to work at the family business, Merrill, his father, insisted that Stephen try another job in business to be certain about his goals. For two years, Stephen worked at an advertising agency in Providence until Merrill brought him on board as his assistant in 1964.

When Stephen started, Hasbro was bogged down with demands for a product that had become an overnight success—G. I. Joe. The first toy of its kind, G. I. Joe was an action figure that initially, and unexpectedly, provoked the same groundswell of excitement generated by rival Mattel's Barbie doll. The action figure plunged Hasbro into the playing field of the major toy companies. During Stephen's initial years with the company, he was placed in the Romper Room division, which owned the television show of the same name and manufactured a line of Romper Room toys geared toward the preschool market.

By the mid-1970s, G. I. Joe had become a casualty of the Vietnam War with antiwar sentiment affecting how the public perceived the influence of militaristic toys. Sales of the doll dropped from $23 million in 1965 to $7.5 million in 1970, and in 1978 G. I. Joe was taken off the market.

In 1974, Stephen was made president of Hasbro Toys. Though he would eventually restore the company's status and financial standing, he initially made a number of judgment errors and unwisely moved the company into ownership of day-care centers and housewares. Within two years, those endeavors were closed down. After Merrill's death in 1979, Harold Hassenfeld, who ran the Empire Pencil division of Hasbro, refused to recognize Stephen as the chief executive officer of Hasbro Industries. Stephen became Merrill's successor only to Hasbro Toys. Stephen underwent a period of deep contemplation and determined to turn the toy company around.

After studying Hasbro's business strategy and management style, Stephen took stock of the company's flaws. He believed that Hasbro attempted to produce too many types of toys. Stephen identified three market niches. Toys that did not fall into the categories of preschool toys, 3-D skill and action games, and design toys were eliminated altogether. This decisive action produced solid results. By 1980, Hasbro, without ever entering the trendy arena of electronic games, had become a profitable company, earning $4.6 million on sales of $104 million.

At this juncture, Stephen began negotiations with his uncle to split the two main branches of Hasbro, the toy company and the pencil manufacturer, into two separate companies. Newly confident of the toy division's ability to succeed without the steady income provided by Empire Pencil, Harold agreed to the split.

Within a few years, Hasbro was considered by financial analysts to be the fastest-growing firm in the industry. In 1982, the hype surrounding the Star Wars movie and action figures convinced Stephen to bring back G. I. Joe. In conjunction with a Marvel Comic Book series, the retooled Joe was released along with a new set of characters and story lines befitting the cold war patriotism of the Reagan era. Within two years, sales of the doll tripled, inspiring Hasbro to launch the syndicated animated children's show, *G. I. Joe: A Real American Hero.*

Prior to this time, toys based on TV and movie characters had become quite popular. Hasbro's G. I. Joe cartoon was one of the first TV shows to be launched based on a popular toy. This concept allowed Hasbro to integrate advertising for a product directly into the context of the show's plot. This would happen with a number of other Hasbro products, such as My Little Pony and the Transformers. The lines became so blurred that Hasbro executives would frequently dictate the emphasis of a story line to the show's writers in order to promote sales of particular toys.

Stephen was critical in fostering Hasbro's growing understanding of demographics and the marketplace. His leadership took the company to new heights in terms of inventive advertising and vigorous market analysis for new products. In 1987, his inauguration of the company's flashy New York City showroom was also a presentation of a company that had been re-created and redesigned. Under Stephen, Hasbro expanded dramatically, acquiring such giants as Milton Bradley and Tonka Toys. The merger with Milton Bradley increased Hasbro's sales to $760 million annually, placing it squarely at the head of the toy industry.

Despite the success and the satisfaction he took in revitalizing the company, Stephen was a driven workaholic who derived little joy from an industry based on fun and games. A bachelor who lived much of his life with his parents before enjoying a long-term relationship, Stephen made his work central to his life.

Hasbro would continue to experience the success made possible by his efforts, but Stephen Hassenfeld's years at the helm ended prematurely. After battling illness for several years, he died on June 25, 1989, leaving his brother Alan to continue the family legacy.

BIBLIOGRAPHY

Atlantic Monthly, October 1986; *Forbes*, May 25, 1981; *Fortune*, April 25, 1988; Miller, G. Wayne, *Toy Wars: The Epic Struggle between G. I. Joe, Barbie, and the Companies That Make Them*, 1988.

Hearst, William Randolph

(April 20, 1863–August 14, 1951)
Publisher

From the late 1800s into the early 1900s, William Randolph Hearst reshaped American journalism with his newspapers the *San Francisco Examiner* and the *New York World*. His adherence to low prices, quality writing, and sensationalist reporting won millions of readers.

Hearst was born on April 20, 1863, into a wealthy family in San Francisco, California. His father, George Hearst, had made a fortune in mining. His mother, Phoebe (Apperson) Hearst, took young Hearst to Europe at age 10 for his early education. He entered Harvard in 1882 but was expelled two years later for a prank he pulled on his teachers.

While at Harvard, Hearst had worked on the *Lampoon* (the college's undergraduate humor magazine) and obtained his first training in journalism. After his expulsion, he convinced his father to let him run the *San Francisco Examiner*, which the elder Hearst had purchased several years earlier and operated at a loss.

The first *Examiner* under Hearst appeared on March 4, 1887, and he quickly reorganized the paper to reflect his formula for success: attract talented writers, combine insightful stories with sensationalist ones, and use the paper to advertise itself by heralding its own achievements. He used the *Examiner* for political purposes also, criticizing the Southern Pacific Railroad, then a power in California.

Triumphant in his first foray into journalism, Hearst decided to challenge JOSEPH PULITZER's dominant position in New York City. With a fortune of more than $7 million obtained from his father, who died in 1891, and from his mother, who sold her inheritance in the Anaconda Mining Company, Hearst bought the struggling *New York Journal* for $180,000 and remodeled it after the *Examiner*. He brought with him some of his writers from San Francisco and raided Pulitzer's *New York World* for others. He added comics to the *Journal*, used bold headlines, printed morning and evening editions, and lowered the paper's price to one penny—a move Pulitzer was forced to copy.

Most significantly, however, Hearst developed what one critic called "yellow journalism"—exaggerated, sometimes faked, stories, that appealed to people's emotions and, in particular, the large number of immigrants who made up an important part of the city's expanding population.

Hearst's most spectacular stories covered the ongoing Cuban revolution. Hearst sided with the rebels then trying to gain independence from Spain. He did

William Randolph Hearst (Library of Congress)

so as much from the desire to promote an exciting story that would boost circulation as he did from any commitment to Cuban liberty. As a result, he portrayed the Spanish as evil oppressors and kept prodding the American government to support the Cuban freedom fighters. When the U.S. battleship *Maine* blew up in Havana harbor in 1898, Hearst accused Spain of having attacked the ship—a charge that lacked convincing evidence.

Hearst beat the war drums louder, as did other yellow journalists, and the U.S. government reacted by declaring war on Spain, thus beginning the Spanish-American War. Other developments, of course, contributed to the war, but Hearst must be included among the causes of the conflict. By late 1898, his New York newspapers, the morning and evening *Journal*, had a daily circulation of 1.25 million or what he called "the largest circulation in the world."

A Democrat, Hearst entered politics when he won election to the U.S. House of Representatives from Manhattan in 1902. The following year, he married Millicent Willson, a Broadway dancer, and they eventually had five sons.

Hearst served one undistinguished term in Congress. Despite his lackluster record, he vied for the Democratic Party presidential nomination in 1904, but lost to Alton B. Parker, a judge. Hearst ran for mayor of New York City in 1905, only to lose by a slim margin. There followed a race for governor of New York in 1906, which turned out to be another loss in a tight contest.

In the years before World War I, Hearst expanded his communications empire. He bought newspapers in Chicago, Boston, Los Angeles, and Atlanta, founded two prominent nationwide news systems (King Features Syndicate and the International News Service), and acquired several magazines, including *Cosmopolitan*, *Good Housekeeping*, and *Harper's Bazaar*.

Hearst began a long romantic relationship with Marion Davies, a showgirl with the Ziegfield Follies, in 1917, and tried, but failed, to get his wife to agree to a divorce. From that point on, his marriage existed in name only.

Hearst inherited substantial wealth when his mother died in 1919, and he continued to build his holdings. He owned more than 20 newspapers and several magazines and invested in New York real estate. He lived on a 375-square-mile ranch at San Simeon, California, collected art and antiquities, and bought a castle in Wales.

In his later years, Hearst developed a reputation for arbitrary promotions and demotions at his newspapers. He also moved from a progressive Democratic ideology to a conservative one and in the 1930s severely criticized President Franklin Roosevelt's efforts to end the Great Depression, telling his writers to call the president's New Deal the "Raw Deal." He even expressed views sympathetic with Adolph Hitler.

The Great Depression severely hurt Hearst, and in an attempt to stem his financial losses, he organized his newspapers and magazines in 1935 under American Newspapers, Inc., a business worth nearly $200 million. Revenues continued to drop, however, and Hearst was forced to relinquish control of American Newspapers to a bank representative, who sold many of the holdings.

Hearst recovered financially with the national economic boost caused by World War II and regained some power over his holdings. He suffered a heart seizure in 1947 that made him an invalid, and he died on August 14, 1951, in Los Angeles. Today, many Americans remember Hearst as the character Citizen Kane, which was played by Orson Welles in the classic 1941 movie of the same name. Kane's story in the movie was based closely on Hearst's life.

BIBLIOGRAPHY

Chaney, Lindsay, *The Hearsts: Family and Empire, the Later Years*, 1981; Littlefield, Roy Everett, *William Randolph Hearst: His Role in American Progressivism*, 1980; Procter, Ben, *William Randolph Hearst: The Early Years, 1863–1910*, 1998; Swanberg, W. A., *Citizen Hearst*, 1961; Tebbel, John, *The Life and Good Times of William Randolph Hearst*, 1952.

Hefner, Hugh

(April 9, 1926–)
Publisher

Curtains drawn, sunlight shut out, clocks covered—Hugh Marston Hefner worked in a strange atmosphere, putting together *Playboy* magazine (noted for its nude photographs of women) and building its readership into the millions. His publishing empire seemed impregnable until a bold competitor, ROBERT GUCCIONE, published his racier material in *Penthouse* magazine and knocked *Playboy* from the top.

Hugh was born on April 9, 1926, in Chicago, Illinois, to Glenn Hefner, an accountant, and Grace (Swanson) Hefner. His parents, devout Methodists, raised him in a setting that repressed him sexually and caused him to fear girls. In fact, he did not go out on his first date until he entered his senior year at Steinmetz High School. After graduation, he entered the University of Illinois to be with his girlfriend, Millie Williams. Hefner studied psychology, obtained his bachelor's degree in 1949, and, after marrying Millie, held various jobs to support her and their two children.

Hefner's marriage ended in divorce after just three years, while his job as a subscription promotion writer at *Esquire* magazine convinced him that he wanted to enter publishing. He believed that a market existed for a sophisticated magazine that would publish photos of nude women, discuss sex, and present quality writing. Although the conformist atmosphere that prevailed in the 1950s suppressed anything middle-class society considered deviant, Hefner banked on the increasingly younger population and the media's exploitation of Marilyn Monroe that had whetted appetites for more explicit sex.

He banked right. With $600 of his own money and $10,000 raised by selling stock to friends, he launched the first issue of *Playboy* magazine in 1953, featuring a nude calendar photo of Monroe, rights to which he had acquired for a mere $200. The issue sold well and from then until the early 1970s, *Playboy*'s circulation climbed. Prior to Hefner's venture, nude photos of women had appeared in trashy, poorly produced magazines, peddled as illicit items stashed beneath store counters. Hefner used only professional photographs, mainly color, and had them airbrushed to remove skin blemishes. Thus, he sold fantasy as much as he did nudity and went so far as to prohibit any advertisements that might remind readers of bodily imperfections—both those of the readers and those of the models. No acne remedy advertisements appeared in *Playboy*.

Hefner presented his first Playmate of the Month in 1956 when he convinced Janet Pilgrim—subscription manager at the magazine and a woman whose name ironically conjured up thoughts of the puritanical attitudes Hefner challenged—to pose nude. As with his previous editions, he included literary articles that gave *Playboy* a reputation for good writing and that elevated its overall reputation.

By 1960, *Playboy*'s circulation topped 1 million, and two years later, Hefner decided to found two other publications, *Show Business Illustrated* and *Trump*, a humor magazine. Both failed, however, with *Show Business Illustrated* losing $3 million. Hefner had more success when he opened Playboy Clubs International, which operated as combination night clubs and restaurants, in the United States and overseas. Rather than food and drinks, "Bunnies," derived from the rabbit symbol Hefner used for his magazine, were the main attraction—hostesses and waitresses who wore magenta satin corsets with cotton tails attached and bunny ears atop their heads.

Hefner opened Playboy hotel-resorts in Jamaica, the British West Indies, and other locations, and his wealth enabled him to buy a 48-room mansion in Chicago, a house known for the darkened rooms where he did most of his work and where Playboy models cavorted.

A serious challenge arose to Hefner, however, in 1969 when Guccione began publishing *Penthouse* magazine in a move to dislodge *Playboy* from its commanding position. *Penthouse* won a large readership by publishing more explicit photographs of its nude models.

Hefner responded slowly to Guccione and did not allow full frontal nudity in *Playboy* until 1972. This flesh competition between the two magazines was dubbed the "pubic wars" by the media. At the same time, Hefner's operations expanded to include the Playboy TV channel, movies, and records, but they produced mixed results, with the movies and records losing millions. Annual profits at Playboy tumbled from $20 million in 1973 to $2 million in 1975. Hefner had to fire 100 employees in 1976 as his money woes mounted, and the following

year—soon after he moved from his Chicago mansion to luxurious digs in Los Angeles—he brought in a new president to turn the situation around but to no avail.

As the crisis worsened, Hefner turned to his daughter Christine Ann (Christie) Hefner for help. She had suggested that she take over as president, and in 1982 Hefner agreed. As a child, Christie had hardly known her father, visiting him only occasionally. But while a student at Brandeis University, she got to know him better. She graduated from Brandeis in 1974 with a bachelor's degree in literature and in 1975 joined Playboy as a special assistant. She advanced to the vice presidency in 1977. As president she cut the firm's debts, donated the Chicago mansion to that city's Art Institute, and in 1986 closed the Playboy clubs. The business still lost $62 million.

Hefner took a less active role at Playboy in 1988 after he assumed the more limited position as editor in chief of the magazine. The following year, he married Kimberly Conrad, the 1989 Playmate of the Year. The couple had two children. Meanwhile, Christie Hefner became CEO, and the business began returning a profit. *Playboy* magazine obtained a circulation of about 3 million in 1997, and the company's net revenues reached $297 million.

BIBLIOGRAPHY

Miller, Russell, *Bunny: The Real Story of Playboy*, 1985; Ramsey, Douglas K., *The Corporate Warriors*, 1987.

Heinz, H. J.

(October 11, 1844–May 14, 1919)
Manufacturer

The "Pickle King" and "57 varieties"—that is how millions of Americans once recognized Henry John Heinz, the business leader who turned a small garden plot into a huge corporation that bottled and canned fruits and vegetables.

Born to Henry Heinz and Anna Margaretha (Schmidt) Heinz on October 11, 1844, in Birmingham, Pennsylvania (near Pittsburgh), Henry grew up in Sharpsburg, the town his family moved to when he was only 5. His mother had a large garden, and at age 8, the youngster began selling produce from it, going from house to house, basket in hand. His success caused his parents to allocate him his own three-quarter-acre plot. He built hotbeds and expanded his yield to three crops per year. As he sold more, his acreage expanded, and by age 16, he had several employees and was making wagon deliveries to grocers in Pittsburgh.

After attending Duff's Business College, Heinz worked in his father's brickyard as a bookkeeper and became a partner when he was 21. He improved the business by installing heating flues at the plant that enabled it to operate year-round.

Heinz's main interest remained food, however, and in 1869, he relinquished his share of the brick business and formed a partnership to make and sell grated horseradish. He called his product Anchor Brand, and although the business at first did well, it suffered amid an economic depression and went bankrupt in 1875.

While paying his debts, Heinz began a new business in 1876 with his brother John and his cousin Frederic Heinz, called the F. & J. Heinz Company. Heinz bottled pickles and more: he had many recipes and used them to make chili sauce, tomato sauce, mincemeat, and other mixes. By 1879, he had left his indebtedness behind and reported he was solvent and stable. "All are busy and really driving a good business and profitable," Heinz said, "more so I think than ever before in my life."

Heinz reorganized the firm in 1888 as the H. J. Heinz Company and, repulsed by the labor strife then sweeping America, decided to build a showcase factory along with a progressive industrial welfare program. The facility that arose along the Allegheny River on 24 lots next to his vinegar factory comprised Romanesque buildings, all made of hard brick and oak posts. The first plant opened in 1889, and eventually 17 buildings surrounded a grassed courtyard.

Heinz's plant had the most advanced kitchens and bottling and packaging departments. He provided employees with a restaurant, dressing rooms, rest rooms, a roof garden, and a gymnasium. The workers—mainly young immigrant women—could participate in classes held on the premises: dressmaking, millinery, cooking, drawing, and music. As sounds from an organ mingled in the air with the odors from condiments, the immigrant workers received instruction on how to attain American citizenship. One newspaper summed up the conditions at Heinz's plant by saying that a working woman found "kindly care and fair treatment."

The sight at the pickle plant attracted tourists then and would impress us as peculiar today: 100 white-frocked women sitting in rows behind tables in a vast room, each worker using a wooden paddle to take pickles from large bowls and pack them in empty jars, along with a red pepper, which they placed against the glass to make the product look attractive. From the factory, salesmen traveled in horse-drawn wagons with Heinz pickles pictured on the side. Although Heinz made more than 200 products, people called him the "Pickle King." And, despite the size of his product line, he coined the advertising slogan "57 varieties" because he thought the number and phrase catchy. The slogan soon beamed down on New Yorkers from that city's first large electric sign, six stories high with 1,200 bulbs.

In the 1890s, Heinz led efforts to end the adulteration of packaged food. Some of his competitors used chemicals to change the way food looked, such as by making green beans greener. Heinz believed these practices damaged the entire industry, and so he encouraged Congress to pass the Pure Food and Drug Act, which it did in 1906.

Heinz had over 6,500 employees in 1919, along with 25 branch factories and his own seed farms. Each year, more than 100,000 acres of fruits and vegetables wound up in Heinz barrels, bottles, and cans. Besides his business interest, Heinz donated money to found a settlement house to help the poor, and he served as a Sunday-school superintendent for 25 years. He died in Pittsburgh on May 14, 1919, from pneumonia, and left an estate valued at more than $4 million. In addition to its American factories, Heinz currently has processing plants overseas and owns Weight Watchers, which runs weight-reduction programs and sells frozen food.

BIBLIOGRAPHY

Alberts, Robert C., *The Good Provider: H. J. Heinz and His 57 Varieties*, 1973.

Hershey, Milton

(September 13, 1857–October 13, 1945)
Manufacturer

When Milton Hershey found that milk added to caramel made the candy tastier, he discovered a recipe that earned him millions and led to his founding of the Hershey Chocolate Company.

Milton was born on September 13, 1857, in Derry Church, Pennsylvania, to Henry H. Hershey and Fannie (Snavely) Hershey. His father moved frequently, and, as a result, young Hershey attended seven schools within an eight-year period. He never made it past the fourth grade, since his father put him to work as a printer's apprentice in Gap, Pennsylvania.

Disliking the trade, Hershey left the printer's shop in 1872 to apprentice in a confectioner's shop in Lancaster, Pennsylvania. There he discovered his calling and four years later opened his own candy shop. The extremely competitive environment took its toll, however, and in 1882 the business failed.

Seeking new opportunity, Hershey moved to Denver, Colorado, where his father had recently relocated. There he worked for a caramel manufacturer and discovered that fresh milk could enhance the flavor of candy. Hershey moved to Chicago in 1883, and he and his father opened a candy shop that prospered, until the elder Hershey made a financial blunder. After that shop closed in 1886, Hershey went briefly to New Orleans, Louisiana, and then to New York City, in each instance trying to resume his candy business.

Hershey finally settled in Lancaster, Pennsylvania, in 1886 and once again made caramels with fresh milk in the recipe. This time, success came quickly. Within three years, his Lancaster Caramel Company prospered, bringing him wealth. In 1893, Hershey visited the Chicago World's Fair and was so impressed with some German chocolate-making machinery on exhibit that he bought his own. Early the following year, he founded the Hershey Chocolate Company as a subsidiary to his caramel company and began making caramels with chocolate coatings, along with breakfast cocoa, sweet chocolate, baking chocolate, and novelty chocolate candies.

In 1900, the year Hershey began making milk chocolate bars, he sold the Lancaster Caramel Company for $1 million to his main competitor, the American Caramel Company, but retained his chocolate manufacturing machinery and the right to continue making and marketing his chocolate. He then returned to

Milton Hershey (Corbis/Bettmann-UPI)

Derry Church, and amid Pennsylvania's dairy farms, he built a chocolate factory. With construction completed in 1905, Hershey moved into mass production. Sales grew rapidly, even without advertising, which Hershey rejected in favor of reputation spread by word of mouth.

New products soon followed: Hershey Kisses in 1907, Hershey's Almond Bars in 1908, and Mr. Goodbar in 1925. At the same time, Hershey built around his factory an entire town, converting Derry Church into Hershey, Pennsylvania. The town had churches, schools, a park, a zoo, a football field, and many amenities. He provided his workers with low-cost housing, and during the Great Depression, he fought unemployment by expanding his construction projects. But the townspeople had little influence—they had no mayor or council since Hershey ran everything—and they received only modest wages. As a result, in 1937, workers staged a strike, and in 1940 they won recognition for their union. As the labor strife appeared, so did new products: Krackel in 1938 and Hershey's Miniatures the following year. Sales went from $30 million in 1931 to $55 million in 1941.

Hershey also engaged in philanthropy. He had married Catherine Sweeney in 1898, and, unable to have their own children, in 1909 they housed and educated four orphan boys. From this experience emerged the Hershey Industrial School (later the Milton Hershey School) to provide schooling and training for orphans. In 1918, three years after his wife died, Hershey placed most of his fortune in a trust for the school. Today, the school provides education for 1,100 children, and through the Hershey Trust Company, it owns 35.5 percent of Hershey Foods stock.

Hershey died on October 13, 1945, about one year after he retired as chief executive officer of the Hershey Chocolate Corporation. After Hershey's death, the company faced enormous competition from FORREST MARS and other candy makers who advertised their brands. Hershey finally began its own advertising in 1970. In 1998, Hershey Foods consisted of three divisions: Hershey Chocolate North America (the largest division, which included Hershey's, Reese's, and Cadbury's candies), Hershey Pasta and Grocery Group (which made dry pasta products), and Hershey International (which oversaw the company's interests in Germany, Japan, and Italy).

BIBLIOGRAPHY

Hinkle, Samuel, *Hershey*, 1964; Shippen, Katherine B., and Paul A. W. Wallace, *Biography of Milton S. Hershey*, 1959; Snavely, Joseph, *An Intimate Story of Milton S. Hershey*, 1957.

Hill, George

(October 22, 1884–September 13, 1946)
Tobacco Executive

As president of the American Tobacco Company for 21 years, George Washington Hill led the tobacco industry in marketing savvy with an emphasis on advertising and promotion of the Lucky Strike cigarette brand. Hill capitalized on the potential of marketing the mass-produced cigarette brand on a national scale and then used extensive advertising to improve its market share.

Born on October 22, 1884, in Philadelphia, Pennsylvania, George was one of three children born to Cassie Rowland and Percival Smith Hill. Percival sold his carpet business when George was six and joined the Blackwell Durham Tobacco Company as sales manager two years later. Percival eventually bought a partnership in the company, and when the Blackwell Company was absorbed by the

American Tobacco Company in 1898, Percival became an executive of American Tobacco, relocating his family to New York City.

George attended the Horace Mann School in New York and after graduating in 1902, enrolled at Williams College. In 1904, George left college in his sophomore year and began a job in the factories and leaf markets of the American Tobacco Company in North Carolina. In that same year, he married Lucie Langhorne Cobb. The couple would eventually have two children before their marriage ended in divorce in 1920.

In 1907, American Tobacco acquired the small firm of Butler and Butler, which produced the Pall Mall brand of cigarettes, an expensive Turkish blend. George was put in charge of sales of Pall Mall. Promoting the brand through advertising became his driving mission. In just a few years, Pall Mall became the number-one brand among high-end Turkish blends. In 1911, the American Tobacco trust was partially dissolved by spinning off several separate companies. Percival was appointed president of what remained of the American Tobacco Company, and George became vice president and manager of sales.

In 1913, the R. J. Reynolds Company introduced the first mass-produced, blended cigarette brand, which was called Camel. This product was initially ignored by American Tobacco until George, identifying the potential of the growing market for this type of blended cigarette, convinced the rest of the company's management to aggressively manufacture and promote their own blended brand to compete with Camel's rising success. Lucky Strike was introduced on a national scale in 1917, and George per-

sonally oversaw most of the promotional aspects, from packaging design to advertising slogans. In 1922, George married his second wife, Aquinas M. Heller, who died just three years later. She bore him two children.

Hill's father, Percival, also died in 1925, and Hill replaced him as the president of the American Tobacco Company. In this post, he continued to focus heavily on advertising Lucky Strike with an unprecedented annual advertising budget of $20 million. At the beginning of 1927, Hill launched an advertising campaign using endorsements from foreign female opera stars in order to target women, a previously untapped and vast market. The investment paid off when in 1930 Lucky Strike briefly surpassed Camel as the nation's leading cigarette brand. Hill was also highly regarded for maintaining American Tobacco's profitability during the Great Depression. During this time, he became one of the highest-paid executives in the country.

In the 1940s, Hill continued to juggle his aggressive attempts to dominate the market with his desire to avoid encroaching government regulation. He ultimately lost this battle in 1946, when the U.S. Supreme Court upheld an antitrust ruling against the American Tobacco Company and two other companies for setting up a price monopoly on leaf tobacco. The companies and their executives, including Hill, were fined for the collusion. During this time, one of the principal types of promotional tools Hill employed was radio commercials. He was one of the first to extensively sponsor feature shows and develop musical jingles for a product.

Hill was a hardworking and private man. He drew his friends from a circle of colleagues who shared his zeal for tobacco and its promotion. On July 8, 1935, he married his secretary, Mary Barnes, in London. In his spare time, Hill enjoyed fishing, dancing, and reading detective stories. He died from a heart attack on September 13, 1946, at his vacation home near Matapedia, Quebec, and was buried at Sleepy Hollow Cemetery in North Tarrytown, New York.

BIBLIOGRAPHY

Current Biography, 1946; "Gone—One of Advertising's Great Teachers," *Printer's Ink*, October 4, 1946; "He Makes America Sit Up and Buy," *Forbes*, January 1, 1933; *New York Times*, Obituary, September 14, 1946.

Hill, James J.

(September 16, 1838–May 29, 1916)
Railroad Executive, Financier

James Jerome Hill helped organize major new transportation systems in Canada, the upper Midwest, and the Pacific Northwest. In one of the most impressive engineering and financial feats of the nineteenth century, Hill relentlessly expanded the Great Northern Railroad west from Minnesota to Puget Sound, building a transcontinental route that would substantially aid settlement and growth in the northern United States and southern Canada.

Hill was born on September 16, 1838, in the small town of Wellington in the province of Ontario, Canada. His father, James Hill Sr., had emigrated from northern Ireland to Ontario with his own parents in 1829. In 1832, the elder Hill met and married Anne Dunbar, whose family had also recently emigrated from northern Ireland. The family lived a typical frontier lifestyle. The third of four children, James Jr. later recalled that his father was not very successful in working the land. The young James acquired a taste for hunting, which would be one of his pastimes throughout his life. In an unfortunate hunting accident when he was nine years old, his bow snapped, destroying the sight in his right eye.

Hill's education began in the local public school, but he transferred to the newly established Rockwood Academy at age 11. In 1852, the death of his father necessitated Hill leaving school to work as a clerk in the village store. During his four years as a clerk, he was encouraged by the principal of Rockwood Academy to continue his studies and to read actively.

At the age of 18, Hill began to seek his own fortune. Inspired by his extensive reading about India, China, and Japan, he set out for the Atlantic ports of the United States, hoping to secure passage to the Orient. After no such opportunity presented itself, Hill decided to head west, intending to look for passage to Asia from a Pacific port. He reached the city of St. Paul, Minnesota, too late in the year to begin the perilous trip to the West

Coast. Instead, he settled in St. Paul and found work as a clerk for a steamboat line, during which time he initiated his first independent venture in commodities trading in 1865. Two years later, Hill contracted to supply fuel to the St. Paul and Pacific Railroad. Realizing that coal would eventually replace wood as fuel for locomotives, Hill steadily took in partners to supply capital for expanding the fuel business to include coal.

Although Hill devoted himself to business, family remained important to him. On August 19, 1867, he married Mary Theresa Mehegan, a woman who shared Hill's Irish heritage. She bore him 10 children, and the couple enjoyed a long and happy union.

By 1875, Hill was successful enough to buy out his partners in the fuel business. He formalized his activities in the supply business by forming the Northwestern Fuel Company. During his efforts to build the company, Hill recognized that the St. Paul and Pacific Railroad was poorly organized and in terrible physical condition. By pooling his assets with the capital of three friends, Hill purchased the St. Paul and Pacific in 1878. Many viewed the deal as a reckless endeavor, but it demonstrated Hill's astute business instincts.

Under Hill's able management, the aging rail lines were rejuvenated and extended into an integrated system, eventually leading to the formation of the Great Northern Railway Company in 1890. The Great Northern consolidated into one vast entity, the St. Paul and Pacific Railroad, with a number of smaller systems that ran across the Northwest and Canada. Under Hill's leadership, the Great Northern laid down additional lines that enabled travel from Minnesota all the way west to Puget Sound, in Washington.

James J. Hill (Library of Congress)

Hill served, at various times, as general manager, vice president, president, and chairman of the board for the company and served as the guiding spirit for the railroad. He was involved in every facet of the railroad—from construction to selection of routes to the design of terminal facilities. He insisted that operating costs be the lowest in the industry. In addition, Hill's management of the railroad was unique among transcontinental lines, mainly because the railroad maintained constant earnings and dividends despite the tumultuous economic climate. This economic stability was even more remarkable given that the Great Northern did not receive any government assistance or financial aid, as had the Central and Union Pacific Railroads when they built their lines from Omaha, Nebraska, to Sacramento, California.

In addition to his role in the Great Northern, Hill was instrumental in the formative years of the Canadian Pacific Railway, a vast system that reached across Canada from coast to coast by 1885. Hill served for several years as director and made key decisions regarding the selection of routes for this railway.

Building on the success of the Great Northern, Hill was able to acquire a substantial stake in the Northern Pacific Railroad, the only other major rail line serving the Northwest at the time. In 1901, Hill tried to consolidate the Great Northern, Northern Pacific, and other railways into one massive holding company, the Northern Securities Company. The new holding company was short-lived, however; in 1904, the Supreme Court declared that the company was in violation of the Sherman Antitrust Act of 1890 and ordered that it be broken into smaller, independent companies.

This legal defeat disappointed Hill greatly, but he continued to control the Great Northern and Northern Pacific Railroads. Hill's style of management placed great emphasis on detail, particularly with regard to costs. He required that all superintendents be familiar with accounting and statistics. Often characterized as harsh, he deplored incompetence and frequently stated that management "must be based on exact knowledge of facts. Guesswork will not do."

In 1907, Hill resigned the presidency of the Great Northern and became chairman of the board. His son, Louis, assumed the company's presidency. In 1912, Hill retired as chairman of the board.

In addition to his business interests, Hill was an advocate for the conservation of natural resources, becoming involved with the national conservation movement in 1908. His concern for the environment and other reform subjects led to the publication of his book, *Highways of Progress*, in 1910. He was also active in finance, serving as director and board member for a number of banks. Hill remained interested and active in the railroads' affairs until only a few days before his death. He died after a short illness on May 29, 1916.

BIBLIOGRAPHY

Holbrook, Stewart Hall, *James J. Hill: A Great Life in Brief*, 1967; Kerr, Duncan J., *The Story of the Great Northern Railway Company—and James J. Hill*, 1936; Malone, Michael P., *James J. Hill: Empire Builder of the Northwest*, 1996; Martin, Albro, *James J. Hill and the Opening of the Northwest*, 1991; Pyle, J. G., *The Life of James J. Hill*, 1917.

Hillman, Thomas

(February 2, 1844–August 4, 1905)
Manufacturer

Thomas Hillman represented a New South born from the Civil War, one intent on reviving its economy through industry. He helped make Birmingham, Alabama, the iron manufacturing center of the region.

Thomas was born on February 2, 1844, in Montgomery County, Tennessee, to Daniel Hillman and Ann (Marable) Hillman. Daniel Hillman owned an iron furnace in Kentucky, and young Thomas learned the trade from him. As a boy, Thomas suffered a back injury when he was thrown from a horse, but he still liked to hunt, and his father helped him in that pursuit by having slaves carry the youngster through the woods on their shoulders.

After limited schooling, Hillman joined his father's Empire Coal Company in Trigg County, Kentucky, a thriving business that made bar and sheet iron for the Southern market. He managed the company during the Civil War, after which his father gave him an interest in the firm. Hillman married Emily S. Gentry in July 1867.

Hillman made a foray into the mercantile business in 1879, but the following year, the prominent business leader H. F. De Bardeleben interested him in beginning an iron-making company in Birmingham, Alabama. Hillman moved there and with De Bardeleben built Alice Furnace No. 1, which began operating in November 1880. Hillman built a second furnace, called Big Alice, in 1883 and the following year joined his business with the Pratt Coal & Iron Company, controlled by Enoch Ensley.

Hillman and Ensley had several disagreements, however, and in 1886 Hillman helped the Tennessee Coal & Iron Company buy into Pratt Coal and force Ensley out. With Ensley gone, the Tennessee Company made Hillman vice president, and he directed the building of four furnaces in Birmingham. Before long, the Tennessee Company emerged as the largest iron company in the South.

Hillman joined several partners in 1904 to found the Pratt Consolidated Coal Company, which controlled 54 coal mines. In addition, he was a director of the Birmingham Railway, the Light & Power Company, and the First National Bank.

Hillman died in Atlantic City, New Jersey, on August 4, 1905. Two years later, the world's largest corporation, United States Steel, bought the Tennessee Company. In developing his iron and coal businesses, Hillman had pursued the idea advocated by Henry Grady (editor of the newspaper the *Atlanta Constitution*) and other prominent Southerners that the region should replace its antebellum agricultural economy with industries, transportation, and cities, thus building a New South.

BIBLIOGRAPHY

Henley, John C., *This Is Birmingham: The Story of the Founding and Growth of an American City*, 1960.

Hilton, Conrad

(December 25, 1887–January 3, 1979)
Hotel Executive

From helping his father rent rooms at a small adobe inn, Conrad Hilton built the Hilton hotel chain.

Conrad was born on December 25, 1887, to Conrad Hilton and Mary (Laufersweiler) Hilton in San Antonio, New Mexico. Hilton Sr. operated several small businesses, among them a five-room adobe inn, for whose guests young Conrad carried luggage from the local train. Conrad attended St. Michael's College in Santa Fe from 1900 to 1902 and the New Mexico School of Mines from 1907 to 1909. After graduation, he worked as a cashier and then as president at the small New Mexico State Bank operated by his father. At the same time, he joined his father's mercantile business, A. H. Hilton & Son. Hilton later remarked: "I was peddling sowbelly bacon, grits, beans, and coffins in my father's general store." In 1912, he won election as a Republican for a term in the state legislature.

After serving in World War I, Hilton went to Cisco, Texas, in 1919 to buy an interest in a bank, but when his effort failed, he instead bought the aging but busy Melba Hotel, a stark two-story building. A few months later, he purchased another hotel in Fort Worth, and in 1920 he bought the 140-room Waldorf in Dallas.

Through the 1920s, Hilton bought and sold several hotels in Texas, in each case displaying a keen ability to assay their potential and determine when to sell them for a profit. For example, in the 1940s—after having endured a sharp drop in business during the Great Depression that forced him to remove the phones from his hotel rooms in order to save money—he bought the Town House in Los Angeles for $175,000, and in 1953 sold it for a profit of $1.8 million. Indeed, throughout the 1940s, he expanded and acquired such prominent hotels as the Palmer House in Chicago and the Plaza in New York City (which he remodeled at a cost of $2 million). In 1949, he fulfilled a long-held quest when he bought New York City's Waldorf-Astoria Hotel. With his acquisitions, he obtained national prominence, and the attention intensified when he divorced his first wife, Marry Barron, and entered a short, tempestuous marriage to the actress Zsa Zsa Gabor.

In managing his hotels, Hilton stressed using as much space as possible by placing lounges, stores, and garages in the buildings. After founding Hilton International in 1948 and opening a hotel in San Juan, Puerto Rico, and other overseas locations, Hilton made a mistake when in 1967 he sold the company and the right to use his name on overseas hotels and on other hotels built in the future to Trans World Airlines. His decision meant that he missed out on the tremendous growth in international tourism that occurred in the following decade.

In fact, since Hilton franchised the Hilton Inns that opened in cities around America (he had 136 hotels by the late 1970s), his empire relied on 18 hotels that accounted in 1978 for 90 percent of his corporation's sales, and most especially on 2 highly profitable establishments in Nevada: the Las Vegas Hilton and its neighbor, the Flamingo Hilton.

Hilton, who had remarried in 1977, died on January 3, 1979.

BIBLIOGRAPHY

Bolton, Whitney, *The Silver Spade: The Conrad Hilton Story*, 1954; Dabney, Thomas Ewing, *The Man Who Bought the Waldorf: The Life of Conrad N. Hilton*, 1950; Hilton, Conrad N., *Be My Guest*, 1957.

Hooker, Elon

(November 23, 1869–May 10, 1938)
Engineer, Manufacturer

Elon Huntington Hooker was considered one of the leading American figures in the field of electrochemistry, primarily for the civil engineer's role in realizing the commercial possibilities for producing chemicals by an electrolytic process. The Hooker Electrochemical Company at Niagara Falls was one of the first electrochemical plants in the United States. The company was renowned for its role in the chemicals and plastic industry.

Elon, the third of eight children of Horace B. and Susan Pamelia Huntington Hooker, was born in Rochester, New York, on November 23, 1869. Horace, an acting captain of engineers during the Civil War, was a chronic tinkerer whose enthusiasm for inventing did not translate into the success he dreamed would free him from his struggling nursery business. The young Hooker, on the other hand, displayed an early aptitude for engineering. While in high school, Hooker attended night classes at Rochester's Mechanics Institute. An energetic youth, he also took jobs lighting street lamps and delivering newspapers to earn money.

In 1891, Hooker earned a two-year degree from the University of Rochester. Having spent summers working for Rochester's city engineer, he decided to study civil engineering at Cornell University. In 1894, he earned his bachelor's of science degree in civil engineering and remained at Cornell for a graduate fellowship in hydraulic engineering. During his fellowship, he also studied at the Zurich Polytechnicum and the École des Ponts et Chausées in Paris. In June 1895, Hooker received a doctorate in civil engineering.

Hooker's first job after graduation was with a construction company, a position followed by an appointment to serve on a private commission investigating the feasibility of building a canal route through Nicaragua or Panama. Hooker's acclaim built quickly, and in 1899 he was appointed by Theodore Roosevelt (then the governor of New York) to serve as deputy superintendent of public works for New York State.

In January 1901, Hooker married Blanche Ferry, the daughter of the founder of the Ferry Seed Company. The Hookers had four daughters—Barbara, Adelaide, Helen, and Blanchette (who would later marry John D. Rockefeller III). In the first year of his marriage, Hooker left his government job in favor of a corporate role as the vice president of the Development Company of America, a holding company that loaned support and management to struggling, but potentially profitable, undercapitalized businesses. Hooker enjoyed the work and in 1903 left to form a similar firm, the Development and Funding Company.

Hooker's company considered various research possibilities, deciding after examining 250 potential projects to manufacture chemicals using an electrolytic process invented by Clinton P. Townsend and ELMER SPERRY. The procedure involved passing an electrical current through brine (a saturated solution of salt) to produce chlorine, caustic soda, and hydrogen. Though the principle of electrolysis had been demonstrated in 1807, it was not until the development of the electric dynamo in the late 1800s that electricity became inexpensive to generate and thus readily available commercially. Townsend developed a "cell" in which the electrolysis could take place.

Though Townsend and Sperry were already very successful (by the turn of the century, Sperry himself had over 100 patents in his name), Hooker's development company had gained a reputation for revolutionary tactics in investing and managing. The inventors were impressed not only with Hooker's financial resources but his bold, assertive style and technical expertise. After tests of the Townsend cell in 1904, the Development and Funding Company began construction of one of the first electrochemical plants in the United States.

The early years of the plant proved so successful, and so busy, that the company in 1909 established an offshoot, the Hooker Electrochemical Company, to administer the plant, which was located at Niagara Falls. The plant prospered, quickly becoming a principal supplier of chloralkali chemicals as well as plastics. Over the next 50 years, the company, using modified versions of the original Townsend cell, produced over 100 types of chemicals and reached employment levels of 7,000 people.

As the company continued to grow steadily, Hooker turned his attention to politics, though he continued to remain involved in professional associations, serving as president of the Research Corporation from 1915 to 1911 and of the Manufacturing Chemists' Association from 1923 until 1925. In 1912, Theodore Roosevelt, with whom Hooker had remained friends since his years in Albany, appointed him national treasurer of the Progressive Party. Though Hooker was unsuccessful in his 1920 bid for the Republican nomination for governor of New York, his interest in politics remained undeterred. Throughout his life, Hooker wrote articles to address political and social issues.

Hooker was a tall and self-assured man with diverse interests and talents. In addition to his keen intellect, political insight, and organized manner, he was a devotee of the arts. He was a trustee of both the Eastman School of Music and his alma mater, the University of Rochester. Though Hooker was a generally healthy man (he abhorred alcohol and did not smoke), he fell victim to a severe bout with pneumonia and died while in Pasadena, California, on May 10, 1938.

BIBLIOGRAPHY

Hooker, Edward, *Descendants of Rev. Thomas Hooker*, 1909; *Elon Huntington Hooker: A Tribute to Our Founder*, 1938; Hughes, Thomas Parker, *Elmer Sperry: Inventor and Engineer*, 1971; Thomas, Robert E., *Salt & Water, Power & People: A Short History of Hooker Electrochem. Co.*, 1955.

Hopkins, Johns

(May 19, 1795–December 25, 1873)
Merchant

Johns Hopkins, a prominent nineteenth-century merchant, was a principal investor in the nation's first major railroad, the Baltimore & Ohio. After attaining wealth through his trade enterprises, the railroad, and other investments, Hopkins became known for his financial generosity. His gift of $7 million for the founding of the Johns Hopkins University and Medical School was the largest philanthropic bequest in American history until that time.

Johns, the second of the three sons of Samuel and Hannah Hopkins, was born in Maryland's Anne Arundel County on May 19, 1795. He was raised at Whitehall, his father's tobacco plantation. Hopkins's education ended at age 12, when he left the South River School and went to work at the family's plantation. His parents, devout Quakers, had decided on the basis of their faith to free their slaves, and Hopkins and his brothers were thus needed to work the fields.

In 1812, Hopkins went to Baltimore to work in his uncle's wholesale grocery and commission merchandise business. He was a quick learner and managed the business well during his uncle's absences. In 1819, he and his uncle parted ways, due to both personal and business conflicts. When he was 24, Hopkins fell in love with his cousin, Elizabeth, but his uncle forbade the marriage. Neither Hopkins nor Elizabeth ever married, and they remained friends for life. Hopkins and his uncle also disagreed on the practice of accepting whiskey as payment for goods, a policy Hopkins viewed as necessary based on the economic hardships of the time.

Johns Hopkins (North Wind Picture Archives)

The split was amicable. With his uncle's loan of $10,000, Hopkins established his own business, selling $200,000 worth of goods in his first year. A short time later, he and his brothers (Philip, Gerard, and Mahlon) launched a new firm—the Hopkins Brothers—with an investment of $20,000 from their mother and uncle. The firm sold groceries for both money and liquor, reselling the whiskey under the name "Hopkins' Best."

The company grew rapidly throughout the regions of Maryland, Virginia, North Carolina, and Ohio. Hopkins, eager to find new endeavors, bought up business notes and became, in essence, a banker. He helped the budding city of Baltimore to grow commercially by building warehouses.

Understanding early on the potential of the West and the need for adequate transportation to reap the benefits of the region, Hopkins was a significant investor in the Baltimore & Ohio Railroad, the nation's first major line. He served in numerous committee positions on the board, and by the time of his death in 1873, he was the third largest stockholder after the state of Maryland and the city of Baltimore.

Hopkins had two standards for his spending habits. In his personal life, he tended toward the miserly, walking everywhere to save money and never buying an overcoat. Yet he loaned money liberally to community institutions, and even, on several occasions, advanced large sums (often without full reimbursement) to the city of Baltimore.

Hopkins's greatest act of philanthropy came about after a great deal of contemplation. He had decided that while he would leave a substantial sum of his fortune to relatives, he wanted to endow the bulk of his $8 million estate to a worthy cause. It is likely that his own lack of education weighed heavily in his ultimate decision to give much of the money for the founding of the Johns Hopkins University in Baltimore. The rest of the sum went to the creation of the Johns Hopkins Hospital and a number of smaller youth education agencies.

Hopkins died on December 25, 1873.

BIBLIOGRAPHY

Baltimore Sun, Obituary, December 25, 1873; Bernheim, Bertram Moses, *The Story of the Johns Hopkins: Four Great Doctors and the Medical School They Created*, 1948; Hawkins, Hugh, *Pioneer: A History of the Johns Hopkins University, 1874–1889*, 1960; Thom, Helen Hopkins, *Johns Hopkins: A Silhouette*, 1929.

Hormel, George

(December 4, 1860–June 5, 1946)
Meat Packer

A rapidly industrializing, late-nineteenth-century America, which was becoming increasingly far removed from its rural origins, needed processed meat, and George Albert Hormel responded by establishing one of the largest packing houses in the nation.

George was born on December 4, 1860, in Buffalo, New York, to John Hormel and Susanna (Decker) Hormel. The youngster grew up in poverty after his father's tannery in Toledo, Ohio, the town to where the family had moved, failed during the 1873 depression. George was forced to quit school and hold unskilled jobs. In 1875, he went to Chicago and worked in a packinghouse that processed meat products.

By that time, America had shaken its depression, and the industrializing economy offered opportunities Hormel was determined to pursue. In 1880, he bought wool and hides for a Kansas City company and in 1881 for one based in Chicago. He settled in Austin, Minnesota (a town near the nation's cattle lands in 1887), and founded a business to butcher and package meat with a partner. After the partnership dissolved in 1891, he began his own packinghouse, George A. Hormel & Company. The next year, he married Lillia Belle Gleason, a teacher. They eventually had one child.

Hormel's business, located in an abandoned creamery along the Cedar River, grew slowly at first, and in his first year, he slaughtered only 610 hogs. He supplied the nearby market of Minneapolis-St. Paul with hams and sausages, however, and sales soon grew rapidly. In 1900, while his bicycles and horse carts traversed the twin cities, the company's annual sales reached $1 million.

Hormel subsequently expanded his market across the nation and overseas, and competed formidably with the meat giant GUSTAVUS SWIFT. In 1927, with the help of his son JAY HORMEL, to whom he had turned over much of the company's operation, Hormel produced the first successful canned ham in the United States. The product sold well before being overwhelmed by Swift. Hormel also began making canned soups in the 1920s, although he faced stiff competition from those produced by Joseph Campbell and H. J. HEINZ. In 1937, Hormel started selling a canned spiced pork shoulder loaf called Spam. The product soon became a household word, sometimes used derisively to indicate a cheap meal.

Throughout his leadership, Hormel treated his workers liberally. Although he could sometimes be tyrannical, he pushed within the industry for shorter workweeks and higher wages. During the Great Depression, he advocated federal programs for unemployment relief and retirement pensions. In 1931, he established at his plant a "straight time plan" that provided 52 equal paychecks a year, despite the number of hours worked in a given week. Although he opposed unions, he was reluctantly forced to accept one at his company in 1933.

By that time, Hormel had relinquished the presidency in favor of his son, although he continued as chairman of the board until his death in Los Angeles on June 5, 1946.

BIBLIOGRAPHY

Dougherty, Richard, *In Quest of Quality: Hormel's First 75 Years*, 1966; "The Name Is HOR-mel," *Fortune*, October 1937.

Hormel, Jay

(September 11, 1892–August 30, 1954)
Meat Packer

A shrewd businessman with an inventive marketing sense, Jay Catherwood Hormel was an entrepreneur who will be forever remembered, after his most successful product, as the "Father of SPAM." The Hormel Company's processed, canned, meat product has fed generations of income-conscious families, nourished the troops of every war since World War II, commands impressive international name recognition and affection as an icon of American pop culture, and still generates millions of dollars in earnings. Hormel's business legacy is his innovative search for new and quality products, his flair for marketing, and his contribution to fair labor practices.

Born in Austin, Minnesota, on September 11, 1892, Jay Hormel was the son of GEORGE HORMEL and Lillian Belle Gleason Hormel. An early entrepreneur, the young Hormel earned spending money by contracting to paint automobile gas cans and collecting grease to be used in soap making. At the age of 12, he was introduced to the meatpacking business at the family's Hormel Provision Market, where he learned about by-product manufacture. After attending Austin's public school and the Shattuck Military School for Boys in Faribault, Minnesota, he entered Princeton University.

After three years of college characterized by nonacademic ventures (such as running a laundry business), he left school and went to work for his father at the Hormel plant. A thorough man, Hormel learned the business from the ground up. Even in his early career, his attention to detail and aversion to waste were evident. For example, Hormel observed that when the hogs were herded into pens, they were prodded with heavy canes and kicked, resulting in severe bruising that later caused large chunks of the meat to be discarded. Viewing the practice as both inhumane and wasteful, he changed the policy, thus producing a higher quantity of useable meat. Hormel shortly became superintendent of the plant, and by 1916 had been made vice president.

During World War I, Hormel served in the army as a first lieutenant with the Quartermaster Corps in France. In 1922, after the war, Hormel returned to France to marry Germaine Dubois, a miller's daughter. The couple had three sons, George A. Hormel II, Thomas Dubois Hormel, and James Catherwood Hormel.

Upon his return to the family business, Hormel's managerial skills and leadership abilities began to receive notice. In 1921, he unearthed evidence that a top company official had embezzled more than $1 million. Hormel then instituted an executive training program and streamlined many of the company's personnel policies. He pushed the company to earmark funds for product development and marketing research. In 1926, these years of experimentation paid off with the incredibly popular response to the introduction of "Hormel Flavor-Sealed Ham," America's first canned ham.

In 1929, after his father retired, Hormel became the new president of the Hormel Company. His place in business history is assured not only for his leadership in the meatpacking industry but also for his innovative reforms in employment and salary practices. Believing strongly that job security promoted employee loyalty and productivity, Hormel originated the concept of the annual wage. In an era where laborers were paid hourly and weekly and often laid off seasonally, Hormel provided a steady income based on an annual rate with the expectation that the workload would vary according to business needs. He implemented incentive pay, a system of bonuses linked to meeting performance goals that would soon become the model for many other American firms. Hormel was also ahead of his time in promoting employee savings plans, a pension plan, and profit sharing, which allowed employees to supplement their income with dividends from stocks.

Hormel realized that to make such programs economically feasible for the company, he needed to develop products that would become household staples, unlike the popular, but costly, canned ham and chicken. Hormel created the Dinty Moore line of affordable soups, as well as the extremely popular chile con carne. In 1936, the introduction of Hormel's newest product, Spam, assured the company a future of guaranteed revenue. Unable to market the canned meat as a ham product due to the inclusion of pork shoulder meat, Hormel instead copyrighted the name Spam and marketed the can graced with a picture of a sliced ham. He then launched an unprecedented, diverse advertising campaign. Hormel's sponsorship of the Burns and Allen comedy show constituted the first singing radio commercial. Hormel advertisements enticed people to give their opinion of Spam by paying them $1 or $2. During World War II, Hormel appealed to America

to conserve beef for the war effort by eating Spam. After the war, Hormel capitalized on America's patriotism with the singing "Hormel Girls." This traveling caravan of all-American girls gave performances and surprise door-to-door appearances.

Hormel's efforts to position the product as a household name were enormously successful. By 1959, the Hormel Company had produced its one-billionth can of Spam. Sales of the product would continue to escalate; the Hormel company claims that every second in the United States 3.8 cans are consumed.

In 1946, upon the death of his father, Hormel handed over the reins of the presidency and became the chairman of the board. The move allowed him to focus on product development and long-range planning. The company expanded rapidly and diversified by manufacturing meat by-products and developing frozen food products.

Though the business had always been the dominant force of Hormel's life, he devoted a fair amount of time to outside interests. He established the Hormel Institute for research in chemistry and biology. He was a trustee of the Shattuck School for Boys and the Committee for Economic Development, as well as a member of the National Council of Boy Scouts of America. He sat on the board and acted as an adviser to many industry-related committees. In 1940, he was a delegate to the Republican National Convention.

On August 30, 1954, Hormel died in his Austin, Minnesota, home of heart trouble.

BIBLIOGRAPHY

Blum, Fred, *Toward a Democratic Work Process: The Hormel Packinghouse Workers' Experiment*, 1953; Dougherty, Richard, *In Quest of*

Quality: Hormel's First 75 Years, 1966; Lewis, George, "Spam: An American Tradition," http://www.worldandi.com/archive/cldec97.htm; MacCormack, Zeke, "Spam Smorgasbord Stuns the Senses," *Austin-American Statesman*, April 11, 1994; *New York Times*, Obituary, August 31, 1954.

Houghton, Amory

(July 27, 1899–February 21, 1981)
Manufacturer

As president of Corning Glass Works, Amory Houghton established a management style noted for its heavy emphasis on research and for its cordial relations with workers.

Amory was born on July 27, 1899, in Corning, New York, to Alanson Houghton and Adelaide Louise (Wellington) Houghton. He graduated with a B.A. from Harvard in 1921 and then worked for Corning Glass as the fourth generation of his family associated with the company. (His great-grandfather, Amory Houghton, had founded Corning as a glass company in 1851.) Amory faced a substantial challenge when he became president of Corning Glass in 1930, as the onset of the Great Depression threatened the business.

Despite economic hard times, Houghton had faith in glass as crucial to America's industrial development, and rather than reduce expenditures on research and development—the practice followed by most companies—he increased it. Between 1930 and 1941, the money the company spent on research grew from $578,000 to $925,000. One observer said that for years Houghton's tactic "hurt quarterly earnings" but he was "looking at the long term." Even in 1932, while in the depths of the depression, Corning still managed to make a profit of $808,000 on revenues of $7 million.

Houghton's research team developed innovations that expanded business, and he soon began joint ventures new to the glass industry. Thus, he created Pittsburgh Corning to manufacture and market glass building blocks in 1937, Owens Corning to make fiberglass in 1938, and Dow Corning to make silicones in 1943. *Fortune* magazine declared in 1945 that Corning's laboratories "have consistently produced one good idea after another for improving glass and have been especially productive in the last fifteen years."

Houghton established a benevolent atmosphere for his workers. For example, during the Great Depression, when sales declined, rather than fire people, he cut everyone's workweek by a day, thereby maintaining jobs. The Flint Glass Workers unionized the company in 1943, but labor relations remained largely harmonious and no strikes ensued.

In 1952, Houghton's laboratory developed a way to evaporate molten glass and condense it into a highly purified form. A decade later, the company adapted the process to make fiber-optic cable, important in the modern communications revolution. In 1958, the company began making Corning Ware cooking utensils using a new type of glass ceramics.

Houghton served as U.S. ambassador to France from 1957 to 1961 and then returned to Corning. He retired in 1964 and by that time had increased the company's yearly sales from $2.4 million in the World War II era to $328 million. Houghton died in Charleston, South Carolina, on February 21, 1981.

BIBLIOGRAPHY

"Amory Houghton," *Newsweek*, March 9, 1981; Nulty, Peter, "The National Business Hall of Fame," *Fortune*, April 5, 1993.

Hubbard, Gardiner

(August 25, 1822–December 11, 1897)
Communications Executive

Gardiner Greene Hubbard, most noted for his role in the early organization of the telephone industry, pursued diverse interests throughout his life. He enjoyed a lengthy career as a lawyer before becoming involved in establishing the early telephone system, was active in many scientific societies, and founded the National Geographic Society. Hubbard was also an outspoken advocate for educating the deaf after his daughter lost her hearing at an early age.

Hubbard was born in Boston, Massachusetts, on August 25, 1822, the son of Massachusetts Supreme Court Justice Samuel Hubbard and his wife Mary Anne. He was named for Mary Anne's father, Gardiner Greene. The young Hubbard proceeded through the Boston school system and went on to Dartmouth College. After graduating from Dartmouth in 1841, he studied law at Harvard for one year.

In 1843, Hubbard joined a Boston law office. He would go on to practice law for

Gardiner Hubbard (Library of Congress)

over 30 years in the Boston and Washington, D.C., areas. On October 21, 1846, he married Gertrude Mercer McCurdy and moved with his new wife to Cambridge, Massachusetts. Hubbard became well known in Cambridge for his improvements to the city's infrastructure. By 1857, he had introduced the use of natural gas for lighting in the city. He also established one of the original streetcar lines between Boston and Cambridge.

After his young daughter lost her hearing from scarlet fever in 1862, Hubbard became interested in the education of the deaf and aided in the creation of the Clarke Institute for Deaf Mutes. He was president of the Institute from 1867 until 1877 and also served on the Massachusetts Board of Education for 12 years.

Hubbard met the young Alexander Graham Bell in 1871, when Bell visited the Horace Mann School for the Deaf in Boston. Hubbard was fascinated with Bell's invention of the telephone in 1875 and joined with him to develop the first telephone organization, which eventually became the Bell Telephone Company. Hubbard's wisdom and pragmatism were key to the development of the business. He made the decision to lease rather than sell the telephones, a practice that led to the integrated "Bell System." In 1878, he helped recruit THEODORE VAIL to expand and unify the early telephone agencies into a public utility. Hubbard shortly yielded control of the company entirely to Vail and William H. Forbes.

Hubbard had made a series of studies of the postal service and the effectiveness of the telegraph in the period between 1867 and 1876. In 1876, President Ulysses S. Grant, recognizing Hubbard's extraordinary ability, appointed Hubbard to a commission assigned to investigate and recommend improvements in the postal system. Hubbard relocated to Washington, D.C., in 1879 and lived there the rest of his life. His business and personal lives came together in an interesting fashion in 1877, when his daughter Mabel married Bell.

Once in Washington, D.C., Hubbard pursued a variety of activities to benefit the public welfare. In 1883, he and Bell cofounded the journal *Science*, which eventually became one of the most prestigious scientific publications in the world. Hubbard also worked with Bell in the establishment of the American Association to Promote the Teaching of Speech to the Deaf in 1890. He founded the National Geographic Society in 1888 and served as its first president until 1897. He was a trustee of the Columbian University (now George Washington University) for 12 years and served as president of the commission that formed the Washington Academy of Sciences. Hubbard was held in high esteem throughout the Washington, D.C., area for this wide range of ambitious activities. At the end of his full and successful life, he died at home on December 11, 1897.

BIBLIOGRAPHY

Day, E. W., *One Thousand Years of Hubbard History*, 1895; Hubbard, Gardiner Greene, "Our Post-Office," *Atlantic Monthly*, January 1875; Waite, Helen Elmira, *Make a Joyful Sound: The Romance of Mabel Hubbard and Alexander Graham Bell, an Authorized Biography*, 1961; Yale, Caroline A., *Years of Building*, 1931.

Hudson, Joseph

(October 1, 1846–July 5, 1912)
Merchant

Joseph Lowthian Hudson worked his way from a job as a clerk in a clothing store at age 15 to the owner of a chain of successful department stores, one of which was the third largest retail store in the nation during his lifetime.

Joseph, the son of Richard and Elizabeth Lowthian Hudson, was born on October 1, 1846, in Newcastle-on-Tyne in England. The family immigrated to Hamilton, Ontario, Canada, in 1855 but by 1860 had settled in Grand Rapids, Michigan. Joseph left school at age 13 to work as a telegrapher for the Grand Trunk Railroad. He subsequently worked as a grocery store clerk and a farm laborer before securing work as the clerk in a clothing store in 1861.

By 1866, Joseph's father, Richard, had joined with Christopher Mabley, Joseph's employer, to purchase a small clothing store in Ionia, Michigan. Shortly after employing his son as manager, Richard bought out his partner's interest in the store. The Hudsons began to diversify their business holdings by purchasing a flour mill and timberlands. When Richard died in 1873, Joseph inherited 50 percent of R. Hudson and Son, while his brothers, James and William, split the remaining interest in the $40,000 enterprise.

The next few years were financially turbulent, causing the brothers to bankrupt the mill and timber enterprises. The clothing store survived, and in 1877 Hudson left the management of it to his brothers and moved to Detroit to manage a new retail clothing store owned by his former employer, Christopher Mabley.

Though he was made a partner within a year, Hudson longed to become independent. He realized this dream in 1881 with the establishment of J. L. Hudson, a clothing store for men and boys. Hudson, who believed that customer loyalty was pivotal to retail success, introduced a number of novel customer-friendly merchandising practices. Unlike the majority of retailers, he maintained a full inventory to avoid delivery delays, kept prices consistently low, and marked prices clearly on all merchandise. The store had a liberal return policy, and Hudson put a premium on a well-trained, friendly sales staff. The store grew rapidly, enabling Hudson to diversify merchandise until J. L. Hudson became a full-fledged department store.

In 1895, the store was incorporated as J. L. Hudson and Company. By this time, Hudson had opened chain stores in St. Louis, Cleveland, Toledo, and Buffalo. Expansion continued at a rapid pace. Taking great pride in the diversity of goods available, Hudson advertisements touted the store's supply of items "from A to Z—from antimacassars to zippers, aspirin to zwieback, an African mask to Zeurcher cheese." In the store's heyday, the largest bookstore, toy store, and drugstore in Detroit were all departments of Hudson's. Customer service was continually stressed, with Hudson hiring bilingual clerks who between them spoke 14 different languages.

Another sales tactic of Hudson's was to lay emphasis on the marketing of related items; for instance, bedding and all related merchandise such as pajamas and alarm clocks were displayed together. Hudson's store also included a planning center for home building, frequently enabling the store to sell to one customer every item for the home.

As business remained strong, Hudson continued to enact innovative policies. In 1905, he shortened the stores' hours, stating that "it has been shown that we can produce with the same labor in eight hours what we used to produce in twelve."

As Hudson never married and had no children, he turned many of the responsibilities of the company over to his nephews as he sought out new interests for himself. Largely because one of his nieces married Edsel Ford (the son of HENRY FORD), Hudson became interested in the automobile industry. In 1909, after supplying the capital for the company's creation, Hudson became the chairman of the board of the Hudson Motor Car Company. The firm proved quite successful, making increasingly large profits until it was sold many years after Hudson's

death to Nash Kelvinator in 1954 to create American Motors, Inc.

Hudson was involved in a number of civic institutions and sat on the board of many banks, including the Dime Savings Bank, the American Exchange National Bank, and the Third National Bank of Detroit. A great philanthropist, Hudson aided hospitals, orphanages, scientific research, and needy individuals.

Hudson's stores continued to profit, and when he died on July 5, 1912, while on vacation in England, Hudson's Detroit store alone had annual profits of nearly $3.5 million.

BIBLIOGRAPHY

Noble, Joseph T., "Joseph L. Hudson, Jr., Detroit's Merchant Prince," *Detroit News Pictorial Magazine*, September 12, 1965; Sloane, Leonard, *The Great Merchants*, 1955; Sloane, Leonard, "In Detroit—Hudson's," *New York Times*, December 10, 1965; Webber, Oscar, "J. L. Hudson, the Man and the Store," Address to the Newcomen Society, November 8, 1954.

Hughes, Howard

(December 24, 1905–April 5, 1976)
Oil Industrialist, Airline Executive

Howard Hughes had no respect for the feelings of others, believed money could buy everything, and lived his last years as an eccentric recluse, yet he created the nation's largest transcontinental airline and a far-flung, multibillion-dollar empire.

Howard was born on December 24, 1905, to Howard Hughes and Allene

(Garo) Hughes in Houston, Texas. Hughes Sr. had founded the Hughes Tool Company and made a fortune providing the oil industry with a drill bit that could cut through bedrock. Howard attended the California Institute of Technology, but when his father died during his freshman year at the college, he took command of Hughes Tool and guided it to even bigger profits with little difficulty. Howard hired Noah Dietrich to be his accountant, and over the years, Dietrich played an instrumental role in handling his employer's finances—some observers even called him the brains behind many an investment.

Two years after acquiring Hughes Tool, Hughes decided he needed a challenge, preferably a glamorous one, and so went to Hollywood and began producing movies. Only *Hell's Angels* and *Scarface* were memorable, but after a marriage to Ella Rice in 1929 that quickly ended in divorce, he lived flamboyantly, attracting headlines as a playboy.

In the 1930s, Hughes turned to his first love, aviation. He had begun flying at age 14; now he founded an experimental aviation company and acted as his own test pilot. From this endeavor came Hughes Aircraft, begun in 1934 to manufacture airplanes for civilian and military use, which soon became a giant in the field. Hughes personally set several world records during the decade, including flying around the world in 91 hours, 14 minutes at an average speed of 202 miles per hour.

Also in the 1930s, Hughes bought into Transcontinental and Western Air (TWA). Within a few years, he acquired controlling interest and made TWA the leading transatlantic airline. Meanwhile, during World War II, Hughes Aircraft obtained lucrative contracts to provide the military with reconnaissance planes. At that time, Hughes involved himself in a boondoggle when, with shipbuilder HENRY KAISER, he constructed the Hughes Hercules, a giant flying boat. The heaviest aircraft ever built, and made entirely from laminated birch veneer, it was intended to carry troops across the Atlantic, safe from German submarines. Numerous de-

Howard Hughes (Archive Photos)

lays meant that it failed to make its maiden flight until 1947, however. By then, the aircraft, derisively dubbed the Spruce Goose by newspapers, had been made obsolete by large land planes.

After the war, Hughes Aircraft continued to obtain government contracts even though a congressional investigation in 1947 revealed that the company had received millions of dollars for planes never delivered. In the 1950s, Hughes exhibited eccentric and indecisive behavior, and as a result, TWA fell behind other airlines in buying jet aircraft. When Hughes finally bought several of the planes, he did so without the money to pay for them. Consequently, several bankers stepped in and gained an interest in TWA that allowed them to oust Hughes in 1960. They then turned around and sued him for having harmed TWA when he allowed only Hughes Tool to sell supplies to the airline. Hughes countersued, and although a lower court ruled against him, the U.S. Supreme Court ruled in his favor.

As Hughes built an ever larger empire in the 1960s and 1970s—including casinos, hotels, land, and West Coast Airlines (renamed Hughes Air West)—stories circulated about his odd behavior. He lived reclusively at hotels in the United States and overseas, telephoned people in the middle of the night, grew his hair and fingernails long, and refused to touch anything without wearing gloves due to an obsession with germs. Amid a legal fight over the way Hughes had taken over West Coast Airlines, he died on April 5, 1976, after a prolonged illness.

BIBLIOGRAPHY

Brown, Peter H., *Howard Hughes: The Untold Story*, 1996; Drosnin, Michael, *Citizen Hughes*, 1985; Higham, Charles, *Howard Hughes: The Secret Life*, 1993; Maheu, Robert, *Next to Hughes: Behind the Power and Tragic Downfall of Howard Hughes, by His Closest Advisor*, 1992; Rummel, Robert W., *Howard Hughes and TWA*, 1991.

Huizenga, Wayne

(December 29, 1937–)
Waste Manager, Merchant

From a single garbage truck purchased with borrowed money, Harry Wayne Huizenga built businesses attuned to post–Word War II suburbia: Waste Management, Blockbuster Entertainment, the Florida Panthers, and the Miami Dolphins.

Wayne was born on December 29, 1937, in Evergreen Park, Illinois, to Gerrit Harry Huizenga and Jean Huizenga. His father, a contractor, built ranch houses in the Chicago suburbs and, at age 14, young Huizenga began operating a bulldozer to help clear land. Around 1953, Harry Huizenga moved his family to Fort Lauderdale, Florida, where he hoped to save his faltering marriage. That attempt failed, and in 1954 he and Jean divorced. Wayne graduated from Pinecrest High School, and after returning to Chicago where he held various construction jobs, he entered Calvin College in Grand Rapids, Michigan, in 1957. He stayed only briefly, however, before joining the U.S. Army reserves, and then went back to Florida, where he managed a garbage company and married Joyce VanderWagon in 1960.

Huizenga had returned to Fort Lauderdale at a heady time—an influx of northerners seeking warm temperatures and sunshine had produced an economic boom, and each new house that popped from the sand and palmetto represented a household that needed its garbage collected. Huizenga, who had relatives in the Chicago-area garbage business, convinced his father-in-law to loan him $5,000, and in 1962 he purchased his first garbage truck and the accounts for a route operated by Wilbur Porter. Huizenga quickly expanded his firm, Southern

Sanitation Service, with additional loans from his father-in-law and from area banks, and boosted his revenues by renting dumpsters to businesses. All the while, he made political contacts in getting garbage contracts from city and county governments.

When Huizenga obtained capital by selling an interest in Southern Sanitation to his relatives, Waste Management, Incorporated emerged. By 1970, Waste Management had five offices in south Florida, and its annual revenues exceeded $3 million, despite competition from BFI, Sanitas, and other large garbage haulers. In 1971, Waste Management went public and offered stock, with Huizenga as executive vice president and chief deal maker. Huizenga soon acquired garbage companies in Jacksonville and Orlando, Florida, and in Toledo, Ohio. The strain from business affected his personal life, and in 1972 he divorced his wife and married Marti Goldsby.

By 1974, Huizenga had guided Waste Management to incredible growth: 35 percent per year, with annual revenues exceeding $132 million, with Huizenga's own holdings valued at $2.5 million. At this point, the Securities and Exchange Commission investigated Waste Management's acquisitions as to whether illegal payoffs had been made to politicians. In 1976, Huizenga signed a consent decree, promising not to violate any securities laws but admitting no wrongdoing.

Meanwhile, amid national concern over environmental pollution, Huizenga formed Chemical Waste Management as a subsidiary of Waste Management, and he formed ChemNuclear to handle low-level nuclear waste. This turned out to be Huizenga's last big deal with Waste Management. He decided to leave the company in 1983, at the same time that the *New York Times* and the *Wall Street Journal* criticized the firm for violating environmental laws at landfills. Waste Management admitted that some mistakes had been made. (The company bought several businesses that drained its profits in the late 1980s and early 1990s, and in 1998 announced it would merge with USA Waste Services, Incorporated.)

Huizenga pursued several different businesses, among them a company that rented portable toilets (Port-O-Let International) and companies that sold bottled water. In making deals, he showed a keen ability to discern exactly what the other side wanted in order to strike a bargain, a talent that served him well when he completed a deal in 1986 for the Blockbuster Entertainment Corporation. David and Sandy Cook had begun Blockbuster in 1985 as a video rental store that used an innovative computer system. Huizenga bought 60 percent of Blockbuster stock, and his purchase and options soon made him a multimillionaire.

Huizenga's entry into the video market coincided with Americans buying videocassette recorders in record numbers. However, Huizenga knew that Blockbuster existed in a highly competitive field in which an innovation by one video store could be easily duplicated by another. To offset this, he decided to overwhelm his competition by expanding rapidly. He bought competing chains, most notably Major Video and the Super Club, and opened new stores. Whereas Blockbuster had 19 stores at the end of 1986, three years later it had 1,079 and opened its first one overseas in London.

Huizenga scored an advertising coup in 1990 when he paid millions of dollars to sponsor a college football bowl game that carried his company's name. When network sports shows referred to the Blockbuster Bowl, they popularized Blockbuster.

Huizenga diversified Blockbuster in 1992 when he signed a deal with Virgin Music that brought the video company into the retail music field. Blockbuster Music Plus stores began opening that year. In 1993, Huizenga bought an interest in Republic Pictures and 48 percent of Spelling Entertainment, producer of television shows.

These purchases characterized Huizenga's investment in high-profile businesses, evident when in October 1992 he acquired the Florida Panthers professional ice hockey team and shortly after announced his intention to build a 20,000-seat arena within a 2,500-acre sports and entertainment theme park to be owned by Blockbuster. He never built the theme park—partly because environmentalists opposed construction at the site in northwest Dade County, but mainly because yet another deal, this one with Viacom, got in the way.

Huizenga maneuvered to dominate the south Florida sports dollar when in January 1994 he bought the Miami Dolphins football team for $128 million (he had already purchased a minority interest) and Joe Robbie Stadium for $12 million. Much to the disgust of the Robbie family, he sold the stadium name to a corporate sponsor, Pro Player. He also acquired the Florida Marlins baseball team and attempted but failed to acquire the Miami Heat professional basketball team.

Huizenga arranged his biggest deal when, in 1994, he merged Blockbuster with Viacom, a company that operated syndicated television shows, cable systems, and the cable networks Showtime, MTV, and Nickelodeon. Viacom wanted an infusion of money to buy Paramount Pictures, while Huizenga wanted the merger to boost the value of Blockbuster stock. The deal ended his leadership of Blockbuster but enhanced his personal wealth.

Ever pursuing opportunities, Huizenga acquired Republic Waste Industries later in 1994, thus marking his return to the garbage business that had started his career. In 1995, the company's stock value rose more than 850 percent. With Huizenga as chairman and CEO, Republic bought a dozen businesses, mostly garbage haulers and electronics security firms. The following year, Republic entered the used-car market with AutoNation USA, superstores that each had 1,000 "reconditioned-to-be-like-new" vehicles. It remained to be seen, however, whether he could affect the car market as much as he had the other endeavors important to suburban America.

BIBLIOGRAPHY

DeGeorge, Gail, *The Making of a Blockbuster: How Wayne Huizenga Built a Sports and Entertainment Empire from Trash, Grit, and Videotape*, 1996.

Hunt, H. L.

(February 17, 1889–November 29, 1974)
Manufacturer

Harold Lafayette Hunt Jr. turned from card shark to oil businessman and amassed a fortune that ranked among the greatest in the world.

H. L. was born on February 17, 1889, to Haroldson Lafayette Hunt and Ella Rose (Myers) Hunt near Vandalia, Illinois. His father owned a farm and a market, through which he bought and sold local produce and speculated successfully in commodities futures. Young H. L. obtained little formal schooling, but his mother taught him—so well, in fact, that he excelled on state exams. Restless in his late teens, he wandered about the country and held many odd jobs, among them mule-team driver, lumberjack, and crop picker.

When the elder Hunt died in 1911, the younger Hunt inherited $5,000 and with that money bought a 960-acre cotton plantation near Lake Village, Arkansas. A flood soon wiped him out, but as an excellent card player, he made money gambling, traveling up and down the Mississippi River. Many people commented on his quiet demeanor, to which he responded: "What I've learned, I've learned from listening."

With his funds replenished, Hunt speculated in cotton and timberland in Louisiana and married Lydia Plummer in 1914. They eventually had seven children. Hunt's finances suffered again, however, when cotton prices plummeted, and in 1921 he traveled to El Dorado, Arkansas, an oil boomtown. There he plied his trade as a card shark and owned gambling halls. With his profits, he entered the oil business, retiring from gambling

H. L. Hunt (Archive Photos)

in 1922. That same year, he settled in El Dorado, and by the next year, he owned 44 wells in the town and in nearby Smackover.

Hunt sold his oil wells in 1925 for $600,000 and went to Florida, where he met Frania Tye. They exchanged vows before a justice of the peace and within a few months had their first child. Although Hunt claimed he had never "officially" married Frania, his relationship had all the earmarks of bigamy. (In 1942, Frania and Hunt separated, and after receiving a cash settlement, she signed a paper saying she had never married him.)

Hunt returned to his oil investments in the late 1920s and owned wells in Arkansas,

Oklahoma, and Louisiana. His big deal developed, however, in 1930. That year, C. M. "Dad" Joiner discovered a vein of oil on 4,000 acres in east Texas. The well produced erratically, however, and many oil experts thought it would go dry. Hunt believed otherwise and made a deal with Joiner. Under its terms, Hunt got an oil lease in return for $30,000 cash and $1.3 million in future oil payments. Hunt's bold gamble paid off when Joiner's discovery turned out to be the largest oil find in the world at that time and top quality, too, with a low sulphur content. Hunt eventually made more than $100 million from the deal. Critics claimed he had originally lied to Joiner by claiming that tests had revealed little oil in the area when in fact they had shown otherwise, a charge never verified and eventually denied by Joiner.

Hunt founded the Hunt Oil Company in 1936, with headquarters in Dallas, Texas. In 1951, he used his fortune to begin a controversial organization, Facts Forum. Amid the cold war, Facts Forum produced and distributed radio shows that condemned communism and anything Hunt believed seemed Communist, including the United Nations. To the amazement of observers, Facts Forum received tax-exempt status from the Internal Revenue Service (IRS) despite the organization's political line. In 1958, Hunt discontinued Facts Forum and replaced it with Life Line. This time, the IRS declared it too political for a tax-exempt status.

Through Life Line, Hunt continued his crusade against communism. He championed far-right causes and considered himself a savior who would lead the free world to victory. Observers labeled him "self-deluded" and commented that:

> Once he heard what he wanted to hear, he stopped listening.
>
> He believed the world was the way he wanted it to be, not the way it is.
>
> He thought he was a second Jesus Christ.

Meanwhile, Lydia Hunt died in 1955, and Hunt continued seeing Ruth Ray, a secretary with whom had had been having an affair for several years. He married her in 1957.

Partly to support Life Line, and partly to show that he still could build a business, Hunt founded HLH Products in 1960, a food company that manufactured canned chicken, canned tomatoes, aspirin, vitamins, and toothpaste. (HLH Products was not the same as Hunt-Wesson, a firm independent of H. L. Hunt.) He fed money from HLH into Life Line, but HLH drained Hunt's oil company through corruption and misspending, and in the early 1970s he divested it. After Hunt died of heart failure on November 29, 1974, his family continued operating the oil firm and entered other endeavors, most notably the soybean and world silver markets.

BIBLIOGRAPHY

Hunt, Harry III, *Texas Rich: The Hunt Dynasty from the Early Oil Days through the Silver Crash*, 1981.

Huntington, Henry

(February 27, 1850–November 23, 1927)
Railroad Executive, Transportation Executive

Known in his later years for his tremendous art collection, Henry Edwards Huntington headed railroads and developed a streetcar empire in Los Angeles.

Born on February 27, 1850, in Oneonta, New York, to Solon Huntington and Harriet (Saunders) Huntington, Henry worked at an early age as a clerk in a hardware store in his hometown. When he was 20, he moved to New York City, where he joined a larger hardware company. In 1871, however, his businessman uncle, Collis P. Huntington, hired him to direct a sawmill in St. Albans, West Virginia. Collis Huntington's mill was supplying lumber to railroads, and it prospered so much that Henry obtained ownership of the business.

Collis Huntington, also an investor in railways, hired Henry in 1881 to superintend construction of a portion of the Chesapeake, Ohio & Southern Railroad. After that, Henry held several posts with the Kentucky Central Railroad: superintendent of construction in 1884, receiver in 1886, and vice president and general manager from 1887 to 1890. His uncle then involved him in the powerful San Francisco–based Southern Pacific Railway, a company that dominated the California legislature. From 1892 to 1900, Henry served successively as assistant to the president, second vice president, and first vice president as the company developed a transcontinental rail system.

While in San Francisco, Henry helped develop that city's street railways. In 1898, however, he focused on Los Angeles and began buying and consolidating transportation companies there. When Collis Huntington died in 1900, Henry inherited a fortune and assumed leadership of the Southern Pacific. He quickly sold control of the railway to EDWARD HARRIMAN, however, and used his inheritance to develop a streetcar system in Los Angeles. By 1910, his lines traversed 35 miles and boosted the value of real estate that he owned in the area.

Huntington sold his urban lines in 1910 to the Southern Pacific Railway, developed electric power, and continued to buy real estate that made him for several years the single largest landowner in southern California. He built a mansion in San Marino adjacent to Pasadena, where he also built a library and art gallery to which he devoted his last years. He collected books and manuscripts relating primarily to England and America, while in art he collected English painters. Shortly before his death, he signed deeds that placed his collections and his estate in the hands of trustees.

When Huntington died in Philadelphia on November 23, 1927, he left a library and art collection valued at $30 million. He had married twice—in 1873 to Mary Alice Prentice, whom he divorced in 1906, and in 1913 to Arabella Duval (Yarrington) Huntington, his uncle's widow.

BIBLIOGRAPHY

Dickinson, Donald C., *Henry E. Huntington's Library of Libraries*, 1995; Friedricks, William B., *Henry E. Huntington and the Creation of Southern California*, 1992; Marcosson, I. F., *A Little Known Master of Millions: The Story of Henry E. Huntington, Construction Capitalist*, 1914; Thorpe, James Ernest, *Henry Edwards Huntington: A Biography*, 1994.

I

Iacocca, Lee

(October 15, 1924–)
Manufacturer

Known as the "father of the Ford Mustang," Lido (Lee) Anthony Iacocca took over the nearly bankrupt Chrylser Company and, in what financial analysts called a miraculous turnaround, saved it.

Lee was born on October 15, 1924, in Allentown, Pennsylvania, to Nicola Iacocca and Antoinette (Perrotto) Iacocca, who were immigrants from San Marco, Italy. The elder Iacocca prospered as the owner of several small businesses until the Great Depression almost ruined him.

After graduating from high school, Iacocca entered Lehigh University in nearby Bethlehem, Pennsylvania, and as a freshman boasted to his friends that he would be a vice president at the Ford Motor Company by the time he reached age 35. He graduated from Lehigh in 1945 and the following year received a master's degree in mechanical engineering from Princeton University in New Jersey.

Iacocca entered an engineer-training program at Ford in 1946 but disliked the work and transferred to fleet sales. He turned out to be a phenomenal salesperson, and in 1949 the company made him zone manager in Wilkes-Barre, Pennsylvania. By 1953, he earned promotion to assistant sales manager of the Philadelphia district. Three years later, when he married Mary McCleary, he developed an innovative sales promotion, "56 for 56," that allowed consumers to purchase a car by paying $20 down and $56 a month over three years. The promotion made the Philadelphia district number one at Ford in national sales and resulted in Iacocca's promotion to sales manager for Washington, D.C.

Within a short while, Ford brought Iacocca to its headquarters in Dearborn, Michigan, to direct national marketing for the company's trucks. In 1960, he obtained the goal he had pronounced years earlier and was named a vice president at age 36, just one year behind the schedule he had so confidently pronounced as a college freshman.

Iacocca displayed a knack for knowing what the public wanted, and after perceiving that an enormous youth market had emerged, he pushed Ford to produce a sporty, speedy, inexpensive car. He once told the recalcitrant company president ROBERT MCNAMARA "safety doesn't sell." In April 1964, well after McNamara's departure, the first Mustang appeared, and over the next 12 months, it broke the record for sales of a first-year model, thus topping the record set by HENRY FORD's original Model T.

Iacocca was named executive vice president of North American automobile operations in 1967 and revived the Lincoln-Mercury line, introducing such cars as the Mercury Cougar. Success led to his appointment in 1970 as president.

Iacocca introduced several new models, including the best-selling Pinto. That car, however, proved an engineer's nightmare when it was discovered to have gas tank leakage. In addition, safety tests showed that in rear-end collisions, the Pinto's gas tank exploded and engulfed the car in flames. Ford had to issue 1.5 million recalls but even that failed to end criticism of the car.

A dispute with Henry Ford II in 1978 (partly resulting from the Pinto's failure) forced Iacocca from the presidency, but Chrysler quickly hired him as its president and chief executive officer. Iacocca faced an enormous challenge, for Chrysler tottered near bankruptcy with outdated plants and bloated inventory. In 1979, a gasoline shortage additionally hurt the sales of Chrysler's large cars. The company's debt approached $5 billion, and in desperation, Iacocca turned to the federal government to guarantee loans made to the company. In a move critics called risky, Congress agreed, and over $1 billion soon flowed to Chrysler.

What followed has been called "one of the most dramatic events in American corporate history." Iacocca laid off workers, reduced wages, and closed or consolidated plants. He later stated:

> During 1980, I went to every single Chrysler plant in order to speak directly to the workers. At a series of mass meetings, I thanked them for sticking with us during these bad times. I told them when things got better, we'd try to get them back to parity with Ford workers, but that it wouldn't happen overnight.

He hit the airwaves, too, with an advertising campaign that featured himself assuring consumers that Chrysler would survive. His straightforward image appealed to audiences, and in 1982 he announced that Chrylser had made a profit. The following year, he paid all the outstanding government-backed loans in full. Not only had Chrysler been saved but the federal government also made $500 million in interest.

Chrysler's sales surged again in 1984 when Iacocca introduced a car that in appeal fit somewhere between a station wagon and a van—the minivan—that could conveniently fit in a garage. The profits that Chrysler made enriched Iacocca, too, and in 1986 his earnings from salary, bonuses, stocks, and stock options exceeded $23 million. With his adroit knack for public relations, he defused a potential disaster when it was revealed that Chrysler had been turning back odometers on its test vehicles and selling the cars as new. Iacocca called the action stupid and apologized—and consumers accepted his apparent sincerity.

Meanwhile, Iacocca wrote an autobiography that reached the best-seller lists. He also married Peggy Johnson in April 1986, three years after his first wife died. The couple filed for divorce a few months later, however.

Iacocca retired from Chrysler in 1992. The following year, President Bill Clinton recruited him to help lead the successful effort to have Congress approve the North American Free Trade Agreement.

BIBLIOGRAPHY

Iacocca, Lee, *Iacocca: An Autobiography*, 1984; Wyden, Peter, *The Unknown Iacocca: An Unauthorized Biography*, 1987.

Icahn, Carl

(1936–)
Financier

Tappan Appliances, ACF Industries, Trans World Airlines (TWA) —these and other corporations have all encountered attacks by a master corporate raider, Carl Icahn.

Icahn was born in 1936 in the borough of Queens, New York. His father, Michael Icahn, worked for a while as a lawyer and then as a chemistry teacher but, according to some accounts, for many years did nothing, thus leaving it up to young Icahn's mother, Bella, to earn money for the family. The youngster lived in a comfortable middle-class household and graduated from Far Rockaway High School in 1953, before majoring in philosophy at Princeton University. While in college, he excelled at chess and tied for the state championship. He later said that chess taught him two qualities he applied to business: rational analysis and planning.

After receiving his B.A. degree in 1957, Icahn enrolled at the New York University School of Medicine. He hated his studies, however, and quit after three years. He then entered the army, where he won substantial money playing poker—a thrill that later motivated him to gamble with stocks.

When Icahn left the army in 1961, he joined Dreyfus & Company in New York City as a trainee stockbroker. He invested his own money on the stock market and did well before losing everything in 1962. The experience taught him to pursue strategies largely ignored by other investors. As a result, he plunged into the little-understood world of option trading (that is, he traded the right to buy or sell securities within a specific time and at a specific price) and in 1963 managed the Option Department at Tessel, Patrick & Company, and the following year, at Gruntel & Company.

In 1968, Icahn borrowed $400,000 from his uncle, Elliot Schnall, and began his own brokerage firm, called Icahn & Company. He mainly handled option trades and entered a new practice called risk arbitrage.

In 1978, Icahn stumbled into the profitable and controversial practice of corporate raiding when he discovered that the price of stock in Tappan Company (the giant appliance maker) stood at 60 percent below its book value. He could buy the stock at $8 per share when it actually was worth closer to $20. With the mergers then under way in the appliance industry, Icahn figured that before long another corporation would be eager to buy Tappan stock near book value. As a result, he bought nearly 300,000 shares in an attempt to take over the company, then won election to the board of directors and found a corporation willing to pay $18 per share. The sale netted a huge profit for Tappan stockholders, with Icahn grossing nearly $3 million.

Icahn became determined to pursue other corporations that had undervalued stock, and his ability to do so and to mobilize investors in helping him raid companies made him a high-profile financier similar to IVAN BOESKY. Critics attacked Icahn for driving up the price of a company's stock and then selling without any concern for the business itself. He wanted, they charged, to simply make a quick buck. Icahn admitted his desire for profit but replied that his investments boosted previously undervalued stock to its rightful level, and made a company leaner and better able to meet its competition. About the prevailing corporate environment, he observed:

> Just like college, where the president of the fraternity is a real likable guy, the president or the CEO of the company is usually a likable guy. . . . But they're not the cleverest, because clever guys, intelligent guys, are often abrasive and they're not well-liked . . . what has happened in management is that the guys who got to the top are the guys that the board liked.

> We can't have people on the dole. But when you have ten layers of bureaucracy in a corporation, isn't that the same as the dole?

> The problem we have with managerial society today is that there is no accountability because corporate democracy is a travesty.

Other buyouts and attempted takeovers followed. Icahn made $100 million, usually by buying shares and then selling them to a higher-bidding rival, or through greenmail. In 1983, he actually bought a business outright—ACF Industries, a railroad car manufacturer. He surprised observers by proving to be an able manager, selling unprofitable holdings and streamlining the entire operation to boost profits two years later by 40 percent.

Icahn's most famous acquisition, though, occurred when he gained control of TWA Airlines in 1985. He did so with the help of the pilots' and machinists' unions, who wanted to prevent a takeover by FRANK LORENZO, known for his union-busting tactics. In TWA, Icahn acquired a financially troubled company and in order to boost passenger volume, he bought a rival, Ozark Air Lines, in 1986. Under Icahn, TWA at first lost more than $200 million, but late in 1986 it started to show a profit. Icahn sold his 42 million shares of TWA in 1989 for $2 billion.

In 1997, Icahn was elected chairman of the board at the Marvel Entertainment Group, a company that despite its popular comic books had recently filed for bankruptcy. Married and with two children, Icahn had a reputation for seclusion and associating with people only when he could make a profit from them.

BIBLIOGRAPHY

Dye, Thomas R., *Who's Running America?*, 1995; Johnston, Moira, *Takeover: The New Wall Street Warriors*, 1986.

Inman, Samuel

(February 19, 1843–January 12, 1915)
Merchant, Financier

Samuel Martin Inman, the son of a wealthy merchant and planter, built his father's cotton commission firm into one of the largest cotton dealers in the world in the late 1800s. Inman helped to organize the Southern Railway Company and served on the boards of a number of banks.

Samuel, the son of Shadrach and Jane Martin Hamilton Inman, was born in Jefferson County, Tennessee, on February 19, 1843. Samuel first attended Maryville College and later went to Princeton in 1860. A year after entering Princeton, Samuel left to enlist as a private in the Confederate army. He attained the rank of lieutenant in the war. When the conflict was over, Samuel moved to Augusta, Georgia, for a year. In 1867, he moved to Atlanta to open a cotton commission business with his father, whose farm had been destroyed in the war. The following year, Samuel married Jennie Dick of Rome, Georgia. His father remained in Atlanta for three years before retiring to Tennessee.

At this juncture, Samuel restructured the commission firm, renaming it S. M. Inman and Company. With his able management, the firm grew to become one of the world's principal cotton dealers. S. M. Inman and Company operated from branch offices around the South. Between Samuel and his brother John, the Inman name was central to the post–Civil War cotton industry. In the late 1870s, John became an influential leader in the cotton industry, forming the firm of Inman, Swann and Company, organizing the New York Cotton Exchange, and be-

Samuel Inman (North Wind Picture Archives)

coming a major figure—known as "the Cotton King"—in the development of the New South.

In 1891, Samuel served as the treasurer of the International Cotton Exposition in Atlanta. He also assisted in 1895 with the Cotton States and International Exposition. In 1892, two years after the death of his first wife, Samuel married Mildred McPheeters from Raleigh, North Carolina, with whom he had three children.

By 1896, though he continued to maintain some interests in conjunction with his brother, Samuel retired from actively working in the cotton trade, turning to other financial and industrial ventures. Samuel was one of the founders of the Southern Railway Company, and his role in organizing the railroad's network earned him the honor of a station named after him in Atlanta. The Southern Railway was most notable for the bankruptcy of its backbone station, the Richmond Terminal. The terminal, a project undertaken by John Inman and others, attempted to link the Danville Railroad, the East Tennessee Railroad, and the Central Railroad of Georgia into one system under the Richmond and West Point Terminal and Warehouse Company.

During the latter years of his life, Samuel was a director of several banks, the Equitable Life Assurance Society, and the *Constitution* (an Atlanta newspaper). As Samuel withdrew from his business activities near the end of his life, he be-

came more active in civic duties. He influenced the founding of the Georgia Institute of Technology and made generous donations to Oglethorpe and Emory Universities. He was also an active member of the Presbyterian Church until his death on January 12, 1915.

BIBLIOGRAPHY

Klein, Maury, *The Great Richmond Terminal*, 1970; *National Cyclopedia of American Biography*, 1921; Stover, John F., *The Railroads of the South*, 1955; Woodman, Harold, *King Cotton and His Retainers*, 1968.

Insull, Samuel

(November 11, 1859–July 16, 1938)
Utilities Investor

An immigrant who came to America with little money, Samuel Insull amassed a fortune only to lose it in the Great Depression, undergo trial for fraud, and find his name vilified throughout the nation.

Samuel was born on November 11, 1859, in London, England, to Samuel Insull and Emma (Short) Insull. His father was a preacher, and his mother operated Insull's Temperance Hotel. He left school at age 14 to work as a clerk in an auction company. Four years later, George E. Gourard (the London representative for THOMAS EDISON) hired Samuel to be his

personal secretary and bookkeeper. Samuel so impressed Gourard with his sharp mind and hard work that he sent him to New Jersey to work as Edison's private secretary in 1881.

Edison soon made Insull the head of the struggling Edison General Electric Company, and within 10 years, Insull had made it profitable. Ambitious, Insull won appointment to the presidency of Chicago Edison and in 1892 convinced the small Commonwealth Electricity Company that he should head it, too. He expanded Chicago Edison by acquiring smaller companies and in 1907 merged the firm

Samuel Insull (Library of Congress)

with Commonwealth Electricity to form Commonwealth Edison, giving him a monopoly in Chicago.

Meanwhile, in 1899, Insull had married Margaret Bird, an actress. They eventual-

ly had one son, Samuel, who ultimately joined his father's utilities business.

With Chicago's electricity under his control, Insull penetrated surrounding towns and consolidated several utilities into the Public Service Company of Northern Illinois. Insull's companies eventually brought electricity into several states and served millions of Americans. Beyond a genius for finance, Insull understood technology and recognized the potential of a new compound steam turbine that could generate more electricity over longer distances than standard turbines. Its use dropped electric rates in Chicago from 20 cents per kilowatt-hour to 2.5 cents.

Insull applied his financial acumen to other businesses, helping turn them around as well. These included Peoples Gas, Light & Coke Company (through which he brought natural gas from Texas to Chicago by pipeline), and Chicago's streetcar and elevated railway systems.

Insull created a complex network of holding companies that attracted investors (including many small investors who bought securities) and that relied on his companies buying the stocks of other companies that were added to the empire. Generally, for every dollar Insull invested in his businesses, he controlled $20 of assets. His personal wealth peaked at about $150 million.

When the economy expanded in the 1920s, Insull and his investors made a fortune. For example, Insull Utility Investments—one of his companies—saw its stock rise in 1929 from $30 a share to $147. The Great Depression changed all that, however, and changed it quickly. In 1932, Insull failed to make a $10 million loan payment, and his empire collapsed, taking with it the many investors who had thought the business and its creator invincible.

An outraged public demanded retribution, and state and federal grand juries indicted Insull for embezzlement, mail fraud, and conspiracy to evade the national bankruptcy act. Afraid he would not get a fair trial, Insull fled the country but after several months was kidnapped in Turkey, placed into custody, brought back to Chicago, and unceremoniously placed in Cook County jail.

Had Insull acted illegally as a business leader? Insull's holding structure involved many unsound practices, and several of his companies reported phony profits. In a largely unregulated market, however, he may have done nothing illegal. In any event, he went through three court trials and won acquittal each time.

A few years later, on July 16, 1938, he died of a heart attack at a subway station in Paris. When found, his body had been rifled by thieves, and his pockets contained only eight francs.

BIBLIOGRAPHY

Fuhrman, Peter, "Do It Big, Sammy," *Forbes*, July 13, 1987; Gordon, John Steele, "The Farthest Fall," *American Heritage*, July–August 1997; McDonald, Forrest, *Insull*, 1962; Michaels, James W., "History Lesson," *Forbes*, December 24, 1990.

Jackson, Patrick

(August 14, 1780–September 12, 1847)
Manufacturer

Patrick Tracy Jackson, a cheerful, spirited man of Irish descent, was instrumental in the expansion of the textile industry in the nineteenth century. His factory at Waltham, Massachusetts, was one of the first in the world to combine under one roof all operations involved in the conversion of raw cotton into finished cloth. Jackson and his brother-in-law, FRANCIS LOWELL, were the founders of the city of Lowell, Massachusetts, a town that would come to be a manufacturing epicenter known as the "Manchester of America," after the booming industrial town in England.

Patrick, the youngest of three sons of Jonathan and Hannah Tracy Jackson, was born in Newburyport, Massachusetts, on August 14, 1780. His father was, at various times, a supervisor of internal revenue in Boston, the treasurer of Massachusetts, the treasurer of Harvard College, and a member of the Continental Congress. After attending public schools and the Dummer Academy, Patrick left school at age 15 to begin an apprenticeship with William Bartlett, the richest merchant in Newburyport.

Within five years, Jackson had so impressed his employer that he was assigned to a voyage to St. Thomas in the West Indies with authority superceding that of the captain. After successfully proving his leadership ability, Patrick's elder brother, Capt. Henry Jackson, offered him in 1799 the position of captain's clerk aboard Henry's own ship for a voyage to the Far East.

Over the next few years, Jackson commanded the ship and its cargo for three additional voyages. His final journey lasted four years. Upon his return to Massachusetts in 1808, Jackson used his savings to set up a mercantile enterprise devoted to trade with the East and West Indies.

On November 1, 1810, he married Lydia Cabot, with whom he had nine children. Though his personal life had gained some structure, Jackson's business was suffering; by 1811, he was almost penniless. Though nearly bankrupt, Jackson had built an impressive reputation as a trustworthy, knowledgeable trade specialist. Gradually, the status of the company improved, despite a curtailment of shipping activities during the War of 1812. He eventually amassed a small fortune.

Patrick Jackson (North Wind Picture Archives)

During a hiatus in trade activities due to the war, Jackson and his brother-in-law, FRANCIS LOWELL, became enthusiastic about the textile manufacturing industry. In 1813, Jackson, Lowell, Nathan Appleton, and others established the Boston Manufacturing Company. A mill was built in Waltham, Massachusetts, alongside the Charles River. Jackson was in charge of the mill's operations, and Lowell, in collaboration with textile machinist Paul Moody, designed and built the mill's machinery. By 1816, the factory also owned the local resources for power generation. Jackson's enthusiasm for cotton manufacturing had by this time motivated him to focus solely on the mills and give up his trade career.

Over the next few years, the factory and its operations continued to grow. Faced with the increased need for space and other resources, Jackson and his partners purchased in 1820 a large piece of land in East Chelmsford, on the banks of the Merrimac River. The cotton factories, and associated residences and support businesses, formed a new community, which the partners named Lowell. Jackson was active in the new city's founding, and also helped establish the Appleton Company and smaller local business enterprises.

Over the next decade, the burgeoning community's need for improved communication and transportation facilities inspired Jackson to study the feasibility of building a steam railroad from Boston to Lowell. After persuading his associates of the value of the project, Jackson took the helm of the construction process. Though he planned to retire after completion of the Boston & Lowell Railroad's construction, Jackson was faced with economic hardship after becoming involved in failed real estate speculations. Ironically, the ill-fated land arrangements were related to the much more successful railroad endeavor. As some of the land required for the route was swampland that needed to be filled in, Jackson had bought another piece of land to use as a resource for the gravel needed for filler. He then built houses on the land, but took a loss on all of them due to the widespread financial instability during the Panic of 1837.

The blow to Jackson's financial resources, combined with the death of the most talented of the Lowell mill managers, motivated him to postpone retirement. His energetic pursuit of administering the enterprises at Lowell took a toll on his health, and he died from a fatal bout of dysentery on September 12, 1847, at his home in Beverly, Massachusetts.

BIBLIOGRAPHY

Appleton, Nathan, *Introduction of the Power Loom, and Origin of Lowell*, 1858; Lowell, J. A., "The Late Patrick Tracy Jackson," *Merchant's Mag. and Commercial Rev.*, April 1848; Putnam, E. C., and J. J. Putnam, *The Hon. Jonathan Jackson and Hannah (Tracy) Jackson: Their Ancestors and Descendants*, 1907; Ware, C. F., *The Early New Eng. Cotton Manufacture*, 1931.

Jobs, Steven

(1955–)
Manufacturer

The computer age owes as much to Steven Jobs as anyone else. With the formation of his Apple Computer Company, he made computers accessible to teachers, students, and millions of other everyday people.

Born in 1955, Steve was adopted in February of that year by Paul Jobs, a machinist, and Clara Jobs of Mountain View, California. While a student at Homestead High School in Los Altos, the town where his family had moved—he dabbled in electronics and obtained a part-time job at Hewlett-Packard. He met Stephen Wozniak, a computer whiz who also worked at Hewlett-Packard, and the two became friends. They entered into their first moneymaking venture when they manufactured a "little blue box" that they sold to college students. The box enabled callers to illegally bypass long-distance phone charges.

Jobs entered Reed College in Oregon in 1972 but quit his classes after one semester. He had always enjoyed art and literature and had a contemplative nature, so for the next few months, he hung around the campus and experimented with psychedelics, learned the *I Ching* (a mystical book of divination), and associated with a Hare Krishna sect. In 1974, he worked as a video game developer at Atari but then embarked for India, where he shaved his head, backpacked, and searched for spiritual enlightenment.

Jobs returned to California later that year, underwent primal scream therapy, worked at Atari, and joined a Palo Alto hobby group (the Homebrew Computer Club) that his friend Wozniak had also

Steven Jobs (Reuters/Lou Dematteis/Archive Photos)

joined. By that time, Wozniak and Bill Fernandez had designed a personal computer—they called it the Cream Soda Computer—and discovered a way to add graphics to the screen. "We had no idea," Wozniak recounted, "that people were going to be able to write games with animation and little characters bouncing all around."

Jobs made some improvements to the machine and suggested that they should market it, using their connections at the Homebrew Computer Club. Jobs and Wozniak raised money by selling some of their personal possessions and went to work developing the computer in the family garage, which Jobs's father had renovated for the project. They called their computer Apple, a name Jobs likely chose in memory of a summer that he spent in Oregon as an orchard worker.

The two entrepreneurs sold their first Apples to an electronics store and, in all, sold about 200 of the machines that year. The following year, they introduced the advanced Apple II, faster and complete with color graphics, although as with the first Apple, it still required the user to hook it up to a television set for output. Consumers liked Apple II for its low price, compactness, and simplicity that made it possible to run computer programs without having to know a computer language. To help with financing Apple, Jobs brought in a former marketing manager at Intel, A. C. Markkula, who invested heavily, attracted other investors, and became chairman of what was by then officially the Apple Computer Company. At a time when few people owned their own computers, Apple experienced nothing less than phenomenal growth. The company's sales hit $7.8 million in 1978 and $117.9 million in 1980, while more than 16,000 software programs developed by independent producers complemented the computer. Apple reached the *Fortune* 500 quicker than any other new company in the history of the list.

Jobs, however, had his critics. They claimed he lacked managerial ability, that he could not take advice, and would not keep appointments. At times, Apple seemed more chaos than order. The company introduced Apple III complete with a monitor, but the machine flopped due to inexplicable program crashes, and a shake-up brought Jobs back to the chairman position that he had held when the company first started. Meanwhile, Markkula became president.

Apple sold well in schools and homes, but International Business Machines (IBM) had reacted quickly to the challenge by producing its own personal computer (called the PC), which businesses favored. In 1983, Jobs recruited John Sculley from Pepsi-Cola as the new president to replace Markkula, while Jobs focused on designing a new computer, the Macintosh.

Macintosh sold well in 1984, boosted in its first 100 days by a $15 million advertising blitz, but IBM still recorded gains and in 1985 had 40 percent of the personal computer market compared to Apple's 24 percent. With Apple struggling, Jobs resigned under pressure in 1985 (Wozniak had left earlier) and started an educational computer company, NeXt, Incorporated.

Jobs sold NeXt to Apple in December 1996 and bought Pixar (a computer animation firm) for $10 million. Pixar produced *Toy Story*, the first entirely computer-generated full-length movie. Although Jobs pumped $50 million into Pixar, the firm never made a profit.

Jobs returned to Apple in 1997 as a part-time adviser and temporary chairman at a time when Apple, besieged by its competitors, was suffering a large loss of market share and flirting with collapse. The company counted on Jobs to keep it afloat, or even save it, while searching for a permanent chairman.

In August of that year, Jobs stunned the business world when he entered into a deal with Apple's main competitor in software, Microsoft. He and Microsoft's leader, BILL GATES, formed a partnership between their two companies, in which Microsoft invested $150 million in Apple and agreed to let Apple remain largely autonomous. (Gates's motivation was unclear—he may have feared that if Apple collapsed, Microsoft would be accused of operating a monopoly and thus would face legal action.) In late 1997, for the first time in months, Apple showed a substantial increase in its profits.

BIBLIOGRAPHY

Freiberger, Paul, and Michael Swaine, *Fire in the Valley: The Making of the Personal Computer*, 1984; Moritz, Michael, *The Little Kingdom: The Private Story of Apple Computer*, 1984.

Johnson, George

(October 14, 1857–November 28, 1948)
Manufacturer

George Francis Johnson, an entrepreneur who became successful in the shoe manufacturing business, was a firm believer in a type of "welfare capitalism" that stressed the importance of a happy workforce. While Johnson emphasized a sound bottom line, his early implementation of such employee-friendly practices as profit sharing, the 40-hour workweek, comprehensive medical care, and higher-than-average wages marked a new trend in labor relations.

Johnson, the son of Francis A. and Jane Aldrich Johnson, was born on October 14, 1857, in Milford, Massachusetts. George, his three brothers, and his sister came from a long line of New England working-class families. His father worked at a boot factory.

Johnson's working career began early. He left home at age 13 to work for the Seaver Brothers Boot Factory in Ashland, Massachusetts. On December 22, 1876, Johnson married Lucy Anna Willis of Braintree, Massachusetts. Though the couple eventually divorced, they had five children—Walter, George, Zaida, Irma, and Ernest.

By 1881, Johnson was working at the Lester Brothers Boot Factory in Binghamton, New York. While in Binghamton, Johnson remarried. He and Mary Ann McGlone had one child, Esther Lillian.

By 1890, when the boot company was bought by Henry Endicott, Johnson had earned a reputation as an innovative, hard worker. Endicott rewarded his diligence with a promotion to production and sales manager. Impressed by Johnson's work ethic, Endicott sold Johnson half the company in 1899. Johnson's new position of authority enabled him to develop the business along his ideas of industrial democracy. He felt that the ideal factory was "a shop out in the open country, with the homes of the workers built around it in a little village." The new company carried out this vision of "welfare capitalism" by building factories with affiliated towns in the New York countryside. The towns of Endicott and Johnson City emerged in this fashion.

Endicott-Johnson built a number of houses, offering them to employees with affordable mortgages. The company also established utilities and other community services such as libraries, recreational facilities, schools, and stores. Johnson remained accessible to the workers. He became president of the firm in 1920, a year after the company had incorporated and Endicott had died.

Johnson had a very specific sense of fairness in labor issues. He paid wages higher than the subsistence pay that was misleadingly considered a living wage at the time. Even during the Great Depression, he paid higher-than-average salaries. Though the depression years were tight, he kept workers on the payroll by reducing hours. He also opened up the company's dining room to the unemployed.

The Endicott-Johnson Company was the first in the shoe industry to embrace the 8-hour day and 40-hour work-week. It was a pioneer in providing free health care for its employees. Johnson also established a profit-sharing plan whereby workers and executives alike received shares based on the number of weeks they had worked during the previous year.

Despite Johnson's demonstrated concern for a stable and content workforce, he was not a proponent of labor unions. As he structured his company to be a community workplace with great employee involvement, he did not see the need for unions. Though he supported labor unions as a tool against unfair employers, he viewed his own company in a different light. This viewpoint was validated in 1940, when his workers voted down the formation of a union by a five-to-one ratio.

In addition to a thriving business career, Johnson was active in politics. Registered as an independent, he was a supporter of Democratic President Woodrow Wilson and later of the New Deal measures of President Franklin Roosevelt. He also endorsed policies that attempted to equitably redistribute wealth.

Johnson relinquished control of the company in 1930, handing over the reigns to his son George. He remained active as chairman of the board until he suffered a heart attack in 1937, which caused him to retire. Johnson died in Endicott of a second heart attack on November 28, 1948.

BIBLIOGRAPHY

Dictionary of American Biography, supplement IV, 1974; Inglis, William, *George F. Johnson and His Industrial Democracy*, 1935; Saul, Richard S., "An American Entrepreneur: George F. Johnson," unpublished Ph.D. dissertation, 1966.

Johnson, Herbert

(November 15, 1899–December 14, 1978)
Manufacturer

As president and chairman of the board of the Johnson Wax Company, Herbert Fisk Johnson continued the family tradition of manufacturing quality cleaning products for the home. Johnson guided the company through the Great Depression by introducing new products and increasing its advertising budget. In the latter half of his career, Johnson met the challenges of changing market demographics by branching out with new types of cleaning, personal hygiene, and insect control products.

The son of Herbert Fisk Johnson Sr., Herbert was born on November 15, 1899, in Racine, Wisconsin. The Johnson Wax Company was founded by Herbert's grandfather, Samuel Curtis Johnson, in 1886. Originally a carpenter, Samuel Johnson began marketing his floor wax products by giving them away as free bonuses with parquet floor purchases. Herbert Fisk Johnson Sr. took over the presidency of the company from his father, and the young Herbert would follow in the family tradition.

Herbert attended public schools in Racine and worked during the summer at the family factory making wax, packaging products, and loading freight cars. He attended Cornell University and after graduating in 1922, began working full-time for the family business. He first worked on product development in the laboratory and then moved into sales and purchasing. Upon his father's death in 1928, Herbert became president and chairman of the board.

When Johnson assumed control of the Johnson Wax Company, it had 500 employees and subsidiaries in three foreign countries. Johnson's leadership was almost immediately tested when the Great Depression began in 1929, just one year after he became president. Sales dropped sharply, but Johnson refused to lay off any workers and instead attempted to revive the company by introducing new products and increasing advertising.

Johnson introduced the first single-step floor polisher called "Glo-Coat" in 1932 and backed the product with aggressive advertising through the growing medium of radio. Johnson was the first to establish independent sponsorship of a radio program, and this approach was amazingly successful in making Johnson Wax products into household names. The company was thus able to maintain its financial strength through the depression years, and the investment in advertising continued to pay returns as the business grew rapidly after the depression. Johnson believed in maintaining excellent labor relations, and there was never a strike at a Johnson factory under his management. In 1917, the company first instituted a profit-sharing plan for employees, and Johnson added a pension and medical plan in 1934.

In 1956, Johnson expanded the company further by introducing additional household products. Until that time, the product line was entirely based on wax, but in the next decade he added several aerosol and spray products including "Raid" (bug killer), "Off!" (the first aerosol insect repellent), "Pledge" (furniture polish), "Glade" (air freshener), and "Glory" (the first home carpet cleaner). These new products allowed the company to compensate for the drop in sales caused by the introduction of "no-wax" floors in the 1960s.

Johnson also faced falling profits when the women's movement changed attitudes about the need for fastidious housekeeping. To adjust to this new market, Johnson developed a line of personal care products for women including shampoos and conditioners, promoting these items with extensive advertising. The company also created a subsidiary, Johnson Diversified, which bought up several small recreation equipment companies specializing in hiking and camping equipment, kayaks, and scuba gear. By 1979, Johnson Diversified had acquired 15 small recreation companies, establishing it as one of the leaders in the outdoor recreation equipment sector.

Outside of company life, Johnson served as director of the Office of Indus-

trial Resources in 1954 during the Eisenhower administration. He also established the Johnson Foundation to fund charitable and educational projects. After stepping down as president of Johnson Wax in 1958, he continued as chairman of the board and chief executive officer until 1966. Johnson and his wife Gloria had two children; their son Samuel Curtis Johnson II took over management of the company when his father retired. Herbert Johnson died on December 14, 1978.

BIBLIOGRAPHY

Johnson, Samuel C., *The Essence of a Family Enterprise: Doing Business the Johnson Way*, 1988; Moskowitz, Milton, et al., eds., *Everybody's Business*, 1980; "SC Johnson Wax On-line History," http://www.scjohnsonwax.com/scjhist.html.

Johnson, Howard

(1897–June 20, 1972)
Restaurant Executive, Hotel Executive

From a modest pharmacy, Howard Deering Johnson developed the nation's first franchise restaurant chain based on flavorful ice creams and distinctive orange-roofed buildings.

Johnson was born in 1897 in Wollaston, Massachusetts. After fighting in World War I, he returned home, where he was forced to liquidate a cigar store that he had operated with his father. Despite a sub-

stantial debt that he owed creditors, Johnson forged ahead and in 1924 bought a run-down, debt-laden pharmacy near the town's railroad station. There he sold patent medicines, magazines, newspapers, and stationery. At his soda fountain, he served sandwiches and ice cream.

Seeking to build his soda fountain business, Johnson purchased a secret ice cream recipe for $300 from a German pushcart vendor. Johnson liked the ice cream's distinctive taste, and with the purchase, he discovered that the product's delicious flavor derived from a formula that used twice as much butterfat as was typically used in commercial ice cream, along with natural rather than artificial flavors.

Beginning in 1925, Johnson made ice cream in his basement and sold it at his pharmacy. Before long, he developed 28 flavors that went well beyond the standard chocolate and vanilla, and they became a trademark for his business. He consumed plenty of ice cream himself—at least a cone a day—and after he became wealthy, kept 10 flavors in the freezers of his Manhattan penthouse.

In the summer months, Johnson opened ice-cream stands at the beaches in Boston and Wollaston, and his product proved so popular that in 1928 his sales topped $200,000. His success led him to open a family-style restaurant in nearby Quincy in 1929, but the venture failed.

Undaunted, Johnson reentered the restaurant business but with a different twist when a family friend, Reginald Sprague, proposed that he allow him to open his own restaurant under the Johnson name. The two men reached an agreement whereby Sprague paid Johnson a fee for the use of Johnson's name, bought his ice cream from Johnson, and allowed Johnson to establish the standard for food served at the restaurant. Thus began the first step toward a franchise chain.

By 1935, 7 franchised Howard Johnson restaurants had opened in Massachusetts. In a rapid expansion, 135 company-owned and franchised restaurants existed by 1940. Johnson opened each with a

Howard Johnson (Archive Photos)

distinctive architecture intended to draw motorists from the highways: a bright orange roof topped by a cupola and weathervane. A street sign displayed his symbol: Simple Simon and the Pieman. The increasingly mobile American population responded by flocking to his eateries.

Johnson kept a tight hold on quality. He often made unannounced visits to the restaurants and inspected their kitchens. Although gas rationing during World War II forced him to close many of his restaurants, he quickly rebounded in the 1950s with more eateries, while entering the motel business and operating motor lodges. After Johnson retired in 1964 and turned over control to his son, Howard B. Johnson, the company continued to grow, and by the following decade, more than 1,000 Howard Johnson restaurants and 500 motels spanned the landscape.

Johnson continued to scout for restaurant and motel sites into the early 1970s. He died on June 20, 1972, in New York City. Johnson once said: "I've spent my life developing scores of flavors, and yet most people still say, 'I'll take vanilla.'"

The Howard Johnson chain experienced serious challenges in the 1980s from fast-food restaurants, new brands of ice cream, and a slackening of the quality control that its founder had prized. In 1980, the Imperial Group of Britain bought the company. Five years later, the Marriott Corporation purchased it and sold the lodging and restaurant franchising system to Prime Motor Inns.

BIBLIOGRAPHY

Fucini, Joseph J., and Suzy Fucini, *Entrepreneurs: The Men and Women behind Famous Brand Names and How They Made It*, 1965; Sprague, J. R., "He Had an Idea: Howard Johnson's Roadside Restaurants," *Saturday Evening Post*, July 19, 1958.

Johnson, Robert

(February 15, 1845–February 7, 1910)
Manufacturer

As incredible as it might seem today, before the 1880s, unsanitary conditions characterized surgery: surgeons operated in street clothes, wore blood-splattered frock coats, and dressed wounds with unclean cotton. Robert Wood Johnson and his brothers changed all this when they founded a company—Johnson & Johnson—and developed the first practical application of antiseptic wound treatment.

Born on February 15, 1845, in Carbondale, Pennsylvania, to Sylvester Johnson and Elizabeth (Wood) Johnson, as a young man Robert attended the Wyoming Seminary in nearby Kingston. He later worked in an apothecary shop in Poughkeepsie, New York, before helping to found a Brooklyn pharmaceutical firm, Seabury & Johnson, noted for making medicinal plasters from an improved India rubber base.

In 1876, Johnson heard a speech by Sir Joseph Lister, a noted English surgeon, who argued that airborne germs plagued operating rooms with infections. At that point, Johnson decided to develop an antiseptic surgical dressing, and he recruited his two brothers, James Johnson and Edward Mead Johnson, to help him. James and Mead founded Johnson & Johnson in 1885, and the following year, Robert sold his interest in Seabury & Johnson and joined his brothers. They housed their business in a former wallpaper factory in New Brunswick, New Jersey, and incorporated in 1887 with Robert as president.

That same year, the Johnsons developed an antiseptic surgical dressing made from cotton and gauze and sealed in individual germ-resistant packages. Concurrently, they promoted their Lister-based philosophy by publishing a book,

Modern Methods of Antiseptic Wound Treatment, which was considered a pioneering work in medicine.

Gradually, doctors and hospitals ordered Johnson & Johnson's new product, and in 1891 the company opened a bacteriological laboratory that allowed them to produce cotton and gauze that was not only antiseptic but also sterile—the result of a process that used steam and pressure. The brothers called their company "The Most Trusted Name in Surgical Dressings," and made additional contributions to surgery when they developed an improved technique for sterilizing catgut sutures in 1897 and introduced a zinc oxide adhesive plaster known for its quick-stick quality in 1899.

Under Robert's leadership, the company expanded to a 40-building complex. Mead disliked his brother's domination, however, and shortly before 1900 left the firm and founded his own business, Mead & Johnson, which manufactured baby formula.

Robert died on February 7, 1910, and James succeeded him, holding the presidency until 1932. During those years, Johnson & Johnson developed the product that consumers most remembered it for when in 1920, Earl Dickson, a cotton buyer in the purchasing department, showed James a small gauze pad he had attached to a thin strip of surgical tape to form a cover for minor cuts and bruises. James decided to market the innovation under the brand name Band-Aid.

Over the years, Johnson & Johnson expanded into a worldwide corporation with 180 subsidiary companies marketing health-care products in 175 countries today. Johnson & Johnson has over 91,000 employees and makes products ranging from baby-care, first-aid, and hospital supplies to prescription pharmaceuticals, family planning, and feminine hygiene.

BIBLIOGRAPHY

"The 88 Ventures of Johnson & Johnson," *Forbes*, June 1, 1972; Fucini, Joseph J., and Suzy Fucini, *Entrepreneurs: The Men and Women behind Famous Brand Names and How They Made It*, 1965.

Kaiser, Henry

(May 9, 1882–August 24, 1967)
Engineer

Few people, if anyone, could surpass Henry John Kaiser's role from World War I into the 1960s as a builder of America—dams, bridges, ships, hotels, and cement and aluminum plants all came from his work as engineer, contractor, and business executive.

Born on May 9, 1882, at Sprout Brook, New York, to Francis J. Kaiser, a shoe factory mechanic, and Mary (Yopps) Kaiser, a practical nurse, Henry grew up in humble surroundings. Forced for economic reasons to leave school at age 13, he labored in a dry-goods store.

After discovering an interest in photography, Kaiser hit the road as a salesman of photographic supplies, and then, with a partner, opened a photography shop in Lake Placid, New York. Displaying the success that would characterize his career, he soon opened branches in Florida and in the Bahamas. In 1906, however, he sold his business to move out West, where he believed he could make money that would enable him to marry Bessie Fosburgh, whose wealthy father demanded that Kaiser be able to support his daughter in comfort.

Settling in Spokane, Washington, Kaiser married Bessie in 1907 and, after working for a hardware business, joined a construction company as a salesman in 1912. Two years later, he founded the Henry J. Kaiser Company and began building highways when automobiles created the demand for paved roads.

Kaiser moved his company headquarters to Oakland, California, in 1921 and six years later obtained his biggest contracting job to that time: building 200

Henry Kaiser (Library of Congress)

miles of highway and 500 bridges in Cuba. He later claimed that the Cuba project taught him more about road building than anything else he had done.

In the early 1930s, Kaiser built levees along the Mississippi River, and over the next decade, his firm and its affiliated companies engaged in a string of massive construction projects, helping to build, among others, the San Francisco Golden Gate Bridge, Boulder (later Hoover) Dam on the Colorado River, the Bonneville Dam on the Columbia River, and the Grand Coulee Dam near Spokane.

To provide material for still more projects, Kaiser constructed a cement plant in world-record time—between August and December 1939. Permanente

Cement soon became the largest supplier of building materials in the West.

Perhaps Kaiser achieved his most spectacular feat, however, when he built merchant ships during World War II. He had never seen a shipyard, yet in the early 1940s at sites in California and the Northwest, he completed 60 cargo ships for Britain, and reduced the time for constructing such a vessel from 105 days to 56 by using mass-assembly techniques. During the war, spurred by lucrative defense contracts, Kaiser's company produced one-third of the American merchant ships. Also during the war, he built a steel mill in Fontana, California, the first in the state.

Kaiser encountered one of his few failures when he began making automobiles in 1946. Although his Kaiser-Frazer Corporation had turned out 300,000 cars by 1948, it lost money, and in 1953 he stopped production. (His Willy Motors, however, continued to make the Jeep, then a commercial vehicle.) Meanwhile, with the help of two government-built aluminum plants that he bought, Kaiser created the Kaiser Aluminum & Chemical Corporation, which over the following decade captured a quarter of the nation's primary aluminum production.

Kaiser built houses and hotels, too, notably the Hawaiian Village resort and a resort-residential city on Hawaii's Oahu Island. In 1961, he sold the Hawaiian Village to Hilton Hotels for over $21 million.

Remaining heavily involved in his companies until 1959, when he relinquished many of his responsibilities, Kaiser reshaped America through his construction projects. He died on August 24, 1967, survived by his second wife, Alyce Chester (whom he had married in 1951 after his first wife's death), and two sons. Although Kaiser considered himself a paragon of free enterprise, his success in most instances relied on the federal government, or as one historian observed: "Energy, ability, ambition, those things Kaiser had; but government supplied his capital, furnished his market, and guaranteed his solvency on the cost-plus formula—and so spared him the need for cost efficiency, rewarded speed at any price, and came close to guaranteeing his profits."

BIBLIOGRAPHY

Adams, Stephen B., *Mr. Kaiser Goes to Washington: The Rise of a Government Entrepreneur*, 1997; Foster, Mark S., *Henry J. Kaiser: Builder in the Modern American West*, 1989; Heiner, Albert P., *Henry J. Kaiser, Western Colossus: An Insider's View*, 1991.

Kellogg, Will

(April 7, 1860–October 6, 1951)
Manufacturer

The Kellogg brothers made a picture in contrasts: John Harvey was outgoing and fitful while Will was reserved and orderly. With these personalities, they had a volatile relationship. Together, they accidentally discovered breakfast cereal, but as competitors, they fought a protracted legal struggle over the family name.

Will was born on April 7, 1860, in Battle Creek, Michigan, to Ann Janette (Stanley) Kellogg and John Preston Kellogg, a Seventh-Day Adventist who operated a small grocery store and broom factory. Will received little formal education, and at age 19 went to Texas, where he took a faltering broom factory owned by an Adventist leader and saved it. He then returned to Michigan and began working at the Battle Creek Sanitarium in 1880.

The Battle Creek Sanitarium was run by Will's older brother, John Harvey, who had embraced the vegetarian health principles advocated by the Adventist leader Ellen G. White and edited the Adventist monthly, *Good Health.* After the Adventists appointed John Harvey superintendent of their Western Health Reform Institute in Battle Creek, which stressed providing natural remedies to sickness, he renamed it the Battle Creek Sanitarium, and publicized it as a health refuge dedicated to a largely vegetarian diet, fresh air, sunshine, and exercise.

Will was a quiet man, and his brother paid him just $87 a month and often forced him to do menial chores. Will's contributions to the sanitarium went well beyond such work, however. While his brother flitted from one project to another, Will kept the sanitarium and John's other endeavors running smoothly.

The brothers made their accidental discovery that resulted in breakfast cereal in 1894. They had been experimenting with boiled wheat, pressing it through rollers to make sheets of food, when they mistakenly left some of it atop a baking tin overnight. The next morning, when they passed the wheat through the rollers, it crumbled into flakes. After they fed the wheat flakes to patients at the sanitarium and received demands for more, John founded the Sanitas Food Company to sell the product. With John writing more than 50 books over the next few years and earning a reputation as an accomplished surgeon, the business management fell largely to Will, who grew increasingly frustrated with his brother's failure to protect and promote their food-making process. Despite the Kelloggs' discovery, the cereal industry quickly became dominated by their neighbor CHARLES POST. In fact, 42 brands of wheat flakes soon emanated from Battle Creek.

In 1902, Will perfected corn by using the heart of the corn mixed with added malt to make them soft. He decided that the company would not lose control over this market as it had over the wheat flakes market. In addition, he saw great potential in cereals in general as at this time Americans, in their industrializing phase, had moved to the cities and had the money for quick, ready-made breakfasts and the desire to consume them.

Consequently, Will reached an agreement with John to start his own company and in 1906 began selling corn flakes. Will's genius at advertising produced a resounding success. Within three years, his company was selling 1 million cases of corn flakes annually. This worldly endeavor irritated the Adventists, however, and in 1907 the church expelled both Will and John over religious issues and an alleged failure to maintain their faith.

With Will's business triumph, John decided to sell breakfast flakes under the Kellogg name, too, and this led, throughout the 1910s, to the brothers engaging in acrimonious legal battles over control of the company and the Kellogg name. Will finally won the right to use the name in 1921. He retired from the company presidency in 1939 and from the board of directors in 1946.

Will had a turbulent personal life. His first wife, Ella Davis, whom he had neglected, died in 1912. He married Dr. Carrie Staines, a physician at the sanitarium, in 1918, but their marriage soon ended in divorce. None of his children or grandchildren, who he had hoped would follow him in the company, did so.

In his later years, Will began the W. K. Kellogg Foundation—to which he contributed $47 million—as an organization to help agricultural, educational, and health programs in the United States and foreign countries. Both brothers lived to the age of 91, with John dying on December 14, 1943, and Will on October 6, 1951.

BIBLIOGRAPHY

Powell, Horace B., *The Original Has the Signature—W. K. Kellogg*, 1956; Rowsome, Frank, Jr., *They Laughed When I Sat Down*, 1959.

Kelly, William

(1906–January 3, 1998)
Employment Company Founder

William Russell Kelly changed the American employment scene when he founded a company that supplied businesses with temporary workers.

Kelly, born in 1906 in British Columbia, Canada, came from a wealthy family. His father had struck it rich as an oil prospector, and at one point, Kelly lived with his parents in a hilltop castle in France. Kelly attended the University of Pennsylvania but had to drop out after his father became ill and the family's finances suffered. In the 1920s and 1930s, he worked as a car salesman and, after that, as a staff accountant with the Great Atlantic and Pacific Tea Company.

During World War II, Kelly joined the Army Quartermaster Corps and in that position learned about labor-saving equipment. When the war ended, he moved to Detroit with the idea that he would provide the many businesses growing up around the automobile industry with machines and services they needed in their offices. Consequently, he leased equipment such as calculators and provided workers who took inventory and typed.

Much to his dismay, Kelly discovered that the businesses preferred to buy their own equipment. To his pleasure, however, he found they needed his workers, the "girls" who helped operate the office machines. Quite inadvertently, then, Kelly learned he could make money by providing temporary workers. He soon changed his company's name from Russell Kelly's Office Service to the Kelly Girl Service.

The times provided Kelly with a great opportunity. For one, post–World War II economic expansion meant more businesses needed more bookkeepers, file clerks, stenographers, and typists. For another, many housewives wanted a chance to work outside the home without being tied to a permanent job that would restrict their family activities. Temporary employment seemed to meet this requirement, and employers considered women best suited to the jobs that they needed filled.

Kelly Girl Service flourished, and in 1952 Kelly opened his first office outside of Detroit in Louisville, Kentucky. By the end of the 1950s, the phrase "Kelly Girls" had become widely recognized and even informally applied to temporary office workers who were not a part of Kelly's company.

Kelly operated his business by advertising for women in newspapers and then screening each applicant in order to match the person's talent with prospective openings at various companies. He then placed each woman with a business, charged the business an hourly rate, and paid the employee 75 percent of the rate while keeping 25 percent for himself. In this way, many women obtained jobs they might not otherwise have had. Critics, however, noted that Kelly Girls received no benefits, worked for low wages, and had little opportunity to advance.

Kelly's company expanded in the 1960s and began two new divisions, Kelly Marketing in 1962 and Kelly Labor and Technical in 1964, which provided businesses with a more diverse and more male labor force, including technicians. In 1966, Kelly again changed his company's name to Kelly Service, a move that eliminated any connotations of gender bias.

By this time, Kelly, who had married Margaret Adderley, had stepped down from the daily operation of the company—although he took the post of chairman—and turned it over to his adopted son, Terrence E. Adderley. In 1986, Kelly Service became the first temporary employment company to exceed $1 billion in revenues, and the following year, the firm inaugurated its Encore Program to recruit retired workers for the temporary market. The company had by then more than 525,000 people holding temporary jobs. At his death on January 3, 1998, Kelly's fortune stood at several hundred million dollars.

BIBLIOGRAPHY

Crozier, Michael, *The World of the Office Worker*, 1971.

Kendall, Donald

(March 16, 1921–)
Manufacturer

For years, Pepsi-Cola ranked a distant second in soft-drink sales to Coca-Cola. Then Donald Kendall arrived, an abrasive white-haired executive, who plied the youth market, opened factories overseas, and so ruthlessly reorganized the company that he received the nickname "White Fang." His tactics worked, and soon Pepsi often outsold Coke.

Donald was born on March 16, 1921, in Sequim, Washington, to Carroll Kendall and Charlotte (McIntosh) Kendall, and grew up on his parents' dairy farm near that town. After graduating in 1941 from high school, where he earned honors as a football player, he entered Western Kentucky State College. He left after three semesters to join the navy in 1942, and as a bomber pilot during World War II, he won two Distinguished Flying Crosses and three Air Medals.

Following the war, Kendall obtained a job on Long Island, New York, selling fountain syrup for the moribund Pepsi-Cola Company. The business had been founded in the 1890s when, impressed by the popularity of Coca-Cola, Caleb D. Bradham, a pharmacist in New Bern, North Carolina, concocted a syrup he called Pepsi-Cola. Bradham went broke after World War I, however, and Pepsi-Cola nearly disappeared until the Loft Candy Company marketed it as a 12-ounce drink to contrast with Coke's standard 6-ounce size. In the 1950s, Pepsi's new leader, Alfred Steele, revitalized the drink when he advertised it as the cola for "those who think young."

As Pepsi showed signs of life, Kendall showed he could sell the syrup in quantities far exceeding other salespeople. His success, which he attributed to working long hours and "always wanting to be No. 1," made him branch plant manager for fountain sales in 1949, corporate vice president for national accounts in fountain sales in 1952, and head of Pepsi-Cola International in 1953, thus making him responsible for sales outside the United States and Canada. In this position, he again worked wonders, doubling the number of countries in which Pepsi did business, tripling overseas revenues, and quintupling profits—all within six years. He gained international attention when, at a highly publicized meeting in Russia between Soviet leader Nikita Khruschev and American Vice President Richard Nixon in 1959, he provided Khruschev with Pepsi, who promptly drank nine bottles.

Kendall assumed the presidency of Pepsi-Cola in 1963 and two years later merged the company with Frito-Lay, a snack food business, to create PepsiCo. With the merger, he became chairman of the board and chief executive officer. His personal life changed, too, when he married Sigrid Ruedt von Collenberg in December 1965. The couple subsequently had four children.

In 1967, Kendall began Pepsi Generation advertising, tying the soft drink to baby boomers—"Come Alive! You're in the Pepsi Generation!" the company proclaimed, and "You have a lot to live, and Pepsi has a lot to give!" A few years later, in 1974, he opened a soft-drink factory in the Soviet Union, the first Western consumer product manufactured in that nation and the first international soft drink manufactured there. At the same time, he built a management team that became the envy of other companies for its effectiveness.

PepsiCo launched its Pepsi Challenge in 1975, an advertising campaign that cut deeply into Coke's sales by showing that in blind taste tests consumers usually preferred Pepsi to Coke. One year later, Pepsi supplanted Coke as the single largest soft-drink brand sold in U.S. supermarkets. (Coca-Cola, however, still dominated as a fountain drink.) Pepsi's dynamic growth forced Coke under ROBERTO GOIZUETA to strike back with its own aggressive marketing.

Kendall diversified further in the late 1970s when he acquired Taco Bell and Pizza Hut fast-food restaurants. At that time, PepsiCo had 416 plants in the United States bottling Pepsi, Diet Pepsi, Mountain Dew, Pepsi Light, Teem, Patio, and Aspen. Overseas, 600 plants made Pepsi, with PepsiCo owning 34 of them outright. In addition, Frito-Lay produced more snack foods than any other company, with 38 American manufacturing plants.

A scandal rocked PepsiCo in 1982, however, when an employee revealed that executives in the Philippines and Mexico had kept false books to overstate sales and profits. Problems also arose when Frito-Lay reported slow growth for its snacks, and Wilson Sporting goods, also owned by PepsiCo, suffered from excess inventory. Yet PepsiCo rebounded with Pepsi Free (a caffeine-free cola) and with brisk sales at its restaurants. In 1986, Kendall, then chief executive officer at PepsiCo, saw his company's revenues finally exceed Coke's—$9.3 billion as opposed to $8.7 billion. Kendall retired from PepsiCo that May.

PepsiCo's growth continued, and that same year, the firm bought Kentucky Fried Chicken, the nation's largest quick-service chicken restaurant, and signed pop star Michael Jackson to advertise Pepsi. In 1997, PepsiCo spun off its restaurants as an independent company, sold its food distribution business, and focused on its beverages and snack foods, the core of its success. In 1998, PepsiCo filed suit against Coca-Cola for unfairly pressuring independent food-service distributors to carry Coke over Pepsi. As to Kendall's legacy, the relatively small company he had taken over in the 1950s now had 140,000 employees and sales topping $20 billion.

BIBLIOGRAPHY

Enrico, Roger, *The Other Guy Blinked: And Other Dispatches from the Cola Wars*, 1988; Mack, Walter, *No Time Lost*, 1982; Martin, Milward W., *Twelve Full Ounces*, 1962; Stoddard, Bob, *Pepsi: 100 Years*, 1997.

Kendall, Henry

(January 15, 1878–November 3, 1959)
Manufacturer

Henry Plimpton Kendall was a leading textile manufacturer whose innovative ideas about management styles and labor conditions revolutionized the social conditions of mill workers throughout the South and the Northeast.

Henry, the son of Henry Lucian Kendall (a Congregational minister) and Clara Idella Plimpton Kendall, was born on January 15, 1878, in Charlestown, Massachusetts. After attending the Lawrenceville School in New Jersey, Henry went to Amherst College. After graduating in 1889, he obtained work at his uncle Herbert's company in Norwood, the Plimpton Press.

Kendall was a hard worker, and by 1910 he had become the general manager and treasurer of the firm. Early in his career, Kendall's imagination was fired by the industrial engineering and scientific management principles espoused by Frederick Winslow Taylor. With Kendall's encouragement, Plimpton became one of the first plants to set Taylor's notions in action. Kendall, though inspired by Taylor, enacted modified versions of Taylor's theories. He believed that workers would be more productive and happier when matched with a type of duty that suited their temperament. To this end, Plimpton Press was an early pioneer in establishing a personnel department. Though Kendall promoted the human element in industrial management, he was extremely antiunion, differing from Taylor in this regard.

After several years with Plimpton Press, Kendall began exploring additional business opportunities. In 1903, at the suggestion of another uncle, George Plimpton, Kendall became interested in an unsuccessful manufacturing firm, the Lewis Batting Company, located in Walpole, Massachusetts. As their treasurer, he eliminated many of their product lines and developed a new line to target the hospital supply market. Working with Taylor, Kendall improved the firm's management practices and developed more efficient methods of bleaching cotton to improve the work flow. During the building of the Panama Canal, Kendall secured the army medical contract to supply gauze. In 1912, Kendall purchased the company.

A year later, Kendall became part owner of the Plimpton Press and remained an active participant in its affairs for the next decade. Ever the entrepreneur, he continued to look for new ventures. In 1915, he bought the Saltersville Finishing Company of Rhode Island. A firm believer in improving social conditions and updating physical infrastructure, Kendall dropped the workweek from 60 to 48 hours without a corresponding reduction in pay. He also repaired company houses, built a community church, and constructed recreational facilities for the employees.

Kendall's next purchase came in 1916, when he bought a cotton mill to provide the raw materials for the Walpole plant's gauze production. Additional purchases during this period included the Bauer and Black Company of Chicago and the Bike Web Company of South Bend, Indiana.

During World War I, Kendall was called upon to coordinate hospital supply companies in the United States to supply the needs of the armed forces. Almost all of the participating firms faced potential bankruptcy when, at the end of the war, the Red Cross surplus of bandages was to be distributed to hospitals around the country. Kendall was instrumental in negotiating with the Red Cross to slow the distribution of the surplus in order to allow the firms a place in the bandage market.

In 1925, Kendall consolidated the five mills he owned into Kendall Mills, which would be renamed the Kendall Company three years later. On February 11, 1926, he married Evelyn Louise Way, the daughter of a railroad executive from Montreal, Quebec, Canada. The couple had three children—Henry Way, John Plimpton, and Helen Louise.

Over the next few years, Kendall, determined to improve the conditions at mills in the South, instituted a program of constructing model mill villages across the region. The workweek was curtailed to 50 hours with no loss of pay, and women and children were no longer made to work night shifts. Always absorbed by labor issues, he wrote a treatise in 1926 entitled "Sharing and Stock Ownership for Employees."

Over time, the Kendall Company became a major supplier of textiles developed for industrial and consumer purposes, with products such as Curity diapers and Curad bandages. Kendall's success was largely based on his continued adherence to principles of scientific management in all phases of product development, manufacturing, and sales. The firm ballooned in size from a 75-person outfit to a conglomerate consisting of 13 factories in six states, as well as plants in Canada, Mexico, and Cuba. Another addition to the firm was the purchase of the Brown Company, an unprofitable paper manufacturing business that was nonetheless the largest employer in the state of New Hampshire. With Kendall's vigorous reorganization, the company's management and marketing focus was revolutionized.

During the 1920s, Kendall found time to participate in the affairs of the Cotton Textile Institute, an industrial trade association. He was also a catalyst for textile industry support of labor during the Great Depression. While other manufacturers agreed with Kendall that collaborating to reduce hours in order to keep more people employed would be an appropriate response to the poor economic situation, many of the executives feared that such collusion would expose them to government antitrust claims. Kendall allayed fears of government interference by meeting with President Herbert Hoover to facilitate an agreement between the administration and the cotton manufacturers to shorten the workweek without lowering pay.

Kendall remained active after retiring from direct management of his business concerns, giving lectures, sitting on educational and government boards, and establishing a museum to house his extensive collection of whaling artifacts. Kendall died on November 3, 1959.

BIBLIOGRAPHY

Ingham, John N., ed., *Biographical Dictionary of American Business Leaders*, 1983; Kendall, Henry P., "Discussion of Robert G. Valentine, Scientific Management and Organized Labor," *Bulletin of the Taylor Society*, 1915; Nelson, Daniel, *Managers and Workers*, 1975.

Kennedy, Joseph

(September 6, 1888–November 18, 1969)
Financier

Through a variety of investments and businesses, Joseph Patrick Kennedy amassed money that he later used to help his son John F. Kennedy win election as president of the United States.

Joseph was born on September 6, 1888, in Boston, Massachusetts, to Patrick Joseph Kennedy and Mary (Hickey) Kennedy. His father, a successful tavern keeper and owner of wholesale liquor houses, entered politics, gained prominence as a ward boss, and served in the state legislature. Joseph graduated from Boston Latin School and then attended Harvard. He obtained his B.A. in 1912 and through his father's connections was appointed state bank examiner.

Two years later, Kennedy became president of a small bank, the Columbia Trust Company, founded by his father and several partners—making him at 25 the youngest bank president in the state, and probably in the nation. He married Rose Fitzgerald in October 1914, and they eventually had nine children. Their marriage, however, had to endure his infidelity as, over the years, he had had several lovers, among them the actress Gloria Swanson.

In 1917, Kennedy was elected a trustee of the Massachusetts Electric Company, the most powerful utility corporation in New England. During World War I, he helped manage Bethlehem Steel's shipyards in Quincy, Massachusetts, and formed a friendship with Assistant Secretary of the Navy Franklin D. Roosevelt. After the war, Kennedy managed the Boston branch of Hayden, Stone, an investment banking firm. There he made a fortune through activities that today would be illegal but at that time were widespread, particularly using insider information to gain advantages in buying and selling stock.

Beginning in 1926, Kennedy entered the motion picture business when he bought several small movie theaters in New England and soon after, gained ownership of Film Booking Offices (FBO), a motion picture producer. As chairman of the board at Keith-Albee-Orpheum theaters, he helped arrange a merger of that firm and FBO that created RKO Pictures.

Meanwhile, Kennedy continued to invest wisely and heavily in the stock market. Controversy still exists as to how many of his stocks he unloaded before the Crash of 1929, but he still held shares in 1930, and one historian claims that Kennedy, in order to protect his position and make more money, engaged in "some of the most unsavory trading in the history of American business." In any event, by the time of the Great Depression, he had already made some $10 million.

During the 1930s, Kennedy used his political connections to obtain liquor distributorship franchises as Prohibition neared its end. He even obtained "medical" permits to bring in two huge shipments of Scotch prior to Prohibition's repeal—a move that gave him an advantage over his competition when the liquor market reopened.

At the same time, Kennedy entered politics, contributing heavily to Roosevelt's campaign fund and holding three positions in the government, most notably, ambassador to Britain beginning in 1938. While serving as ambassador, Kennedy made several statements indicating a desire to appease Hitler—Kennedy himself condemned Jews for dominating the American press and believed that the greatest threat to American security came not from Germany but from Russian communism—that led to his return to the United States in 1940. He supported Roosevelt for the presidency that year, but relations between the two had clearly cooled. Kennedy held no important government position after that time, and in the 1950s he supported right-wingers such as Senator Joseph McCarthy.

As Kennedy's second son, John, entered politics, the wealthy patriarch supported him with money and political contacts. Kennedy's conservatism tainted his son and made him suspect among liberals, but John won the presidency in 1960, fulfilling one of his father's greatest ambitions. A few months into his son's presidency, on December 19, 1961, Kennedy suffered a coronary thrombosis that left him an invalid. Friends and family tried, unsuccessfully, to keep from him the news in 1963 that John Kennedy had been assassinated. Kennedy himself died at Hyannisport, Massachusetts, on November 18, 1969.

Joseph Kennedy (John F. Kennedy Library)

BIBLIOGRAPHY

Beschloss, Michael, *Kennedy and Roosevelt*, 1980; Goodwin, Doris Kearns, *The Fitzgeralds and the Kennedys*, 1987; Kessler, Ronald, *The Sins of the Father: Joseph P. Kennedy and the Dynasty He Founded*, 1996; Koskoff, David E., *Joseph P. Kennedy*, 1974; Whalen, Richard J., *The Founding Father*, 1964.

Kerkorian, Kirk

(June 6, 1917–)
Financier

An investor who went from airlines to Hollywood, Kerkor "Kirk" Kerkorian purchased Metro-Goldwyn-Mayer (MGM) studios three different times.

Kirk was born on June 6, 1917, in Fresno, California, to Armenian immigrants Ahron and Lily Kerkorian. His father owned a successful fruit merchant business in the San Joaquin Valley, until a recession in 1921 wiped him out. The elder Kerkorian tried several other businesses over the following years, but none prospered. Kirk, meanwhile, had a troubled childhood. He was expelled from junior high school for fighting and truancy, and sent to a school for delinquents. From there, he entered a high school where he could study automotive repair, but he quit and in the 1930s held many odd jobs—from cleaning auto engines to boxing to working as a bouncer at a bar.

Then, Kerkorian found something that changed his life—airplanes. He obtained his commercial pilot's license in 1940 and worked as a flight instructor and then, at Morton Air Academy in California, as a flight commander. During World War II, he served as a captain in Britain's Royal Air Force Transport Command, for which he was paid $1,000 a month, the most money he had ever seen.

In 1944, Kerkorian opened an instrument-training school for pilots and a few months later bought several DC-3 aircraft, remodeled them, and sold them at a considerable profit. He used that money to buy three more planes and in 1948 founded the Los Angeles Air Service, which operated on an irregular schedule.

In 1960, Kerkorian changed the name of his company to Trans International Airlines (TIA) and flew charters to Hawaii. Two years later, he bought a DC-8 jet and started hauling cargo for the military. Consequently, his company's earnings jumped from $236,000 in 1961 to $1.1 million in 1962.

Kerkorian issued stock in TIA in 1965 and in 1968 sold his shares to the Transamerica Corporation for $85 million of their stock. He turned around and sold that stock in 1969, making over $100 million on the deal.

At the same time, Kerkorian pursued real estate in the burgeoning gambling city, Las Vegas. He bought land along the Las Vegas Strip and purchased the Flamingo Hotel. For $5 million, he sold a plot of land to the interests building Caesar's Hotel. With the money from that sale and from his lucrative deal with Transamerica, he formed the International Leisure Corporation and built the International Hotel—then the world's largest hotel and casino.

Kerkorian obtained a controlling interest in Western Airlines in 1970 and increased its operating revenues while maneuvering to enter Hollywood by buying stock in MGM, a major movie studio founded decades earlier by MARCUS LOEW and LOUIS MAYER. Four years later, Kerkorian controlled a majority of the MGM stock and immediately moved to diversify the company by buying luxury cruise liners and building a resort hotel (the MGM Grand), which opened in Las Vegas in 1973 with more than 2,000 rooms and a huge casino.

Problems with financing used in his acquisitions caused Kerkorian to lose almost $400 million in securities in the early 1970s, but he recovered, in part by selling his International Leisure Corporation to Hilton Hotels. Kerkorian continued to head MGM until 1978, retaining a commanding financial interest in the firm after that date. In 1981, he directed the company's merger with United Artists.

Kerkorian then began a peculiar financial dance. First, he sold MGM/UA to television network mogul Ted Turner for $1.5 billion in 1986. Five months later, he bought it back from Turner, minus television film broadcast rights, for $480 million. He sold it again in 1990 to Pathé for $1.3 billion.

Kerkorian subsequently joined LEE IACOCCA in a controversial attempt to buy the Chrysler Motor Corporation. That effort failed in 1996, but a few months later Kerkorian again bought MGM (beating out Australian millionaire Rupert Murdoch) for $1.3 billion. All the while, he continued his ownership of the MGM Grand. In 1997, *Forbes* magazine placed Kerkorian on its list of the world's 200 richest people, estimating his wealth at $3.8 billion.

BIBLIOGRAPHY

Torgerson, Dial, *Kerkorian: An American Success Story*, 1974.

Kerr, Robert

(September 11, 1896–January 1, 1963)
Oil Industrialist

After briefly pursuing a law career that had been interrupted by World War I, Robert Samuel Kerr found his calling in the oil industry. He began working at an in-law's oil drilling company and soon bought out the firm. His business grew dramatically after making deals with the Phillips Petroleum Company to drill for oil in Oklahoma City. After building his wealth in oil, he turned his attention to politics and served as governor of Oklahoma and as a U.S. senator.

The second of seven children of William Samuel and Margaret Eloda Kerr, Robert was born on September 11, 1896, near Ada, Oklahoma. William was a self-educated man who worked at various times as a farmer, teacher, and merchant. The young Kerr was educated in the public school at Ada and then studied at the East Central Normal School from 1909 to 1911. He attended Oklahoma Baptist University for one year and then returned to East Central for three more years. He worked as a rural teacher for two years and was a student once more at the University of Oklahoma for one year.

Kerr moved to Webb City, Missouri, and began working in the law office of B. Robert Elliott until the United States entered World War I in the spring of 1917. After entering the officers' training camp at Fort Logan H. Roots in Arkansas, Kerr was sent to Europe in August 1918 as a second lieutenant of field artillery. The war ended before he saw active combat duty. He remained in the Officers' Reserve Corps after his return to the United States and joined the Oklahoma National Guard in 1921.

On December 5, 1919, Kerr married Reba Shelton. After her death in February 1924, he married Grayce Breene on December 26, 1925. Their union produced four children, all of whom grew to be over six feet tall like their father. In returning to civilian life, Kerr and two friends opened a wholesale produce business in Ada but lost their money when their warehouse burned down.

Kerr then restarted his law career by working and studying in the office of J. F. McKeel, subsequently passing the state bar exam in 1922. He practiced law in Ada as a partner in the firm of Kerr, Lambert, and Conn. In 1925, Kerr went to work for a brother-in-law who owned a small oil drilling business. Just one year later, he bought out the business with a loan and then borrowed working capital to move the business to Oklahoma City where oil had recently been discovered. Kerr struck it rich after being asked by the Phillips Petroleum Company to persuade Oklahoma City voters to approve drilling projects in the city. As a reward for his efforts, Kerr was employed by Phillips to drill their wells and share the profits. In 1936, he joined a Phillips employee, D. A. McGee, to form Kerr- McGee Oil Industries, Incorporated, and later Kerr's personal wealth increased to about $10 million.

After making his fortune in the oil industry, Kerr enjoyed a lengthy political career. In the spring of 1942, he ran as the Democratic candidate for governor of Oklahoma and won by only 16,000 votes. As governor, he was successful in achieving his stated campaign goals, which included elimination of the state debt, a businesslike administration, and a sound fiscal policy. It was Kerr's record as governor as well as his vigorous support of Franklin D. Roosevelt that led to his selection as keynote speaker at the Democratic National Convention in 1944.

Kerr's name was then mentioned in the press as a possible vice presidential candidate, but he denied any such lofty goals. He did seek a seat representing Oklahoma in the Senate, which he won handily by 170,000 votes in 1948. In the Senate, he generally sided with the administration of President Harry Truman and was a socially minded Democrat, favoring a women's equal rights amendment and the creation of a Department of Welfare. However, his voting record also reflected his campaign pledge to uphold the strict racial segregation laws of Oklahoma. One of the biggest issues in the 1950 congressional session involved Kerr's own "natural gas bill," which would have excluded natural gas producers who did not distribute their own gas from federal rate regulation by the Federal Power Commission. Congress passed the bill by a narrow margin, but it was vetoed by President Truman.

A devout Baptist all his life, Kerr was active in the church and became president of the Oklahoma Baptist General Convention in 1944. He also supported charities such as the YMCA and the Red Cross. For recreation he enjoyed fishing, playing cards, and flying his own airplane. He died on January 1, 1963.

BIBLIOGRAPHY

Morgan, Anne Hodges, *Robert S. Kerr: The Senate Years*, 1977; Moskowitz, Milton, et al., eds., *Everybody's Business*, 1980; Stephenson,

Malvina, *King of the Senate: The Early Life of Robert S. Kerr and Other Insights with His Wit and Humor*, 1995.

Kettering, Charles

(August 29, 1876–November 25, 1958)
Inventor

Perhaps the most prolific inventor since THOMAS EDISON, Charles Kettering used a strange method to convince a doubter that he had built a machine that could paint cars rapidly. While eating lunch with the man, Kettering had accomplices repaint the doubter's car. Then he walked him to the parking lot and watched bemused as the doubter looked around and confessed he could not find his car. Kettering finally pointed to a vehicle and asked: "Isn't that yours?" "It looks like mine," the doubter replied, "but my car isn't that color." Kettering responded: "It is now."

Charles was born on August 29, 1876, in Loudonville, Ohio, to Jacob Kettering and Martha (Hunter) Kettering. After graduating from Loudonville High School, he taught for three years in country schools. In 1898, he entered Ohio State University to study engineering, but eye trouble caused him to drop out. He worked on a telephone construction crew for a while and then reentered Ohio State. Still suffering from myopia and inflamed eyes, he received help when the engineering department waived its drafting requirement and when friends read each day's lesson aloud to him at night. He finally received his engineering degree in 1904.

Kettering then worked for the National Cash Register Company (NCR) in Dayton, Ohio, and the following year married Olive Williams. They subsequently had one son.

NCR, led by JOHN PATTERSON, assigned Kettering to discover a way to electrify the cash register. That accomplished, Kettering earned a reputation for leadership, brilliance, and an ability to understand what consumers wanted. In 1908, while still working at NCR, he and a friend, Ed Deeds, opened a shop in a barn behind Deeds's house where they made inventions for the automobile. In the summer of 1909, Kettering invented a battery-powered electric ignition system that Cadillac adopted.

Deeds and Kettering formed the Dayton Engineering Laboratories Company, better known as Delco. Kettering next invented an electric starter for automobiles, eliminating the cumbersome practice of cranking up a car to get it going. One historian claims that "Kettering's system was probably the most important single step toward making the motorcar practical for everyone."

As car companies ordered the starter, Delco boomed, and Kettering worked full-time for it and for three other businesses he and Deeds had started—one to make generating systems for farm lighting, a second to build aircraft engines for fighter planes, and a third for pure research. In 1916, United Motors bought Delco. Two years later, General Motors (GM) bought United Motors. In 1919, GM hired Kettering to head its new research division, a position he held for 25 years. Kettering first tackled the problem with auto paint. With the prevailing method, it took over a month to paint a car, but he applied a weather-resistant gloss through a high-speed process.

At the same time, Kettering and his team of engineers pursued the problem of engine knock, a sound that indicated problems with compression and that prevented engines from pulling more power. In 1921, a Kettering researcher, Caroll Hochwalt, applied a newly synthesized compound, tetraethyl lead, to the gasoline in a test engine. The lead created a high-octane gasoline that solved the problem of knock and resulted in higher compression.

The Ethyl Gasoline Corporation was formed to produce the additive, and Kettering served as the company's first president. Kettering later claimed that the antiknock discovery saved consumers $5 billion to $8 billion a year through more efficient engines. That assessment, however, ignored the later evidence that lead deposited on the ground and in the air from automobiles caused many illnesses.

Kettering failed at a project in the 1920s to develop an air-cooled engine that would eliminate the need for radiators. GM lost $31 million in the effort, but Kettering achieved another success when his engineers developed a diesel engine that could be used on locomotives. In 1934, a diesel-powered locomotive traveled from Denver to Chicago in about 13 hours, almost half the time it took using a steam engine.

Kettering used his wealth to support many community organizations and projects. He gave money to Antioch College and with his friend ALFRED SLOAN endowed the Sloan-Kettering Institute for Cancer Research. He retired from GM in 1947 and died in Dayton on November 25, 1958. As a sought-after public speaker in his later years, he told an audience:

> I think it was the Brookings Institution that made a study that said the more education you had the less likely you were to become an inventor. The reason why is from the time a kid starts kindergarten to the time he graduates from college he will be examined two or three or four times a year, and if he flunks once, he's out. Now an inventor fails 999 times, and if he succeeds once, he's in. An inventor treats his failures simply as practice shots.

BIBLIOGRAPHY

Bernstein, Mark, "A Self-Starter Who Gave Us the Self-Starter," *Smithsonian*, July 1988; Boyd, Thomas A., *Professional Amateur*, 1957; Boyd, Thomas A., *Prophet of Progress*, 1961; Kettering, Charles, *Short Stories of Science and Invention*, 1945.

Kimberly, John

(July 18, 1836–January 21, 1928)
Manufacturer

Under the direction of John Alfred Kimberly, the paper manufacturing company of Kimberly-Clark became one of the largest of its kind in the world. As a principal supplier of newsprint, as the developer of Kleenex tissues, and as the innovator of a substitute for surgical cotton that became the material for Kotex sanitary napkins, Kimberly created a company that catered to a wide array of consumer needs.

Kimberly was born to John Robbins and Aurelia Aldrich Kimberly on July 18, 1836, in Troy, New York. After Kimberly's early education in Troy, the family moved to Neenah, Wisconsin, in 1847. Kimberly graduated from St. Lawrence College in nearby Appleton and in 1857 joined with his cousin, Havitah Babcock, in taking over their parents' Neenah store, J. and H. Kimberly.

In 1865, Kimberly married Helen Cheney, of Logansport, Indiana, with whom he had seven children. Three years later, Kimberly and his father purchased a flour mill. Though the mill, renamed J. R. Kimberly and Company, maintained a profitable trade with England, Kimberly sold it in 1872 to become involved in the lumber industry. In that year, Kimberly and his cousin Babcock, along with Charles Clark and Frank Shattuck, invested $7,500 each to start a mill for the purpose of making newsprint from linen and cotton rags. The paper mill, which was the first of its kind in Wisconsin, manufactured two tons of the newsprint daily.

Kimberly and Clark, as the company's managers, divided the administration ac-

John Kimberly (UPI/Corbis-Bettmann)

cording to their talents. Clark, who was energetic and a natural leader, oversaw operations at the mill. Kimberly was the financial whiz of the two, and he concentrated on sales and management. By 1880, the business had dramatically expanded operations, and it incorporated, with Kimberly as president, as Kimberly-Clark. The only one of the original partners to remain with the company for a long period, Kimberly held the post of president until his death. Despite the eventual turnover in partnerships, the firm's early precedent for emphasizing teamwork over individual control became a management style that remained consistent over the years.

In addition to newsprint, Kimberly-Clark made stationery and wrapping paper. The company was an innovator, becoming the first mill to produce paper for printing photographs on a rotary press, a technique known as rotogravure. Kimberly-Clark remained the leader in this market for many years.

Research and development during World War I yielded some strange, yet immensely profitable results for the company. Kimberly-Clark researchers, in trying to develop a substitute for the surgical cotton in short supply during the war, came up with a creped cellulose wadding, called "cellucotton." Army nurses discovered that the cotton substitute made perfect disposable sanitary napkins. Though the company was embarrassed enough to feel compelled to house the product under a separate sales unit, International Cellucotton Products, Kimberly-Clark marketed the new product, Kotex, as the first disposable sanitary napkin.

In 1924, another Kimberly-Clark product mainstay got its start by being marketed for a different purpose than its eventual application. Kleenex tissue was intended as a substitute for the towels that were used to remove cosmetics. After consumer testing caused the company to market Kleenex as a disposable handkerchief, sales skyrocketed. Soon Kotex and Kleenex were Kimberly-Clark's most lucrative products. During these years, Kimberly also opened the company's first foreign branch, in Ontario, Canada. By 1925, foreign sales of Kotex and Kleenex had taken off.

Kimberly, a Presbyterian and a Republican, was very civic-minded. He was a longtime member of Neenah's board of education and was pivotal in the establishment of the town's high school.

In addition to his dedication to business, Kimberly founded the First National Bank of Neenah in 1861 and served as either president or chairman of the board for every year until his death. By the time of his death on January 21, 1928, gross sales of Kimberly-Clark exceeded $18 million, and the number of employees totaled 3,000.

BIBLIOGRAPHY

Glaab, Charles N., and Lawrence H. Larsen, *Factories in the Valley*, 1969; Moskowitz, Milton, et al., eds., *Everybody's Business*, 1980.

Klein, Calvin

(November 19, 1942–)
Manufacturer

As a fashion designer, Calvin Klein combined a simple, even puritan, style in clothes with a sensational appeal to sex that made his business rank among the world's leading clothiers and among the most prominent influences on popular culture.

Calvin was born on November 19, 1942, in the Bronx, New York, to Leo Klein and Flore (Stern) Klein. As a boy, Klein displayed a talent for judging clothes when he accompanied his mother on shopping trips and selected outfits for her to wear. Rather than play sports, he liked to sew and sketch clothes. After graduating from high school, he remained in New York City and attended the Fashion Institute of Technology, from which he earned a degree in 1962. He then worked as an apprentice designer in the garment district. At that time, a childhood friend, Barry Schwartz, inherited his family's grocery store and offered to take Calvin in as a partner. Calvin responded by suggesting they form a fashion business, and Schwartz agreed. Calvin invested $2,000, and Schwartz contributed $10,000 to found Calvin Klein Limited.

Klein first earned notice in the late 1960s when he designed a women's trench coat. After 1972, he emphasized women's sportswear and gained a following with his belief that form should follow function, and that, unlike European designers, fashion should stress simplicity and clean lines. "I've always believed in simplicity," Klein once said. "I've never been one to see women in ruffles and all kinds of fanciful apparel. To me it's just silly."

Klein stripped away excess to the point that observers called him the "puritan of design" and "Calvin Clean." Although Klein won election in 1975 to the American Hall of Fame of Fashion, he never won awards in Europe, where clothiers considered him more a marketer than a designer. Nevertheless, his clothes gained a mass following beyond the United States and especially changed the way young people overseas dressed.

Klein expanded his appeal in 1978 when he took jeans, a standard product largely undifferentiated among manufacturers, made them more stylish, and sold them for $50 a pair. Although Klein had earned a reputation for "puritan styling," he launched a series of provocative advertisements that were far from puritan in tone and that appealed directly to sexual longing among young people. In one notorious advertisement, actress Brooke Shields appeared in a provocative pose on TV and asked, "What comes between me and my Calvins? Nothing."

Klein grew wealthier and moved easily throughout the flashy celebrity scene. For years, he partied at Studio 54 and other nightclubs. He indulged in drugs and alcohol and eventually had to enter a rehabilitation center to break an addiction to Valium and vodka.

After resolving his drug and alcohol problem, Klein faced another one in the early 1990s when his company neared financial collapse. He and Schwartz had, a few years earlier, bought Puritan Fashions (the business that manufactured jeans for them), but a sharp decline in the market made what had appeared to be a good investment turn out to be a bad one. Salvation came in the form of David Geffen, a record company millionaire, who saved Klein when he invested in the clothier's company.

As Klein's business affairs began to improve, a controversy broke out in the mid-1990s when he ran advertisements on TV and in newspapers and magazines that presented models who looked no older than their mid-teens in scenes that showed more skin than they did clothes and suggested sexual licentiousness. Many parents complained that Klein was exploiting children, although young people thought differently. Said one teenager about a Klein model: "I think she looks cute there. All my friends wear pants down past their underwear."

The controversy may have helped Klein more than hurt him. His revenue climbed upward, and in 1994 he introduced CK perfume, which grossed $60 million in its first three months on the market, followed the next year by a 20,000-square-foot CK store on Madison Avenue, and entry into housewares with such items as tablecloths, bedsheets, and pillows. After divorcing his second wife in 1996, Klein continued to live luxuriously on a $6 million summer estate at Long Island's East Hampton.

BIBLIOGRAPHY

Gaines, Steven S., *Obsession: The Lives and Times of Calvin Klein*, 1994; Walz, Barbara, and Bernardine Morris, *Fashion Makers*, 1978.

Kluge, John

(September 21, 1914–)
Financier

Restaurants, telephones, radio and TV stations, movie studios, the Harlem Globetrotters—these and many more attracted the investments of John Kluge and resulted in his ranking among the richest people in America by the early 1990s.

John was born on September 21, 1914, in Chemnitz, Germany, to Fritz Kluge, an engineer, and Gertrude (Donj) Kluge. In 1922, after his father had died, John and his mother immigrated to the United States and settled in Detroit, Michigan, then a booming city tied to the automobile industry. There he worked on the assembly line at the Ford Motor Company before obtaining a scholarship to Columbia University in New York City.

Five years after graduating from Columbia in 1937 with a degree in economics, Kluge entered the U.S. Army and served in an intelligence unit during World War II. Discharged in 1945, he began working as a food broker and from 1947 to 1955 served as president of New England Fritos in Boston. In 1956, he and

David Finkelstein formed Kluge, Finkelstein & Company, a wholesale food business located in Baltimore.

At the same time, Kluge showed his amazing ability to engage in diverse enterprises when he acquired a radio station in Silver Spring, Maryland, for $15,000. In 1959, he deepened his involvement in broadcasting when he bought a controlling interest in the Metropolitan Broadcasting Corporation that owned television stations WNEW in New York and WTTG in Washington, D.C., and radio station WHK in Cleveland, Ohio. Within months, Kluge added stations in Los Angeles and Sacramento, California; Boston, Massachusetts; and Kansas City, Missouri. He renamed the operation Metromedia, Incorporated.

With Metromedia, Kluge took unprofitable stations and turned them around by revising their programming. At WTTG, for example, he used television reruns from the 1950s to attract viewers.

Kluge diversified further while developing Metromedia when he bought the General Outdoor Advertising Company and several other firms. By 1964, Metromedia had become the nation's largest outdoor advertising company with 35,000 billboards.

Metromedia's profits exceeded $9 million in 1968 and continued to grow in the 1970s. Kluge then stunned the business world when in 1984, he borrowed $1.2 billion to buy Metromedia outright and convert it into a private company. Many financial analysts called him foolish and said he would never be able to meet his loan obligations. However, Kluge began selling Metromedia's holdings—7 television stations, 11 radio stations, the outdoor advertising firm, the Harlem Globetrotters, the Ice Capades, and a cellular

John Kluge (Frank Capri/Saga/Archive Photos)

telephone business that he had bought. By 1988, he had acquired $2.5 billion in cash.

Kluge then founded Metromedia Technologies, a company that painted billboards with computer-generated designs. In 1988, he bought the Ponderosa steak house chain and followed that with several other restaurant acquisitions: Bonanza steak houses, Steak & Ale, and Benigan's. Yet this highly competitive business proved more difficult for Kluge, and he earned nowhere near the returns he expected.

In 1989, Kluge merged Metromedia Long Distance, a company he had formed three years earlier, with the long-distance divisions of the International Telephone and Telegraph Corporation to create Metromedia-ITT Long Distance, later renamed WorldCom.

In a struggle with investor SUMNER REDSTONE, Kluge bought a 70 percent interest in Orion Pictures and then struggled to make the faltering studio a profitable one. In the early 1990s, he founded International Telcell to establish wireless cable TV stations in Eastern Europe. Again, some financial analysts questioned Kluge, claiming that the region lacked money to support such a business. "There may be obstacle courses," Kluge responded, "but you've got to believe these countries eventually will succeed, and that's why we're there."

Back in the United States, Kluge bought the Empire, a deteriorating 30-room New York City hotel, for about $64 million. He borrowed another $64 million and added $25 million of his own to renovate it. After that, the Empire began running at nearly 80 percent occupancy, well above the industry average of 60 percent.

In 1991, *Forbes* magazine estimated Kluge's net worth at nearly $6 billion and declared him the nation's wealthiest person. He used this money in part to expand his investments in Eastern Europe by purchasing radio stations there.

Kluge sold WorldCom for $1.2 billion in 1993, and in 1996 *Forbes* declared his net worth to be over $7 billion. Kluge, married three times and last divorced in 1990, lives on a 10,000-acre Virginia estate with a vintage carriage museum and working farm. Over the years, he has given $110 million to Columbia for minority scholarships, declaring, "It is incumbent on those who have benefited from a private education to see that others get the chance."

BIBLIOGRAPHY

Coleman, Lisa, "What's Up John?," *Forbes*, November 25, 1991; Marsh, Ann, "Over $7,000,000,000," *Forbes*, October 14, 1996; Michaels, James W., "Billionaire on a Shoestring," *Forbes*, February 26, 1996.

Knapp, Joseph F.

(July 1, 1832–September 14, 1891)
Printer, Insurance Company Executive

Joseph Frederick Knapp was a well-rounded businessman who succeeded in such diverse enterprises as lithography and the insurance trade. Under his management, the lithographic firm of Major & Knapp became one of the most prestigious in the industry in its time. Knapp's dedication to innovative techniques as the director of the Metropolitan Life Insurance Company enabled the firm to surpass the industry leaders, Prudential and John Hancock.

Joseph, the son of William and Antoinette Chichester Knapp, was born in New York City on July 1, 1832. After receiving an education at a boarding school in North Adams, Massachusetts, Knapp entered the business world with a job at the lithographic firm Saroney & Major. Knapp was a quick study and was promoted frequently. By 1854, he had become a partner in the firm.

During these early years with Saroney & Major, Knapp was married to Phoebe Palmer of New York City, with whom he had a son and a daughter. In 1864, the year his son, JOSEPH P. KNAPP, was born, Saroney & Major became Major & Knapp. Knapp's responsibility grew, and under his eventual direction as the sole owner, the company expanded to become one of the most successful lithographic companies in the nation.

With his company doing strong business, Knapp became interested in the insurance trade. In 1868, he became a director of the Metropolitan Life Insurance Company, becoming the firm's president in 1871. Though the early years of his leadership were financially turbulent, his guidance eventually enabled the company to achieve financial stability. After two years under his direction, the company had doubled the number of policies in force, becoming the third largest seller of life insurance policies nationwide. During the 1870s, however, the firm was hit hard by an economic depression.

In search of a means to break the stagnation, Knapp traveled to England to study that country's insurance industry. Termed industrial insurance, the companies involved issued low-cost policies but had agents collect premiums on a weekly basis by calling at the home of the policyholder. Encouraged by the success of this system, Knapp hired experienced English agents, and in 1879 Metropolitan Life began issuing industrial life policies in the United States. The plan was immediately successful, and before long the company had surpassed Prudential and John Hancock, major competitors and former industry leaders.

By this time, Knapp's son Joseph had entered Columbia University. Joseph was unhappy at Columbia, and his father became increasingly frustrated with his poor academic performance. In 1881, Joseph dropped out and was apprenticed at his father's company at the low salary of $5 per week. Knapp was impressed with Joseph's ambition and hard work. Shortly after Joseph began earning important contracts with companies like the American Tobacco Company, his father changed the company name to Knapp & Company. He also allowed his son to accept stock in lieu of commission, enabling Joseph to work his way toward ownership of the company.

Joseph's aggressive sales techniques and savvy understanding of printing and publishing techniques encouraged Knapp to delegate more duties to his son. By 1891, Knapp had sold his interest in the company to Joseph. Later that same year, on September 14, Joseph Frederick Knapp died.

BIBLIOGRAPHY

An Epoch in Life Insurance: Twenty-five Years of Administration of the Metropolitan Life Insurance Company, 1917; Ingham, John N., ed., *Biographical Dictionary of American Business Leaders*, 1983; Marquis, James, *Metropolitan Life*, 1947.

Knapp, Joseph P.

(May 14, 1864–January 30, 1951)
Publisher

In addition to his success in building a large publishing empire, Joseph Palmer Knapp developed a revolutionary multicolor printing press. Knapp was an extremely successful businessman whose holdings included the well-known Collier publications.

Knapp, the son of JOSEPH F. KNAPP and Phoebe Palmer Knapp, was born in Brooklyn, New York, on May 14, 1864. His father was the president of the Metropolitan Life Insurance Company from 1871 to 1891, in addition to being a partner in the lithographic company of Major & Knapp.

After a stint at the Brooklyn Polytechnic Institute and a year at Columbia University, Knapp went to work with his father's printing company in 1881. By this time, Major & Knapp had grown and been reorganized under the new name Knapp & Company.

Knapp's father, unhappy with his son's academic performance, apprenticed him to the company at the low salary of $5 per week. After learning the fundamentals of the printing business, Knapp began to demonstrate his managerial skills. He pursued new business contacts while on his lunch break, and after work rapidly built a good base of high-profile clients like JAMES BUCHANAN DUKE of the American Tobacco Company.

In 1886, Knapp married Sylvia Kepner, with whom he had two children before they divorced in 1903. He married again to Elizabeth Laing McIlwaine, but the date of their marriage remains obscure. They were married until her death, which was sometime before 1923, but the exact date is unknown.

Knapp continued to excel at increasing the company's sales, and, in 1891, after years of accepting stock in lieu of commission, he bought out his father's interest in the firm. Deciding to move the business toward publishing, Knapp joined forces with Duke to put out a daily newspaper, the *New York Recorder*, which was published from 1891 to 1896.

During this time, Knapp also expanded the company's printing facilities, buying out a number of other businesses and creating the American Lithographic Company in 1895. It was during this phase that Knapp invented a multicolor press, which operated by means of six cylinders of different color inks that created distinct color impressions.

In 1903, Knapp used the new press to establish the *Associated Sunday Magazine*, which became the first syndicated insert for Sunday newspapers. The magazine was very successful, reaching a circulation of over 1.5 million despite an increase in the price for newspapers when World War I caused a rise in the cost of paper.

In 1906, Knapp took over the Crowell Publishing Company. He and his associates in the purchase—THOMAS LAMONT and Samuel Untermyer—acquired all publications of the company, including *Farm and Fireside* and *Woman's Home Companion*. Later, Crowell bought the company of P. F. Collier and Son, a purchase that brought *Collier's Weekly* and a book subscription business into the Knapp fold.

In 1923, Knapp wed a third time, to Margaret E. Rutledge. He continued to expand his company with his new Sunday syndicated magazine, *This Week*, succeeding so well that by the time of his death in 1951, circulation had reached 6 million. Knapp set up a holding company called Publication Corporation to manage the magazine and other projects. This corporation also managed the Crowell-Collier Publishing Company. With all of his holdings, Knapp dominated a publishing empire.

Knapp's magazines focused on success and opportunities in a free-market economy. He did not encourage political or issue-oriented journalism. Despite his firm belief in the free enterprise system, he felt personally obligated to use his wealth to support philanthropic causes. He established the Knapp Foundation of New York and North Carolina to fund education and ecology causes. Knapp died on January 30, 1951.

BIBLIOGRAPHY

Dictionary of American Biography, 1977; Mott, Frank Luther, *A History of American Magazines, 1885–1905*, 1957; *National Cyclopedia of Biography*, vol. 39, 1954; *New York Times*, Obituary, January 31, 1951; Peterson, Theodore, *Newspapers in the Twentieth Century*, 1956.

Knight, Jack

(October 26, 1894–June 16, 1981)
Publisher

Shortly after John S. "Jack" Knight bought the *Miami Herald* in 1937, he toured the newspaper's aging plant and discovered a coop filled with pigeons and emitting a powerful stink.

> "What are these for?" he asked the business manager.
> "To carry news from reporters, in case conventional methods are unavailable," came the reply.
> "Well," said Knight, "I don't believe we'll require pigeons for our news coverage operations."

Knight envisioned a modern newspaper built not with gimmicks but with sound reporting. With that, he laid the foundation for today's giant Knight-Ridder communications company.

Jack was born on October 26, 1894, in Bluefield, West Virginia, to Charles Landon Knight and Irene (Sheifly) Knight. Six years later, the family moved to Akron, Ohio, when Charles Knight accepted a position as advertising manager of the *Beacon-Journal*. The elder Knight rose quickly and in 1915 gained full control of the newspaper while earning a reputation for writing blunt editorials.

As a boy, Jack worked in the newspaper office during the summers, and in 1914 he entered Cornell University. Before he could complete his college education, however, the United States entered World War I, and in 1917 he joined the army. By war's end, he was in the Army Air Corps training to be a gunner.

After returning home, Knight hesitated about rejoining the newspaper. He doubted he had the talent for journalism and feared that should he sign on, his father would give him special treatment. Finally, in 1920, he accepted his father's offer to work for the paper, but only on condition that he be evaluated like any other employee.

Knight had a talent for writing—his commentaries would win the Pulitzer Prize in 1968—and management. In the early 1920s, he worked for two other Knight newspapers, the *Springfield Sun* and the *Massillon Independent*. In 1925, Charles Knight named him managing editor of the *Beacon-Journal*. After the elder Knight died in 1933, Knight inherited the family newspapers and amid the Great Depression worked hard to improve the *Beacon-Journal*, adding feature stories and providing more news than his competitor did. These changes and others made the *Beacon-Journal* Akron's leading newspaper.

Knight extended his newspaper holdings in 1937, when he bought the *Miami Herald* for $2.25 million. His younger brother, Jim, moved to Miami to take charge of the *Herald*. Over the years, Jim directed its emergence as an award-winning newspaper and handled the fiscal matters for which Knight had little interest.

Soon after acquiring the *Herald*, Knight bought a competitor, the *Miami Tribune*, and closed it so there would be only one other competing newspaper in the city, the *Miami News*. In 1938, he eliminated his competition in Akron by buying the *Times Press*. He made a major acquisition in 1940 when he bought the prestigious *Detroit Free Press* and continued his expansion by purchasing a controlling interest in the *Chicago Daily News* in 1944 (which he sold in 1959).

Knight allowed each newspaper to pursue an independent editorial policy, and he emphasized extensive local news so that each would remain distinct. He bought many other newspapers over the years, and in 1969, after he purchased the *Philadelphia Inquirer* and the *Philadelphia Daily News*, he merged his company with Ridder Publications to create a firm that was truly national in scope.

Knight retired in 1976, and by the time of his death on June 16, 1981, Knight-Ridder owned 32 newspapers in 17 states, becoming the nation's largest newspaper chain in terms of weekly circulation. Today, along with newspapers, Knight-Ridder owns a business information service and a computer network service.

BIBLIOGRAPHY

Smiley, Nixon, *Knights of the Fourth Estate: The Story of the* Miami Herald, 1974.

Knight, Philip

(February 24, 1938–)
Manufacturer

Using endorsements and advertising involving superstar athletes, Philip Hampson Knight took the athletic shoe company he founded, Nike, from the brink of collapse in the mid-1980s to the height of popularity—to the point that 77 percent of American boys in 1993 said that they wanted to wear Nikes.

Philip was born on February 24, 1938, in Portland, Oregon, to William W. Knight, a lawyer and magazine publisher, and Lota (Hatfield) Knight. He attended the University of Oregon and ran as a miler on the school's track team under championship coach Bob Bowerman. After graduating in 1959, Philip entered the graduate program at Stanford University, receiving his M.B.A. in 1963. He then obtained a job at an accounting firm, Coopers and Lybrand.

While employed as an accountant, Knight decided to pursue an idea he had developed for his graduate thesis—that America would soon enter a health-conscious era that held prospects for business. Consequently, he founded Blue Ribbon Sports and imported Tiger running shoes, manufactured by the Onitsuka Company, which was located in Japan. He sent two sample pairs to Bowerman for a reaction and was surprised when the coach wrote him back and intimated they should go into business together. After Knight met with Bowerman, the two men put up $500 each and made Blue Ribbon a partnership. Knight placed his first order in February 1964—$1,107 worth of Tiger shoes.

At this time, Addidas dominated the athletic shoe market and showed little concern with Blue Ribbon. Knight, however, set his sights on Addidas, confident that by using low-cost Asian manufacturing and by providing a better shoe he could unseat the leader. He concentrated on selling shoes to athletic teams, and his company grew steadily. In 1972, however, Onitsuka demanded a majority interest in Blue Ribbon, prompting Knight to make a momentous decision to find another supplier and market his own brand.

As he sought a new supplier, Knight and his colleagues, along with Carol Davidson, an art student, sat around a table discussing logos that Davidson had drawn, including one that looked like a check mark. Criticisms included: "I don't like it. It looks like an upside down Puma stripe." "Looks like the logo from a Chrysler campaign a few years back." Knight, however, offered his halfhearted endorsement: "I don't love it. But I think it will grow on me." For reasons still unclear, they soon started calling the logo "Swoosh."

Knight still needed a name for his company, and Jeff Johnson provided it. Johnson, first employed by Knight as a salesman, had a dream in which the word Nike, the winged goddess of victory from Greek mythology, came to him. Knight accepted Johnson's suggestion, although, as with the logo, halfheartedly and intending to eventually change it.

Later that year, Knight received a boost when at the trials for the 1972 Olympics, four of the top seven finishers in the marathon wore Nikes. Then, in 1975, Bowerman developed a revolutionary waffle sole design after he made a mold from liquid urethane on his wife's waffle iron.

The springy sole turned out to be ideal for the many casual runners involved in that decade's jogging boom, and Nike experienced incredible growth from sales of $2 million in 1972 to $200 million in 1979 and $1 billion in 1984. By that time, it had become the number-one athletic shoe company in the nation and had 8,000 retail accounts, 140 shoe models, 130 sales representatives, and 2,700 employees. The company had also begun selling athletic wearing apparel.

Knight, who had imported some of his early shoes from Mexico, expanded his contacts with Far East manufacturers, a move that allowed him to keep production costs lower than if he had established his own plants, although he also began making some shoes in the United States. In terms of promotion, he used endorsements from athletes (with tennis star Ilie Nastase among the first), gave money to track clubs, and paid runners to wear Nike shoes.

Despite all this expansion, Nike suffered a massive setback in the mid-1980s when Knight underestimated the aerobics craze. He failed to realize that women who participated in aerobics would want a shoe made expressly for the activity, but a competing company, Reebok, did and made a shoe geared to comfort. Dealers, annoyed with Nike by what they considered the firm's arrogant attitude, flocked to Reebok, and Nike struggled to make a profit.

Knight, however, rebounded with Air Jordan, a basketball shoe sponsored by the sport's new star, Michael Jordan. Jordan promoted the shoe assiduously, even wearing it on the court after its red-and-white design had been declared illegal by the National Basketball Association. (The controversy surrounding it only helped to get it more publicity.) Near the same time, Knight introduced AirMax, a running shoe. With these innovations and an advertising budget that grew from under $20 million to over $150 million, Nike took off. From the late 1980s to the early 1990s, its annual sales went from $1 billion to nearly $4 billion. Knight, chairman of Nike, emerged as one of the 200 richest people in the world.

In the process, Knight made sure Nike led in getting superstar endorsements, as when it paid tennis player Jim Courier $27 million. Due to Nike's efforts, endorsements ruled athletics, which became blatantly apparent when at the 1992 Summer Olympics in Barcelona, Spain, Michael Jordan refused to wear the USA team uniform on the victory platform because it bore the Reebok logo.

BIBLIOGRAPHY

Katz, Donald, *Just Do It: The Nike Spirit in the Corporate World*, 1994; Strasser, J. B., and Laurie Becklund, *Swoosh: The Unauthorized Story of Nike and the Men Who Played There*, 1991.

Knox, Rose

(November 18, 1857–September 28, 1950)
Manufacturer

About cooking for her husband and writing a booklet, Rose Markward Knox said: "I spent all that first summer writing out my favorite gelatin recipes for him. I thought I had a tremendous number of them, but when the book came out it was so tiny I almost shed tears. I still remember that awful moment." Yet her *Dainty Desserts for Dainty People* sold widely and spurred sales of the gelatin that she and her husband made a household item.

Rose Knox was born on November 18, 1857, to David Markward, a druggist, and Amanda (Foreman) Markward in Mansfield, Ohio. In her early twenties, she moved with her parents to Gloversville, New York, and worked sewing gloves. She met Charles Briggs Knox, a glove salesman, and in February 1853 they married. They lived in New York City and Newark, New Jersey, and eventually had three children, one of whom died in infancy.

In 1890, Rose and her husband decided to invest their savings in a gelatin business in Johnstown, New York. They established their company in a four-story wooden building near the foot of Montgomery Street, close to the railroad tracks. Johnstown was an ideal location for their business because its tanneries provided the animal skin, bones, and sinew from which the Knoxes extracted gelatinous protein.

At that time, most people considered gelatin a delicacy, for the difficulty in making it made it rare. The Knoxes determined to change that by making gelatin readily available and by popularizing it through promotional stories, advertising (including the Knox Gelatin blimp that visited several cities), and recipes. Rose's *Dainty Desserts for Dainty People* appeared in 1896 and was soon read by hundreds of thousands of people.

By 1908, the Knoxes had made their company the largest maker of unflavored gelatin in the world, while Charles operated several other businesses: a newspaper, a hardware store, and a power company. Soon after he died in 1908, Rose sold these interests to focus on making gelatin. She built a new factory, completed in 1911, and established a research kitchen to find additional ways to use her product. Progressive in her labor policies, she gave her workers a five-day workweek and two weeks' paid vacation. She made it known, however, that in the company her word ruled.

Rose rejected her husband's flamboyant advertising and instead developed promotions that emphasized nutrition and recipes that appealed to women. Her book *Food Economy* (published in 1917) and her newspaper columns (headed "Mrs. Knox says") taught women how to use gelatin.

To meet an increasing demand, during World War I, Rose began acquiring gelatin from Kind & Landesmann, a company in Camden, New Jersey. In 1916, she bought a 50 percent interest in the firm, and in 1930 she became vice president of the Kind & Knox Gelatin Company. At about the same time, she won election as a director of the American Grocery Manufacturers' Association, the first woman to serve in that position. In 1936, she built a new plant in Camden, at which she soon made all her gelatin, and converted the Johnstown plant into a packing and distribution center. More than half the gelatin she sold was as food, while the rest went to industry for use primarily in photography. During the 1930s, she began making artificially flavored gelatin for households.

By 1947, Rose suffered so severely from arthritis that she relinquished the company presidency to her son, James. She continued to serve as chairman of the board, however, and in that position still ran the business, giving James little real authority. She died on September 28, 1950, in Johnstown, remembered as the "first lady" of that city. Never a feminist reformer, she nonetheless urged women to stand tall in a man's world. "Every woman, if forced to, can do more than she ever thought she could," she said. "In running my business I just used common sense; a man would call it 'horse sense.'"

BIBLIOGRAPHY

Asbury, Edith, "Grand Old Lady of Johnstown," *Collier's*, January 1, 1949.

Knudsen, William

(March 25, 1879–April 27, 1948)
Manufacturer

Rising from obscurity as an immigrant shipyard worker to become the president of General Motors, William Signius Knudsen personified the American Dream. While working at an automobile parts plant, Knudsen's talents were recognized by the plant's biggest customer, HENRY FORD, who hired him to manage 14 of his assembly plants. By 1921, Ford and Knudsen had strong disagreements on production issues, and Knudsen was lured to General Motors, where he achieved great success in improving sales to surpass Ford's. During World War II, Knudsen served on two commissions distributing wartime production contracts and then returned to General Motors and served on its board of directors until his death.

On March 25, 1879, William was born in Copenhagen, Denmark, as Signius Wilhelm Poul Knudsen, the first and only son of six children born to Augusta and Knud Peter Knudsen, a customs inspector. The family also included three sons and a daughter by a previous marriage. The young Knudsen was raised with values of frugality and self-reliance, and he began working after school at age six to supplement the family income. He earned honors in mathematics in high school and became interested in mechanical design, accepting an apprenticeship in a bicycle shop for two years while attending night classes at a government technical school in Copenhagen. In 1898, he joined an import firm that dealt with bicycles and then immigrated to the United States in 1899.

After arriving in New York City, Knudsen worked in a shipyard and changed his name to William Knudsen, although

William Knudsen (Library of Congress)

this did not become official until he was granted citizenship in 1914. He returned to the bicycle business in 1902 by joining the John R. Keims Mills, which specialized in bicycle parts, and he rose to become assistant superintendent of the factory in a few years. After the initial popularity of the bicycle faded, the plant converted to the manufacture of automobile parts. Henry Ford took over the Keims plant in 1911, and recognizing Knudsen's industriousness and talent, hired him to oversee the layout and installation of manufacturing operations at 14 new or expanding Ford factories in 1913. Knudsen married Clara Elizabeth Euler on November 1, 1911, and the couple had four children.

As a master mechanic, Knudsen felt completely at home on the shop floor, and at the Ford Motor Company he also mastered the art of mass production. His gift for refining and applying complex mechanical techniques on a broad scale made him one of the principal figures in the expansion of American industry in the first half of the twentieth century.

During World War I, Knudsen's improvements to mass-production proved invaluable to the U.S. war effort. Ford received numerous military contracts and put Knudsen in charge of projects to build aircraft motors, ambulances, and submarine patrol vessels. After the war, Knudsen inspected and reorganized Ford's European operations, but after returning to the United States in 1920, his ideas and orders were increasingly vetoed by Henry Ford. Before Knudsen could resign in 1921, Ford fired him.

Knudsen joined General Motors one year later, after briefly working for a Detroit auto parts firm. After just three weeks at General Motors, he was named vice president of the Chevrolet division, which was struggling to produce lower-priced cars to compete directly with Ford's Model T. Knudsen quickly increased Chevrolet's sales more than 10-fold in his first five years by networking dealers, surveying consumers, and making mechanical and styling improvements to the vehicles.

In January 1924, Knudsen was made president and general manager of Chevrolet, as well as a vice president and director of General Motors. In that year, he set out to overtake Ford's sales by redesigning the Chevrolet automobiles and production lines to allow for fast retooling to adjust to market conditions. Chevrolet surpassed Ford in sales in 1927 and would remain the leader for the rest of Knudsen's career. Chevrolet was hit hard by the Great Depression but still continued to make a profit every year in the decade from 1927 to 1937. In the latter year, Knudsen ascended to become president of General Motors and was one of the 10 highest-paid men in the country.

With the advent of World War II, Knudsen was called upon to serve on various special committees to oversee the nation's military production needs. President Franklin Roosevelt appointed Knudsen to the National Defense Advisory Commission as a production specialist, and Knudsen accepted the position. He resigned from all his posts at General Motors in September 1940 to devote his full attention to his new role. As commissioner of industrial production, Knudsen held the key responsibility of awarding military production contracts for aircraft, transports, and other heavy machinery. Knudsen favored using existing industrial resources rather than expanding factories, an attitude that made many of his decisions controversial among liberals within the government and labor unions alike.

In January 1941, Roosevelt created the Office of Production Management with Knudsen as director general, and the new office assumed responsibility for industrial mobilization. In April 1941, Knudsen arranged for a 20 percent reduction in automobile manufacturing to allow for new military production capacity, but this was regarded as grossly inadequate by the Roosevelt administration, and Knudsen's reputation among policymakers declined. Following the attack on Pearl Harbor in December 1941, the War Production Board was established in January 1942 and overtook all military supply duties. Knudsen pondered returning to General Motors in Detroit. Instead, he accepted a commission as a lieutenant general in the army and was placed in charge of purchasing and maintaining all of the aircraft used by the Army Air Forces.

Knudsen retired from the military in May 1945 and returned to General Motors after being elected to the board of directors. He served in this position until his death from a brain hemorrhage at his Detroit home on April 27, 1948.

BIBLIOGRAPHY

Beaseley, Norman, *Knudsen: A Biography*, 1947; Borth, Christy, *Masters of Mass Production*, 1945; Kennedy, E. D., *The Automobile Industry*, 1941; Wilkins, Mira, and Frank Ernest Hill, *American Business Abroad: Ford on Six Continents*, 1964.

Kohler, Walter

(March 3, 1875–April 21, 1940)
Manufacturer

While transforming his father's plumbing business into a manufacturing empire, Walter Jodok Kohler built one of the most livable industrial cities of his era. Like many other capitalists of the time, Kohler was a staunchly conservative Republican, whose brief political career culminated in a term as governor of Wisconsin.

Kohler, the third of six children, was born to John Michael and Lillie Kohler on March 3, 1875, in Sheboygan, Wisconsin. In 1873, his father, an Austrian immigrant, began a foundry and shop for the production of farm machinery. Over time, the product line was expanded to add enameled ware and plumbing fixtures.

After completing his education in the Sheboygan public school system at the age of 15, the young Kohler joined his father's foundry. He was promoted to foreman three years later and by age 25 had become the superintendent of the plant. On November 30, 1900, Kohler married Charlotte H. Shroeder, a union that produced four sons.

Kohler and his two brothers, Robert and Carl, took over the management of the business when their father died in

1900. Robert was the company's president until his untimely death in 1905. Kohler then succeeded him and remained president until 1937.

Ambitious research and product development were initiated under Kohler's management. The factory was expanded, and progressive policies were instituted to deal with labor issues. Kohler's practices regarding wages and work hours, as well as insurance, safety, and recreation, were quite advanced. By 1912, the company had grown so large that Kohler made grand and somewhat paternalistic designs to create the Kohler Village, a planned industrial community, for his employees. On the outskirts of Sheboygan, the village was engineered to include zones for the business as well as houses, churches, parks, and schools. Unlike other company towns, the employees were able to buy their homes rather than just rent them. The village also defied the stereotypical monotony of other industrial towns by varying the architecture and including landscaping.

Kohler received the first National Service Fellowship Medal from the Society of Arts and Sciences in 1934 for his development of the Kohler Village. But that same year his workmen unionized under the American Federation of Labor, and when he refused to bargain with them. A violent strike ensued.

A conservative Republican, Kohler began dabbling in politics in 1928 as a delegate to the Republican National Convention. He won the delegate election in such a landslide that he was then urged to run for governor of Wisconsin. During the campaign, he was faced with a legal challenge from the progressives based on his high campaign expenditures. The Wisconsin Supreme Court, however, ruled in his favor, and he won the election handily.

Kohler served only a single two-year term as governor. He was popular for his reductions of expenditures and superfluous state agencies as well as for his creation of a state highway commission and refined budget system. Despite his popularity, Kohler was defeated in his bid for reelection in the turbulent political climate of 1930. He regained the gubernatorial nomination two years later only to be defeated in a Democratic landslide. Despite his electoral defeat, his name was mentioned as a potential presidential candidate in 1936.

Outside of his political and business interests, Kohler found time to serve on the board of regents of the University of Wisconsin from 1918 to 1924 and was a trustee of Lawrence College. He also served as chairman or president of various charitable organizations and was remembered fondly for his generosity, dignity, and amiability.

Kohler died suddenly of a coronary embolism on April 21, 1940, at his country estate near Kohler Village.

BIBLIOGRAPHY

Geiger, G. L., "Kohler: A Planned Village of Beauty and Neighborliness," *American City*, August 1930; Holmes, F. L., ed., *Wisconsin: Stability, Progress, Beauty*, 1946; *Kohler Village: A Hopeful and Stimulating Example of American Community Life*, 1925; *New York Times*, Obituary, April 22, 1940; Uphoff, W. H., *The Kohler Strike: Its Socio-Economic Causes and Effects*, 1935.

Kraft, James

(November 11, 1874–February 16, 1953)
Manufacturer

Thanks largely to James Lewis Kraft, cheese consumption in the United States skyrocketed when, through his Kraft Cheese Company, he revolutionized the market with new techniques.

Born in Fort Erie, Ontario, Canada, on November 11, 1874, to Franklin Krafft, a farmer, and Alice (Tripp) Krafft, James—who later changed the spelling of his last name—graduated from high school, worked as a clerk, and in 1903 moved to the United States. The following year, he settled in Chicago, and in 1911 he became a naturalized American citizen.

In Chicago, Kraft bought a horse and wagon and delivered cheese that he purchased from wholesalers and sold to grocers. His first year in business resulted in his losing $3,000 and his horse, but he quickly turned the situation around and recruited his four brothers to help him, forming J. L. Kraft Brothers & Company in 1909. That same year, he married Pauline Elizabeth Platt. They eventually had one child.

For several years, Kraft experimented with making and packaging cheese that would result in little waste or spoilage. Traditionally, cheese was formed into large wheels and shoppers who wanted some would ask the grocer to cut a wedge for them. The section of the wheel around the cut, however, would get crusty and have to be thrown out, and the cheese as a whole had a short shelf life. Kraft solved these problems by pasteurizing cheese. In that form, it could be conveniently marketed in containers. Pasteurization produced another benefit in that it reduced the risk of disease, particularly salmonella.

Purists balked, though, and called Kraft's cheese inferior, for pasteurization damaged flavor-producing enzymes and thus altered the flavor. One observer later said "Kraft has been responsible for the decline of the quality of cheese made in the U.S." When Kraft began packing cheddar cheese in four-ounce cans in 1916, however, consumers flocked to buy it. After overcoming competitors who infringed on his patent, Kraft's gross sales reached $2 million in 1917 and an astonishing $22 million a short six years later.

In 1928, Kraft merged with a rival company, Phoenix Cheese, and together, they accounted for 40 percent of America's cheese consumption, while boosting that consumption by 50 percent per capita over the next two decades. In 1930, the National Dairy Products Corporation acquired Kraft Cheese but kept Kraft in charge of its operations.

Kraft expanded sales through extensive advertising and by introducing new products. During the 1930s, Velveeta, Miracle Whip, Parkay margarine, and Kraft caramels appeared. Kraft Cheese was one of the earliest advertisers on radio as sponsor of the Kraft Music Hall.

Kraft retired as director of National Dairy in 1948 and as chairman of the board of Kraft Foods in 1951, at which time his brother John briefly succeeded him. Kraft died on February 16, 1953. National Dairy adopted the name Kraftco in 1969 before changing it to Kraft, Incorporated in 1976.

BIBLIOGRAPHY

Baum, A. W., "Man with a Horse and a Wagon,"
Saturday Evening Post, February 17, 1945.

Kresge, Sebastian

(July 31, 1867--October 18, 1966)
Merchant

Developing Kmart, a multimillion-dollar discount chain, from a single variety store, Sebastian Spering Kresge exploited America's population shift to the suburbs and helped reshape the way consumers shopped.

Born on July 31, 1867, in Bald Mount, Pennsylvania, to Sebastian Kresge and Catherine (Kunkle) Kresge, Sebastian attended the Gilbert Polytechnic Institute in Gilbert, Pennsylvania, before enrolling at the Eastman Business College in Poughkeepsie, New York, from which he graduated in 1889. Raised in a poor family, Sebastian worked his way through school as a clerk and in 1890 joined the Howley Brothers Store in Scranton, Pennsylvania, as a bookkeeper.

From 1892 to 1897, Kresge sold hardware in New England for W. B. Bertels & Sons Company of Wilkes-Barre, Pennsylvania. While on that job, he met FRANK WOOLWORTH, who had become famous for his five-and-dime stores. Kresge resolved that he would be as successful as Woolworth, and amid a devastating depression in the 1890s, he saved $8,000 and invested it in the J. G. McCrory Company, a dry-goods firm.

With that investment made, Kresge operated McCrory's Jamestown, New York, store and then joined him as a partner in opening stores in Memphis, Tennessee, and Detroit, Michigan. In 1899, he bought out McCrory's interest in the Detroit property and promoted it as a five-and-dime store—"Nothing over 10 Cents," he proclaimed, a limit he upheld for two decades.

In partnership with his brother-in-law, Charles J. Wilson, Kresge opened a second store in Port Huron, Michigan, in 1900. There soon followed additional stores in Indianapolis, Indiana; Toledo, Ohio; Pittsburgh, Pennsylvania; Chicago, Illinois; and Cleveland and Columbus, Ohio. Seven years later, Kresge bought out Wilson, and in 1912 he incorporated his company as S. S. Kresge, which comprised 85 stores with annual sales topping $10 million.

Amid inflation in 1920, Kresge raised the price limit in his five-and-dime stores to 25 cents and opened his "green-front stores" that sold more expensive items. In 1925, Kresge relinquished his company's presidency to serve as chairman of the board. Four years later, he opened his first store in a shopping center at the Country Club Plaza in Kansas City, Missouri. The opening occurred as Americans had begun moving from the cities

Sebastian Kresge (Corbis-Bettmann)

into surrounding suburbs, shifting their shopping away from downtown districts. That trend accelerated after World War II, and Kresge would continue to reap benefits from it.

Kresge owned considerable real estate as well, and during the 1920s he purchased such other stores as the Fair in Chicago and Stern Brothers in New York City. He participated in social reform, too, and ardently supported Prohibition through the Anti-Saloon League and the National Vigilance Committee for Prohi- bition Enforcement. During that decade, his first wife, Anna Emma Harvey, who he had married in 1897 and by whom he had five children, divorced him. Kresge married Doris Mercer in 1924, but four years later, that marriage also ended in divorce. He married Clara Katherine Zitz in 1928.

In 1962, Kresge and HARRY CUNNINGHAM, the company president, took the next step in appealing to suburban America when they began building discount stores called Kmart, the first one opening in Garden City, Michigan. The idea developed from the nation's first discount store, the Ann and Hope Mill Outlet in Rhode Island, which had opened in 1953. With their emphasis on reduced prices, self-service, and large parking lots convenient to motorists, Kmarts prospered. By 1966, the Kresge Company operated the second largest retail chain in America with 670 variety stores, 162 Kmarts, and several Jupiter discount stores.

Kresge maintained a progressive labor policy in his stores. He gave his employees sick leave and paid holidays long before other businesses, and he established profit-sharing bonuses and retirement pensions. He also involved himself in many civic endeavors and with a $1.3 mil-lion gift established the Kresge Foundation, a philanthropic organization. Over the years, Kresge provided the foundation with another $60 million—most of his personal fortune—and, on his death, willed it 2.5 million shares of Kresge stock worth $100 million. Kresge died on October 18, 1966, in East Stroudsburg, Pennsylvania.

Today, in addition to its discount stores, Kmart (the company officially changed its name from S. S. Kresge in 1977) owns other chains, among them Office Max.

BIBLIOGRAPHY

Kresge, Stanley S., *The S. S. Kresge Story*, 1979.

Kress, Samuel

(July 23, 1863–September 22, 1955)
Merchant

Through diligence and careful management, Samuel Henry Kress built up an empire of discount variety stores (also known as "dime stores"). The success of the Kress stores was based on their ability to offer a wide range and large quantity of household goods at reasonable prices. Later in life, having secured his fortune, Kress became an avid art collector and philanthropist.

Kress, the son of Margaret and John Franklin Kress, was born in Cherryville, Pennsylvania, on July 23, 1863. At the age of 17, Kress began a short-lived career as a teacher at a school near Slatington, Pennsylvania. His father owned a drugstore and two mine commissaries in Slatington, and the young Kress would eventually follow his father's lead with a career in merchandising. By age 24, Kress had saved enough money to purchase his first store, selling novelties and stationary, in Nanticoke. In just three years, Kress was able to purchase the second S. H. Kress & Company store, located in Wilkes-Barre. His brother Claude joined him in managing it.

There were two keys to the early success of Kress's merchandising operations. First, Kress was a diligent and disciplined worker who sank nearly all profits back into further improvements and expansion. Second, he was determined to obtain his inventory directly from the manufacturers, eliminating the middleman. In so doing, Kress was able to offer his high-volume goods at discounted prices. Kress's marketing strategy came to fruition when he opened a very popular store in Memphis, Tennessee, in 1896. The high volume of sales compensated for low profit margins, and in the first year alone, the store grossed $31,000. This tremendous success prompted Kress to expand with another store in Nashville, Tennessee, also operated by his brother Claude.

In subsequent years, Kress successfully continued his expansion, fostered by the stable economic growth of the country as a whole. The expansion was cautious in that Kress believed in owning rather than renting his store properties, but this approach was risky due to the small amount of working capital available at any given time. By 1900, the chain consisted of 12 stores, and Kress soon moved the company headquarters to New York City to maintain closer ties with all of his manufacturing sources. Further growth of the chain was achieved throughout the southern states, and the number of stores reached 51 by 1907 with revenues of $3 million.

Even as the discount chain grew, Kress wisely kept a great degree of control over the quality, procedures, and service at each store. Employees were trained according to guidelines handed down from the corporate headquarters. In addition, Kress traveled extensively to inspect the operation of his stores.

All the Kress stores shared a similar design and nearly identical operating procedures. The two front windows displayed goods to entice customers who, once inside, would find a high-ceilinged, warehouse-style store with large stocks arranged on orderly tables. Each store also contained a soda fountain and lunch counter. The external features of the stores, however, varied greatly. Kress buildings were envisioned by the owner as works of art to contribute to the civic landscape. The exterior of each store was visually distinct, and all buildings bore the name Kress. While S. H. Kress & Company would eventually become part of the Genesco corporation, and some of the stores sold, many buildings have retained the Kress name though they currently house law offices, movie theaters, or museums.

As the Kress store chain continued to be successful, Kress's interests turned to art collecting after he met an art dealer named Alessandro Contini while traveling in Italy in 1921. Kress began importing all types of classic European art including paintings, statues, medallions, and textiles. Pieces from his personal collection were occasionally displayed in Kress store windows during holiday seasons. Ultimately, most of the paintings would be donated to public art galleries; by the time of his death, 14 galleries owned sizable Kress collections.

Kress's philanthropy was also routed through the Kress Foundation, which he established in 1929. The foundation was responsible for transferring his art collections to public institutions as well as supporting medical research. The foundation was given 40 percent of the company's voting stock. Kress gradually withdrew from the leadership, leaving his brother Claude to assume control.

After Claude's death in 1940, Kress returned as chief executive officer and president until he suffered a stroke in

1945. His younger brother Ross then took over the direction of both the company and the Kress Foundation. A very private man, Samuel Kress never married, and upon his death in New York City on September 22, 1955, the remainder of his $17.5 million estate was given to the Kress Foundation.

BIBLIOGRAPHY

"Great Kress Giveaway," *Life*, November 16, 1953; Rieser, C., "S. H. Kress: Who's in Charge?," *Fortune*, November 1957; Thomas, Bernice L., *America's 5 & 10 Cent Stores: The Kress Legacy*, 1997.

Kroc, Ray

(October 5, 1902–January 14, 1984)
Merchant

At age 51, Raymond A. Kroc went from selling milk-shake machines to making McDonald's the largest fast-food franchise in the world.

Kroc was born on October 5, 1902, in Chicago, Illinois, and grew up in the lower-middle-class Oak Park section. His father worked for the American District Telegraph Company. While in his teens, Kroc left high school and, with World War I under way, volunteered for the Red Cross. He went to Europe, where he served briefly as an ambulance driver, and then entered special duty as a piano player. After he returned to Chicago, he played for a prominent orchestra but quit in 1922 when he married Jane Dobbins and tired of the nightlife.

At that point, Kroc joined Lily-Tulip (makers of paper cups) as a salesman, while also working for WGES (Chicago's first radio station) where he again took up the piano. In 1925, Kroc left Chicago and went to Florida, where he sold real estate during a land boom. He did well, but the following year, the boom went bust, and he once again resorted to playing the piano, this time in nightclubs. During the Great Depression, he returned to Chicago, resumed his job with Lily-Tulip, and earned promotion to Midwest sales manager.

Then a discovery changed Kroc's course. In 1937, he stumbled across the Multi-Mixer, a machine recently invented by Earl Prince of Prince Castle Ice Cream. Kroc marveled at the machine's ability to make several milk shakes at the same time, and he convinced Prince to appoint him as an exclusive sales agent. In this capacity, Kroc traveled the nation, acquainting himself with different restaurants and concluding that they could benefit from standardization. He did not, however, immediately act on his idea.

After World War II, the environment grew conducive to Kroc's concept. In the early 1950s, prosperity encouraged conformist behavior and people bought suburban houses and big-finned automo-

Ray Kroc (Corbis/Bettmann-UPI)

biles. Out in Downey, California, two brothers, Maurice and Richard Mc-Donald, exploited these developments when they opened a hamburger stand geared to the new mobile suburbanite—as evident in its fast, drive-up self-service. McDonald's, as they called it, sported a spotlessly clean building and two large, golden-colored arches. The brothers cleared $75,000 per year from their hamburgers, shakes, and french fries.

McDonald's caught Kroc's attention when the brothers ordered eight Multi-Mixers. Kroc later said: "In that moment, I suppose, I became an entrepreneur. I decided to go for broke." He convinced the brothers to assign him the right to license their restaurant as franchises in return for their getting a percentage of the franchise fee.

Kroc did not invent franchising—it had been around since the late 1800s, when Singer Sewing Machine franchised dealerships. The McDonald brothers had already begun limited franchising on their own, but Kroc saw a golden opportunity with the golden arches. Although the McDonald brothers agreed, they soon had several differences with Kroc. For example, he thought he had an exclusive nationwide right to license the business, only to discover that the brothers had granted a right to someone else for the Chicago area. Getting this territory cost Kroc an additional $25,000.

In April 1955, Kroc opened his first McDonald's in Des Plaines, Illinois—a building resplendent with its red-and-white tile front and large golden arches. A short time later, he sold his first franchise in Fresno, California. Kroc reflected homogeneous America when, in discussing his franchises, he declared: "We will make conformists out of them in a hurry. . . . The organization cannot trust the individual; the individual must trust the organization [or] he shouldn't go into this kind of business."

As Kroc continued to sell more franchises—228 by 1960—he asked the McDonald brothers to sell him their trademarks, copyrights, recipes, and the golden arches for his exclusive use. In 1961, the brothers did so for $2.7 million. Kroc raised the money with the help of Harvey Sonneborn, former vice president of Tastee Freez. Sonneborn secured several loans and became Kroc's partner. For a short while, the McDonald brothers operated a hamburger stand under a different name, then they retired to New Hampshire.

Kroc worked on perfecting the assembly-line production of hamburgers—complete with specific requirements as to patty size—and considered a low, uniform price essential, which he fixed at 15 cents per burger (a price originally set by the McDonald brothers and one maintained until 1967). He trained franchise owners at his "Hamburger University" in Elk Grove, Illinois, where his pupils earned a "Bachelor of Hamburgerology with a minor in French fries." Kroc prided himself in producing "the greatest French fries in the world," and assured freshness for his food by requiring that cooked burgers be disposed when 10 minutes old, fries when 7, and coffee when 30.

Kroc insisted that each McDonald's be super clean, with gleaming stainless steel, and that employees be well groomed and polite. (Several years earli-

er, he had adopted the motto "Q. S. C. & V.—Quality, Service, Cleanliness and Value.") To discourage teenagers from loitering, he prohibited pay telephones and, at first, refused to hire young girls, who he thought would attract mischievous boys.

Despite the company's growth in the early 1960s, Kroc found that the limited franchise fee that he collected in his original deal with the McDonald brothers restricted his income. At this point, Sonneborn decided that the company should purchase the land required by each new McDonald's and then rent the site to the franchisee for a percentage of income. His plan, which put McDonald's into real estate, boosted profits. By 1962, the total food sales at McDonald's restaurants reached $76 million, and by the end of 1965—two years after the company had introduced Ronald McDonald as a clown-suited promotional figure—McDonald's had 710 stores in 44 states with plans to open 100 more. In just 20 years, Kroc had made McDonald's an American symbol.

Kroc began relinquishing his control over McDonald's in 1968, and although he remained company chairman, his protégé Fred Turner (a former McDonald's cook) succeeded him as president. Under Turner's leadership, McDonald's built a large headquarters building in Oak Brook, Illinois. The company continued to emphasize standardization and still charged considerable money for its franchises, requiring $200,000 up front, a 3 percent franchise fee, and 8.5 percent annually of gross revenues.

Turner, though, brought changes. He deserted Kroc's simplicity and replaced the red-and-white tile stores with brown brick and plate glass, while expanding the menu. In another move, he placed a 20-year limitation on all franchise contracts and began buying back franchises so that by 1973 the company owned one-third of the restaurants.

McDonald's had its critics. Some complained that it indoctrinated children through the Ronald McDonald symbol and through the playgrounds the company built adjacent to many of its restaurants. Others assailed the food, asserting that the Big Mac burger consisted of "cheese made of glue, [and] Russian dressing three generations removed from the steppes," and that the "whole thing tasted like a charcoal-broiled roll garnished with day-old salad."

In a continuing effort to improve public relations, McDonald's sponsored many community events—including fire prevention, bicycle safety, and litter cleanup campaigns—and urged its franchisees to support the United Way and other voluntary organizations. At the same time, Kroc donated heavily to the Republican Party and campaigned to exempt teenage workers, who were important in the McDonald's labor force, from the minimum wage.

Meanwhile, Kroc broadened his business interests in 1974 when he purchased the San Diego Padres baseball team for $10 million. Until he relinquished operating control five years later, he ran the club much as he did McDonald's, expecting perfection from his players.

Kroc suffered a stroke in December 1979. He died on January 14, 1984, from his heart ailment while living in La Jolla, California, and serving as senior chairman at McDonald's. His efforts at standardization had revolutionized the restaurant business and made McDonald's a fast-food empire.

BIBLIOGRAPHY

Boas, Max, and Steve Chain, *Big Mac: The Unauthorized Story of McDonald's*, 1976.

Kroger, Bernard

(January 24, 1860–July 21, 1938)
Merchant

Bernard Henry Kroger had a temper that could explode: more than once he fired a manager on the spot for keeping a dirty store. But such exacting demands coupled with shrewd selling tactics enabled him to build his Kroger Grocery Company into a national chain of stores.

Kroger's environment at birth may have predisposed him to a mercantile future. He was born on January 24, 1860, to John Henry Kroger and Gertrude (Schlebbe) Kroger in a flat above his father's small dry goods store in Cincinnati, Ohio. After the Panic of 1873 ruined the elder Kroger, Bernard began working at a grocery store, delivering orders. At age 16, he worked for the Imperial Tea Company, selling coffee, tea, and spices from their wagons. When the company found itself in financial straits, he reached an agreement with the owners to manage it for a share of the profits. Kroger worked 16-hour days as he studied each product to make sure it met the quality standards he desired. After one year, Imperial made a profit, but Kroger quit when the company's owners rejected his demand for a bigger share.

Then, with a partner, Kroger formed the Great Western Tea Company, a small store in Cincinnati, and almost lost everything. At a railroad crossing, a train rammed into their horse and wagon, killing the horse and destroying the wagon. Shortly thereafter, the Ohio River flooded and heavily damaged their store. Kroger fought back, though, and bought out his partner.

Kroger worked day and night, demanding high-quality goods for his grocery and besting his competitors with new forms of promotion: advertisements in newspapers and "loss leaders"—such items as heads of lettuce sold at a loss—to lure customers into the store so they would buy other products. By 1885, Kroger had four stores, all small and all painted bright red, inside and out. The following year, he married Mary Emily Jansen, who subsequently bore him seven children.

In the 1890s, Kroger expanded his business into other Ohio cities and started his own bakery, selling bread at 2.5 cents a loaf. In 1902, he incorporated the Kroger Grocery and Baking Company while opening yet additional stores and buying other smaller chains. He was the first to open meat departments in his grocery stores—consumers traditionally went to butcher shops.

By 1928, Kroger owned thousands of grocery stores and several bakeries, along with packing and beverage plants. That year, he sold his stock in the company and married Alice Farrington Maher. (His first wife had died in 1899.) For a brief time, Kroger headed the Provident Bank in Cincinnati. On July 21, 1938, he died at his summer home in Wianno, Massachusetts.

BIBLIOGRAPHY

Moskowitz, Milton, et al., eds., *Everybody's Business*, 1980.

L

Lamont, Thomas

(September 30, 1870–February 2, 1948)
Banker, Financier

Thomas William Lamont, an associate of noted financier J. P. MORGAN SR., was an extremely influential banker, famous for his role in financing industry and foreign governments. Originally a journalist, Lamont was respected and well connected in many circles of society, as well as reputedly being one of President Herbert Hoover's closest advisers.

Born in Claverick, New York, on September 30, 1870, Thomas was the son of Thomas and Caroline Deuel Lamont. The son of a Methodist minister, Lamont grew up in a strict parsonage, turning to books for his escapist pleasures. Though the family was strict and of simple means, Lamont remembered his upbringing with great affection.

Lamont earned scholarships both to Phillips-Exeter, an elite preparatory school, and Harvard College, which he entered in 1888. At Harvard, Lamont began his journalism career, serving as editor of the college newspaper and holding various correspondent jobs with Boston newspapers. After graduating in 1892, he worked for two years at the *New York Tribune*, initially as a reporter, and then as city editor. On October 31, 1895, Lamont married Florence Haskell Corliss with whom he would have four children—Thomas Stillwell, Corliss, Austin, and Eleanor. Over the next few years, Lamont decided to change his career track, signing on in 1894 as a secretary with Cushman Brothers, a New York food products distribution agent.

After some years with the company, one of its major creditors asked for Lamont's assistance in reorganizing and managing the firm to help it regain its financial footing. To do so, Lamont established, with his brother-in-law, the firm of Lamont, Corliss and Company. His restoration of the firm's status proved so successful that Lamont began to win acclaim from a number of prominent New York bankers. In 1903, he was invited, despite his protests that he was no banker, to join the Bankers Trust Company as treasurer and secretary. By 1905, he had become a vice president and director of the company. From 1906 until 1911, he served in a similar capacity for the First National Bank, leaving the post to become a partner at J. P. Morgan's private investment banking firm.

Lamont's work of the Morgan years was the most significant of his career, positioning him as the consultant of presidents, prime ministers, and bankers alike. He was an articulate mouthpiece for Morgan's firm; his strict control over the firm's publicity and information prompted the conventional wisdom that "Mr. Morgan speaks to Mr. Lamont and Mr. Lamont speaks to the people." Lamont's reputation was largely established on the strength of his dealings with industry and foreign governments.

When World War I began, the House of Morgan (as J. P. Morgan's firm was known) was appointed by Britain and France to be their American purchasing agent and representative. Lamont was an integral part of the $500 million Anglo-French Loan of 1915. Once the United States entered the war, he served on the Liberty Loan committees that helped the Treasury Department sell bonds. In 1917,

Thomas Lamont (Library of Congress)

After the war, Lamont returned to J. P. Morgan and Company, where he played a substantial part in the company's ability to offer the public almost $6 billion in securities. Lamont was critical of the negotiations with foreign banks, governments, and companies to include their securities in Morgan's portfolio. By the late 1920s, Lamont had become one of the most influential bankers in the world.

It became evident during and immediately after the war that Lamont's sphere of influence was not limited to banking. A staunch supporter of the League of Nations effort, Lamont bought the *New York Evening Post* in 1918 with the specific intention of curbing the torrent of anti-Wilson commentary that reflected the views of the paper's owner, Oswald Villard. He sold the newspaper in 1922.

When the stock market crash of 1929 resulted in the convening of congressional committees to investigate banking practices, J. P. Morgan's firm came under scrutiny. Lamont successfully demonstrated that the firm had avoided abuses of authority and financial mismanagement. However, by 1933, all banks were required to separate commercial and investment banking functions under the Glass-Seagall Banking Act. Largely due to Lamont's advice, Morgan chose to remain a bank of deposits and cease its security underwriting function. Later, in 1943, after Morgan's death, Lamont was made the chairman of the board of J. P. Morgan and Company.

During the Great Depression, Lamont shared President Hoover's conviction that the economic decline needed to run its course; he served as one of Hoover's key advisers during this period.

Over the years, Lamont became a generous philanthropist, endowing a $500,000

he was also assigned by President Woodrow Wilson to the team negotiating the details of the Allies' coordinated war effort. These influential advising posts led to a higher-profile role at the Paris Peace Conference as representative of the United States Treasury on the American delegation, a role that allowed Lamont to participate in determining the specifics of Germany's reparation payments to the Allied countries.

chair at Harvard for political economy studies and $1 million for an undergraduate library. He also donated $500,000 to help restore the Canterbury Cathedral in England, which was damaged in World War II. After suffering from a heart ailment, Lamont died at the age of 77 in Boca Raton, Florida, on February 2, 1948.

BIBLIOGRAPHY

Lamont, Edward M., *The Ambassador from Wall Street: The Story of Thomas W. Lamont, J. P. Morgan's Chief Executive: A Biography,* 1994; Lamont, Thomas, *My Boyhood in a Parsonage,* 1946; *New York Times,* Obituary, February 3, 1948.

Land, Edwin

(May 7, 1909–)
Manufacturer

Edwin Herbert Land never suffered any adolescent turmoil about what he would do for a living. While still in his teens, he dedicated himself to science and believed he would make important contributions to the field. And he did, as an inventor and a manufacturer of Polaroid cameras.

Born on May 7, 1909, to Harry and Martha Land, Edwin grew up in a comfortable middle-class setting in his hometown of Norwich, Connecticut, where his father owned a thriving salvage and scrap-metal business. An extensive reader, young Land developed a liking for science at an early age. After graduating from Norwich Academy in Norwich, Connecticut, with an outstanding academic record, he entered Harvard in 1926, where he continued work he had begun several years earlier on polarization. Land wanted to perfect a filter and envisioned developing one that could be used by the auto industry to reduce glare from headlights.

Land never graduated from Harvard. Instead, he left there and in 1932 joined with George Wheelwright III (a physics professor) to found Land-Wheelwright Laboratories in Boston, Massachusetts. Two years later, Land manufactured a polarizer made from plastic that altered the transmission of light waves so as to eliminate glare. He called this device the Polaroid J-sheet—the word Polaroid coined by a Smith College professor, Clarence Kennedy. The Eastman Kodak Company, founded by GEORGE EASTMAN, used Land's research to place polarized filters in its cameras in 1935, and the American Optical Company began making polarized sunglasses.

In 1937, with financial backing from major Wall Street investors, Land began the Polaroid Corporation in Cambridge, Massachusetts. During World War II, he invented optical elements for use in infrared night-vision devices, and his company produced filters for periscopes, range finders, aerial cameras, and other items used by the military.

Land later reported that the idea for a camera able to develop film instantly came from a question posed to him by his young daughter who wondered why it took so long for snapshots to be made into pictures. After World War II, when his company's profits tumbled, he turned full attention to inventing a new camera. In 1948, one year after Land demonstrated his invention at the American Optical Society, Model 95 entered the market. This "Land camera," which was a big hit with consumers, produced fully developed sepia-toned prints one minute after a picture was taken. In 1950, Land replaced the sepia with black-and-white film. "All that should be necessary to get a good picture," said Land, "is to *take* a good picture, and our task is to make that possible."

Polaroid manufactured millions of special polarized glasses during the 3-D movie craze of the 1950s, while Land pursued the next step in photography and in 1963 unveiled color film for his cameras. He worked to make Polaroid cameras more easily available and as a result introduced the Swinger in 1965, which sold for $20 and produced black-and-white pictures. An updated Swinger soon followed that produced color prints.

In 1972, Land's SX-70 camera appeared. It used 17 layers of chemical compounds to eliminate the previous procedure of having to hold the print while waiting for it to develop and then having to tear paper to reveal the photo. Now the print popped from the camera fully developed.

Land's one great failure occurred in 1977 when he tried to sell the Polavision movie camera. His invention lost out to videotape cameras. Land retired from his company in 1982. During that decade Polaroid won a lawsuit against Eastman Kodak that upheld its instant photography patents and forced its competitor to stop making Polaroid-type cameras.

BIBLIOGRAPHY

Olshaker, Mark, *The Instant Image*, 1978; Wensberg, Peter, *Land's Polaroid: A Company and the Man Who Invented It*, 1987.

Lannom, George, Jr.

(February 22, 1885–February 13, 1953)
Manufacturer

At a time in the early 1900s when America was adopting baseball as a recreational sport, George Sharp Lannom Jr. converted his leather-making business into a baseball-making one. He created Worth, which is today one of the nation's leading sporting goods manufacturers.

Born on February 22, 1885, in Humboldt, Tennessee, to George Sharp Lannom and Mary Narcissa (Chappell) Lannom, George Jr. grew up in a comfortable middle-class setting. His father traveled extensively as a dry-goods salesman. After graduating from Branham and Hughes Preparatory School in nearby Spring Hill, the young George attended Bethel College in Russellville, Kentucky, but left without having earned a degree. He briefly rode the range for a cousin in Oklahoma and then returned to Tennessee, where he worked as a salesman for the Robinson-McGill Company—jobbers of knitted fabrics, harnesses, and horse collars. After he moved back to Tennessee, he married Martha Louise Killough.

In 1912, Lannom founded his own business when he bought a small tannery in Tullahoma, Tennessee, for $3,000 and with several partners began operating as the Lannom Manufacturing Company. He quickly learned tanning, helped by an experienced tanner who oversaw production, and in 1915 produced a net income of about $1,500.

Two national developments soon greatly affected Lannom. For one, the spreading use of automobiles depressed his tanning business by reducing demand for the horse collars he made. For another, the popularity of baseball opened another possible market for leather. Lannom began making baseballs not from any sentimental attachment to the sport or even from any particular fondness for it but from a desire to save his tannery and guide its expansion.

Although by 1923 Lannom was producing an assortment of products under the Worth label that included basketballs, footballs, fielder's gloves, and boxing gloves, baseballs and softballs occupied an ever-greater share of his product line. In 1928, a local newspaper claimed that Lannom had shipped to New York a railroad boxcar loaded with over 130,000 baseballs. By 1930, he was exclusively manufacturing baseballs, softballs, and cheaper balls used at carnivals and by children at play.

Lannom ruled his factory in Tullahoma with an iron hand, making his word law, and established a firm policy against unions. He provided employment in a job-starved region and created a paternalistic environment. To put his business on a firmer financial footing, Lannom merged it in 1923 with a glove manufacturer in Grinnell, Iowa, named Morrison-Ricker. Much to his dismay, four years later, he discovered that Morrison-Ricker owed the federal government substantial back taxes, whereupon he took over the company and straightened it out. By 1931, Lannom Manufacturing thus consisted of the dress glove factory in Grinnell (its name changed to Morrison-Shults) and the Worth baseball factory in Tullahoma.

At first, Worth baseballs had a poor reputation. According to one story, after customers complained about the leather on several balls being too fuzzy, a Worth salesman sarcastically proposed that the company provide in each box a razor blade. By 1940, however, Worth's league-quality balls improved and gained wider acceptance. The following year, Lannom founded a factory in Puerto Rico to sew baseball covers.

After the death of his first wife, Lannom married Edith Kavanaugh, a wealthy widow from Dallas, Texas, in 1944. He continued to expand his business and in 1949 established another plant in Barrie, near Toronto, to make baseballs and softballs for the Canadian market. By 1950, he had created a network of small industries that, taken together, composed a wealthy manufacturing empire. In 1952, Worth produced 12,000 baseballs and softballs a day—one every two seconds.

Lannom died on February 13, 1953, at his beach house in Puerto Rico. His enterprises, particularly Worth, continued to flourish. Lannom's grandson, Sharp Lannom IV, directed Morrison-Shults from making gloves to making sports jackets under the name DeLong. In the 1970s and into the 1990s, Worth manufactured a wider array of sporting goods, including a popular aluminum bat, named the Tennessee Thumper, which is used in softball. "Where there is life there is struggle," said Lannom, "and that is the way it should be." These words reflect his fight to build a thriving business from the tiny tannery in Tullahoma.

BIBLIOGRAPHY

Hamilton, Neil A., *Visions of Worth: The Life of G. S. Lannom, Jr., Independent Entrepreneur*, 1988.

Lasker, Albert

(May 1, 1880–May 30, 1952)
Advertising Executive

Albert Davis Lasker transformed the very nature of the advertising business by emphasizing a more persuasive advertising approach based on catchy phrases and hooks. Diverted from a journalism career by his father, Lasker quickly prospered in the advertising business and soon owned the first firm where he was employed. After many years and many successful campaigns, Lasker was worn down by the stress of the business and left it to pursue his love of art and philanthropy.

Albert Lasker was born on May 1, 1880, in Freiburg, Germany, while his parents, Morris and Nettie Lasker, both Americans of German-Jewish descent, were taking an extended trip abroad. Six weeks later, the family returned to their home in Galveston, Texas, where Morris Lasker was a successful businessman and banker. Albert attended the local school, but studying bored him, and his grades were only average.

Albert's thirst for business experience manifested itself at the age of 12, when he launched his own successful weekly newspaper called the *Galveston Free Press*. The paper earned him a profit of $15 per week, but his father did not approve of Albert's budding journalism career. Albert was sent to Chicago after graduating from high school in 1898 to take a $10-a-week job arranged by his father with the prestigious advertising agency of Lord and Thomas.

When Lasker began his new job, the primary role of an advertising agency was to use copy prepared by the advertisers themselves and simply place the advertisement in appropriate periodicals. Lasker began to question this approach and stressed the agency's participation in creating more catchy advertisements, which were then pitched to the advertisers.

Because of Lasker's influence, agencies around the world began to use active salesmanship rather than passive advertising techniques. In particular, Lasker popularized the technique of using product testing and sampling information in advertising. By 1905, he was a partner in the firm and in charge of copywriting, and by 1912 he had acquired sole ownership of the agency. In just five years, Lord and Thomas was the most celebrated advertising agency in the world, and Lasker himself was earning $1 million per year.

Lasker did little of the copywriting himself but instead recruited the best writers in the business with very lucrative offers. Lasker remained the "idea man" and directed many successful campaigns for such products as Palmolive Soap and Quaker Oats. He was also responsible for popularizing the Kotex and Kleenex brands as well as Sunkist orange juice. His largest account, procured in 1923, was the American Tobacco Company, maker of Lucky Strike cigarettes. In the next three years, Lucky Strike became the best-selling brand in America, and sales rose more than sixfold.

Much of Lasker's success came from his mathematical aptitude. He was quite conservative with money but had a keen sense of what was a valuable investment. He was known to be a generous man but was notoriously obsessed with thrift, agonizing over high phone or electric bills while simultaneously engaging in the purchase of high-priced artwork or a new wing for a hospital.

Lasker became actively interested in politics after the outbreak of World War I. He financially supported the Republican Party and used his advertising prowess to publicize its isolationist views, which he shared. He became assistant to the chairman of the Republican National Committee from 1918 to 1920. As he aged, however, his views became more

Albert Lasker (Library of Congress)

liberal and international in nature, and he supported Democratic Presidents Franklin Roosevelt and Harry Truman.

Lasker's first marriage to Flora Warner lasted from 1902 until her death in 1936, a union that produced three children. He was married again in 1938 to actress Doris Kenyon, but their tumultuous relationship ended one year later. In 1940, he married Mary Woodard Reinhardt, a businesswoman, who helped Lasker deal with the psychological blows caused him by the stressful advertising business. Lasker had suffered three nervous breakdowns, claiming at the time that his therapy was needed to "get rid of all the hate the advertising business put in [him]." With the encouragement of his third wife and the help of psychoanalysis, he developed a new relaxed attitude. He became disenchanted with the decline of creativity and the rise of expensive research in the advertising business and ceded control of his agency in 1942 to three associates—Foote, Cone, and Belding.

In his final years, Lasker became interested in philanthropy and art collecting. He established major awards for medical research and became a vocal supporter of the state of Israel. Lasker was an avid sports fan and acquired a large stake in his favorite team, the Chicago Cubs. He also developed an eye for modern art and assembled an impressive collection. He died of cancer in New York City on May 30, 1952.

BIBLIOGRAPHY

Cone, Fairfax M., *For All Its Faults*, 1969; Gunther, John, *Taken at the Flood*, 1960; Hopkins, Claude C., *My Life in Advertising*, 1936; Lasker, Albert, "The Personal Reminiscences of Albert Lasker," *American Heritage*, December 1954.

Lauder, Estée

(July 1, 1908–)
Manufacturer

Although Estée Lauder came from a humble background in Corona, located in the borough of Queens, New York, she built a thriving business in cosmetics through fanciful stories about her origins and the allure of her products.

Lauder was born Josephine Esther Mentzer on or about July 1, 1908. As an adult she portrayed her parents as wealthy immigrants who frequented European spas, but in actuality her mother, Rose (Rosenthal) Mentzer, and father, Max Mentzer, although both immigrants, had a more pedestrian life. Max Mentzer, a Hungarian Jew, owned and operated a hardware store in the Italian working-class neighborhood of Corona, above which the Mentzer family lived.

As a teenager, Estée (she dropped Esther for the French-sounding name) had a transforming experience when an uncle, who worked in a Hungarian chemical laboratory, visited the family and showed her how to make beauty creams. Enthralled, Estée decided she would one day make and sell skin-care products. (For years she sold her uncle's creams without, critics claim, adequately compensating him.)

She married Joseph Lauter in 1930, a garment district businessman of modest wealth. Soon the couple changed Lauter's family name back to the way it had been spelled in Austria—Lauder. Ambitious, Lauder convinced her husband that they should go into business together, and in 1932 they opened a cafeteria. But Lauder's thoughts remained with beauty creams, and she soon began making the lotions in her kitchen, selling them to beauty parlors in and around Corona. She related well to her clients, especially to Jewish women, who liked the confidence she showed in her products and her friendly, often gushing, demeanor.

The long hours she spent at her business hurt her marriage, and in 1939 she and Joseph Lauder divorced. Three years later, however, they remarried, and at that point Estée and Joseph operated the beauty cream business as a family enterprise. Lauder sold four basic skin-care lotions and some makeup products, all encased in a distinctive and expensive-looking shade of greenish blue packaging. She soon began dressing in that color to convey a sense of class and wealth, and she spun unfounded stories about her past or often refused to reveal anything about her early life so as to build a mystique about her. While some criticized her for this behavior, it fit the world of cosmetics where women bought products as much for the atmosphere they promoted as for how effective they were.

Estée and Joseph formed Estée Lauder, Incorporated in 1946, and soon after convincing Bonwit Teller to carry their product line, they obtained their biggest break when Saks Fifth Avenue agreed to do the same. This associated Lauder's creams with class, an image Lauder reinforced when she took a different path from her main competitors, HELENA RUBINSTEIN, Revlon, and Max Factor, and decided to stay away from drugstores and beauty salons and sell her products only in department stores.

Lauder introduced her first fragrance, Youth Dew, in 1953, and the perfume soon accounted for 80 percent of her business at Saks. Overall, Youth Dew made Estée Lauder, Incorporated a major player in the cosmetics industry. Lauder widened her offerings again in 1967, when she introduced men's toiletries under the Aramis label. In 1968, she began appealing to the health-conscious with Clinique allergy-tested cosmetics. Aramis and Clinique took several years, however, to earn a profit.

Estée Lauder (Tom Gates/Archive Photos)

Promotions for her products, as indeed for those of other companies, made specious claims about protecting youthful appearances and renewing skin cells, claims about which one leading dermatologist said: "Puffery is understood, but there are boundaries. And it looks as if Lauder may exceed these boundaries."

Throughout her company's expansion, Lauder maintained a high public profile, making it a point to associate with the rich and famous, thus attaching a glamorous image to her business. She owned expensive homes in New York, London, Palm Beach, and on the French Riviera, and counted among her friends the Duke and Duchess of Windsor and Princess Grace of Monaco.

Lauder largely retired from her company in 1973 and chose her son Leonard Lauder to take command. *Forbes* ranked him in 1997 as among the nation's 800 top executives. Under his direction, Estée Lauder Companies bought the Aveda Corporation, maker of shampoos and other hair-care products, and Sassaby, Incorporated, maker of cosmetics. Now widowed (Joseph died in 1983), Lauder continues to take an interest in product development.

BIBLIOGRAPHY

Israel, Lee, *Estée Lauder: Beyond the Magic*, 1985.

Lauren, Ralph

(October 14, 1939–)
Manufacturer

From the manufacture of wide neckties, Ralph Lauren built a fashion empire, Polo/Lauren, that made him a multimillionaire.

Lauren was born Ralph Lifshitz in the Bronx, New York, on October 14, 1939. He and his siblings legally changed their last name to Lauren in the mid-1950s. Lauren's father was an artist who painted houses for a living. Lauren had a taste for fashion even while still a child, and when, as a high school student, he worked part-time as a stock boy in a department store, he used his paychecks to buy expensive clothes.

After graduating from high school and serving in the army, Lauren worked as an assistant buyer for Allied Stores in New York. He wanted to design clothes, but had no such experience. Always confident that he had taste, however, he kept trying and in 1967 began designing men's ties for Beau Brummell, Incorporated. Lauren won many admirers and customers for his work when he made his ties four to five inches wide, compared to the three inches then in fashion.

In 1968, with the backing of a clothing company executive, Lauren founded his own company, Polo Fashions. He created suits with a classic design more shapely than traditional American suits but less formal than European ones. As with his ties, Lauren's suits sold well. In 1971, encouraged by the clothes he had designed for his wife, Ricky, he began making a women's line.

In the early 1970s, Lauren's sales neared $4 million, and he opened the first Polo/Lauren store on Rodeo Drive in Beverly Hills. Poor management on his part meant a low profit for his company, until he hired Peter Strom to manage the business. In 1978, when Lauren acquired Lanham Clothing, he became the only American designer to license as well as manufacture his designs. L. Greif & Company manufactured Chaps, his popularly priced men's clothing, and the Hathaway Shirt Company made Chaps shirts, while Warner/Lauren Ltd. produced Polo cologne for men.

In 1983, Lauren started his home collection of sheets, towels, and furniture.

Three years later, he opened his flagship store at 72nd Street and Madison Avenue in Manhattan. Despite the several hundred dollar price for a Polo suit, by 1995 Lauren operated 116 stores, 62 discount outlets, and 1,300 boutiques within department stores. A 45,000-square-foot store opened in London in 1997.

Between 1993 and 1996, Polo/Lauren's revenues increased 30 percent, and its operating profit increased nearly 70 percent, to about $110 million. Much of that came from licensing agreements, with some 26 licensees making Lauren products. While some criticized Lauren for being more derivative than original in his designs, he had the highest sales of any fashion designer in the world.

BIBLIOGRAPHY

Caminiti, Susan, "Ralph Lauren: The Emperor Has Clothes," *Fortune*, November 11, 1996; Trachtenberg, Jeffrey A., *Ralph Lauren: The Man behind the Mystique*, 1988.

Laurens, Henry

(March 6, 1724–December 8, 1792)
Merchant, Planter

Henry Laurens amassed a fortune in early America by trading in rice and slaves and buying plantations. His prominence in business led to his leadership in the American Revolution.

Henry was born on March 6, 1724, in Charleston, South Carolina, to John Samuel Laurens and Hester (Grassel) Laurens. The elder Laurens was a saddler and developed his business into the largest of its kind in the colony. In 1744, he sent young Henry to London to learn about commerce. When his father died in 1747, Henry inherited a substantial estate and shortly thereafter formed a merchant partnership in Charleston with George Austin. Henry married Eleanor Ball in 1750, and they had at least 12 children, only 4 of whom reached maturity. Eleanor died in 1770.

By 1762, Laurens's commercial partnership dissolved, but he continued to work as a merchant, and his wealth exceeded that of most others in South Carolina. Laurens dealt in many different items, usually handling trade on consignment. His most extensive business was exchanging rice for slaves, for which he received especially large commissions. The slave trade disturbed him, however, and he eventually refused to deal in it.

After 1764, Laurens shifted from commerce to buying and managing plantations. He owned "Mepkin," a 3,000-acre rice plantation on the Cooper River, along with two indigo plantations elsewhere in the colony, and several rice plantations in Georgia. In all, Laurens possessed more than 20,000 acres, and his reservations about the slave trade failed to keep him from owning thou-

Henry Laurens (Library of Congress)

sands of slaves to work on his plantations.

Laurens entered politics in 1757, when he won election to the colonial assembly, and as the revolutionary crisis unfolded in the 1760s and 1770s, his political involvement increased. In 1769, he approved South Carolina's nonimportation agreement, enacted as retaliation for taxes imposed by Parliament under the Townshend Acts. In 1774, he was elected to the First Continental Congress, and the following year was chosen its president. He then won election to the Second Continental Congress, and in 1777 succeeded John Hancock as its president, a post he held until December 1778. He strongly supported George Washington against those plotting to remove him as general.

An unusual episode landed him in jail and prompted a war between two nations. In 1780, he set sail for Holland on a mission to secure a treaty with that country to assist the American Revolution. A British ship, however, intercepted his brigantine, captured him, and retrieved from the sea papers he had tried to destroy. The papers included a draft of a treaty with the Dutch, and the British used the proposed alliance as a reason to declare war on Holland. A London publication reported that "the capture of Mr. Laurens, late President of the Congress, on his passage from America, was ... one of those singular instances in which the political situation of no small part of Europe seemed considerably affected by the fortune of a single man."

Laurens languished in jail for nearly 15 months, during which time he petitioned for his release with language so subservient it angered his fellow revolutionaries. He called "the commencement of the present war" a "subject of great grief" to him and assured King George that while in America he had "extended every act of kindness ... to persons called Loyalists, as well as to British prisoners of war."

Despite his controversial statements, the Continental Congress appointed Laurens as a peace commissioner in 1782 following his release, and he helped shape the treaty with Britain, including a provision prohibiting the retreating British forces from confiscating slaves and granting them their freedom. He returned to America in 1784 and the following year retired to Mepkin. By that time his health had declined, and his estate had suffered considerable losses from the war. Although elected to the federal Constitutional Convention in 1787, his illness prevented him from attending. Laurens died on December 8, 1792.

BIBLIOGRAPHY

Laurens, Henry, *Correspondence of Henry Laurens of South Carolina*, 1861; Wallace, David Duncan, *The Life of Henry Laurens*, 1915.

Laybourne, Geraldine

(1947–)
Entertainment Executive

At one point considered the number-one female executive in the television business, Geraldine Laybourne built the children's cable network, Nickelodeon, into a ratings powerhouse.

Born in 1947 in Plainfield, New Jersey, Laybourne, whose father was a businessman, grew up in nearby Martinsville and in 1969 received a B.A. degree in art history from Vassar College. When she met her future husband, Kit Laybourne, in Philadelphia, he was teaching children how to understand electronic media by having them make their own movies. Enthralled by his approach, she returned to college and, in 1971, earned a master's degree in elementary education from the University of Pennsylvania–Philadelphia.

She then began teaching school but, although she liked working with children (and in time had two of her own), she disliked the administrative system. As a result, in 1974, she quit teaching and co-founded the Media Center for Children, a nonprofit group that researched the opinions children held toward the media. She and her husband also established an independent production company and sold two shows to the new children's cable network, Nickelodeon. Impressed with her work, the company hired her in 1980 as program manager.

Although Laybourne did not become president of Nickelodeon until 1989, she soon wielded the most power at the network. Until her arrival, the network had struggled to find an audience, as most children considered its programs boring. Laybourne said: "We were losing money, we had no viewership, and kids hated us."

She changed that by introducing lively shows, beginning with *Double Dare*, which had children running through mazes and being hit with slimy gook. She also introduced *Clarissa Explains It All*, in which a 10-year-old girl pondered questions about life. To help determine programming, Laybourne emphasized a radical concept in the television industry, asking children what they wanted. Each year, she put together dozens of focus groups and surveyed them.

Besides children's programming, Laybourne launched Nick at Nite, a hip repackaging of such old sitcoms as *I Love Lucy*, *The Bob Newhart Show*, and *The Mary Tyler Moore Show*. Said one TV executive: "She wrote the book on how you take pre-existing programming and package it and make it look contemporary." At the same time, she became vice chair of MTV, the rock music video network owned by the same company that owned Nickelodeon, Viacom.

Laybourne displayed business acumen when she convinced Nickelodeon to charge premium prices for advertising during its Saturday morning cartoons. In 1995, Nick's ratings jumped 40 percent, and revenue in 1998 topped $400 million, with profits of nearly $250 million.

Then, in 1996, Laybourne stunned the industry when she announced her departure from Nick to join Disney/ABC Cable Networks as president. SUMNER REDSTONE, the head of Viacom, lamented Laybourne's departure. "Businesswise," he said, "she's a star." Many others doubted whether she could change Disney, a company known for its entrenched mentality. It was a challenging time since Disney's chairman, MICHAEL EISNER, had recently brought in MICHAEL OVITZ to serve as overall company president in an attempt to revitalize the corporation.

The skeptics proved right. Neither Ovitz nor Laybourne lasted long. She quit in 1998, little more than a year after Ovitz, and announced plans to start her own media company to provide programming for both television and the Internet. Whatever the outcome of her new venture, she will be remembered for her work at Nickelodeon. "Except for TED TURNER and his shepherding of CNN," said a writer for *Variety* before Laybourne departed Nick, "since its founding in 1980, no other cable executive is so associated with one network as Laybourne, whose nurturing of Nickelodeon spans . . . 15 years."

BIBLIOGRAPHY

Rose, Frank, "The Eisner School of Business," *Time*, July 6, 1998; Schmuckler, Eric, "From Nick to Mick," *Working Woman*, October 1996.

Lazarus, Charles

(1923–)
Merchant

No matter what the city, customers could enter Charles Lazarus's toy store and find the same toys on the same shelf. In terms of standardization, Lazarus did for toy retailing what McDonald's did for hamburgers through his store chain called Toys 'R' Us.

Lazarus, who was born in 1923 in Washington, D.C., entered the toy business unintentionally. In the late 1940s, he rented his father's bicycle repair shop, located on the ground floor of the house in which he was born, and began selling baby furniture. He sold a few toys, too, and after discovering they made more money for him than did the furniture, he added them to his line on a permanent basis. He called his store the Baby Furniture and Toy Supermarket. As an eye-catcher, the "R" in supermarket was turned backward.

By the 1960s, Lazarus had expanded to four locations, and in 1966 he sold his business to Interstate Stores for $7.5 million. Under the name TOYS, more stores opened—47 in all. But in 1974, Interstate filed for bankruptcy, and Lazarus reentered the scene. He emerged as head of Interstate, and in order to save the toy operation he sold many of the company's other holdings, including all but four of its department stores. By 1978, Interstate emerged from bankruptcy while its toy stores had expanded to 63—called Toys 'R' Us, with the "R" turned backward.

Toys 'R' Us grew behind Lazarus's formula for success. He insisted on huge stores carrying a wide variety of toys, on locations near shopping malls, on standardized floor plans (18,000 square feet) and layouts, and on discount prices. He also used a computerized inventory system, the most advanced in retailing.

By the mid-1980s, Toys 'R' Us had about 200 stores and expanded into Canada, England, and the Far East. One financial writer called the company "the Goliath of American toy retailing." In addition to Lazarus's genius, Toys 'R' Us benefited from minimal competition. Only Playworld, owned by the financially troubled Lionel Corporation, had developed another sizable toy store chain.

After stating, "I don't want to sound complaisant, but we've been looking for something that's more challenging," Lazarus began children's apparel stores called Kids 'R' Us. The move further boosted the value of his company's stock.

Lazarus, who often appeared in TV commercials with his wife and children, relinquished his positions as president and chief executive officer of Toys 'R' Us in 1994 when the company's sales sagged. Although $20 of every $100 spent on toys in the United States was spent at Toys 'R' Us, competition from large retailers, such as Wal-Mart, Kmart, and Target, who expanded their toy selections, had taken its toll. On certain items, those stores even offered lower prices than Toys 'R' Us.

Nevertheless, in 1998, Toys 'R' Us had more than 1,400 stores in over 20 countries. As for his success, Lazarus noted: "Someone . . . once said to me, 'You have a tremendous advantage. You love what you do.'"

BIBLIOGRAPHY

Chakravarty, Subrata, "Toys 'R' Fun," *Forbes*, March 28, 1983; Lubove, Seth, "The Growing Gets Tough," *Forbes*, April 13, 1992.

Lear, William

(June 26, 1902–1978)
Manufacturer

"I remember working out a blueprint for my future when I was 12," William P. Lear recollected. "I resolved first to make enough money so I'd never be stopped from finishing anything; second, that to accumulate money in a hurry . . . I'd have to invent something that people wanted; and third, that if I ever was going to stand on my own feet, I'd have to leave home." Lear left home and developed two inventions that people wanted: an automatic pilot and a small passenger jet.

William was born on June 26, 1902, in Hannibal, Missouri, but grew up in Chicago, Illinois, where his mother had moved after divorcing his father, Otto Kirmse, a German-born plasterer. William left home at age 16 and, with World War I under way, joined the navy. He studied radio technology while in the service, and in the 1920s, after his discharge, applied his inventive mind to design a radio that could be installed in automobiles, another recent invention just gaining popularity. William sold his design to the Motorola Corporation and, over the years, obtained patents for many other inventions in radio, electronics, aviation technology, and auto engineering. During the 1930s, he invented direction finders for aircraft that navigated by using radio signals.

In 1939, Lear founded Lear, Incorporated, which sold supplies to the military during World War II. Shortly after the war, he developed what some observers called his most important invention, a lightweight automatic pilot. The device used electronic impulses to stabilize an airplane and fly it on a fixed course without the pilot having to steer it.

In the late 1950s, Lear envisioned a small private jet for business executives. Impressed with a Swiss fighter, the P-16, he took a team of engineers to Switzerland and studied the aircraft. With modifications, the P-16 developed into the Lear Jet 23. In 1963, Lear began making his airplanes in a building at the Wichita, Kansas, Municipal Airport. The first prototype Learjet flew that year on October 7, and within a short time it became popular because of its speed and relatively low price. The $600,000 aircraft held eight passengers and, at 600 miles per hour, climbed to 40,000 feet in less than 6.5 minutes.

Critics questioned Lear's design, however, and their assessment proved valid when several of the aircraft crashed. With those problems and with competition from other manufacturers, Lear sold his factory in 1967 to the Gates Rubber Company of Denver, Colorado. Gates Rubber revised the design, and the jet regained its popularity.

After a brief retirement, Lear, who had amassed a $75 million fortune, moved to Reno, Nevada, and in the 1970s tried, and failed, to perfect an efficient steam engine for autos. He died in 1978 from leukemia and was survived by his third wife, seven children (three by previous marriages), and several grandchildren.

Lear's former company, Learjet, struggled again in the early 1980s from competition and nearly folded. But Bombardier, Incorporated of Canada bought the company in 1990 and today continues to operate it.

BIBLIOGRAPHY
Boesen, Victor, *They Said It Couldn't Be Done: The Incredible Story of Bill Lear*, 1971; Petrakis, Harry M., *The Founder's Touch: The Life of Paul Galvin of Motorola*, 1965.

Leslie, Miriam

(June 5, 1836–September 18, 1914)
Publisher

Although Miriam Florence Follin Leslie is notable for many of the interesting paths she took in life, she is best known for her impact on publishing and editing. She not only managed a vast and profitable publishing business, but her style of illustrated journalism cultivated the growing American desire for immediate, detailed, and sensational news stories.

Miriam Follin was born in New Orleans, Louisiana, on June 5, 1836. (Miriam cultivated an air of mystery throughout her life, occasionally giving the year 1851 as her birthdate and maintaining for several decades that she was in her thirties.) Her father, Charles Follin, a descendant of Creole immigrants, worked in his family's commission business. Her mother, Susan Danforth, was from New England. Miriam had two brothers—Ormond Weyman Follin and Augustus Noel Follin.

Though the family struggled financially, education was a priority. Miriam learned several languages and was well versed in literature and the classics. The family moved from Louisiana to Ohio in 1846 and by 1850 had settled in New York City.

came the editor of *Frank Leslie's Illustrated Newspaper.*

Miriam, who had been writing for publication since she was 14 years old, began to contribute to the newspaper. By 1863, she was the editor of her own publication, *Frank Leslie's Lady's Magazine.* Over the next few years, she became the successful editor of two more magazines and also became involved romantically with her publisher, Frank Leslie. She divorced Squier in 1873 and married Frank Leslie a year later. The marriage to Leslie made her a wealthy woman, and her lifestyle changed dramatically. Miriam began to entertain extravagantly and wrote several books. An elaborate trip to the West Coast is chronicled in her book, *California: A Pleasure Trip from Gotham to the Golden Gate*, which was published in 1877.

Leslie died in 1880, leaving Miriam with a publishing company that had, by then, begun to struggle. The company's financial problems prompted Miriam to embark on a highly successful foray into the publishing world that would eventually earn her the title "the empress of journalism." She would take over Leslie's publishing business and turn the fortunes of the company around, but before the business could attempt a recovery, Miriam was faced with a tremendous amount of debt. In the period immediately following her husband's death, she demonstrated the resourcefulness, business acumen, and dramatic flair for attention that characterized the woman who was dubbed the "commercial Joan of Arc."

Following Leslie's death, Miriam was frequently in the headlines as the nation followed her court battles to assume the leadership of the publishing house left to

Miriam Leslie (Archive Photos)

Miriam was a curious, beautiful, and impetuous girl, and in 1854 her family learned of her brief love affair with David Peacock, a jeweler's clerk. Though her family successfully pressured her to marry him to avoid scandal, the two separated immediately, and the marriage was annulled two years later.

In 1857, Miriam began a stint on the stage, appearing as "Minnie Montez," the fictional sister of the famous actress and courtesan Lola Montez. After some success in the role, the relationship between the two actresses soured, and Miriam left the act. In 1857, she married Ephraim G. Squier, an archeologist who in 1861 be-her by her husband. It was an inheritance sharply contested by the Leslie relatives. As soon as Miriam won the suit, she assumed full control over the publishing house to ensure that the business would flourish and that her claim to it would prevail. In 1882, she took the unusual step of having her name legally changed to Frank Leslie, thus securing her right to the continued use of the name on the masthead of various publications.

Under her assertive leadership, the publishing house quickly regained its footing. Miriam eliminated six publications and assumed editorial control of the remaining six. Her first publishing coup occurred when President James A. Garfield was shot by an assassin. Within an hour of hearing rumors of the attack, Miriam arranged for artists to go to Washington, D.C. Her staff worked overtime, and by the end of the week, three editions of *Frank Leslie's Illustrated Newspaper* had been released, each one packed with illustrations and sensational details of the crisis. This accomplishment, three illustrated newspapers in a week, was unprecedented in publishing history and was considered "an achievement without parallel" in the newspaper world, marking just one of many occasions where Miriam's intuition and canny business sense enabled her to break new ground in the profession.

Under her direction, the publishing house grew to a circulation of over 250,000, employing 400 people at its peak. Miriam, who continued to be an active socialite while working slavishly at her career, was the subject of intense public admiration and scrutiny. Her clothes, the literary and artistic salons held at her house, her dramatic love affairs, and her own observations on society were frequently the subjects of articles and general conversation.

In 1891, Miriam married William C. K. Wilde, the brother of British author Oscar Wilde. The marriage was short-lived, ending in divorce in 1893. In 1895, Miriam retired, leasing the business to a syndicate. She traveled extensively and became a favorite speaker on the lecture circuit. Crowds of people all over the country turned out to hear her discourse on the newspaper trade, her childhood, her jewelry, politics—everything and anything she chose to discuss.

After several years, however, the failure of the syndicate caused Miriam to resume control of her publishing house. Upon her return, she restored *Frank Leslie's Popular Monthly* to its previous circulation of over 200,000. By 1900, however, she had given up editorial control and relinquished half-ownership of the company.

Once again retired, Miriam remained active, traveling to Europe and entertaining in New York City. After her European trip, she assumed for herself the title Baroness de Bazus, claiming it to be her ancestral legacy.

A firm proponent of women's rights throughout her life, Miriam willed almost $1 million to Carrie Chapman Catt for the woman's suffrage movement. "Frank Leslie," the woman with the man's name who was the leader in a male-dominated industry, died in New York City on September 18, 1914, of acute dilation of the heart.

BIBLIOGRAPHY

Leslie, Miriam, *California: A Pleasure Trip from Gotham to the Golden Gate*, 1877; Stern, Madeleine, *Purple Passage: The Life of Mrs. Frank Leslie*, 1953; Stern, Madeleine B., *Queen of Publishers' Row: Mrs. Frank Leslie*, 1965.

Lewis, David

(July 6, 1917–)
Airline Executive

Most noted for saving the financially troubled Douglas Aircraft Company and General Dynamics Corporation, at the end of his career David Lewis was widely criticized for mismanagement.

David was born on July 6, 1917, in North Augusta, South Carolina, to David S. Lewis and Reuben (Walton) Lewis. After graduating in 1934 from Columbia High School in Columbia, South Carolina, he attended the University of South Carolina before transferring to the Georgia Institute of Technology and receiving a B.S. degree in 1939. The Glenn L. Martin Company then hired him as an aerodynamics engineer in Baltimore, Maryland. He married Dorothy Sharpe in 1941, and they had four children.

In 1946, Lewis left Martin to head the aerodynamics division at the McDonnell Aircraft Corporation in St. Louis, Missouri. At that time, the company had several lucrative contracts with the Defense Department to build the F-3H Demon and F-101 Voodoo jets. Six years later, Lewis was appointed chief of preliminary design, and after that he rose rapidly in the corporate ranks, becoming executive vice president in 1962 and, after James McDonnell retired, president and CEO.

Lewis expanded McDonnell's business when he won a contract from the federal government to build the F-4 Phantom jet. His leadership resulted in the company doubling its size and reaping substantial profits. In 1967, he merged McDonnell with the financially troubled Douglas Aircraft Corporation, then experiencing difficulty meeting deadlines in producing its DC-8 and DC-9 passenger jets. As head of McDonnell-Douglas, Lewis expanded the facilities, hired 10,000 additional workers to meet the deadlines, and matched the competition posed by Lockheed, then marketing its L-1011. In 1969, McDonnell-Douglas earned more than $100 million.

The following year, Lewis accepted an offer to lead the General Dynamics Corporation, which had recently lost more than $6 million. He centralized decision making, improved procurement procedures, tightened inventory controls, and moved the company's headquarters from New York City to St. Louis. In 1971, the firm showed a profit of $22 million.

Despite cost overruns in producing the F-111 jet for the military, Lewis scored what some called "the arms deal of the century" when in January 1975 he obtained a contract from the Pentagon to build 650 YF-16 jet fighters for the air force at a cost of $4.3 billion. Six months later, he arranged to sell 348 YF-16 jets to four European nations for $2.1 billion.

But the cost overruns typical of General Dynamics eventually ensnared Lewis. In 1984, a federal grand jury began investigating the problem, and a few weeks later the navy suspended contracts at two General Dynamics divisions because of overcharges. The navy then canceled two missile contracts worth $22.5 million and fined the company for giving gifts to an admiral who directed the Trident submarine program. Only Lewis's resignation in June 1985—at a time when 80 percent of General Dynamics' sales of $7.8 billion were through government contracts—prevented the government from debarring him and two other General Dynamics executives from negotiating for Pentagon contracts. Since that time, Lewis has been retired.

BIBLIOGRAPHY

Rogers, Michael, "Sudden Changes at General Dynamics," *Fortune*, June 24, 1985; Shaw, Gaylord, "Chairman to Retire at General Dynamics in Wake of U.S. Sanctions," *Los Angeles Times*, May 23, 1985.

Lewis, Reginald

(December 7, 1942–January 19, 1993)
Financier

Wall Street was stunned in 1987 when an African-American attorney and small-stakes financier maneuvered the largest leveraged corporate takeover in business history with his acquisition of Beatrice Foods International for $1 billion. The deal, though spectacular, was just the most visible example of the many accomplishments of the determined, arrogant, generous, and intelligent Reginald Francis Lewis.

Born on December 7, 1942, in Baltimore, Maryland, Reginald was the son of Clinton and Carolyn Cooper Lewis. An only child, Reginald had six cousins, one of whom, James, became an older brother figure to Reginald. His parents divorced when he was young, leaving Reginald to be raised by his mother and his maternal grandparents and, eventually, his stepfather, Jean Fuget. His family's work ethic and pride instilled in the young Reginald an early appreciation of financial independence and hard work.

Lewis attended Catholic schools and demonstrated his entrepreneurial streak through his work on a paper route at the age of 10. When he tired of the route, he sold it to his friend, a sale that would be his first of many leveraged buyouts. In high school, Lewis was active in sports and was a serious student. He also cultivated expensive tastes after observing the customers at the country club where he worked.

In 1961, Lewis entered Virginia State University, where he began an anticipated career in football until an injury to his shoulder changed his plans. During college, he juggled vigorous studying with a demanding sales job. Initially driven purely by a desire to do well, Lewis decided by his senior year to pursue law school. Despite an uneven academic record, he negotiated his way into the group of students selected to participate in a Harvard University summer law program for minorities. Confident by the end of summer that Harvard Law School was his path, Lewis managed to gain admission even though the program was never intended to be used as a springboard for minority admissions. Lewis became the first law student to attend Harvard without submitting an application, a feat he achieved largely through the force of his dynamic personality.

One of only 17 African-American students in a freshman class of 500, Lewis quickly developed a strong social network that transcended ethnicity. Though known as a ladies' man and an extrovert, Lewis was very focused. By his third year at Harvard, Lewis knew that he wanted to become involved in corporate finance.

After graduating in 1968, Lewis obtained a job with the New York City law firm of Paul, Weiss, Rifkind, Wharton, and Garrison. The following year, he married Loida Nicolas, a law student from the Philippines, with whom he had two daughters. Just two years after joining the firm, Lewis shocked his colleagues by leaving to start the first African-American law firm on Wall Street, with partners Charles Laurence, Rita Murphy, and Josephine Thorpe.

During the first few years of the firm's operation, associates came and went, and the partnership eventually was split between Lewis and a college friend, Charles Clarkson. Initially, most of the work came from servicing the New York Urban Coalition's low- and moderate- income housing program. Within a few years, however, Lewis had landed some high-profile corporate clients including General Foods, Aetna Life, and the Ford Foundation.

Anxious to move into the high-stakes field of corporate finance, Lewis cut his teeth on a number of attempts in the late 1970s. Though unsuccessful, he learned lessons about timing, strategy, and raising investment capital that prepared him well for the ambitious endeavors he would soon undertake. When a deal dissolved in 1978, Lewis used the disappointment to take stock and decided that he was not yet ready for high-stakes negotiations. He soon became a self-proclaimed "prospectus junkie," devoting himself to learning every detail publicly available about companies of inter-est. He also realized that serious deal makers involved themselves full-time. He continued with the legal work but began to seriously seek an opportunity to propel himself into the ranks of serious venture capitalists.

In 1983, Lewis found his vehicle. After identifying the potential in McCall's Pattern Company, he set up TLC Pattern, Inc. to use as the mechanism for purchasing McCall. Though he had virtually no track record in venture capital, Lewis put together a loan package of $23 million and raised $1 million in cash to purchase McCall. Over the next few years, through brilliant management in reducing costs, he sold the company, including its $32 million debt, for $63 million. Though Lewis had bigger surprises to spring on Wall Street in his future, this was the deal that catapulted Lewis into the elite group of corporate takeover players.

In 1987, Lewis, with the confident backing of the king of the corporate acquisitions, MICHAEL MILKEN, acquired Beatrice Food International, a massive conglomerate with 64 separate companies in 31 countries, for $1 billion. With over 20,000 employees, the purchase made Beatrice the largest African-American-owned firm. Though Lewis was uncomfortable with the media focus on the racial aspects of his financial coup, he was pleased that the deal added to the visibility of African-American accomplishment.

Unlike the acquisition of McCall, which was a means to an end, Lewis became very interested in the long-term management of Beatrice. He moved quickly to sell off many of the foreign branches and tighten up the company. In 1992, TLC Beatrice earned $1.542 billion in sales and had over 5,000 employees.

Lewis was very involved in family activities, spending as much time as possible with his wife and children at Broadmoor, their Long Island estate. He was a loyal friend and throughout his career was a generous, though low-profile philanthropist who gave millions to charities and worthy enterprises. Though he was not especially political, Lewis was a solid supporter of the presidential campaigns of Jesse Jackson, with whom he became friends.

Long after securing his wealth and celebrity status, Lewis continued to work at a frenetic pace. On January 19, 1993, less than a year after his fiftieth birthday, Lewis died from a brain tumor.

BIBLIOGRAPHY

Business Week, June 3, 1985, and August 24, 1987; Lewis, Reginald F., and Blair S. Walker, "Why Should White Guys Have All the Fun?" How Reginald Lewis Created a Billion-Dollar Business Empire, 1995; *USA Today*, January 20, 1993.

Lilly, Eli

(April 1, 1885–January 24, 1977)
Manufacturer

After working at his family's pharmaceutical company as a youngster, Eli Lilly led it through the Great Depression of the 1930s and oversaw its development of new drugs.

Born on April 1, 1885, in Indianapolis, Indiana, the son of Josiah K. Lilly and Lilly (Ridgely) Lilly, Eli grew up in a business environment. His grandfather had founded Eli Lilly & Company as a drug firm, and his father was president. Eli first worked at the company at age 10, when he helped out on Saturdays and, later, during the summers. In 1907, he received a degree in pharmaceutical chemistry from the Philadelphia College of Pharmacy and Science. He then immediately joined the company full-time.

At first placed in charge of efficiency, in 1909 Lily was made superintendent of the manufacturing division. In that

Eli Lilly (UPI/Corbis-Bettmann)

capacity, he modernized the firm's practices. He became general superintendent in 1915 and vice president in 1920. In 1932, he succeeded his father as president. By that time, the Great Depression had overtaken America, and it fell on Lilly to guide his company through the difficult times. He did so successfully and avoided layoffs by putting his employees to work painting walls, washing windows, and sweeping floors, and by expanding his sales force. His aggressive marketing resulted in an increase in sales from $13 million annually in 1932 to $117 million annually in 1948.

During that same period, he and his company contributed to the development of such new drugs as barbiturates in the 1930s and penicillin and other antibiotics in the 1940s. During the following decade, Eli Lilly & Company produced LSD in a controversial, top-secret program with the Central Intelligence Agency, which hoped the hallucinogen would act as a mind-control drug. Scientists at Eli Lilly & Company assured the government agency that "in a matter of months LSD would be available in tonnage quantities."

Meanwhile, Lilly relinquished the presidency in 1948 to serve as chairman, a position he held until 1961, when his brother, Josiah K. Lilly Jr., succeeded him. After Josiah died in 1966, Eli Lilly resumed the chairmanship and held it for three years, until his retirement.

Lilly also engaged in philanthropy, establishing the Lilly Endowment, which provided money to hundreds of colleges and universities. He also wrote several books and articles that reflected his interest in history. Lilly died on January 24, 1977.

BIBLIOGRAPHY

Clark, Roscoe Collins, *Threescore Years and Ten: A Narrative of the First Seventy Years of Eli Lilly and Company, 1876–1946*, 1946; Kahn, E. J., *All in a Century: The First 100 Years of Eli Lilly and Company*, 1975; Lilly, Eli, *Early Wawasee Days*, 1960; Lilly, Eli, *The Lilly Church on the Circle*, 1957; Lilly, Eli, *Prehistoric Antiquities of Indiana*, 1937; Lilly, Eli, *Walam Olum*, 1954.

Ling, James

(December 31, 1922–)
Financier

James Ling represented the type of 1980s business leader who often got the most public attention: a financial dealer less concerned with managing a firm than with forming conglomerates, selling, buying, moving on, and selling and buying again.

James was born on December 31, 1922, in Hugo, Oklahoma, to Henry William Ling and Mary (Jones) Ling. His father, of Bavarian ancestry, worked as a railroad fireman and later as an oil field roustabout. At age 11, Ling's mother died, and his life turned upside down. First his father sent him to a boarding school in Ardmore, Oklahoma. Later the youngster lived with an aunt in Shreveport, Louisiana, and attended a prep school. Then his father entered a Carmelite monastery and lived in seclusion, never again seeing James. With no money coming in from his father, James was forced to leave school at age 14. Over the next several years, he held various odd jobs and got married in 1939 before entering the navy in 1944.

Upon his discharge in 1946, James used money from the sale of a house he owned to start an electrical contracting business in Dallas, Texas. At first he handled only home service, such as repairing household wiring. Later he acquired industrial contracts, and his business boomed. By 1955, his gross annual income reached $1.5 million. Meanwhile, his first marriage ended in divorce, and in 1956 he married Dorothy Hill, his secretary. Ling had two sons by his first marriage and a stepson by his second.

The following year, Ling bought an electronics business and merged it with his contracting company to form Ling Electronics. He made vibration testing equipment for the aerospace industry, and by 1959 his annual revenues neared $7 million. Over the next two years, more acquisitions followed: Altec Company, makers of speakers and other sound equipment; University Loudspeakers; Continental Electronics; Temco, makers of electronics reconnaissance equipment for the military; and Chance-Vought Aircraft Corporation. The Ling-Temco-Vought (LTV) merger formed a conglomerate that represented the accelerating post–World War II trend toward ever-larger business units.

Ling directed LTV to even greater expansion in 1965 when he bought the Okonite Company, Kennecott Copper's power cable division. Two years later, he acquired Wilson and Company, which was involved in the making of a variety of products, from meatpacking to sporting goods. Ling's acquisitions in the late 1960s continued at a rapid pace, including the Great American Corporation, a bank and insurance holding business, and the Jones and Laughlin Steel Company, a deal that required him to relinquish some of his holdings. All these maneuvers ranked LTV among the nation's largest corporations and made Ling a multimillionaire.

Yet he encountered problems. In 1969, an economic recession combined with his company's heavy indebtedness to force retrenchment, and he laid off workers and sold properties. The crisis worsened to the point that in 1970 Ling was removed as chairman of LTV and lost his Dallas mansion to creditors.

He recovered, however, and in a settlement with his creditors became chairman of Omega-Alpha, Incorporated, a holding company. Then in 1971, he bought Okonite from LTV. Ling took little interest in management. Instead, he pursued finance and the hunt for combinations, often through risky, heavily indebted deals.

Perhaps Ling's biggest challenge, though, came in 1981 when a rare disorder, Gullain-Barre Syndrome, racked his nervous system. The disease paralyzed him, yet he still made business decisions from an intensive-care unit by blinking to signify words as his wife pointed to a letter board.

After his recovery in 1983, Ling handled finances for the L. G. Williams Company, a firm dealing in oil leases. He said about his business pursuits in the wake of his disease: "It is not completely honest to say that money doesn't interest me. Now, though, it's just a way of keeping score. My illness has given me a sense of values that I simply did not have before."

BIBLIOGRAPHY

Angrist, Stanley, "The Return of Ling," *Forbes*, January 3, 1983; Sobel, Robert, *The Age of Giant Corporations*, 1972.

Loew, Marcus

(May 7, 1870–September 5, 1927)
Entertainment Executive

Marcus Loew once attributed his success to the good fortune of living when the new technology of motion pictures transfixed America. He made a fortune by building theaters and forming a giant studio, Metro-Goldwyn-Mayer.

Marcus was born on May 7, 1870, in New York City to Herman Loew and Ida (Lowenstein) Loew. His parents, immigrant Austrians, struggled to make a living on the city's East Side, and Marcus was forced to leave school at about age 10 to find a job. For a while he worked in a printing shop, and later he published his own weekly newspaper, but neither these nor other endeavors proved profitable, and at about age 20 he declared bankruptcy.

Shortly thereafter, Loew went into business processing furs and used his earnings to buy real estate. At about the same time, he married Caroline Rosenheim, and they had two sons. In the early 1900s, Loew's real estate investments brought him into contact with an actor, David Warfield, and they began investing in the penny arcades. After a brief partnership with businessman Adolph Zukor, they formed their own company, capitalized at $100,000. In 1904, they opened an arcade in Cincinnati, Ohio, in a storeroom where they placed penny peep machines, shooting galleries, mechanical fortune-tellers, and fun-house mirrors.

After a few months, Loew received a new machine that showed moving pictures. He outfitted a second-floor loft above his arcade with folding chairs and a large white sheet to serve as a screen. For five cents, audiences saw a half-hour silent movie accompanied by piano music. The movies typically showed speeding locomotives, bathing beauties, and news events.

Customers flocked to Loew's new offering, and he and Warfield sensed that motion pictures had a future well beyond lofts over arcades. As a result, they began buying stores in New York City and remodeling them for movies. Soon they made more money from the theaters than they did from the arcades.

As Hollywood studios began producing full-length motion pictures, Loew bought a playhouse in Brooklyn and readied it for the new technology. He presented movies and vaudeville acts, a combination so popular that shortly before and during World War I, he opened many more small theaters in New York City and elsewhere.

Loew then expanded into movie production. Upon learning that the Metro Film Corporation was in financial trouble due to cost overruns from making *Four Horsemen of the Apocalypse*, Loew bought the company in 1920. Four years later, he merged Metro with the Louis B. Mayer Company and Goldwyn Pictures, creating Metro-Goldwyn-Mayer, or M-G-M as it was renamed in 1926, a subsidiary of Loew's, Incorporated. Loew handled his diverse operations from New York City, while LOUIS MAYER and Irving Thalberg oversaw production at the California studios.

Loew's then began building large, elaborate movie palaces, replete with velvet curtains, Oriental carpeting, balconies, even chandeliers. The most famous of Loew's theaters included the State, Roxy, and Paramount in New York City; the Palace in Dallas; the Chicago, Oriental, and Tivoli in Chicago; and Fox Theaters in Atlanta, Detroit, and St. Louis. The movies together with the ornate surroundings provided a luxurious escape for thousands of middle-class patrons.

Loew died on September 5, 1927, just weeks before the first full-length movie containing sound, *The Jazz Singer*, swept America. His successors, however, continued to expand his business, even during the Great Depression of the 1930s. In 1989, Loew's Theaters became a part of Sony Pictures Entertainment.

BIBLIOGRAPHY

Bowers, Q. David, *Nickelodeon Theaters and Their Music*, 1986; Hampton, Benjamin Bowles, *A History of the Movies*, 1932; Irwin, Will, *The House That Shadows Built*, 1970.

Lorenzo, Frank

(May 19, 1940–)
Airline Executive

Francisco Anthony Lorenzo ripped through airline companies like a scourge, plundering them and leaving their skeletal remains as his trophy. He bought and operated Texas International Airlines, Continental Airlines, and Eastern Airlines, expanding them briefly, but then contributing to their collapse.

Francisco was born on May 19, 1940, in New York City to Olegario Lorenzo and Ana (Mateos) Lorenzo, immigrants from Spain. His father was a hairdresser and owned a beauty shop in Manhattan. After completing high school, Francisco studied economics at Columbia University and received his undergraduate degree in 1961. Two years later, he obtained his M.B.A. from Harvard.

He then worked as a financial analyst at Trans World Airlines (TWA). In 1965, he left TWA and joined the financial analysis department at Eastern Airlines as its manager. By this time, he desired to go into his own business, and in 1966 he and a classmate from Harvard, Robert Carney, established Carney & Company, a financial advisory firm. With the modest profits they earned, in 1969 they formed

Frank Lorenzo (Corbis/Bettmann-UPI)

a holding company, Jet Capital Corporation. They offered stock and raised more money to further their business of leasing planes, but their biggest deal came in 1971 when Chase Manhattan Bank asked them to help save Texas International Airlines (TXI), a company near bankruptcy. Jet Capital arranged a refinancing plan, and in August 1972 Lorenzo became TXI's president and chief operating officer. Two years later, he married Sharon Neill Murray. The couple had four children.

Lorenzo needed help in turning TXI around, and for this he turned to Donald Burr, who in 1977 devised "peanuts fares," superlow discounts on certain routes. TXI's earnings consequently doubled in 1977 and again in 1978, and observers hailed Lorenzo as a brilliant business leader. Often overlooked, however, was the important contribution made by the federal government when the Civil Aeronautics Board (CAB) decided to increase the subsidies it paid to TXI for losses on short-haul routes. In fact, over the years Lorenzo developed a cozy relationship with the CAB, even employing its former general counsel as TXI's executive vice president.

While TXI expanded in profits and size, it fell victim to some disturbing developments. Complaints about service became endemic, and questions arose about safety. Nevertheless, Lorenzo wanted to gain control of a larger airline, and in 1980 he established a holding company, Texas Air Corporation, that in its turn formed a subsidiary, New York Air, to run a shuttle service between New York City and Washington, D.C. After the CAB granted approval, New York Air began offering cheap fares, accomplished in part by using poorly paid, nonunion pilots. Building on this success, in early 1981 Lorenzo and Texas Air bought an interest in the nation's tenth largest airline, Continental.

From here, there was no turning back. Lorenzo bought more shares of stock until he forced the company's president, Alvin Feldman, and its unions to acquiesce in his control (a deal that so shattered Feldman, he committed suicide). In 1982, TXI merged into Continental (by then controlled by Texas Air).

Continental suffered enormous losses and plunged into a dispute with its unions. In 1983, when the machinists' union struck, Lorenzo sought reorganization under Chapter 11 of the federal bankruptcy laws, a move that voided all of the airline's labor contracts. He then fired 12,000 employees and invited 4,000 to return with substantially lower wages. With its payrolls pared and superlow fares, Continental soon began showing a substantial profit.

Lorenzo aimed for another conquest in 1986 and went after Eastern Airlines, also a struggling company involved in labor disputes. He acquired Eastern in February for $640 million, followed in September by People Express, which was merged into Continental in a move that made Continental the largest airline in the nation.

Before long, a war erupted between Lorenzo and the unions at Eastern. Lorenzo considered the labor costs at Eastern excessive, while the unions refused to make any substantial concessions. As a result, Lorenzo decided to transfer Eastern's assets to his other holdings and reduce Eastern's flights while increasing Continental's. When Lorenzo tried to transfer Eastern's lucrative air shuttle system, which served several northeastern cities, to Texas Air, the machinists' union got a federal court to block the move.

In 1987, Eastern lost more than $180 million while, as with TXI and Continental, passengers complained about poor service. Lorenzo had miscalculated when he concluded there would be no complaints as long as fares remained low. By 1988, Continental began to unravel, and the airline lost nearly $100 million. Later that year, Lorenzo tried to save Eastern by selling its air shuttle system to financier DONALD TRUMP.

This done, he raised fares at both Continental and Eastern. He also pressured his pilots for more and more flights, to the point that they complained about unusually long shifts of up to 90 hours in the air a month. In 1989, a strike by the machinists' union at Eastern caused Lorenzo to again file for Chapter 11 bankruptcy. Unlike the time he filed for bankruptcy at Continental, the strategy failed. Lorenzo's airline empire was losing too much money, and investors had little faith.

Eastern, placed in the hands of a court-appointed trustee, struggled for two more years and then collapsed. Removed from Continental, Lorenzo saw his reputation change from financial genius to financial charlatan. When in 1994 he tried to start a new short-haul carrier on the East Coast, the Department of Transportation rejected his application. A federal court upheld the decision, declaring that while Lorenzo was head of Eastern and Continental, he had acted in a confrontational and cavalier manner.

BIBLIOGRAPHY

Ramsey, Douglas K., *The Corporate Warriors*, 1987.

Love, James

(July 6, 1896–January 20, 1962)
Manufacturer

James Spencer Love, one of the first in the textile industry to produce the synthetic fiber rayon, built a small cotton mill into Burlington Industries, the world's largest maker of textiles. At the time of his death, Burlington Industries, with over 65,000 employees, became the first textile company to exceed $1 billion in annual sales.

The son of Julia James and James Lee Love, a professor of mathematics at Harvard University, James was born on July 6, 1896, in Cambridge, Massachusetts. After attending Cambridge Latin School, James completed a bachelor of arts degree in just three years at Harvard during 1914–1917. A year at the Harvard Graduate School of Business was followed by service in the military during World War I. While assigned to the adjutant general's office, he served a term in Europe, earning promotion to major and a citation.

After the war, Love was surprised to encounter difficulty finding a job in the Boston area, later reminiscing that he was astonished to discover that "no-one gave much of a damn about [his] brand-new Harvard degree or even [his] war record." Sometime in late 1917, he moved to North Carolina to work for his uncle as a payroll clerk for the Gastonia Cotton Manufacturing Company. Eager to advance his position, Love persuaded his father and other investors to join him in purchasing the firm a year later. Love's father became president with Love as secretary-treasurer and general manager. The cotton industry proved unsteady, however, and in 1923 Love shut down the firm, selling the building and the equipment for $200,000.

Love decided to move to Burlington, North Carolina, with his new wife, Sara Elizabeth, whom he had married on January 25, 1922. The couple later had four sons—James Spencer, Robert Lee, Richard, and Julian. In Burlington, after encountering support from a group of local textile manufacturers, Love opened the new Burlington Mills Company in October 1924. With the popularity of cotton in decline, Love decided to gamble on the production of a new, man-made fabric called rayon, which was made from a chemically produced material called cellulose. Though criticized by some as being too shiny and of cheap appearance, Love found the fabric to be a great product for weaving bedspreads. The low-cost spreads sold rapidly, and Love continued to seek out new products from rayon, achieving success rapidly as demand necessitated the construction of additional mills around the nation.

By 1936, Love had turned Burlington Mills into a textiles giant, despite the Great Depression that had rocked the country. The following year, the mills' headquarters moved to Greensboro, where, in 1939, Love established six mills solely for the manufacture of hosiery. On July 23, 1944, four years after divorcing his first wife, Love married Martha Eskridge, with whom he had three children—Charles, Martin, and Cornelia Leila.

During World War II, Burlington Mills made cloth and yarn for a number of war products, grossing $150 million annually by the end of the war. This positive financial status encouraged Love to begin a planned expansion of the company through acquisition of other firms. He bought Cramerton Mills, which focused primarily on cotton and twill, marking a departure from Burlington's synthetics focus. In 1948, May-McEwen-Kaiser (a hosiery company) was brought on board. Over time, other subsidiaries were added, propelling the company in 1955 to become incorporated as Burlington Industries, Inc.

Aside from his dedicated pursuit of business objectives, Love was involved with the governing bodies of the University of North Carolina, Davidson College, and the New York Trust Company. His drive to succeed and his zeal for self-improvement were also evident in his great enthusiasm for sports such as golf and tennis. At the time of his death from a heart attack during a tennis match on January 20, 1962, he was the president of a company with over 65,000 employees in 130 plants in over seven countries.

BIBLIOGRAPHY

Business Week, November 5, 1955; Hallett, Anthony, *Entrepreneur Magazine: Encyclopedia of Entrepreneurs*, 1997; Moskowitz, Milton, et al., eds., *Everybody's Business*, 1980; *New York Times*, February 8, 1957.

Low, Isaac

(April 13, 1735–July 25, 1791)
Merchant

A prominent colonial merchant, Isaac Low gained political prominence during the American Revolution as a voice against the movement toward independence.

Isaac was born on April 13, 1735, near New Brunswick, New Jersey, to Cornelius Low Jr. and Johanna (Gouverneur) Low. As a young man, he moved to New York City and before long made a fortune as a merchant. He also obtained an interest in a slitting mill, and had numerous other commercial connections. He was married in 1760 to Margarita Cuyler, the daughter of the mayor of Albany, New York.

Low's economic prominence involved him in politics, which was not an unusual development given the community leadership provided by many merchants in colonial America and the measures passed by Parliament that directly affected trade. As disputes between the colonies and Britain intensified in the 1760s, Low served as a delegate to the Stamp Act Congress, which protested the British tax on items printed within the colonies. In 1768, after Parliament passed the Townshend Acts, he headed a committee to enforce a boycott of British goods.

Yet revolutionaries questioned Low's radicalism. Massachusetts leader John Adams, for one, believed Low to be insincere in his protests against Britain. Whether he lacked sincerity or simply cooled to the possibility of breaking with Britain, Low began to take an increasingly conservative position, and after the first shots of the Revolution were fired in 1775 at Lexington and Concord, he worked to dissuade the Second Continental Congress from declaring independence.

When British troops occupied New York City, Low supported them. Elected president of the New York Chamber of Commerce in 1775, he led its Loyalist wing and in 1779 expressed sympathy for England. The revolutionaries confiscated his lands that same year, and in 1783, as the war neared its end, Low moved to England. He died on July 25, 1791.

BIBLIOGRAPHY

Abbott, Wilbur Cortez, *New York in the American Revolution*, 1929; Rosebrock, Ellen, *Farewell to Old England: New York in Revolution*, 1976.

Lowell, Francis

April 7, 1775–August 10, 1817)
Manufacturer

Through his founding of the Lowell Mills in the early 1800s, Francis Cabot Lowell changed the character of textile manufacturing and contributed significantly to America's early industrialization.

Born on April 7, 1775, in Newburyport, Massachusetts, to John Lowell, a judge, and Susanna (Cabot) Lowell, Francis was raised in Boston. In 1789, at age 14, he entered Harvard where he excelled at mathematics and graduated in 1793.

After leaving Harvard, Lowell entered a merchant house owned by his uncle, William Cabot. Ill health in 1810 forced Lowell to journey to England to seek recovery. There he saw great factories whose prosperity convinced him that America should industrialize to develop national wealth. He especially studied the textile machinery used in Lancashire, and upon his return to Massachusetts in 1812 went to work developing plans for his own factory.

The War of 1812, which disrupted trade with England, further convinced him that America needed its own textile mills. He formed the Boston Manufacturing Company and in 1813 began building his plant. Relying on memory from his observations in England, he designed the power loom and added improvements that made it operate faster.

Lowell opened his factory at Waltham, Massachusetts, in 1814, the first mill in the world that converted raw cotton into finished cloth at a single location. For laborers he hired mainly young, single women who lived in company housing under strict supervision. Lowell was de-

Francis Lowell (Library of Congress)

termined that his factory and American industrialization would avoid the English system, which relied on workers from slum neighborhoods and perpetuated and worsened their living conditions.

Thus, the "Lowell girls," as they were called, adhered to curfews, attended church, and avoided all "disorderly or improper conduct." Lowell's system, however, proved to be an anomaly, and American industrialization, like its English counterpart, in time resorted to cheap labor recruited from among the poor. In any event, by the time of his death on August 10, 1817, Lowell had founded America's textile manufacturing system and moved the nation toward an industrial future.

BIBLIOGRAPHY

Coburn, Frederick William, *History of Lowell and Its People*, 1920.

Lucas, George

(May 14, 1944–)
Producer

Best known for writing and directing the movie *Star Wars*, through his Lucasfilm company George Lucas exerted an influence in Hollywood film production perhaps second only to WALT DISNEY.

Born on May 14, 1944, in Modesto, California, Lucas grew up on his father's walnut farm near town. At first, young George aspired to race cars, and as a teenager often sped along the local highways in a modified Fiat. He changed his goal just days before his high school graduation, however, when he wrapped his car around a walnut tree and landed unconscious in the hospital. He later said, "The accident made me more aware of myself and my feelings. I began to trust my instincts. I had the feeling that I should go to college, and I did. I had the same feeling later that I should go to film school, even though everybody thought I was nuts. I had the same feeling when I made *Star Wars*, when even my friends told me I was crazy. These are things that have to be done, and I feel as if I have to do them."

After attending Modesto Junior College, Lucas, who had barely passed high school, gained admission to the University of Southern California's film program. There he impressed director Roger Cor-

man, who allowed him to shoot a short documentary about another director, Francis Ford Coppola. Coppola, in turn, helped get Lucas a contract with Warner Brothers so the neophyte could write a plot for a science fiction movie, *THX 1138*.

Released in 1971, *THX 1138* received generally poor reviews, yet some saw potential in Lucas, and *Newsweek* magazine called the movie "an extremely professional first film." Lucas shot his second movie, *American Graffiti*, which he wrote and directed, on a low budget, but critics praised it, and in 1973 audiences flocked to see it. At that point, Twentieth Century–Fox signed Lucas to shoot *Star Wars*. He wrote the screenplay over three years and shot the movie in Tunisia and England. A spectacular presentation, its advanced technology and modernized Flash Gordon–type science fiction story made it an instant hit, breaking all box office records in 1977 and becoming a classic. He followed *Star Wars* with the equally successful *The Empire Strikes Back*.

Lucas founded Lucasfilm, a private company with himself as chairman of the board. Located in San Rafael, California, Lucasfilm consisted in the early 1980s of five stucco buildings that housed, in addition to a studio, Industrial Light & Magic (ILM), an optical research lab. At the time, Lucasfilm had average annual revenues of $26 million, and Lucas was worth $60 million. He expressed his preference, however, for directing and editing movies, rather than executive work. "Running the company to me is like mowing the lawn," he said. "It has to be done; I semi-enjoy it, once in a while."

A private person, Lucas avoided the Hollywood limelight and preferred staying home with his wife Marcia, a film editor, and their adopted daughter. That relationship, however, unraveled in 1983, and the couple divorced.

For Lucas, professional success came again with the third movie in the *Star Wars* trilogy, *Return of the Jedi*, which in its first three weeks at the theaters in 1983 grossed $100 million. At the same time, Lucas guided ILM into new technology, creating special effects for movies such as *E. T.*, *Poltergeist*, *Raiders of the Lost Ark*, and two other Indiana Jones movies that he produced (with Steven Spielberg directing).

Over the next decade, Lucas poured $200 million into ILM so his technology could revolutionize Hollywood. *Forbes* magazine claimed in 1996 that ILM was changing the movie business "as radically as did talkies and Technicolor." ILM special effects appeared in *Forrest Gump* and *Jurassic Park*, among other motion pictures. Lucas had developed a way for computers to digitally alter film, after which a technician using software could transpose and create images within the film's setting.

Thus, for example, in *The American President*, Lucas digitally re-created the House of Representatives, wrapping it around the movie's star, Michael Douglas, who in the role of president, presented his State of the Union speech there. Without Lucas's technology the director would have been required to film on location, a difficult task given the public building involved. In another movie, *Cliffhanger*, star Sylvester Stallone performed apparently death-defying stunts along the sides of mountains, but he was actually suspended from wires and protected by nets that, on the film, Lucas digitally erased.

In 1996, *Forbes* estimated that Lucasfilm, with 1,200 employees, had sales of $300 million, with the company's total value at about $5 billion. Lucas observed: "I'm very aware as a creative person that those who control the means of production control the creative vision. It's not a matter of going down and saying, 'You're going to let me have the final cut.' Because no matter what you do in a contract, they will go around it. Whereas if you own the cameras and you own the film, there's nothing they can do to stop you."

BIBLIOGRAPHY

Champlin, Charles, *George Lucas: The Creative Impulse*, 1992; Ebert, Roger, *The Future of the Movies: Interviews with Martin Scorsese, Steven Spielberg, and George Lucas*, 1991; Lane, Randall, and James Samuelson, "The Magician," *Forbes*, March 11, 1996; Pollock, Dale, "A Man and His Empire," *Life*, June 1983; Pollock, Dale, *Skywalking: The Life and Films of George Lucas*, 1983; Zoglin, Richard, "Lights! Camera! Special Effects!," *Time*, June 16, 1986.

Luce, Henry

(April 3, 1898–February 28, 1967)
Publisher

Henry Robinson Luce produced America's first weekly newsmagazine, *Time*, and from that beginning built a publishing empire that included *Life* and *Sports Illustrated*.

Henry was born in Tengchow, China, on April 3, 1898, the son of Henry Winters Luce, a Presbyterian missionary, and Elizabeth Middleton (Root) Luce, a former social worker. After attending Chefoo, a British boarding school, Henry traveled to England at age 14 and then on to the United States, where he continued his schooling on a scholarship at Hotchkiss in Lakeville, Connecticut. He showed a fondness for journalism at an early age when he edited the school paper.

Henry Luce (Archive Photos)

Luce enrolled at Yale in 1916 and edited the *Yale Daily News* until called into the army in 1918 to serve in World War I. After his discharge the following year, he returned to Yale and received his B.A. degree in 1920. He then spent a year in England studying history at Oxford.

On his return to the United States, Luce joined the *Chicago Daily News* as a reporter, but left after two months for the *Baltimore Sun*. There he and a friend from Hotchkiss, Briton Hadden, developed a plan to start a magazine. They had noticed that although the nation had a large number of newspapers, it lacked a weekly publication that could summarize the news for busy readers. The two men borrowed $86,000, and published the first issue of *Time* in February 1923. In December, Luce married Lila Holtz, with whom he had two children.

Luce and Hadden struggled to keep *Time* afloat, but they benefited from relatively low operating costs. At first they had no reporters since they and three staff writers simply summarized from news clips and did their own research. Over the next few years, circulation grew rapidly, helped by the magazine's unique format. It also drew attention with distinctive language that often reversed the normal word order in sentences and coined its own words.

After Hadden's death in February 1929, Luce gained majority control of Time Incorporated and named John S. Martin managing editor of the magazine. Martin's editorial talent led to *Time*'s circulation increasing from 300,000 in 1930 to 700,000 in 1936. While this was occurring, Luce founded a second magazine, *Fortune*, to present business news. He began a radio and newsreel service, too, called *The March of Time*, which lasted some 10 years.

Intrigued by a new form of journalism, photo-essays, Luce developed an idea for yet another magazine. While planning it with Clare Boothe Brokaw, former editor of *Vanity Fair*, he fell in love with her, and after obtaining a divorce from Lila Luce in October 1935, he married Clare in November. The following year, he published *Life*, and its photo-essay format proved an immediate hit, with circulation reaching 1.7 million in 1937.

With a missionary zeal perhaps inherited from his parents, Luce approached *Time* and *Life* wanting to communicate more than news. He wanted to present a positive picture of America's business community. Critics called his reporting biased and shallow, but he apparently provided the middle class with what it wanted.

Luce launched *Sports Illustrated* in 1954, with its initial print order of 550,000 exceeding that achieved by *Life*. He bought radio and TV stations, along with two paper companies and an interest in the 48-story Time & Life Building erected in New York City.

Luce was politically influential, generally supporting Republican Party causes and taking a firm stand against communism. He repudiated Republican isolationists, however, and urged heavy American investments abroad to assist non-Communist economies. At one point, Luce referred to "the moral and practical bankruptcy of any and all forms of isolationism." He insisted that the United States must take the lead in defeating the threat presented by the Soviet Union, or, in his words, "to accept wholeheartedly our duty and our opportunity as the most powerful and vital nation in the world and in consequence to exert upon the world the full impact of our influence, for such purposes as we see fit and by such means as we see fit."

Luce largely retired from business in 1964, and he died in Phoenix, Arizona, on February 28, 1967, remembered as one of the most innovative publishers in twentieth-century America. In 1989, Time merged with Warner Communications to create Time Warner, Incorporated, a media giant with interests in magazines, books, videos, recorded music, cable TV systems, and motion pictures.

BIBLIOGRAPHY

Baughman, James L., *Minister of Information*, 1987; Horowitz, Irving Louis, "Histories, Futures, and Manifest Destiny," *Society*, July–August 1994; Kobler, John, *Luce: His Time, Life, and Fortune*, 1968; Swanberg, W. A., *Luce and His Empire*, 1972.

Luckenbach, Edgar

(January 19, 1868–April 26, 1943)
Shipping Executive

After taking over the successful shipping business started by his father, Edgar Frederick Luckenbach continued its expansion. The Luckenbach lines became essential both for efficient peacetime trading and for supplying military goods for America in times of war. A Luckenbach steamship was one of the first commercial vessels to travel across the Panama Canal.

Edgar, the son of Lewis and Mary Frey Luckenbach, was born in Kingston, New York, on January 19, 1868. The Luckenbach shipping legacy had begun when Lewis established his own shipping business with a single tugboat in 1850. He later moved the business to Philadelphia to perform towing and salvage services and joined with several partners to build five tugboats for general harbor work. Over time, oceangoing tugs and barges were added to the fleet, and the company began hauling coal from Norfolk, Virginia, to New England. The company headquarters were moved to New York City, and further salvage work in that area was undertaken. Increasingly, transoceanic voyages were added as steam vessels replaced sailing ships, and the business enjoyed steady growth.

Edgar was raised in Brooklyn, New York, and was educated in the public schools there. He entered his father's shipping business after his schooling. When his father died in 1906, Edgar took charge as head of the business. He married Florence Bissell in 1895, but she died one year later. He then married Susan G. Vickers, and they had one son; they divorced in 1915.

In 1908, Luckenbach devised a plan to reduce shipping times by having his shipping lines from the Atlantic and Pacific coasts meet at the Isthmus of Panama, at which point cargo could be transported the short distance across the isthmus by the Panama Railroad. With increased worldwide business, the company continued to grow and was incorporated as the Luckenbach Steamship Company in 1913 with Luckenbach as president. He remained in this position until his death 30 years later. When the Panama Canal opened in 1914, the first commercial ship to pass through it was a Luckenbach vessel.

At the beginning of World War I, Luckenbach lent a fleet of five oceangoing tugs and 19 barges to the U.S. government to aid the war effort. The rest of the company's ships were employed for many transatlantic voyages hauling war materials. After the war, these same ships were used as troop carriers to bring thousands of American soldiers home. In 1919, Luckenbach married his third wife, Andrea Marie Fenwick of Toronto, Ontario, and they had one daughter and one son, Edgar Jr., who would eventually take over the Luckenbach Steamship Company as president and chief executive officer.

Luckenbach had developed the finest fast freight steamers in the country, and in 1920 he turned them from military use back to commercial intercontinental trading routes. In the ensuing period of peace, the fleet made long-haul routes connecting the Atlantic and Pacific ports of the United States to European and Pacific ports. During World War II, 23 Luckenbach ships were involved in transporting war materials both to Europe and the Pacific theater.

A longtime member of the American Steamship Operators Association, Luckenbach was strongly in favor of federal control of shipping rates. He fought for the regulation of intercoastal trade rates under the Copeland Bill, but his battle was unsuccessful. He died on April 26, 1943.

BIBLIOGRAPHY

Ingham, John N., ed., *Biographical Dictionary of American Business Leaders*, 1983; *National Cyclopedia of Biography*, 1921; Shaw, Japes L., *Ships of the Panama Canal*, 1985.

Lynch, Peter

(1944–)
Financier

As head of Fidelity's Magellan Fund, Peter Lynch compiled one of the most impressive investment records in Wall Street history.

Born in 1944 in Boston, Massachusetts, Peter grew up in nearby Newton. His father, Tom Lynch, taught mathematics at Boston College and later worked as an auditor for an insurance company. He died, however, when Peter was only 10 years old. The youngster then helped out with family finances by obtaining a job caddying. While tending to the golfers at a country club, he listened to their conversations about Wall Street and determined he would one day be an investor. After graduating from Newton High School, Lynch attended Boston College on a scholarship for caddies and in 1965 graduated with a B.A. degree.

While a student, he made his first big investment, buying $1,250 worth of stock in the Flying Tigers air freight company at $7 a share, and watching it rise to $32.75 a share. With the profit, he paid for his studies at the Wharton School of Business. In 1966, he obtained a summer internship at Fidelity Investments, Incorporated, and the following year graduated from Wharton with an M.B.A.

Lynch then served two years in the army before rejoining Fidelity in 1969 as a research analyst. Promoted to research director in 1974, Lynch's successful investments led to his promotion to director of Fidelity Magellan. One of the company's smaller mutual funds, investors bought shares in the fund, and the fund, in turn, used the money to acquire a portfolio of stocks. Lynch decided which stocks to buy and when to sell them. Unlike most money managers, he visited companies before buying their stock and made his decisions based on such personal experiences as watching people shop in a mall to see which stores and products were popular.

He believed in finding stable businesses and holding stock for the long term, but he never hesitated to sell a declining

Peter Lynch (Reuters/Jim Bourg/Archive Photos)

An investment of $10,000 in the Magellan Fund in 1977 would have become $250,000 by 1989.

On occasion Lynch picked a bad stock, and in 1987 the stock market crash caused losses for Magellan and forced him to sell more than $1 billion worth of shares. But he withstood the crisis, reinvested funds, and by 1990 doubled Magellan's assets. At the same time, he wrote *One Up on Wall Street*, investment advice for laymen that became a bestseller.

Lynch stunned Wall Street when, in 1990, he suddenly retired from Fidelity. He announced plans to write another book and spend more time with his wife, Carolyn, and his three daughters. In 1998, he compiled a CD-ROM about investing, called *The Stock Shop*.

stock. He once remarked: "You won't improve results by pulling out the flowers and watering the weeds."

The gains in Magellan's mutual funds surprised investors: 32 percent in 1978, 52 percent in 1979, and 70 percent in 1980. "My stock picking was entirely empirical," he later wrote. "And I went sniffing from one case to another like a blood hound that's trained to follow a scent."

BIBLIOGRAPHY

Frailey, Fred W., "Peter Lynch: Still Hanging around Shopping Mall," *Kiplinger's Personal Finance Magazine*, March 1993; Greenwald, John, "The Wizard Bows Out," *Time*, April 9, 1990; Lynch, Peter, *One Up on Wall Street: How to Use What You Already Know to Make Money on the Market*, 1989; Lynch, Peter, and John Rothchild, *Beating the Street*, 1993.